D0875608

The Legend of
Napoleon

The Legend of
Napoleon

Sudhir Hazareesingh

Granta Books
London

Granta Publications, 2/3 Hanover Yard, Noel Road, London N1 8BE
First published in Great Britain by Granta Books 2004
Copyright © Sudhir Hazareesingh, 2004

A CIP catalogue record for this book is available
from the British Library.

1 3 5 7 9 10 8 6 4 2

ISBN 1 86207 667 7

Typeset by M Rules
Printed in Great Britain by
William Clowes Ltd, Beccles, Suffolk

Table of Contents

France at the end of the First Empire

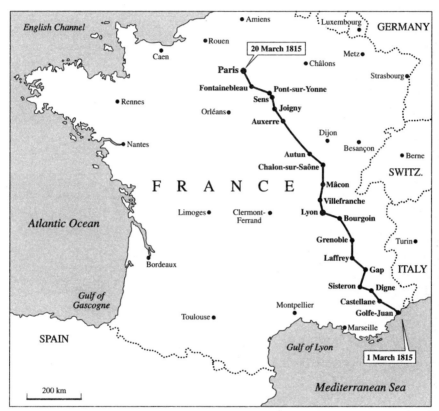

English Channel

Amiens

Luxembourg GERMANY

Rouen

Caen

Metz

20 March 1815

Châlons

Paris

Strasbourg

Fontainebleau Pont-sur-Yonne

Rennes

Sens

Orléans

Joigny

Auxerre

Dijon

Nantes

Besançon

Autun

Berne

Chalon-sur-Saône

SWITZ.

F R A N C E

Mâcon

Villefranche

Limoges

Clermont-
Ferrand

Lyon

Bourgoin

Atlantic Ocean

Grenoble

Turin

Laffrey

Bordeaux

Gap

ITALY

Sisteron

Digne

Gulf of
Gascogne

Castellane

Golfe-Juan

Toulouse

Montpellier

Marseille

SPAIN

Gulf of Lyon

1 March 1815

200 km

Mediterranean Sea

Napoleon's Flight of the Eagle, March 1815

List of Illustrations

Preface

Napoleon figured prominently in my childhood on the Indian Ocean island of Mauritius. My older brother Sandip was a great admirer of the *petit caporal*, as the Emperor was affectionately called by his soldiers, and by my early teens I had read a lot about Napoleon's life and his military campaigns. Most of the television programmes that we received in Mauritius were French, and I still vividly remember the excitement with which I awaited each episode of *Schulmeister, Espion de l'Empereur*. But Napoleon inhabited not only the world of the intellect (or, in the case of the *Schulmeister* series, swashbuckling fantasy); he was also an everyday presence. In our living room hung a framed representation of an *image d'Epinal* of Napoleon at the Boulogne camp, handing out the Legion of Honour to his meritorious soldiers. And my native island was also littered with relics of the Napoleonic era: on a school trip to the Mahébourg museum I remember staring with wonder at the bell of the *Marengo*, a French ship named after Napoleon's famous victory; Mauritius had been its final port of call in the early nineteenth century.

Sandip also constructed our entire universe around Napoleonic personalities, titles, and events. Competent but unimaginative people were named after Napoleon's chief of staff Berthier; and – a fitting combination of our Francophilia with our anti-colonialism – any truly contemptible person was called Wellington. Every member of our family was also given a name from the Emperor's inner circle of Marshals (I was generally known as Ney, Duc d'Elchingen and Prince of the Moskva). My father Lakhan, who was always impeccably dressed, was Murat (although he later, for some unexplained reason, turned into Moncey). We all changed names every now and then, except for my mother Thara: she remained the Emperor.

Without knowing it, our little domestic games were replicating what several generations of French men and women had done for much of the nineteenth century: they lived their lives through the Napoleonic epic. But while writing this book was, in this sense, a return to something familiar, homely even, the exercise was also immensely daunting. In his *Mémoires d'Outre Tombe*, Chateaubriand had noted that the world had slipped from Napoleon's grasp during his lifetime, but that he had finally possessed it in his death. This was certainly true in terms of his ability to capture the imagination of writers. The literature on Napoleon (in French alone) is immense – even more so if one includes works on the French Revolution. I was therefore extremely grateful not to have to enter this world unaccompanied. For their stimulating intellectual support, their encouraging comments and helpful suggestions on the manuscript, I would like to record my warmest gratitude here to David Bell, Malcolm Crook, Alan Forrest, Stéphane Gerson, Robert Gildea, Francisco Gonzalez, Patrice Higonnet, Lucien Jaume, Sheryl Kroen, Karma Nabulsi, Mark Philp, Stuart Semmel, and Marc Stears.

Some of the ideas in the book were discussed with colleagues at conferences and seminars, as well as in less formal settings. I would particularly like to thank David Bell for organizing a day conference on Napoleon at Johns Hopkins, and for providing a setting for stimulating exchanges with some wonderful Napoleonic scholars; Pierre Rosanvallon, who invited me to the Ecole des Hautes Etudes in Paris to deliver a series of lectures on the Napoleonic legend; Steven Englund, with whom it was a great pleasure to discuss our common predilection for all things Napoleonic; and Olivier Ihl, who generously shared his knowledge of the memory of the Emperor in Grenoble. I also record my thanks to the British Academy, under whose Research Readership this book was initiated; and to Balliol College, Oxford, for granting me an extended period of sabbatical leave; especial thanks here to Glynis Baleham, the Senior Tutor's Secretary, for her superbly efficient (and invariably cheerful) help with the production of the final typescript.

Above all, I am indebted to my Granta editor George Miller, without whom this book would not have appeared. His initial enthusiasm for the project, his perseverance in discussing and helping to shape it, and his meticulous comments on an early draft were all invaluable. At Granta my warmest appreciation also goes to Sajidah Ahmad for steering the book through its various stages of production with great efficiency. Finally, I would like to express my gratitude to Frank Pert for producing the index with his customary speed and panache.

As ever, none of my endeavours would have been possible without the love and companionship of Karma Nabulsi: her moral and intellectual support have guided me through every page of this book. It is to her that I dedicate this book.

Sudhir Hazareesingh
Mauritius
January 2004

For Karma
My own *petit caporal*

Introduction

Rethinking the Legend

In September 1815 a judicial official in the rural department of Aude received a letter from Louis Bourges, a villager from Alet. Monsieur Bourges was a fervent supporter of Louis XVIII, who had just acceded to the throne of France after the abdication of Emperor Napoleon Bonaparte. There was bitter local enmity between two rival clans, the 'Bourbons' and the 'Buonapartists' as they were called, and it seemed that in Alet it was the latter who were gaining the upper hand: 'all these Napoleonic usurpers are behaving and acting as if Napoleon's return to power is imminent.' Indeed, the problem was not just with his village: there were 'many inhabitants of the countryside who were repeating every day that King Louis is not the rightful ruler of France.' In order to remedy this 'intolerable situation', Bourges suggested a radical solution: 'I would like to request, beloved father, that you please send us some newspapers carrying the news that this sort of bonnaparte (*sic*) is dead, so that the supporters of this usurper will lose hope.'[1]

The letter is revealing about the political situation in France in the autumn of 1815. It shows the high level of public support enjoyed by Napoleon, especially in parts of rural France, and it also illustrates the difficulties faced by the new royalist government in establishing its popular legitimacy. Most importantly, it demonstrates that the authority of the State was powerless when confronted by the force of popular memory and collective imagination. Napoleon's continuing influence in this area – as in many other parts of France – stemmed not from the social authority, the material wealth, the physical strength, or the degree of organization of his followers, but from the fact that the people attributed extraordinary powers to their former Emperor. The royalists' adversary was no longer a mere mortal: Napoleon, in the popular imagination, had become a legend, a figure of mythical proportions.

This book will tell the story of how Napoleon Bonaparte, First Consul and then Emperor of France between 1799 and 1815, came to be remembered, celebrated and idealized after he lost power, in what was commonly known as his 'legend'. In nineteenth-century France this phenomenon generated a cult whose output and sheer intensity was nothing short of extraordinary. There were poems, books, plays, and pieces of music written in Napoleon's honour; his achievements were immortalized in street names and inscriptions, and on paintings, busts, and public monuments; and his image was affixed to countless objects, ranging from knives and tobacco boxes to scarves and ties. He became a role model for successive generations, idolized by a wide range of groups in society: men and women, members of the bourgeoisie and workers, townspeople and rural dwellers, young and old – and even the insane: according to a study carried out by the physician Esquirol in 1840, most 'megalomaniacs' in France took themselves for Napoleon (or Jesus Christ).[2]

The legend also generated an enormous body of literature. Napoleon's life and political career were comprehensively narrated and commented upon, both within and outside France – by his battlefield companions and civilian collaborators, by contemporaries and successive generations, by memorialists and historians, by artists and writers, and by admirers and adversaries. Every known moment of his childhood and adult life was dissected; every decision he took, whether in his private life, in the political arena or on the battlefield, was scrutinized from all angles, and every conceivable opinion of him was offered. His adulators described him as one of the greatest military geniuses of all time, and the saviour and messiah of France;

his critics responded with a 'black legend', branding him a pervert, a mass murderer, and a ruthless plunderer.[3]

Historians have shown considerable interest in these 'mythological' aspects of Napoleon's legacy.[4] Yet many facets of the legend remain shrouded in darkness – not least its genesis. During most of his reign as Emperor, Napoleon had governed France by despotic means: careful selection and extensive patronage effectively eliminated all opposition to his rule from within the State, and strict censorship prevented any critical voices from reaching the wider public. It was only during his brief return to power in 1815, during the so-called 'Hundred Days', that Napoleon overtly sought to introduce a greater dose of liberalism both within the State and in society, and explicitly to associate Bonapartism with the promotion of greater political freedom. As we shall see in Chapter 1, this experiment in political liberalization was short-lived, and had failed even before Napoleon's abdication in the wake of his defeat at the battle of Waterloo. The Emperor's reputation was now in tatters, and he seemed destined to be remembered, to use a distinction established by the *Encyclopaedia* of 1777, as an 'illustrious villain'[5] rather than as a 'practical genius' who truly deserved to be honoured by the nation.[6]

Yet by the end of 1815 Napoleon's popular image had been radically altered, and his compatriots were celebrating him not only as a fallen hero, but also as a defender of the French Revolution's principles of liberty and equality. As a recent biographer of Napoleon has observed, this remarkable shift in public attitudes towards the Emperor 'frankly defies clear explanation and remains a kind of a mystery'.[7]

The aim of this book is to help resolve this mystery, by locating both the origins and the significance of the 'legend' in the extraordinary growth of 'popular' Napoleonic political mobilizations after 1815. For a long time, French historians believed that the legend was a creation of Napoleon himself, devised from his exile at Saint-Helena.[8] Recent works have rightly cast doubt on this; some sceptics have even questioned the extent to which the Napoleonic cult was authentically rooted in French society after 1815. In her *Napoléon de la mythologie à l'histoire*, Natalie Petiteau chose to narrate the development of the legend through the writings of intellectual and cultural

elites, claiming that 'it is difficult to find evidence of a real
Napoleonic legend among the popular classes'.[9] Others have arrived
at a similar conclusion by suggesting that the legend was largely a
product of the methods of mass manipulation devised by Napoleon
during his reign.

It is true that, even before he became the ruler of France, Bonaparte
was a supremely skilful propagandist, whose masterful promotion of his
military successes (and shrewd concealment of his setbacks) played a
critical role in his ascent to power.[10] Historians have taken their cue
from this proposition to argue that the legend of Napoleon was largely
self-created, drawing from the 'myths' of the warrior and saviour
which were forged during his time as commander-in-chief of the
French Army in Italy;[11] in a similar vein, it has been suggested that
'the military spirit' and the celebration of imperial victories were the
central elements of the legend,[12] together with the successful religious
propaganda of the First Empire, which sought to present Napoleon as
a 'demi-God'.[13]

Although they shed interesting light on Napoleon's methods of rule,
these claims about the genesis of the 'legend' are unconvincing when
extrapolated to the post-1815 period. The argument overestimates
the credulousness of the French people, assuming that they blithely fell
for everything that Napoleon told them – a contention belied by the
growing public disaffection over time for the imperial wars, and the
popular saying: 'to lie like an Army bulletin'.[14] As for the claim about
religious continuity, it is flatly contradicted by the evidence (which we
shall uncover in this book) of widespread anti-clericalism among
Napoleon supporters after 1815.

In truth, the Napoleon of the 'legend' differed in many respects
from the actual ruler; as has been rightly noted, 'Napoleon's myth
reveals much more about the nineteenth century than about the identity of Bonaparte himself'.[15] For this reason, it is more sensible to
distinguish between the 'myth' of Napoleon and his 'legend'. The
former was the attempt by Napoleon to control his public image(s),
from his early military propaganda through his rule as Emperor all
the way up to the publication of the *Mémorial de Sainte-Hélène*. The
latter was a much broader and more heterogenous phenomenon,
which developed spontaneously in France after 1815.[16]

This book will very much take the latter view: although it drew upon the myth, the legend was much more than a celebration of Napoleon's self-image as a military hero and guardian of French national unity, indeed, in many respects the legend represented 'Napoleonic' doctrine and values in ways that the Emperor himself would not have approved. The French historian Georges Lefebvre went even further: 'between [Napoleon's] own inclinations and what the legend would later remember, there is a fundamental contradiction'.[17]

Here the historian stumbles into another minefield: the definition of such terms as 'Bonapartism' and 'Napoleonism'. Bluche suggests that 'Napoleonism' should be defined as a form of sentimental admiration for the person of Napoleon – a feeling which could develop into a veritable cult, but without necessarily assuming any overt political form. 'Bonapartism', in contrast, should be seen as a political doctrine and movement which sought to restore the Empire (or some form of Napoleonic government) in France after 1815.[18]

This distinction may be helpful in some contexts – notably in explaining the attitudes of cultural elites. For example, Balzac, Hugo, and Stendhal were Napoleonists whose novels and poems celebrated the memory and glory of the Emperor; but they were not Bonapartists, since they did little to promote the return of a Napoleonic regime in France. However, this separation is problematic in two ways. Firstly, as we shall see in this book, the term 'Bonapartist' was widely used in French popular discourse after 1815, not only as a label to designate individuals and groups who supported Napoleon 'politically' but also as a wider social and cultural means of self-definition (even by children playing games at school[19]). Bonapartism was more than a 'political' or 'doctrinal' phenomenon, and these wider, popular usages cannot be discounted. Furthermore, it is a mistake to create too rigid a dichotomy between the political aspects of Bonapartism and the 'legend'. For too long, historians have depicted the 'legend' as an essentially literary and romantic phenomenon, a backward-looking idealization of the imperial past, celebrated by artists, poets and songwriters – a nostalgia which generated much sentiment and emotion but very little direct political activity.

Seen in this light, Bonapartism and the legend can appear as not only fundamentally different phenomena, but also as inversely related. The 'peaks' in the legend had no beneficial effects for Bonapartist politics, and conversely, the political successes of Bonapartism occurred independently of the legend. This line of reasoning has led some historians to conclude that there was no significant political character to the Napoleonic legend.[20]

This book fundamentally rejects such a distinction. Instead its aim is to offer an analysis of the Napoleonic legend which sees the politics and the mythology as indissociable. On the one hand, the myths about Napoleon cannot be understood except in fundamentally political contexts – as attitudes shaped by deliberate Napoleonic propaganda; as expressions of firmly held values; and as beliefs which had measurable, practical consequences. On the other hand, the sheer intensity of the legend had a direct bearing on politics, often blurring the boundary between 'history' and 'myth', between actual events and their subsequent perception and representation.

Consider the example of Waterloo. It was known by later French generations as a battle decisively lost by Napoleon in June 1815, and historians of nineteenth-century France often associated its popular memory with feelings of sorrow, grief, and humiliation, and the desire for 'revenge'. But this was not all. In the 'legend', Waterloo also came to be associated with a wider set of notions – courage, determination, self-sacrifice, and patriotism – which in many senses transformed a 'defeat' into something much more positive and even self-affirming.[21] If we take the specific example of the words allegedly uttered by General Cambronne as the French defeat was consummated – 'The Guard dies and never surrenders' – it turns out that this saying not only became an integral part of Napoleonic folklore but was often picked up by ordinary people (peasants, workers, former soldiers) to express their defiance of the French government after 1815.[22] Through Waterloo, later French generations also addressed a host of wider questions about their nation's fate: liberalism, democracy, the destiny of the Revolutionary tradition,[23] and even the threat posed by Protestantism to France's Catholic identity.[24]

The imperial cult was a pervasive phenomenon in nineteenth-century France, with significant ramifications at all levels of society. This book aims to shed as much light as possible upon this breadth of experience of the cult while remaining essentially focused on its political aspects. We shall thus have relatively little to say about the strictly literary dimensions of the imperial cult after 1815; nor is there much about the manner in which the Emperor was portrayed in other artistic forms such as painting and sculpture. These aspects of the 'legend' have been thoroughly covered by Napoleonic scholars.[25]

Considerations of space have also, unfortunately, kept out all material relating to the development of the Napoleonic legend outside France – a wonderful and fascinating subject in its own right. After his death, the Emperor became a cult figure all across Europe – notably in territories which had been subjected to lengthy French occupation, such as the German States,[26] and in countries such as Spain and Russia, where imperial Armies had fought bitter conflicts[27] and where Napoleon had been portrayed as 'the embodiment of all vices and perversions'.[28] Even in *Perfide Albion*, where hostility to the 'Corsican usurper' had reached great heights before 1815, Napoleonic enthusiasm assumed significant proportions during the first half of the nineteenth century.[29] The Emperor's image also consistently inspired Irish republicans and Polish patriots in their struggle for national independence. In the Americas, Napoleon became a legend among Native American tribes, where his exploits were blended into local folklore; and also among other American Bonapartist enthusiasts, who had given the names 'Napoleon' or 'Bonaparte' to fifteen towns in the USA by 1859.[30] Worshipped as a god by Chinese monks and Madagascan rulers, Napoleon was also celebrated as a warrior and liberator by Latin American fighters for independence.[31] In Armenia successive generations idolized a mythical hero named 'Panaporte' whose life was a marvellous blend of Napoleonic biography and local wishful thinking: he conquered the world, burned down the whole of Russia, and strangled the Pope.[32]

Napoleonic mythology was not unique to France; most of the phenomena to which it gave rise were replicated elsewhere across the world. But France was distinctive in the sheer range of the manifestations of the legend, in their social and cultural depths, and (above all) in their overtly political underpinnings. *The Legend of Napoleon* will indeed begin by exploring the realms of popular political belief, as expressed in rumours about Napoleon's return after 1815; the cult of Napoleon through physical objects, as it developed both at elite and mass levels; and the various forms of localized Bonapartist political action, mobilization, and organization. The book then shifts gear by turning to the intellectual development and redesign of Napoleonic political ideas, and the critical role of the legend in the successful emergence of Prince Louis Bonaparte as the pretender to the imperial throne. Having explored the legend both as a mass phenomenon and as the driving force behind the political success of one individual, our story ends with the celebration of the myth throughout the nineteeth century by the ageing veterans of the imperial armies.

There was not, of course, one single coherent vision of what Napoleon represented across these different periods and social groups; but we shall not follow the scholar who, having viewed this diversity, came to the conclusion that 'the legend was transformed and adapted depending on the contexts, each individual or epoch creating for itself a Napoleon consistent, if not with his image, then at least with his desires and needs'.[33] This is an overstatement: there were, as we shall see, clear elements of coherence in the political values and ideals ascribed to Napoleon in the 'legend', which drew essentially from the heritage of the French Revolution.

Since the book relies heavily – especially in its first half, and again in Chapter 9 – on administrative reports compiled by various branches of the French State between 1815 and 1870, it will be helpful to offer a few remarks on the strengths (and limitations) of this type of archival source. In methodological terms, the most original contribution of this book lies in its attempt to narrate the 'legend' by drawing extensively upon administrative reports held in the French National Archives (and in three departmental archives: those of Isère, Rhône, and Yonne). No other book on the Napoleonic legend has attempted to use such sources to tell this story, and in this respect at least *The Legend of Napoleon* can modestly claim to break new ground. The authors of these administrative reports were State employees: members of 'repressive' agencies (police and gendarmerie, judicial and army officials), as well as prefects, subprefects, and mayors. In nineteenth-century France all these functionaries were required to file regular reports on the state of political opinion in their localities, and it was in the course of producing these accounts for their Parisian superiors that they encountered and sought to explain the various manifestations of 'Napoleonic' politics which will be treated in this book.

Naturally, the manipulation of such material requires considerable care; these writings cannot be viewed simply as transparent windows into the state of French public opinion. There were many potential sources of distortion and bias in the system of information-gathering. After 1815, judicial elites were predominantly recruited from the nobility, whose social and political values (a belief in religion and 'order', accompanied by a virulent hostility to all forms of 'popular' intervention in politics) accompanied them into the legal arena, both overtly and subconsciously.[34]

Because they frequently moved around different parts of the territory, elite functionaries – prefects and sub-prefects, military and judicial officials – were often ill-informed and culturally prejudiced about the regions over which they held sway. These characteristics sometimes led them to underestimate the complexities of the events they were experiencing – for example, by ascribing to ignorance, superstition, or drunkenness instances of political activity which may well have been grounded in ideological commitment. Furthermore, at a time when most communities were small and closed, 'foreigners' (i.e. any persons from outside the neighbourhood, or travelling through on their way to other places) were often viewed with suspicion by locals, who were more than happy to ascribe 'seditious' opinions and intentions to them.[35] There was ample potential, in short, for Napoleonic political opinion to be either exaggerated or downplayed in these official reports.

More simply, these functionaries worked in difficult material conditions and were often overworked and understaffed: in 1816, one sub-prefect summed up his pitiful situation in a scrawl on the margin of a letter to his boss:'I am crushed with work, one of my employees is sick and the other is incompetent.'[36] How could these men keep effective track of 'subversion' under such conditions?

The relentless demand for information from Paris produced a heavy reliance on local observers and spies; this, in turn, could create a whole host of problems. These observers (police officers, mayors, informants, etc.) could themselves often be misled about the real extent of Napoleonic support in their localities – either because they were themselves manipulated by Bonapartist agitators, or because they were blinded by their fear and hatred of Napoleon, or (and this was a frequent problem) simply because their very presence led local people to conceal their political opinions.[37]

More subtle forms of bias probably also came into play: like all modern bureaucrats, these men were also self-interested agents and it may well have been the case that they dwelled too much on the manifestations of the 'legend' in their localities because they thought that this was what their superiors in Paris wanted to hear. Especially in the early years of the Restoration, there was a veritable deluge of instructions and circulars from Parisian Ministries demanding that local officials monitor the activities of 'seditious' Napoleonic groups; this exhortation may have become a self-fulfilling prophecy. Likewise, later reports by local officials on the celebrations of the national festivity under the Second Empire may have overplayed the extent of the popular enthusiasm for Napoleonic veterans.

The greatest frustration for the historian is the necessarily fragmentary nature of the information conveyed by these documents. Arlette Farge summed it up succinctly: 'the archive very quickly reveals a startling contradiction: at the same time as it invades and submerges the historian, it also sends him back, by its sheer magnitude, to the seclusion of solitude. A solitude where so many 'living' creatures swarm that it hardly seems possible to account for them, to tell their stories.'[38] Consider a simple example. In April 1821, the police commissioner of Lyons received a brief report to the effect that twenty men had stood on the bridge of La Guillotière and, after joining hands, had proceeded to sing a hymn 'in which the name of Bonaparte appeared frequently'.[39] No further details about this story appear in the folder, and so we are left guessing who these people were, what exactly they sang, and for what purpose. Nor do we know how the police received this information: did it come from one of the singers, acting as an informant? Or from a police official standing on the bridge? Was the song a private homage, intended only for those performing it, or a public performance aimed at demonstrating the continuing strength of Napoleonic support in Lyons?

Official narratives have to be treated sensitively, both for what they contain and for their 'silences'. All of this said, we should not get too defensive about these sources; they contain a substantial mass of information which was clearly *not* distorted or biased. For example, local officials often transcribed the contents of popular Napoleonic utterances and writings ('seditious' shouts, placards, poems, etc.) and these were entirely accurate renderings (as we have often been able to check, since the original versions of the written documents are generally still in the archival folders). Another precious source of information (especially in police and judicial accounts) concerns the social origins and material circumstances of Napoleonic 'activists' – a rich treasure, which can help to isolate the contours of 'popular' Bonapartism during the first half of the nineteenth century.

Most importantly, the large number of reports consulted in the course of writing this book has enabled us to establish clear patterns over time and space, which largely offset the potential problem of individual 'exaggerations'. We shall never really know precisely how many songs were sung in Napoleon's honour, how many cries of 'Long Live the Emperor!' were uttered, how many Napoleonic busts and images were bought between 1815 and 1870, or how many thousands of French men and women turned out to greet imperial veterans during official ceremonies after 1851. But one thing is certain: the scale of these phenomena was absolutely prodigious, as is attested by the mass of bulging folders lying in France's national and local archives (many of which remain completely unexplored – especially for the Restoration and Second Empire periods).

While the political ramifications of the legend constitute the guiding thread of the book, the narrative also has much to reveal about how it functioned at a practical level. Part of the reason why the Napoleonic legend has been so long portrayed as an abstract, free-floating, apolitical phenomenon is that its *modus operandi* has not been closely studied. In this book, we shall find out as much about the content of the legend as about its actual bearers and disseminators. These folk were, some of them, members of the French political elite, but above all they were ordinary workers and peasants from towns and villages; former soldiers and officers; local intellectuals and pamphleteers; doctors and lawyers; schoolteachers and Freemasons. In their celebration of their Emperor, these men and women sang and shouted his name, wrote placards in his honour, spread stories about the imminence of his return, and plotted and conspired against France's political rulers.

These popular manifestations of the Napoleonic cult took myriad forms: individual and collective, open and secretive, spontaneous and ritualized, and expressive and goal-driven. Taken together, they shed revealing light on French political experience in the nineteenth century, most notably concerning the depth of political awareness among ordinary folk, the enduring impact of local memories and traditions, and the inventiveness of Napoleon's supporters.[40] The latter point is particularly worth underlining; the celebration of the imperial cult was very much like a fête – not only in the sense that it elicited feelings of joy and pleasure among its devotees, but also in that it manifested itself in a style of politics which was bold, adventurous, and often playful (even if the French authorities did not always appreciate the humour).[41]

By narrowing the conceptual gap between 'Bonapartism' and the 'Napoleonic legend', this book will also have something to offer about the history and political underpinnings of the Bonapartist movement between 1815 and 1870. In an era in which national, centralized political organizations did not exist, and when self-styled 'Bonapartists', 'republicans', and 'liberals' shared many common values, it was difficult to isolate the specific contours of 'Bonapartism'; and this has often led historians to conclude that there was no such thing as a 'Bonapartist' political movement for much of the pre-1848 period. An additional difficulty was that supporters of Napoleon were not very articulate, tending more towards commemoration and conspiracy than the production of lengthy treatises on the ideal form of government.

Yet, contrary to conventional wisdom, we shall find much evidence of organized Bonapartist political activity after 1815 at local and regional levels, among informal networks and small organizations (often operating in semi-clandestinity, or in associations such as the Freemasonry).[42] And despite the affirmations of their adversaries, these groups had a coherent vision of what Bonapartism represented. This ideal was defined in Napoleon's posthumous utterances; picked up by local activists, who celebrated the memory of the 'liberal Emperor'; and finally repackaged by Louis Napoleon in his successful bid for the French Presidency in

1848. This vision was partly constructed as a rational political discourse, appealing to the interests of particular groups in French society, and partly as an 'imagined' representation of the recent past. This potent combination of ideology and myth was one of the main reasons for the strength of Bonapartism in France for much of the nineteenth century.

Through the Napoleonic legend, Bonapartism (both as ideology and as myth) offered a vision of France as a sovereign, cohesive, and patriotic nation – a theme which has continued to resonate in modern French political discourse. The myths contained in the legend not only expressed the nation's collective identity but also played an important role in shaping it. The imperial cult developed and reached its zenith during a century which also saw the crystallization of mass democratic politics in France. At first glance, these two spheres seemed far removed from each other, indeed polar opposites: the legend was a celebration of the sovereignty of one individual over the nation as a whole, whereas democratic politics expressed the republican principle of 'popular sovereignty' derived from the 1789 Revolution. Indeed, the history of 'Bonapartism' and 'republicanism' during the second half of the nineteenth century was marked by a profoundly adversarial relationship.

Yet this (very real) enmity concealed many elements of overlap and convergence. One of the main reasons why Napoleon's legend thrived in France after 1815 at the political level was because it consistently advocated the adoption of male universal suffrage; it also celebrated Bonapartism as a 'popular' system of rule, both governing in the interests of the people and deriving its legitimacy from their explicit support. Conversely, one of the fascinating political lessons of the nineteenth century was that the Napoleonic legend deeply penetrated the realm of mass democratic politics.

After 1848 millions of voters supported Bonapartism for a range of considerations that included reason and self-interest but also encompassed the memories and mythologies that they had come to associate with Napoleon: the political unity of the nation, the centralization of the State, the modernization of its economy, the promotion of individuals on the basis of merit, and the pursuit of 'grandeur' abroad. Far from abandoning these Napoleonic notions after 1870, France's republican rulers incorporated them all into their political discourse and imagery; the imperial legend was thus blended into the French republic's definition of its own ideals. To this extent, the story of this book is not merely of 'historical' interest; it is a tale about the memory and mythology that continues to underlie modern French identity.

Chapter 1

The Flight of the Eagle

On the afternoon of 1 March 1815, a small flotilla entered the southern French inlet of Golfe-Juan. After anchoring in the bay, the seven ships – clearly seeking to avoid detection – rapidly offloaded their cargo: first around 1,100 men, followed by their military equipment; then, finally, a few horses. An hour later, with the operation almost complete, the ships' artillery fired several rounds to announce the landing of the expedition's leader. Cheered by the assembled group as he stepped ashore, he offered this rousing invocation: 'Land of France! Fifteen years ago I adorned you with the title of *Fatherland of the Great Nation*. I salute you again, and in the same circumstances, one of your children, the most deserving of this beautiful title, comes once again to save you from anarchy.'[1]

These words were spoken by Napoleon Bonaparte, the former sovereign of France. As First Consul, then Emperor, he had risen to the absolute heights of power, and had vastly extended the borders of his 'Great Nation', making France the dominant power in Continental Europe. Symbolized by the eagle, his Grande Armée had been admired and feared across Europe, and Napoleon's own successes on the battlefield had earned him the title of 'the God of War'.

In 1814, however, the Emperor's fortunes seemed to have turned irreversibly: he had been forced to abdicate after suffering a series of defeats at the hands of an Allied coalition led by Britain, Austria, Prussia, and Russia. Even worse, his old enemies the Bourbons, the royal family which had governed France up to 1792, had been brought back to the throne. Napoleon had been sent off to rule the small Mediterranean island of Elba – a demeaning fall for a monarch whose power in Europe had once exceeded even that of Charlemagne. And the prospects for the future seemed even bleaker: as from the end of 1814, there were also worrying rumours that the French government was looking to deport Napoleon even further away; among the destinations mentioned were Malta, Saint-Lucia, and Saint-Helena.[2]

But Bonaparte had never been a man to resign himself to fate, and despite his exile from France and his increasingly precarious position on Elba he still retained intact 'that power to imagine and to act which separated him from the rest of humankind.'[3] Napoleon had always aimed at extraordinary things in his life, as a political ruler and especially as a warrior, but this was perhaps the most audacious scheme ever conceived by his fertile mind: to lead a small expedition onto French soil, to launch an appeal to the people to rally to him, and then to march upon Paris and seize power from the Bourbons – all of this, as he put it to one of the generals accompanying him, 'without firing a single shot'.[4] Confident of the outcome, he issued a proclamation in which he predicted that 'the Eagle with the national colours will fly from steeple to steeple until it alights on the towers of Notre-Dame.'[5]

Thus began the rich, intense, and contradictory period in French history known as the Hundred Days.[6] The Emperor would indeed achieve his return to power, but his second reign would prove short-lived, ending with his defeat at the battle of Waterloo in June that was followed by his definitive exile to the island of Saint-Helena a month later. And yet, even though they included his political demise, the events of 1815 did not result in the end of popular support for Napoleon – quite the reverse. The Hundred Days were critical in shaping the Emperor's image for posterity: they reminded the French people of many of his characteristic qualities (notably his flamboyance, his restlessness, his political shrewdness, and his unerring belief in his good star); they also encompassed some of the most remarkable, as well as the most poignant, moments in his life; and above all they restored the political link between Napoleon and the Jacobin republicans, the militant supporters of the 1789 Revolution.

Until his return in March 1815, the Emperor had portrayed himself as primarily a strong charismatic ruler and as a military conqueror. The events of the Hundred Days would initiate the process through which Napoleon's image would be reinvented. Very soon the creator of a new Empire would come to be seen as an upholder of the Revolutionary principle of equality; the expansive ruler of the world as a patriotic defender of his country; the martialist conqueror as a law-giver; and, perhaps most extraordinarily of all, the autocratic and despotic ruler as the potent symbol of liberty. The manner in which Napoleon's rule ended, in short, proved decisive in the launching of his legend.

From the Golfe-Juan to the Tuileries Palace

By far the most successful aspect of the Hundred Days for Napoleon was the Emperor's journey back to the French capital, many features of which were subsequently immortalized in the 'legend' (see Figure 1). Upon his landing, Napoleon was recognized and generally welcomed, even though some locals told him to his face that his return would only bring trouble. 'We were all living so peacefully,' the mayor of one village told him; 'now you have come to ruin it all!' Suppliers, for their part, took the opposite view, making the most of the business opportunities provided by their august visitor. When a farmer charged him an extortionate price for some eggs, Napoleon asked whether hens were rare in the area. 'No, sire,' the peasant replied tartly. 'But Emperors are.'[7]

It took Napoleon twenty days to journey from the southern French coast to Paris. In order to avoid travelling through royalist areas such as Provence, where he knew the troops would remain loyal to the King,[8] the Emperor decided to take the more arduous route through the heights of the Dauphiné where the people were traditionally hostile to the royalists.[9] This part of the journey was hazardous, as Napoleon and his party had to press ahead over narrow mountain paths, often covered with ice and snow. One mule, carrying over

FIGURE 1

The landing of Napoleon

The popular collection of Epinal images celebrated the Napoleonic cult by representing key moments in the history of the imperial reign. These images were very
cheap and were thus accessible to ordinary folk (peasants, workers, and soldiers). By
the early 1840s, it is estimated that more than 420,000 such prints had been sold in
France. This drawing represents the moment at the beginning of the Hundred
Days when Napoleon's canoe landed on French soil on 1 March 1815. The soldiers
saluting him were part of a small force of around 1,100 men who had accompanied
him from Elba; the flotilla is visible in the background, on the right. The caption
below the drawing narrates the Emperor's journey from Golfe-Juan to Paris, and
ends by quoting Napoleon's statement that his return to Paris on 20 March had been
one of the happiest days in his life.

300,000 francs in gold pieces, fell down a precipice, and only 263,000 francs were recovered; for several decades thereafter, local folk went in search of 'Napoleon's gold'.[10]

In the early stages of Napoleon's progress, most locals simply stared at this strange procession. Yet each day that passed represented a victory, with increasing evidence of support from villagers who brought wine for the soldiers and bunches of violets for the Emperor (thereby initiating, in the French public imagination, the identification of Napoleon with this flower).[11]

There were three major turning points in the course of the 'flight of the eagle'. The first was Napoleon's arrival on 7 March at Grenoble, the first major town to rally to his cause. A large crowd gathered outside one of the gates, and the forces loyal to the King attempted to block Napoleon's entry. Napoleon shouted, 'Open these gates in the name of the Emperor!' The sentry replied, 'I only take orders from my commanding officer.' Without hesitation, the Emperor retorted: 'He is relieved of his functions.' Eventually the gates were smashed, and Napoleon entered a town which was fully illuminated in his honour.[12]

Even more grandiose was Napoleon's arrival and sojourn at Lyons, where he was welcomed enthusiastically and from where he issued a number of imperial proclamations, most notably the decree of 13 March which abolished all royalist emblems and insignia and restored the tricolour as France's national flag; it was also in Lyons that Napoleon announced the dissolution of all royalist assemblies.[13] As the Emperor would later say, he had started the 'flight of the eagle' as an 'adventurer'; by the time he had passed Grenoble, he had become a 'Prince'.[14]

The third key stage of Napoleon's return to power was his encounter with Marshal Ney at Auxerre. Ney was an impetuous man, who had promised the King that he would 'bring back the usurper in an iron cage'. But he had also served the Emperor with distinction and glory, and indeed it was as a commander of the Grande Armée that he had become known as 'bravest of the brave'. Napoleon's return confronted Ney with the most terrible of dilemmas. During the night of 14–15 March, he agonized over the problem before concluding that 'it would be impossible to stop the sea with bare hands'.[15] Ney's decision to rally to the cause of the Emperor sealed the fate of the Bourbons (and his own; he was later executed by the Restoration).[16]

Napoleon reached Paris on 20 March; as he approached the Tuileries (abandoned by the hapless King Louis XVIII on the previous day) he was mobbed by a crowd of several thousand officers and citizens, who carried him in triumph into the Palace. Even men who had seen it all since the 1790s – monarchies overthrown, cities burned, kings executed, Popes kidnapped – were mesmerized by what they saw; one observer noted: 'There was something about this scene which was sensational, out of all proportion with human events.'[17] Another eyewitness agreed: 'It was like witnessing the resurrection of Christ.'[18] (See Figure 2.)

How, then, had such an extraordinary enterprise come to succeed? To royalist opinion after the Hundred Days, it appeared inconceivable that one individual could have landed in the south of France and single-handedly overthrown the legitimate monarchy: it had to have been a conspiracy. Royalist pamphleteers in Paris hammered away at this theme in the immediate aftermath of the Hundred Days;[19] the message was repeated and amplified in the provinces in the months that followed. In a pamphlet published in September 1815, a Bourbon supporter from Besançon alleged that Napoleon's return had been prepared by emissaries sent all over France in the month of February, and supported by 'Jacobin clubs' and 'retired military officers'. Above all, the Hundred Days had been an expression of the Revolutionary tradition, that terrible plague which continued to ravage the nation: 'The revolution of March 1815, it cannot be doubted, is the sister of that of 1789: it had the same fathers, the same executors, and the same supporters.'[20]

Napoleon's followers subsequently denied that the Emperor's return had been part of any conspiracy, underscoring instead the role of chance, and the popular welcome received by the Emperor (especially from the military): 'God, the people, and the Army were the sole conspirators.'[21]

The truth lay somewhere between the two views: contrary to royalist insistence, there had been no systematic and comprehensive plan to assist Napoleon's return, even though there had been much political agitation carried out in the run-up to March 1815 in Paris by the Emperor's former Minister of Police Joseph Fouché, and in the

FIGURE 2

The evening of 20 March 1815: the return of Napoleon to the Tuileries

The scene represents the last few moments of the 'flight of the eagle', as Napoleon was carried in triumph into the Tuileries Palace, which had been vacated by King Louis XVIII the day before. Overnight, Paris had changed its appearance, and royalist emblems and cockades had been replaced by tricolour flags and imperial eagles. Many of the Emperor's former ministers, councillors of State, and valets had already returned to the Palace by the time he arrived, as had his stepdaughter Queen Hortense; they all greeted Napoleon at the top of the stairs. The popular acclamations here symbolize Napoleon's claim to embody the sovereignty of the French nation.

provinces by local Bonapartist networks.[22] At the same time, the Emperor was too wise to rely entirely on popular spontaneity: he had prepared the ground at least for the initial stages of his journey, notably through the correspondence exchanged between the Grenoble-based glove-maker Jean-Baptiste Dumoulin and his military surgeon at Elba, Joseph Emery. Both men discussed, and then planned in minute detail the itinerary of Napoleon's journey through the Alps, in order to avoid passing through hostile royalist areas in the Midi; and they also played a fundamental role in organizing and mobilizing Napoleonic opinion in Grenoble and Lyons ahead of the Emperor's arrival.[23]

The main political factor which ensured the success of the flight of the eagle – and Napoleon himself later admitted as much – was the unpopularity of the royalist government. When Louis XVIII had returned to Paris a year earlier from his English exile in Hartwell House, he had been broadly welcomed by a nation wearied by years of Napoleonic despotism, and the material and human cost of ceaseless warfare. In a pamphlet which caught the spirit of the times, the royalist intellectual Françoise-René de Chateaubriand denounced Bonaparte as a 'tyrant' and appealed to his compatriots to welcome the new Bourbon rulers: 'We shall no longer be the *great nation*, and we shall no longer have an *emperor*, but we shall become *French* again, and we shall embrace our *kings*. Such an exchange will leave us with no regrets.'[24]

Very soon, however, these hopes for a smooth transition were shattered. The obese King was a gentle and moderate individual, but he had none of Napoleon's charisma, especially with the soldiers; they felt little respect for a sovereign who, as they said, 'needed six of us to carry him'.[25] Furthermore, the King's return to the throne 'in the carriages of the foreigners' offended French patriotism; and the monarch exacerbated this sentiment by refusing to wear the Legion of Honour or to recognize the tricolour flag, and by insisting on reinstating the white banner with the fleur-de-lys as France's national emblem. Even worse, his regime was viewed as seeking to bring about the return of *ancien régime* rights and privileges that had been abolished by the Revolution.

The biggest popular fear – which the regime did little to allay – was that the clergy and emigré nobility would seek to reclaim their lands and properties from the million or so Frenchmen who had benefited from their acquisition during the Revolution. This perception was strengthened by the political pressure exerted by a group of ultra-reactionary and revanchist princes (led by the Comte d'Artois) and the relentless propaganda of the clergy; one priest from Savenay bluntly told his parishioners that unless they returned the properties to their former owners 'they would suffer the fate of Jezebel and would be devoured by dogs.'[26]

The Emperor had been kept very well informed of the state of French popular opinion during his time at Elba.[27] The three proclamations he issued on his landing at Golfe-Juan in March 1815 (two signed by him, the third written as an address by his Guard to their fellow soldiers in the French Army) demonstrated both his consummate grasp of the political situation and his masterly capacity to exploit it to his advantage. He savaged the Bourbons, who had acceded to power 'by the force of the very armies which have ravaged our territory';[28] his own defeat in 1814, Napoleon added, had been possible only because of the 'betrayal' by his Marshals who had handed over Lyons and Paris to the advancing enemy forces.[29] Since Bourbon reign had resumed, the Emperor noted in a dictum that would haunt royalists throughout the nineteenth century, 'they have convinced us that they have forgotten nothing, and learnt nothing; they are still driven by prejudice, and they are the enemies of our rights and of those of the people.'[30]

Napoleon also appealed directly to the Army's sense of grandeur and wounded pride: 'Your ranks, your possessions, your glory; the possessions, positions, and glory of your children have no greater enemies than these princes, who have been imposed upon us by foreigners; they are the enemies of our glory.'[31] The Emperor stressed that he was not returning to wage war: 'I come to reclaim my rights, which are also those of the people'. By this wonderfully ambiguous proposition, Napoleon underscored the distinctiveness of his conception of monarchy: he was France's legitimate imperial ruler, but only because he had been recognized as such 'by the people' – unlike the Bourbons, whose claim to rule was founded on 'divine right'.[32]

In these skilful proclamations, the Emperor exposed the most vulnerable flanks of his Bourbon adversaries, while at the same time repositioning himself as the symbol of French patriotism, the champion of the people's rights, and the ultimate guardian of the principles of 1789. 'A feudal King can no longer be accepted by the French people,' Napoleon noted, before concluding: 'she needs a sovereign who has emerged from the Revolution, and I am that sovereign.'[33]

All these political factors notwithstanding, the success of the 'flight of the eagle' was above all a personal triumph for the Emperor. Circumstances might well have been ripe for overthrowing the Bourbons in March 1815, but only Napoleon had the range of qualities (both personal and political) needed to carry through such an extravagant project with such limited means. The most important factor, in this context, was that his prestige remained absolutely intact in the French Army, whose lower and middle ranks had been senselessly alienated by the new regime – especially because of the privileged treatment granted to the King's own military staff in the newly created Maison du Roi. From the moment when Napoleon left France for Elba in 1814, many of his soldiers had begun to predict that he would return 'when the next violets bloomed'; hence his popular nickname of *Père La Violette*.[34]

The Emperor's continuing command over the Army – *his* Army – was critically established in an incident that occurred during the early stages of the 'flight of the eagle', on 7 March: the encounter at Laffrey (on the outskirts of Grenoble) between Napoleon's bedraggled forces and a royalist detachment sent out to intercept them. After a stand-off which lasted an hour, the Emperor broke the deadlock by marching up to the men facing him. Baring his breast to them, he declared: 'Soldiers! If there is any one among you who wishes to kill his Emperor, here I am.'[35] The royalist officers ordered the troops to open fire, only to be met with a deafening shout of 'Long Live the Emperor!'[36] (see Figure 3).

From that moment on, it was clear that Napoleon's former soldiers would not fight his return to power.[37] Indeed, all the troops that the unfortunate King dispatched to intercept Napoleon effectively rallied to him. A Parisian wag affixed on the Vendôme Column a placard that took the form of a message from the Emperor to the King: 'My good brother, there is no point sending me any more soldiers, I have enough already.'[38]

The Laffrey episode in many ways symbolized the essence of the

FIGURE 3

Return from Elba, 7 March 1815

This is a depiction of Napoleon's celebrated encounter with French troops at Laffrey, on the outskirts of Grenoble; this was in many ways the turning point in the 'flight of the eagle'. The Emperor marched up to the soldiers and declared: 'Soldiers! If there is any one among you who wishes to kill his Emperor, here I am!'. The troops responded by shouting 'Long Live the Emperor!' In the background are the mountains of the Dauphiné; Napoleon's officers are standing behind him, bearing the tricolour flag and imperial eagle – the twin symbols of Bonapartist patriotism. In addition to highlighting the enthusiasm of the troops at the sight of the Emperor, Steuben's painting draws attention, in the background, to the local population, who were at the same time witnesses of this epic moment, active contributors to the outcome (they had encouraged the soldiers to rally to Napoleon), and symbols of the 'popular' nature of the Emperor's support.

Hundred Days: it showed that Napoleon's strength in 1815 resided in his authority and not in his brute power. It highlighted his willingness to gamble his fate on one throw of the dice, but it also revealed the mercurial nature of the political situation, and the fluidity of individual and group allegiances. Above all, it revealed the mesmerizing quality of this man from whom the French people could not – despite all his faults – bring themselves to part.

Songs were written to celebrate Napoleon's return from Elba; there were so many of them, and they were performed with such joy as he made his triumphant way through France that by the time he had reached the town of Avallon Napoleon claimed – perhaps with just a touch of exaggeration – that more than three thousand popular songs had been written in his honour since his return in March 1815.[39]

Enthusiasm, Opposition and Passivity

From the moment when he reached Paris, things began to unravel for the Emperor. His monarchical enemies in Europe had lost no time in responding to his escape from Elba. Gathered in Congress in Vienna, the Allied powers (led by Britain, Russia and Prussia) denounced Bonaparte as an 'enemy and disturber of the peace', and reaffirmed their support for the Bourbon monarchy in France.[40] Even before he reached the Tuileries, Napoleon knew that this was tantamount to a declaration of war against him.

In Napoleon's first weeks back in the French capital, his overriding goal was to build as broad a domestic political coalition as possible. He sought in particular to reassure those who feared a return of despotism by stressing that 'popular sovereignty' was the 'only legitimate source of power'; he was especially keen to draw out moderate and elite opinion by emphasizing his commitment to 'the consolidation of liberal institutions'.[41] These progressive aspirations were to be crystallized in a new constitutional arrangement, to be ratified by the people in a plebiscite. When the royalists had returned in 1814, their constitutional Charter had been 'granted' by the King; Napoleon wanted to outflank the Bourbons by presenting a constitution which was both more progressive than the royalist Charter and explicitly grounded in popular consent. And in stark contrast with the authoritarian and intellectually repressive era of the First Empire, when all forms of political and intellectual dissent were proscribed and a strict censorship imposed, Napoleon now granted the press complete freedom.

Unfortunately for the Emperor, his attempt to win over bourgeois and enlightened opinion was a failure. The principal author of his constitutional reform was Benjamin Constant, the liberal philosopher and pamphleteer. As we shall see in Chapter 6, Constant remained a bitter enemy of Bonaparte even as Napoleon journeyed towards Paris during the first weeks of March, but he rallied to the Emperor after meeting him in mid-April. For all his imperfections, the Emperor seemed at that moment the only effective bulwark against extremism and despotism.[42] Napoleon also knew exactly how to appeal to Constant's acute sense of self-interest, appointing him to the Conseil d'Etat and awarding him an immediate advance of 30,000 francs to cover his recent gambling losses.[43]

Despite Constant's best efforts, his fellow liberals did not follow his lead. The document that he drafted, the 'Additional Act', contained notable advances, particularly with respect to individual freedom, religious liberty, freedom of the press, and judicial autonomy from the executive.[44] However, it fell short of offering a genuine constitutional monarchy, and was at best ambiguous on the key issue of whether the people were the effective 'source' of sovereignty.[45] The Emperor himself did not help, refusing to yield to Constant's entreaties for a frank rupture with the imperial tradition, and accepting only an amendment to the existing constitution of the First Empire – change, in other words, rather than transformation[46] (see Figure 4).

While sharing Constant's concerns about the political situation, elite and progressive opinion remained deeply suspicious of Bonaparte. Had he not ruthlessly crushed all opposition to his rule, and severely curtailed the free expression of opinion throughout the First Empire? Some liberals supported the creation of a genuine constitutional monarchy, in which the elected legislative chambers would dominate the executive, essentially reducing Napoleon to the role of a ceremonial head of State.

Such was the view of the most formidable liberal figure, Lafayette, the hero of the American and French revolutions, who even wanted to take away from the monarch his function as commander-in-chief of the Army.[47] A similar plan to emasculate the powers of the

FIGURE 4

Each to his profession

Another *image d'Epinal* depicting the early moments of the Hundred Days. Napoleon is greeted by a woman selling vegetables, who tells him how glad she is that he has returned. As she is about to embark upon a lengthy speech about political matters, she is interrupted by the Emperor: 'Each to his profession: you look after your cabbages and carrots, Madam, and I will take care of politics.' Besides its anecdotal value, this image was a good representation of Napoleon's depoliticized conception of public life. Even in 1815 he believed that political matters were best left to the sovereign and to 'experts'; he disliked elected Assemblies and thought that popular involvement in politics was best limited to the periodic recourse to the plebiscite (referendum).

executive was drawn up by the Grenoble-based liberal Joseph Rey, in a pamphlet entitled *Des bases d'une constitution.*[48]

But many liberals seriously doubted that the Emperor would allow himself to be politically restrained in this way. Charles de Rémusat expressed these reservations, which also captured the complex range of sentiments that assailed men and women of moderate opinion during the Hundred Days:

> 'How could we publicly admit the possibility of the return of the Bourbons? That would be to suppose France defeated, and many who expected such an outcome would have shuddered to contribute to it by confessing their discouragement. But how could we desire absolutely and without concern the victory of the Emperor Napoleon, and how could we desire his defeat? How could we imagine him, with this character and his habits, combining the difficulties and delays inherent in the foundation of a free government with the speed and energy necessary to the defence of the country in its moment of supreme need?'[49]

It was not only a matter of trusting Napoleon's intentions; his promise of a more liberal government was inconsistent with the circumstances of the moment, which required firm leadership and decisive military action. Public discussions held across France in the run-up to the vote mirrored these concerns, suggesting a wide range of views concerning the Emperor's new constitution (known, after its author, as the 'benjamine'). However, a majority of expressed opinions, particularly those printed in newspapers and pamphlets, were critical and often hostile.[50] A cartoon in a liberal newspaper summed up the views of the critics: it showed Napoleon undergoing a medical examination; when he asked how he was faring, the doctor replied: 'Sire, this cannot last. Your Majesty has a very poor Constitution.'[51]

When the document was submitted to the vote, it received majority support (1.5 million 'yeses' to 5,700 'noes'), but only twenty-two per cent of the electorate bothered to vote – a much lower turnout than in Napoleon's plebiscites of 1802 and 1804.[52] The four most enthusiastic departments (Yonne, Côte d'Or, Meurthe, and Haute Marne) were essentially rural; urban and developed parts of the country largely abstained, as did all the royalist bastions in the North, the West, and the Midi.[53]

Napoleon thus lost on all fronts: royalist opponents claimed victory because of the overwhelming number of abstentions; imperial supporters thought the Additional Act was unnecessary; republicans regretted Napoleon's failure to restore the Revolutionary regime, and his restoration of hereditary peers;[54] and for those who were undecided about his return, and his liberal promises, his constitutional amendment was simply insufficient.[55]

Elections to the Chamber of Representatives in May confirmed the anti-Napoleon trend, bringing back into the political fray a number of former critics of imperial despotism; many of them (most notably Lafayette) would play a critical role in pushing for Napoleon's abdication after Waterloo. During the Hundred Days, a Bonapartist woman by the name of Marie-Victorine Perrier had urged the Emperor to govern as a dictator, and dispense once and for all with 'the chatter of elected assemblies'; according to her, its chambers were nothing but 'nests of indolence, treachery, and corruption'.[56] By June 1815 Napoleon probably wished that he had taken her advice.

The Emperor was undoubtedly aware of the bitter hostility to his return in royalist parts of France; in many towns of the Midi, for example, supporters of the Bourbons were so strong that the police were afraid to take down the royalists' anti-Napoleonic proclamations.[57] This opposition was not merely vocal: in May there were insurrections in the Vendée and Brittany, which had to be put down by troops loyal to Napoleon.[58] At a lower level, weapons were frequently discovered during searches of royalist homes; at Bordeaux in April the authorities found twenty-seven rifles on the property of Badin, an 'exalted supporter of the Bourbons'.[59]

Two groups stood out consistently in this agitation: priests and aristocrats, who in many places manifested their opposition to Napoleon 'almost openly'.[60] A 'report on the attitude of the clergy' drawn up by the prefect of the Isère concluded that the vast majority of priests were implacably hostile to the Emperor, especially in the more remote and mountainous parts of the department. Many were actively opposing military recruitment and even encouraging peasants to desert, while in Grenoble it was widely believed that the clergy had hidden weapons in seminaries.[61]

Royalists too sought to spread rumours against Napoleon; the most typical story was that he had been assassinated. Perhaps the most colourful version of this narrative was offered by a man named Glatigny from Chartres, who was arrested for shouting: 'The Emperor has been murdered – Long Live the King!'. Interrogated by the police, he claimed that he had only been repeating the message crowed by his cock that morning.[62]

To some extent, this opposition to Napoleon's return was counterbalanced by the enthusiasm of his supporters. This was, of course, manifest along the trail of the 'flight of the eagle', but was also apparent in localities with distinct Napoleonic memories – such as Toulon, where the entire town celebrated the success of the plebiscite in late May[63] – and above all in his native Corsica. Here the news of his successful escape from Elba was greeted with a proliferation of cockades and tricolour banners; in Bastia there was a fête which lasted until the early hours of the morning,[64] and in Ajaccio a statue of the Emperor was carried in triumph across town.[65]

Among the groups which showed the greatest fervour for Napoleon during the Hundred Days were of course the military (including those still serving in the French Army, but especially the retired soldiers and officers who had fought with him), and also a large number of students. As one Parisian eyewitness noted: 'The great majority of young people aspired to Napoleon's return; some at any cost, and others, including myself, wanting him only if he granted every liberty.'[66]

Such was the strength of support for Napoleon in the Paris Faculty of Medicine that an all-day fête was organized on 7 April; it began with a ceremony at the Carrousel, during which tricolour banners and eagles were distributed, and ended in the evening with a banquet.[67] At the Lycée Sainte-Barbe, the leading secondary school of the capital, opinion was divided between Bourbons and Bonapartists but Napoleon's supporters were buttressed by the young Godefroy Cavaignac, the son of an eminent Revolutionary leader; his support for Bonaparte symbolized the alignment of many Jacobin republicans with Napoleon after March 1815.[68]

Napoleon no doubt welcomed and to some extent even courted this support; at Autun on 15 March he did not hesitate to use Revolutionary language, violently attacking the 'slavery' which the priests and the nobles were seeking to inflict upon the French people.[69] Yet this sort of endorsement proved on balance more problematic than helpful to him. All over France former Jacobin republicans stood behind the Emperor for 'patriotic' reasons: he was fighting to preserve the nation's sovereignty and territorial integrity. Agricol Perdiguier, a young boy at the time of the Hundred Days, had three abiding memories of the events of 1815: his republican father's joy at the return of the Emperor, the public rejoicing that greeted the news in the village, and the tricolour flag which was proudly raised again on the Church steeple.[70]

But the disciples of the 1789 Revolution wanted much more from Napoleon than he was willing to countenance, let alone deliver. During the Hundred Days, local republican leaders agitated for authorities to take strong (and often extreme) measures against priests and aristocrats, the key supporters of the Bourbons. In Avignon, the republicans were led by the notary Vinay who organized processions through the town almost every day, calling for the systematic liquidation of all 'enemies of the people' as in the days of the Revolutionary Terror.[71] In Toulouse, the local republicans carried a bust of the Emperor through the town, shouting 'The aristocrats to the skewer!'[72] In Lyons and Grenoble, republicans were in such a state of agitation in the early weeks of the Hundred Days that police hoped that popular support for Napoleon could be 'dampened down'.

In rural communities, peasant feelings (largely provoked, as mentioned earlier, by fears of the *ancien régime* aristocracy returning to reclaim their lands) were also running high. In the Puy-de-Dôme, a local official reported:

> 'The people of the countryside are manifesting an extraordinary sense of enthusiasm [for Napoleon]; fires are lit every evening on elevated positions, and there are public celebrations in many communes. It is commonly asserted that if the Emperor had not returned to put the aristocrats in their place they would have been massacred by the peasants.'[73]

Although these threats of violence against aristocrats and priests by Napoleon's republican supporters were not acted upon during the

Hundred Days, they did little to calm the situation. Indeed, in many parts of France they created a charged political atmosphere that greatly discouraged local bourgeois notables from rallying to the Emperor after March 1815. The force of these cross-pressures was most tellingly reflected in the fate of the Federations which were established all over France from early May under the supervision of Lazare Carnot, Napoleon's Minister of the Interior, a legendary republican who had played a decisive role in organizing French defences during the Revolutionary years.

These associations were founded at local level to promote patriotic sentiment and mobilize opinion in support of Napoleon's return.[74] Despite the Emperor's wish to see the movement opened to the masses, the Federations remained largely dominated by the petite bourgeoisie; the prefect of the Mont Blanc department noted that 'the main towns in the locality have joined up. But the Federations will be of little use to the administration – few men are taking an active role in it; the mass of the population is abstaining.'[75] Those elements of the bourgeoisie which were not inclined towards republicanism were generally reluctant to join; in Toulouse the police noted that 'there is little civic spirit among the men of the leading class'; this comment reflected the bourgeois defiance of Napoleon in most of urban France.[76]

At the same time, when workers did rally in large numbers (as for example in Paris, where ten thousand men from the Faubourgs Saint-Antoine and Saint-Marcel formed a Federation in May) their revolutionary aspirations inspired fear among the local bourgeoisie.[77] When the Emperor abdicated in June 1815, his strongest support came from these popular republican battalions, who urged him to establish a revolutionary dictatorship. The Federations, in short, symbolized Napoleon's key political dilemma during the Hundred Days: they brought the least support from those social groups he most wanted to rally, and the greatest enthusiasm from those he thought least likely to further his cause.

The general attitude of the French people during the Hundred Days, however, was neither intensely supportive of nor hostile to the Emperor; it was more one of fear, expectation and opportunism. Napoleon recognized as much when he declared to his stepdaughter Hortense: 'I only have the people and the Army up to captain level for me. The rest are scared of me, but I cannot rely on them.'[78]

This was especially true of public officials. After March 1815 Napoleon was in a double bind: the men he appointed at local level (especially the prefects, the chief administrators of the departments) were generally ineffective, while those he allowed to remain in their posts often worked explicitly against him – notably so in the case of the mayors.[79]

Public sentiment among the masses was perhaps best captured by a report from Compiègne in early April, which noted that locals had demonstrated in favour of the Emperor but had only done so in a 'perfunctory' manner. When asked why their enthusiasm had been so guarded, the men and women present had replied that they knew that the King was gathering a large army on France's frontiers, and was preparing to attack Napoleon. The imminence of war bore down heavily on public expectations throughout the Hundred Days.[80]

The End and the Beginning

Throughout his career, Napoleon's immediate political fate had ultimately hinged on his performance on the battlefield, and the Hundred Days would prove no exception. On 18 June, at the end of a battle whose outcome long hung in the balance, he was overcome by a combined force of British, Dutch and Prussian troops.

Napoleon's defeat was to some degree preordained, both by the broader political constraints that he faced in France and by the specific choices he made in preparing for the 1815 Belgian campaign. Rebellions in the Vendée and in Brittany had forced him to deploy some of his troops to contain the royalists; the absence of these forces would be cruelly felt during the battles of June.

The Emperor's choice of commanding officers also left much to be desired. Davout, by far his most capable Marshal – he was still undefeated – was left behind in Paris, a mistake compounded by Napoleon's choice of Soult as his chief of staff, and his unwillingness to reintegrate his brother-in-law Murat (who admittedly had cruelly betrayed him in 1814. But then, so had most of his Marshals.) In place of the flamboyant and energetic Murat, Napoleon put

Grouchy – a man not lacking in talent but one who was overly in awe of the Emperor; his indecisiveness would play an important role in the French defeat at Waterloo.

These 'incoherences' did not augur well for the campaign ahead.[81] It has also been frequently argued that Napoleon himself was morally and physically diminished at the time of the decisive battle, but this is greatly exaggerated. In fact, as he headed towards battle, the Emperor was confident of victory;[82] and his physical stamina during the four days of engagement was undiminished.[83]

Napoleon's battle plan was simple: instead of waiting for his adversaries to attack him on French soil, he decided to surprise them by marching towards the two armies advancing on France from the north-east. His scheme was to cut them off from each other and then to defeat them separately. The first army, made up of British and Dutch troops, was commanded by Wellington, and the second, consisting of Prussian forces, was led by Blücher. The plan was conceived with characteristic Napoleonic aplomb, and immaculately executed inasmuch as neither the British nor the Prussians suspected the Emperor's arrival.[84]

From this moment on, however, almost everything went wrong. A French General (Bourmont) deserted to the enemy, a betrayal which undoubtedly had a demoralizing effect on Napoleon's troops. The first encounter with the Prussians, at the battle of Ligny (16 June) was indecisive: Napoleon pushed back the enemy, but the Prussians managed to retreat in good order.[85] The Emperor here made his first serious mistake: he committed 30,000 men (under Grouchy's command) to pursue the Prussians, thereby weakening his own forces before the decisive battle against Wellington.

This final engagement took place two days later near the village of Waterloo. Napoleon planned to attack his opponents from the centre, and expected Grouchy to deploy his forces to assist him and to prevent the Prussians from coming to their allies' assistance.[86] For reasons that still remain unclear, Grouchy never appeared, even though he was within hearing range of the hostilities. The battle itself consisted of successive waves of French forces led and directed by Jérôme Bonaparte (Napoleon's younger brother), Drouet d'Erlon, and Marshal Ney. But 'the bravest of the brave' was somewhat uninspired on this critical day. Somewhat chaotically executed, Ney's charges were robustly repelled by Wellington's troops, who not only resisted fiercely but also inflicted heavy losses on the French assailants.[87]

Napoleon's rout was completed in the early evening of 18 June when the Prussians – unchecked by Grouchy – made their appearance on the battlefield. As a last resort, Napoleon sent his Guard into the fray, with Ney leading on foot, sword in hand (he had five horses killed under him on the day); but this final charge was also repelled. The terrible carnage wiped out a quarter of the Emperor's armed force of 124,000.

The battle of Waterloo, one of the great 'sites of memory' of modern Europe,[88] was also one of the decisive moments in the French historical experience. For much of the nineteenth century, and well beyond, participants, observers, and historians debated the outcome and its significance. Napoleon, as we shall later see, offered his own (highly tendentious) account of the events.[89] His admirers blamed everyone else but the Emperor: his lieutenants, the weather (it poured with rain before the battle), fate.[90] His adversaries, in contrast, rounded on the 1815 defeat as exemplifying all the flaws in his character.[91] One republican historian, after narrating the campaign of 1815, ended by observing that: 'I contemplate Napoleon defeated, and about to be nailed to his small island, with dry eyes; I reserve all my tears for the victims of his ambitions'.[92]

In his celebrated twenty-volume history of the imperial era, Adolphe Thiers devoted an entire tome to Waterloo, clinically spelling out the numerous mistakes made by the Emperor and his lieutenants on the day of the battle.[93] In truth, even if Napoleon had prevailed his days were almost certainly numbered. The Allied coalition which had resumed the war against France would not have rested until he was defeated, and the French people had no stomach for yet more fighting.[94]

The reaction in Paris in the immediate aftermath of Waterloo was predictable. There was consternation in the imperial court, where news of the defeat came through on the evening of 20 June, just as Benjamin Constant was finishing a reading of his sentimental novel *Adolphe*.[95] Elsewhere, and notably among the elites, it was felt that the time had come to move on. And so, four days later, pressed by the legislators, the Emperor abdicated; thus began a transition phase piloted by his Minister of Police, the wily and perfidious Fouché, which would rapidly see the Bourbons brought back to the French throne.[96]

Louis XVIII returned to Paris on 8 July, and a week later Napoleon left France on board an English ship; he would never see his country again. The Allies eventually decided to banish him to the distant island of Saint-Helena, which the Emperor and his small party of followers reached in October 1815. Just as their commander-in-chief was embarking on his final voyage, his valiant soldiers, discharged from the Army, began their own journey back to their native towns and villages, where many would in effect experience the torments of internal exile. These were the men who would soon become the high priests of the Napoleon cult.[97]

To those who lived through them, the Hundred Days were a strange, paradoxical period. Everything had seemed to revert to the era when the Emperor had ruled supreme, and yet everything was subtly different. There was much more freedom than before – especially for the press. Many publications openly insulted the Emperor every day, calling him a 'monster', a 'modern Tamerlan' or (perhaps worst of all) a 'Corsican';[98] royalist pamphlets typically lumped together, in one terrifying equation, Bonapartism, Jacobinism, and the Terror.[99]

Even Napoleon was not quite his same old self. Carnot later recalled finding him silently contemplating a portrait of his wife Marie-Louise and their son, neither of whom had been allowed by the Austrians to join him: his face was 'flooded with tears'.[100] Perhaps this supremely intuitive man had an inkling that his fortune was finally beginning to turn. After his triumphant return to the Tuileries, his ambitions had been repeatedly thwarted. He had come back seeking peace (and, perhaps for once, really meaning it), but his European enemies had inflicted war upon him. He had tried, again for the first time in his political career, to establish his rule on liberal foundations. But the notables whom he desperately needed to buttress his power had spurned his advances, and withheld all support for him after Waterloo, making his second abdication inevitable.

Was the Emperor mistaken to have pursued the path of liberal reform after his return in March 1815? Napoleon did retain significant popular support among large numbers of peasants and workers, especially the Jacobin republicans; and his brother Lucien had urged him to seek to ground his rule not in the bourgeoisie but in 'the immense party of the Revolution'.[101] But Napoleon was not willing to base his political power on these groups, whom he dismissed as 'terrorists' eager only for a resumption of the civil strife of the Revolutionary era.[102]

The Emperor was still capable of remarkable achievements: his 'flight of the eagle' had been an unparalleled act of political genius. But there was, at the same time, an unmistakable sense that his powers were waning; even his old military touch seemed to be deserting him. Given the balance of forces, it was highly improbable that the battle of Waterloo could have ended in a French victory, but Napoleon committed several tactical mistakes which made his celebrated defeat even more likely. More fundamentally, his error was to devote so much of his time and energy to constitutional reform upon his return from Elba, and to neglect preparations for war. As a sympathetic but critical historian suggested, Napoleon should perhaps have inverted his priorities: the times demanded that he should 'fight first, discuss later'.[103]

Such were the Hundred Days, a period during which events remained fluid and uncertain until the very end. In removing Napoleon from French soil in July 1815, his enemies hoped to rid themselves, once and for all, of the man they saw as 'the most profound corruptive force which ever existed'.[104] Unfortunately for the Bourbon royalists and their allies, things did not prove that simple: the ghost of Napoleon continued to haunt the political scene. The Emperor's return in March had forced the King to flee and then return for a second time under foreign protection – a humiliation with which the Restoration regime would be forever tarred. And, as we shall discover in the chapters that follow, the enduring appeal of Napoleon (and Napoleonic ideas) was largely grounded in the events of March–June 1815. The Emperor's short-lived return to power enabled him to seize the political initiative and to make something of a fresh start, recasting himself in the role of a popular sovereign, liberal reformer, national liberator, and defender of the principles of the 1789 Revolution.

All these images, superimposed upon each other, did not of course cohere – neither with each other nor with Napoleon's earlier self-representations. But in the confused and dramatic context of the time, with France facing the threat of foreign invasion and counter-revolution, these disparities did not matter. Indeed, the very ambiguity which they produced proved highly creative, as it paved the way for the emergence of new forms of Napoleonic support – traditionalist and monarchical, but also popular and neo-republican, liberal and elitist, youthful and romantic.

Born in the troubled context of 1815, these perceptions survived and prospered throughout France in the aftermath of the Emperor's departure to Saint-Helena, thus providing the initial matrix for the legend of Napoleon. They did so through the powerful memories of specific events and incidents, such as the encounter at Laffrey, which highlighted the Emperor's enduring political charisma; through the new political principles and values which came to be associated with Napoleon's rule, notably liberalism and defensive patriotism but also a commitment to the revolutionary heritage; and even through his military defeat and subsequent banishment, which turned him into a martyr in the eyes of enlightened opinion in France (and Europe).

But above all, and despite Waterloo, the events of 1815 resurrected the myth of the Napoleonic Prometheus, of the glorious man who could succeed against all odds and defy the political and physical laws of the universe. As the Restoration authorities would rapidly discover, such powerful beliefs could prove extremely damaging to the order and legitimacy they sought to re-establish.

Chapter 2

Birth of a Legend

In late May 1820 the Baron d'Haussez, prefect of the Isère, decided to leave his office in Grenoble to travel around his department. He had been in his post only for a few months,[1] and knowing the Isère to be a politically 'difficult' region he decided to build a network of personal contacts with the inhabitants.

Initially the trip went quite well, and the Baron even received warm greetings in some localities. But when he reached the area near Laffrey, the scene of Napoleon's epic encounter with French troops in March 1815, there was a perceptible change in the atmosphere. Members of his entourage were threatened as they approached the dwellings, and the prefect's official uniform was mocked by villagers. The worst affront, however, was yet to come. In the village itself, a group of men led by a peasant – clearly a figure of considerable authority in his community – marched up to the Baron to announce that Napoleon would soon be back and would 'chase him away'. As the dismayed officials retreated, they were taunted with chants of 'Long Live the Emperor!'[2]

The story demonstrates the political difficulties encountered by Restoration authorities in dealing with local populations, and the enduring suspicion and hostility towards the Bourbons. Since its second return, the royalist government had done little to bring about

national reconciliation – on the contrary. Some hot-headed supporters of the monarchy, outraged by the events of the Hundred Days,
thirsted for blood and revenge.[3] Indeed, these 'ultra' royalists, as they
called themselves, were profoundly unhappy with the 1814 Charter
granted by King Louis XVIII, which represented in their eyes too
much of a concession to the abhorred principles of the 1789
Revolution.

The dream of the ultras was to turn the clock back to the ancien
régime, with a King ruling by divine right, a political system dominated by the aristocracy, and (above all) a society which repented of
all its sins and was governed by the fear of God. Ultra-royalism poisoned the politics of the Restoration, and helped in no small way to
cement the alliance of liberals, republicans, and Bonapartists[4] (see
Figure 5).

At a more fundamental level, this menace of a resurgent and vin-
dictive royalism also helped to keep alive popular memories of the
Emperor. In many parts of France, this support – as experienced by
the unfortunate prefect of Isère – was coupled with a belief in the
imminence of the Emperor's return. Indeed, this sentiment was
shared by millions of French men and women across the country
after 1815: a matter of hope and anticipation for some, and of fear
and despair for others.

In towns and villages across France, the main sources of such
beliefs were rumours, which swept across the country in a variety of
forms: precise Napoleonic sightings and dates were mixed with vague
and confused tales; realistic accounts with extraordinary and apocalyptic reports; flamboyant adventures with modest and almost
intimate stories; and local fables with legends from far-flung territories. But whatever their form all these rumours shared one central
theme: Napoleon would soon be back in France to reclaim his
throne – and the Bourbons' days were numbered.

These 'seditious' stories, as the authorities called them, posed a
fundamental problem to the Restoration government because they
raised expectations among Bonapartist supporters and spread alarm
(and occasionally panic) among the population. More fundamentally,
this widespread belief in the imminence of Napoleon's 'second
coming' directly challenged the regime's political legitimacy. After all,
why pledge allegiance to Louis XVIII if he was about to be thrown

FIGURE 5

Allegorical representation of the return of the ultras

After 1815 the Bourbon regime came under the increasing political influence of the ultra-royalists, who conducted a 'White Terror' against Bonapartists and Jacobins who had rallied to the Emperor in 1815 and became a vocal lobby for the promotion of the interests of the aristocracy and the Church. The ultras above all sought to destroy all the political and legal achievements of the Revolution, which had been consolidated by Napoleon; this ambition is represented here by a posse of ultra-royalists attempting to deface the Vendôme column in Paris (the symbol of Napoleonic glory). Note the cross in the left background, symbolizing the alliance between the Restoration and the Church; also important is the carriage suspended in the air on the right – a vivid representation of the royalists returning to France 'in the carriages of the foreigners'.

out of the country (again) by the Emperor? And why pay taxes if the royalist administration would soon be replaced?

Although the reactions of Bourbon officials to this predicament varied, in the main their response to these rumours was dismissive. In their view, such stories merely revealed the credulousness of the French population and their capacity to subscribe to 'irrational' forms of belief. In modern parlance, these rumours concerning Napoleon's return appeared symptomatic of a backward mass mentality, of a mindset dominated by traditional values and a belief in the supernatural.

But dismissing these rumours as 'irrational' is far too simplistic. Napoleon had after all returned once from exile, so it was hardly unreasonable for the French people to lend credence to stories that he was about to repeat the feat – especially when we bear in mind that reliable sources of information such as newspapers were available only to a very small minority of the population, mainly in cities and towns, and that literacy levels in some of the less developed regions of France (such as Brittany) were below twenty per cent.[5] Furthermore, as the Restoration authorities themselves acknowledged, these stories did not always spring up spontaneously: they were often planted by Bonapartist agents, with the evident intention of creating social tension and political instability. But even when generated without such an external agency, and even at their most fantastical, these narratives also possessed an inner coherence, revealing the political aspirations and fears of local communities as well as their wider social and cultural values.

Also embedded in these stories were highly structured sets of beliefs about the Emperor himself: about his personality, his state of mind, his military capacities, his political values, and much else. Indeed, when viewed in historical perspective these narratives have much to reveal about the emergence of the Napoleonic 'legend'. It is commonly argued that Napoleon was the creator of his own myth, both through his own systematic use of propaganda and through his careful (and often creative) reconstruction of his political career in the *Mémorial de Sainte-Hélène*, published shortly after his death in 1821.[6]

From this perspective, the legend appears to a large extent as a conscious manipulation 'from above', constructed by literary means and underpinned by a coherent image of Napoleon as an imperial and military hero, the embodiment and saviour of the French nation. If we explore the mythologization of the Emperor which underlay the rumours of his return, however, a rather broader pattern emerges: one that is much more ideologically entrenched in 'the tradition of 1789' and is also grounded in a complex web of national and local popular beliefs. Above all, the rumours of the Emperor's return highlight the central role of the Hundred Days in the emergence of the legend. Politically, 1815 may well have been the end of the line for Napoleon – it certainly was militarily – but in a much more profound sense it really marked a new beginning.

The Ides of March

The wave of rumours concerning Napoleon's return began under the First Restoration in early 1815, just as the Emperor was firming up his plans to escape from Elba and the Bourbons were struggling to establish their hold over France. These stories were often spread by demobilized soldiers, and came with the promise of considerable further upheavals for France (and for the whole of Europe).

In the version peddled by the Mercurin family, ardent Bonapartists from the village of Graveson in Provence, it was stated among other things that: 'The King's promises about forgetting the past are all illusory, and moreover he is intent on destroying all those who believe in the principles of the Revolution; Joachim Murat the King of Naples has seized the whole of Italy, and in alliance with Poland he is about to levy a new army which will burst into France in order to overthrow Louis XVIII and put Buonaparte back on the throne; Napoleon will soon be back in power, and everyone will then have the pleasure of seeing the head of Louis XVIII roll, just as had happened to Louis XVI his brother.'[7]

Napoleon did indeed come back a few months later – and in a way it was the very implausibility of the circumstances of his return in March 1815 which made subsequent predictions or prophecies credible again after his exile to Saint-Helena. And even if the 'accompanying' elements of this particular rumour were not substantiated (Louis XVIII quietly slouched into exile, instead of suffering his brother's fate; and the unfortunate Murat was executed while trying to imitate Napoleon's 'flight of the eagle' in Naples[8]), they underscored many of the key conditions which made possible a widespread belief in the Emperor's reappearance.

Firstly, there were feelings of dissatisfaction with the Bourbons, accompanied by fears that the clock was being turned back to the *ancien régime*. In addition, there emerged a powerful antagonism towards the aristocracy and the clergy, expressed in a rallying of Jacobins to the Napoleonic cause and in frequent calls for the revival of the Terror. Above all, there was a sense that Napoleon, although defeated at Waterloo, retained much of his influence outside France through his international alliances. The broader political backdrop against which the rumours of the post-1815 period proliferated remained essentially the same.

Restoration rumours concerning Napoleon's next return most commonly emerged during the early months of each subsequent year, especially in March. Every anniversary of the Emperor's 1815 landing brought forth a wave of prouncements that Napoleon was on his way to France again. This information was sometimes conveyed on placards, such as the one from Tarbes in 1816 stating, quite simply, that 'Napoleon will be back in March'.[9] Then there were false proclamations purporting to be by the Emperor himself, such as those found pinned to public buildings in Vesoul and Tonnerre in 1817.[10] Word of mouth played its part, as with the former imperial soldier who travelled around the outskirts of Lyons in 1820 declaring that 'Napoleon would be appearing soon; all the former soldiers are for him and he is accompanied by foreign troops who are bringing him back into France'.[11] Songs were written specially for the occasion, as in the tribute to the Emperor which ended by stating that 'every Frenchman will be true to his *patrie* and to his honour if called upon to take up arms again in March'.[12] And at commemorative gatherings, Bonapartists came together to celebrate the 'anniversary of 20 March' and spread the word about Napoleon's imminent return.[13]

The local passage of Napoleon through various towns during the 'flight of the eagle' was also marked. In 1816 a force of six thousand national guardsmen had to be deployed across the main arteries and squares of Lyons to prevent the city from being reclaimed by those celebrating the first anniversary of Napoleon's arrival the year before.[14] These commemorations naturally provided a setting for the dissemination of yet more stories about the Emperor's plans for his imminent return.

By 1817 the police all over France had come to regard the month of March with dread: 'This month, marked several times by extraordinary events, is always chosen by subversive elements who seek to take advantage of the credulous dispositions of the populace.'[15]

Each year between 1816 and 1825, and even beyond, the March rumours re-surfaced.[16] At their peak these tidings were accompanied by spectacular tales of domestic and international turbulence. In Paris during the early months of 1817 stories of Napoleon's return became entangled with accounts of provincial rebellions in Grenoble and Sisteron and riots in Nancy (all imaginary)[17] and in Lyons with graphic details of an (entirely fictitious) army of 40,000 men which had pledged loyalty to the Emperor in the departments of Isère, Ain, and Saône-et-Loire.[18] In Metz, at precisely the same moment, Bonaparte was thought to have arrived in Austria: France was believed to be calm, but Napoleon's escape from Saint-Helena was understood to have triggered revolutions in Spain and in England.[19]

Some historians have noted a particular intensity in the occurrence of rumours in the periods 1816–17, 1819–20, and again in 1823.[20] But even in the relatively 'fallow' years these stories continued to appear in droves; few localities were exempt. In March 1818, for example, the sub-prefect of Chateausalins (Meurthe) noted that a range of different rumours were circulating in his area: 'In some versions, Napoleon is returning to France accompanied by four to five hundred thousand Americans, in others he is being preceded by two to three thousand Spanish clergymen; in others still it is thanks to the efforts of the prisoner of Saint-Helena that the price of wheat has been lowered; and in all of these tales the month of March will not end without some extraordinary events.'[21]

Leaving aside the somewhat odd ratio of American troops to Spanish clergymen, it is interesting to observe here the suggestion of Napoleonic omnipotence – one of the critical components of the 'legend'. Worthy of attention, too, was the mythologization of the month of March itself, which was widely believed to possess almost mystical properties. These rumours, it should also be noted, had few direct connections with any schemes and actions of Napoleon himself, or even with any concrete piece of information about his life at Saint-Helena. Indeed, the prison island itself was occasionally incorporated into the mythology, as in 1817 when stories spread in Valence that an attempted Napoleonic escape had been foiled: the Emperor was now to be deported to the penal colony of Botany Bay, and his aide-de-camp General Bertrand taken to England to face execution.[22]

The disconnection of the mythology from the 'real' Napoleon was most graphically illustrated in the wake of the Emperor's death in 1821 (see Figure 6). When the news reached France, there was very little public reaction – even in 'Napoleonic' strongholds such as Lyons. One police official even sought to provide an explanation: 'The upper class has long believed that Napoleon's career was over; the mass, for its part, has been so often deceived by false rumours that it has become disillusioned and extremely circumspect'.[23]

Then, after months of complete quiet, during which local officials almost boasted of the absence of any political unrest,[24] rumours that Napoleon was still alive and heading back towards France suddenly appeared simultaneously in early to mid-March 1822 all over the nation. In some instances the information was very specific: letters were sent out from Grenoble to Lyons on 15 March announcing that Napoleon had been proclaimed Emperor again, and that he was advancing towards Paris with General Bertrand. The 'news' reached Lyons the following day, and spread so much alarm in the city that the prefect had to issue a public denial two days later.[25]

The Terrain of Rumours

Rumours were not merely verbal abstractions: they were physical realities, comparable to weather systems moving across French territory on a variety of paths. In territorial terms, these storms swirled in

FIGURE 6

Death of Napoleon, 5 May 1821.
Drawing used to illustrate Louis Marchand's account of the Emperor's death
(first published in 1836)

Louis Marchand became Napoleon's principal valet at the time of the Emperor's first abdication in 1814; he never left Napoleon's side from that moment, accompanying him to Elba, then back to Paris during the Hundred Days, and then finally to Saint-Helena. In his will Napoleon rewarded his devotion by a gift of 600,000 francs and a title of Count. Marchand returned to Saint-Helena to bring back Napoleon's remains in 1840. The account of Napoleon's death that he published in 1836 was the first authoritative description of the Emperor's final moments. In this drawing Napoleon is shown on his deathbed. Among those present around him at Saint-Helena were Napoleon's chief of staff Bertrand and his wife, as well as General Montholon and Napoleon's doctor Antommarchi. Among the children sketched is Arthur Bertrand, who was born on the island; Napoleon used to call him his 'little tyrant'.

three sets of directions: from foreign countries into France (most notably through bordering territories such as Switzerland; in parts of the Rhône in late 1815 'everyone believed that Napoleon was in Geneva);[26] from the provinces up to the capital (a report from Lyons in 1816 graphically described the rumours as 'travelling towards Paris');[27] and from provincial urban centres outwards into rural areas (often through markets and fairs, where agricultural workers and farmers picked up the information and avidly disseminated it in their communes).[28] In terms of their specific points of origin, the tales often appeared to emerge from a particular set of provincial localities: Grenoble, Lyons, Strasbourg, and Toulon (often mentioned as the putative port of Napoleon's landing).[29] Toulouse was also an extremely active source of Napoleonic rumours in the early years of the Restoration.[30]

Special mention was also frequently made of Corsica, where authorities lamented that 'a large majority of the population firmly believes in the imminence of the Emperor's return.'[31] Rumours of Napoleon's escape from Saint-Helena continued to circulate in his birthplace until a few months before his death; they were often triggered by false 'proclamations' written by locals or smuggled into the island from Italy or southern France.[32]

Another critical material source of these tales were Napoleonic songs, which described the return of the Emperor in literal or allegorical forms. Police reports in February and early March often directly linked the appearance of rumours to the sale of specific Napoleonic songs; in Chavigny (Bas-Rhin) in 1818 a chant whose theme was 'The Emperor Is Already Back' was the source of a widespread local belief that Napoleon was on French soil.[33] Another song lamented the 'banishment' of the violet, one of the flowers associated with Napoleon since 1815, before concluding that 'this wonderful flower will be returned to us next spring'.[34]

Songs also took the form of classical allegories; one of the most widespread instances of the latter was 'Ulysses and Telemachus', a hymn whose six verses depicted France languishing under tyrannical rule while Ulysses was banished, and ended with the promise of his return. First heard in the immediate aftermath of Napoleon's departure for Saint-Helena, and dismissed by the Minister of the Interior as a classical fable too complicated to pose any serious threat to the regime, 'Ulysses and Telemachus' was by 1819 being sung in over twenty departments; it was most frequently heard around the anniversary of the Emperor's return.[35]

There was also, alongside this 'real' territory in which these tales and songs appeared, an 'imagined' set of locations which figured prominently in the rumours themselves. Paris, as the Emperor's final destination, and the seat of national power, featured in almost every account: sometimes in the form of vague assertions that a Napoleonic insurrection was about to break out in one of the working-class districts, such as the Faubourg Saint-Antoine,[36] and sometimes with very precise additional information: in early 1817 a story went around several departments of the south-east that Napoleon would be in Paris 'on the twenty-fifth of January.'[37] The cities and towns which had been on the path of the 'flight of the eagle' in 1815 – most notably Lyons and Grenoble – also often featured in the rumours. Both towns, as we shall observe in a later chapter, witnessed serious acts of organized rebellion against the Bourbons.

But even more worrying to the authorities was what *might* happen in these various localities. Lyons was described in 1816 by the prefect of the Rhône as 'the central point upon which the thoughts and fantasies of all the conspirators of the country seem to converge'.[38] This dubious honour was in fact shared with another hornets' nest for Restoration authorities: Grenoble. In late February 1818 a story reached several departments of eastern France that the Emperor was already in the capital of the Isère, from which point he would command an army of Turkish soldiers in a push towards Paris.[39]

Stories of Napoleon's return were not always generated spontaneously, even though the tales often took on a life and a momentum of their own once they were 'released' into a particular locality or area. Indeed, from the very outset the Restoration authorities were convinced that these rumours were propagated by 'secret supporters of the usurper'.[40] Evidence confirming this beyond a reasonable doubt was not always available and it is also clear that local authorities often exaggerated the degree of 'organization' of Bonapartist agents. But proof of a coordinated campaign to spread false information was often found. In Grenoble, for example, there were clandestine printers who regularly produced a whole array of literature (false proclamations, alleged newspaper cuttings, etc.) which was used to disseminate the rumours of Napoleon's return in the countryside.[41]

And even when they were not caught by the police, the existence of these 'rumour-mongers' could often be directly deduced by the specific manner in which the tales themselves appeared. In early January 1816 the *procureur* of Fontainebleau reported that a rumour that Napoleon had arrived in Paris had sprung up on exactly the same day (the fourth of January) in Nemours, parts of Burgundy and the Bourbonnais, as well as along the two roads leading to Lyons. The absence of any such story prior to this date and its simultaneous appearance, in the same form and at the same moment, in a range of different but territorially contiguous localities seemed to point to only one possible conclusion: this particular 'rumour' was the work of an organized network of Napoleonic agents.[42]

Some rumours of the Emperor's return were also spread in order to perturb the organization of royalist public events. In the town of Villeneuve (Yonne) local officials were preparing for the visit of the Duchess of Angoulême (scheduled for 25 May 1816) when the story suddenly spread that the person arriving in town on that day would be Napoleon. A woman was eventually arrested for disseminating this rumour; she confessed that her aim in doing so was to 'paralyse the preparations for the royal visit'.[43]

The main culprits in these sorts of incidents were the 'demi-soldes', former imperial officers on half pay, who were among the principal popular disseminators of the Napoleonic 'legend' after 1815. Restoration officials regarded these veterans with veritable dread, as they were both inactive (and thus with much time on their hands) and fanatically devoted to the Napoleonic cause. In early 1816 the prefect of Ain identified half-pay officers in his locality as the main source of the rumours concerning the Emperor's return, and had many of them removed from the department;[44] his colleague in the Doubs likewise described the demi-soldes as the foremost agents of 'political corruption' in his region.[45] The prefect of the Basses-Pyrénées also concurred, adding that these men were proving particularly difficult to handle because of their 'proud and arrogant manners.'[46]

Given their inherently secretive and resilient nature, the specific agents engaged in this sort of rumour-mongering were often difficult to identify. However, the authorities were occasionally successful; in early 1817 an officer by the name of Ségur was arrested and sentenced to five years' imprisonment for spreading the story that Louis XVIII had left France, and that Napoleon was on his way back to Paris to reclaim his throne.[47]

Another group consistently suspected of rumour-mongering were travelling salesmen (*colporteurs*). A police report written in the early years of the Restoration noted that 'travelling salesmen are roaming across town and country, reaching even isolated habitations in order to disseminate deliberately fabricated information, generated so as to alarm feeble minds and entertain the illusions of the supporters of the usurper [Napoleon]'.[48]

Similar reports came in from all parts of France throughout the ensuing decade, sometimes with very specific details. In 1817 the prefect of Isère informed his colleague in Lyons that salesmen from his city had brought six stories with them to the Grenoble fair, which had just opened; one of these rumours concerned Napoleon's alleged flight to Philadelphia.[49] It was also clear that on many occasions these 'travelling salesmen' were in fact thinly disguised political emissaries. In 1827 the prefect of the Côtes-du-Nord reported that 'travelling salesmen seem again to have received the order to disseminate alarming information and seditious songs in the different localities they are visiting'.[50]

In many instances, these itinerant men did not even carry any objects for sale: they devoted themselves entirely to spreading rumours and collecting information. In 1823 the Minister of Interior expressed alarm after reports from all over France suggested that groups of 'travelling salesmen' had been spreading false rumours about the fate of French troops engaged in action in Spain, but also enquiring about the location of gunpowder and munition depots.[51] A military report from the Nièvre described the *colporteurs* who had recently been seen in his department as generally aged between twenty and twenty-five, many of them having served in the French Army; their general attitude was one of 'insolence'.[52]

But the networks that propagated Napoleonic rumours

extended well beyond the officers on half pay and travelling sales-men. Bonapartists all around the country deployed a variety of agents and instruments to spread tales of the impending collapse of the Bourbon regime, and the imminent return of their Emperor. In the Yonne, the mayor of a small town reported that these rumours had 'poisoned the spirits of the great majority of inhabitants'; those responsible were 'several well-off peasants', a priest, and the local schoolteacher Louis-Antoine Guillot and his wife.[53]

This was by no means uncommon; among the fixed agents responsible for conceiving and transmitting these stories, a significant proportion were schoolteachers. In Dieppe an *instituteur* was one of the main activists in an informal group which copied and distributed false Napoleonic proclamations;[54] at Chateau Thierry the school-master was described as 'a very dangerous man who fabricates all the rumours concerning Napoleon and spreads them in the locality';[55] and at Villeneuve-le-Guyard the teacher Monsieur Coutan was known to 'indoctrinate all children with Bonapartist propaganda'.[56]

But Bonapartist agents came from across the social and occu-pational spectrum: in Civrac a barrel-maker was arrested for spreading the story of Napoleon's escape from Saint-Helena;[57] in the Indre, these tales were disseminated by 'a well-spoken and well-dressed man, who was clearly from the bourgeoisie';[58] and in the Somme, the sources of Napoleonic rumours were two officers of the gendarmerie at Abbeville.[59] During the early 1820s a whole subset of men and women seemed to board public coaches travelling from one locality to another only in order to disseminate rumours and false information.[60]

Women were also involved in a significant number of cases, some-times as leaders, on other occasions as accomplices. They were chosen because of their physical attactiveness, or because they were thought to arouse less suspicion, or even because they were sometimes more credible as a source of information. In Marseille a Corsican woman by the name of Catherine Caseneuve was reported to the police for spreading 'exclusive' information about the Emperor's return, which she claimed to have garnered from Napoleon's native island.[61] In Bourg the widow of a Napoleonic officer, who had

accompanied her husband during many of the campaigns of the
First Empire, caused a sensation by revealing the 'secret' plans of
Joseph Bonaparte for the invasion of France and the restoration of
his brother on the throne.[62]

The prize for ingeniousness (and deviousness) must go to a
Bonapartist agent by the name of Baudinot. In his home town of
Chateausalins, he opened a stall in which his wife performed the
function of clairvoyant, using cards and crystal balls to predict
the future. At each of her 'sessions' Madame Baudinot would link
the fate of her individual clients with annoucements of the imminent return of Napoleon, often with very specific dates and precise
locations. Her credibility would no doubt have eventually been
put to the test by the passage of time; however, her reputation was
saved by the police, who arrested her (and her husband) a month
later.[63]

This case of Monsieur and Madame Baudinot draws attention to
the variety of motivations and purposes which could lie behind the
dissemination of Napoleonic rumours. Some Bonapartist agents
spread their stories in the full knowledge that they were false; their
deliberate aim was to foster a climate of fear and uncertainty. This
was the case with a former soldier of the Grande Armée who claimed
that he had recently seen the Emperor in the United States, and that
Napoleon had informed him that he would soon be returning to
France.[64] In Avallon a rumour that the Emperor was back in Paris
spread through cafés and inns between January and March 1817; it
originated from Marie Blondeau, a butcher, who tricked his illiterate
(and, no doubt, intoxicated) audience one evening by claiming to
have just read the news in the copy of the Parisian newspaper he was
holding.[65]

One of the men responsible for the production of a false
Napoleonic proclamation justified this sort of deception by stating
(not without cynicism) that 'all means are good to stir up the
people'.[66] Others, in contrast, caused this very agitation while harbouring exactly the opposite intentions. The prefect of the Meuse
reported in early 1816 that the most consistent source of the rumours
of Napoleon's return came not only from those who hoped for it, but
from those who feared it.[67]

Catholic priests were often the principal agents of Napoleonic rumours in rural localities, provoking alarm by asking their congregation to pray that 'the ogre from Saint-Helena would remain in his cage'[68] – which of course led many of the faithful to believe that his escape was imminent. In the Vendée in February 1819 many panicked priests asked their parishioners to pray fervently 'so as to avert a great disaster which is about to befall France.'[69] With enemies such as these, the Bonapartists clearly needed few friends.

The rumour mill also enabled some entrepreneurial talents to flourish. Many individuals sought to cash in on the appetite of the French public for these stories, claiming to possess specific information which they would pass on to local populations for a modest fee. This was the case with a man who operated in the early months of 1816 on the road between Cahors and Montauban – a lucrative form of seasonal self-employment which came to an abrupt end when he was arrested after being denounced by a dissatisfied customer.[70]

Short, plump, and dark-haired men exploited their physical characteristics (and the credulity of local peasants) to pass themselves off as Bonaparte. Claiming that they had escaped from Saint-Helena, they demanded food and money, and in some cases were extraordinarily successful. A man by the name of Ravier impersonated the Emperor in the rural parts of the Ain, Loire, Isère, Saône-et-Loire, and Rhône throughout the summer and autumn of 1815, generating numerous accounts of Napoleonic sightings in these departments.[71] Hunted down by the police he disappeared for a few months, before re-emerging in the Seine-et-Marne, where his talents brought him a fresh wave of acclamation. He was eventually arrested in February 1816 near Fontainebleau by a rural policeman.[72]

Townsfolk were also taken in: after being released from jail a former convict by the name of Jean Pierre Leclerc successfully passed himself off as Napoleon in various localities in 1821. In Troyes he even managed to deceive the deceivers: he was paraded around town by several local Bonapartists, who showed him 'important papers' and a woman handed over 'all her money and gold'.[73]

Social Consequences

Rumours did not merely live in the realm of the imagination. These stories, as we have just seen, had real social consequences. In the early years of the Restoration news of Napoleon's imminent return altered not only public attitudes but also public behaviour all over the country. At the most immediate level, these tales became the subject of obsessive conversations – in homes, in inns and taverns, in public places.

In January 1816 it was rumoured that the Emperor had landed in Toulon and that his return to the throne was now supported by the Great Powers; soon this tale had reached the department of the Deux-Sèvres, where the prefect issued a proclamation forbidding the local population to discuss the matter. However, the official admitted with resignation that his edict had had little effect: 'This story is the only topic of conversation on the road between Angoulême and Tours.'[74]

In this instance, the rumour no doubt generated a broad and confused range of sentiments among the locals; but in other cases its effects were more precise. In the countryside, some peasants reacted to the same story with practical prudence: in the deepest parts of the Aube and Marne, rural inhabitants carefully hedged their bets by hiding their money (in case Napoleon swooped past to grab it) and slowing down the payment of their fiscal contributions (in case Bourbon rule was nearing its end).[75]

While some greeted the news by withholding everything they had, others in contrast became highly expansive: in the Indre, a wave of peasant marriages was recorded in the weeks following this rumour – a pragmatic response to the conscription which was feared inevitable in the event of the Emperor's return.[76] In this particular case, a large number of children subsequently came to owe their life (literally) to this Napoleonic rumour.

Elsewhere this sort of news provoked scenes of collective enthusiasm, as when a stranger travelling through the Corrèze in mid-March 1816 entered Brive to announce that Napoleon had landed in France and would soon be passing through the town. The story rapidly spread to all the inhabitants, who gathered spontaneously in the public square and raised the tricolour flag on the municipal building. Alerted by the sounds of cheering and beating drums, the mayor arrived to break up the party (and to order the arrest the bearer of false tidings).[77]

Enthusiasm could take the form of eager anticipation: in rural parts of the Var, following suggestions that Napoleon was heading towards France aboard a ship flying the tricolour, groups of villagers were seen heading towards the coast to try and catch sight of the vessel on the horizon.[78]

In some cases, this sort of fervour could also provoke practical gestures of Napoleonic patriotism. In Corsica in late 1816, after persistent rumours that Empress Marie-Louise was gathering troops to invade and liberate France from Bourbon rule, a group of fifty men plotted to seize a vessel in order to travel to Austria to enlist in this force.[79] Some thirty soldiers stationed in the Vendée responded to the same rumour – 'the bird has flown out of his cage' – by deserting and beginning the journey towards Austria.[80]

Enthusiasm in parts of the country, and among some social groups, was mirrored by examples of fear and even collective panic elsewhere. In March 1818 a rumour began to spread in the south-west that some forty thousand Austrian troops were about to pass through France to link up with an army headed by Napoleon (who was believed to be in Spain).[81] The story reached the small town of Pont du Roide during its monthly fair, where several false imperial proclamations were distributed; the news caused so much alarm that 'the fair closed down less than two hours after its opening'.[82]

In many instances, and again mostly in the countryside, sightings of Napoleonic troops were reported – and even of the Emperor himself. In the rural areas around Avallon in early 1816, many peasants swore that they had seen Napoleon riding towards Paris at the head of a small detachment; the story seemed credible enough to the local authorities to warrant the dispatch of gendarmes in hot pursuit.[83] By the time this rumour had travelled up to the Meuse – with the added credibility provided by frantic gendarmes – it caused a considerable number of villagers to flee from their dwellings; they agreed to return only after the prefect issued a proclamation categorically denying that Napoleon was heading towards Paris.[84]

It should not be thought, however, that these sorts of extreme reactions were the preserve of simple-minded country dwellers. In

Lyons the police reported in March 1817 that the whole city was obsessed with Napoleon's return. The bourgeoisie in particular was suffering from paranoia: all those with serious expressions on their faces were thought to be 'conspiring', while those with wry smiles were believed to be harbouring 'seditious hopes'. Unable to cope with the tension, many well-heeled residents of Lyons had departed to their country houses; however, those of a more obstinate disposition had decided to remain on the spot to defend and secure their properties. Many had hired masons to fortify their walls, and some had even built secret hideouts in their own homes, in case the terrible Corsican were to return.[85]

Three years later, there was little sign of improvement in public morale: a large number of citizens lent credence to a story that Napoleon had landed in Bayonne.[86] And in March 1821, following an attempted *coup de force* by Napoleonic activists in Grenoble, 'the most absurd rumours' again circulated in Lyons, forcing the prefect to issue an exasperated proclamation.[87] However, this message arrived too late to stop a large number of inhabitants of Vaize (including the mayor, Monsieur Devarax) from fleeing their village.[88]

Driving Forces

Why did these rumours of the Emperor's return proliferate to such an extent after 1815, causing such widespread and varying reactions – of enthusiasm, anticipation, and fear – among the French population? Historians have suggested several types of explanation. The recurrence of these stories in the month of March has invited quasi-anthropological accounts of rural belief structures, in which the notion of 'cycle' was thought to play a fundamental role.[89] Napoleon's return, from this perspective, was thought to reflect wider patterns of secular understandings about life which fundamentally structured the *Weltanschauung* of the French peasant.[90] Others still have pointed to the continuities in French *mentalités* between the late eighteenth and early nineteenth centuries – a world of millenarian beliefs, parochialism, and irrationalism.[91] In his classic work on the 'Great Fear', Georges Lefebvre highlighted the central role of these phobias in the propagation of rural panic in the run-up to the Revolution of 1789.[92]

There were no doubt some elements of continuity between the 'Napoleonic' rumours of the early Restoration and these earlier manifestations of popular belief. But these connections should not be exaggerated. In order to understand the genesis of these Napoleonic rumours, a greater sensitivity to the specific contexts of the period is needed – especially as the years after 1815 were marked not by continuities (whether with the First Empire or with traditional patterns of belief) but rather by severe social and economic disruptions.

The most important element here was the invasion and military occupation of France by allied forces. Of course, the French people had become accustomed to conscription and troop movements under the First Empire. But for most of the population these were relatively remote occurrences. In contrast, there was a particular immediacy to the events of 1815, which often saw pitched battles on French soil between invading forces of over a million men and national troops (sometimes supported by local militia).

These conflicts were not only destructive – they were also deeply humiliating, all the more so since a considerable number of troops from the British, Russian, and Austrian armies remained on French soil until 1818, imposing considerable hardships on local populations.[93] The presence of these forces, in short, generated feelings of frustrated patriotism and local resentment, and played a particularly important role in changing peasant perceptions of Napoleon. As has been rightly observed: 'The image of Napoleon as ogre disappeared when peasants were confronted by Allied occupation.'[94]

Tales of the Emperor returning to reclaim his throne with the help of various foreign forces emerged against this backdrop: these stories drew upon the existing reality of occupation to construct alternative visions of the post-1815 European and world orders, in which France's international position was reaffirmed through the Emperor. These military fantasies also bear witness to some of the central images that accompanied the Napoleonic 'legend' after 1815: Bonaparte as the incomparable strategist, but also as the heroic and dauntless conqueror of the world.

The range of armed groups and territorial locations which provided the launch pad for Napoleon's return to France in these military rumours was dazzling. In a single twist of the imagination, the Emperor made the leap from feudalism to modernity: his escape from Saint-Helena in one version was organized with the support of the Emperor of Morocco;[95] in another, with the spirited assistance of Latin American revolutionaries.[96] Napoleonic internationalism also knew no bounds: on his journey back towards France the Emperor was reported to be directing armed forces consisting variously of Turks,[97] Indians,[98] Algerians,[99] American negroes,[100] and Africans;[101] mention was made, too, of Persian and even Chinese armies.[102] There were also, of course, ingenious combinations of the above; in the summer of 1816 it was rumoured in the Yonne that the returning Emperor's Army was made up of 'Turks and negroes'.[103]

European forces were not left out: a rumour in early 1817 claimed that Napoleon had formed a new military coalition consisting of Austria, Saxony, Bavaria, and Wurtemberg, and that this force was moving towards France to overthrow the Bourbons.[104] Fuelled no doubt by Bonapartist groups who had settled in the United States after 1815 (notably the one headed by Napoleon's brother Joseph, who had bought a large property near Philadelphia), a variety of stories also placed the Emperor in the New World after he had escaped from Saint-Helena: one had him landing in Boston and another issuing a proclamation from Philadelphia in 1818.[105] Another false proclamation found in the Deux-Sèvres a year later was signed from his military headquarters in the town of Valparaiso by 'Napoleon Bonaparte, Generalissimo of the Federated Army of Western America'.[106] These assorted troops were believed to be about to enter France from a variety of sites: rumours in the south-west of the country had them arriving from Spain;[107] while at precisely the same moment in the northern and central parts of France it was thought that these liberating forces would drive through the Italian peninsula.[108]

Several versions of the plan to restore the Emperor to the French throne involved tactical military support from other members of the imperial family. In 1816 a story went round the Indre that Prince Eugène de Beauharnais, the son of Napoleon's first wife Josephine, had rallied an army in the Rhineland and was preparing to invade France from the east; the force allegedly included 'several of Napoleon's Marshals'.[109] At around the same time the inhabitants of territories bordering Switzerland, and particularly the areas around Gex, heard it said that Joseph Bonaparte was not in America but hiding in the canton of Vaud, preparing an armed force to invade France.[110] The Vaud was known to be a Bonapartist stronghold, and this story caused such widespread alarm by the time it reached the Hautes Pyrénées a week later that it had to be officially denied by the prefect.[111]

The most worrying rumour involving a member of the imperial family other than Napoleon appeared in March 1817, when it was suggested that Lucien Bonaparte, the Emperor's 'republican' brother, was preparing to land a large armed force in the south of France. The rumour originated from the French embassy in Rome (where Lucien lived, along with other members of Bonaparte clan); from there it spread to Corsica, Marseille and Toulon, and then to the rest of the southern French coastal areas. Shortly afterwards, authorities in Antibes, Cannes, Saint-Raphaël, Rocquebrune, Saint-Tropez, and Saint-Maximin all began to report the appearance of tricolour flags in various public places, and to hear dark suggestions that 'extraordinary events were about to take place'. By early April 1817 the story was being taken so seriously that physical descriptions of Lucien were sent out to gendarmes across the entire area, with instructions that he should be arrested if he was seen entering French territory. However, in order to avoid panic among the population, and indeed among the forces of law and order, Lucien's name was not explicitly mentioned.[112]

Napoleon was, in these rumours, irrepressible, literally the stuff of which legends were made: slipping away from his English jailers with devastating ease, galloping across continents while recruiting military support from all nations, races, and tribes, and effortlessly propelling himself back to power in France. One of the striking features of this military image of the Emperor as revealed in these tales was the complete absence of any sense of weakness or vulnerability on his part. It is often claimed that martyrdom was an important ingredient in the legend: Napoleon's defeat and exile, and the humiliations he endured at Saint-Helena, were certainly key elements in the portrait of the Emperor which later emerged in the *Mémorial de Sainte-Hélène*.[113]

But there was none of this fallibility in Napoleon's image in the popular imagination of the early Restoration. Indeed, the rumours celebrated an Emperor with Promethean qualities: like the great conquerors, he was capable of raising colossal armies (two hundred thousand Turks; five hundred thousand Americans and Austrians; and 'two million Indians marching across the Ganges'[114]). But in keeping with his own legend he was equally capable of successfully reclaiming his throne with a few thousand men.[115] One rumour which emerged in early 1816 even credited Napoleon with escaping from Saint-Helena, travelling to Vienna to be reunited with his second wife Marie-Louise and their son, and then capturing his father-in-law the Emperor of Austria – making his wife's father a prisoner in his own country.[116]

The existence of an 'Austrian connection' was one of the most intriguing strands of the Napoleonic-return stories. Some of these tales dated back to the Hundred Days, when Bonapartists themselves spread rumours of Austrian backing as a way of winning over public support for the Emperor's return.[117] But this legend endured after 1815. As we have already noted, many people in France still lent sufficient credence to tales of Austrian military support for Napoleon that they were willing to travel to Vienna to enlist as volunteers. Some of the stories about the size of this liberating army were indeed impressive; according to one account which surfaced in the Indre et Loire in late March 1817 Napoleon was already encamped on French borders with an Austrian force of 530,000 troops.[118]

Interestingly, there is also evidence that many of these return stories originated from the occupying forces themselves – revealing a fascination for the Emperor among the very soldiers and officers who had been fighting against him for years. Already in mid-July 1815, shortly after the Emperor's abdication, rumours had began to circulate in Lyons that Austrian forces were coming to France to impose Napoleon's son as the ruler.[119] While this may have been wishful thinking on the part of Napoleonic enthusiasts, this view appeared to be shared by many Austrian soldiers. Holed up in the town of Saint-Chaumond on the night of 25 July, a group of seventeen Austrian deserters asserted that their entire regiment had been told that they were in France to support the Empress Marie-Louise, as well as Napoleon II's claims to the throne; they stated that they had rebelled when they had found this not to be the case.[120]

This particular instance may well be dismissed as an attempt to curry favour with the local French authorities, or even to give a 'political' explanation for their desertion. Yet it was no isolated incident. As late as March 1818 it was still being reported that Austrian soldiers and officers were spreading rumours of Napoleon's imminent return to France.[121] These stories continued even after the Emperor's death. In 1822, around the time of the celebration of Napoleon's birth in August, Grenoble was suddenly rife with tales of an impending Austrian invasion.[122] Throughout the Restoration years, rumours about the 'Austrian connection' also accompanied stories about Napoleon II: in 1828 the prefect of Loire reported that: 'For some time now it is being said among the people that the son of Napoleon would soon enter France and that he was supported by Austria, which had already deployed troops in the Piedmont for this purpose.'[123]

Sympathy, admiration, and even adulation for Napoleon were also widespread in the ranks of the Russian occupation forces – especially among the Polish contingents. In December 1815 Russian troops passing through the garrison town of Chalon spread the story that the Emperor was about to enter France through its eastern borders 'at the head of a Turkish army'; the source of this story was believed to be a group of Polish soldiers and officers who had served Napoleon, and who were disseminating these tales in the hope of destabilizing the Bourbons.[124] Another group of Napoleonic Poles, based in the Yonne, also spread stories about the Emperor's return, and applauded 'the talents and virtues of the universal scourge of humanity'.[125]

Most remarkably, rumours of Napoleon's return, mingled with expressions of support for the Emperor, were also broadly reported from the ranks of the British occupying forces. Those stationed in northern territories were denounced as the prime instigators of various Napoleonic-return stories in 1815–16; the prefect of the Pas-de-Calais also noted that British troops were among the most avid purchasers of Napoleonic memorabilia.[126]

Evidence of the demand for these objects in Britain was provided by a merchant from Lyons, who went to Paris in 1820 and was offered a range of Napoleonic objects (including tobacco boxes); he was told that 'the English have been ordering large quantities of this material to take home with them.'[127] In the Seine-et-Marne British troops spread the rumour that there had been an uprising against Louis XVIII and that Napoleon was on his way back to Paris;[128] and in the Nord their comrades 'had repeatedly insulted the King and spoken of the usurper [Napoleon] with enthusiasm.'[129] In the Calvados the prefect likewise reported that the British forces were 'directing the movement' of rumours concerning Napoleon's imminent return.[130]

In some parts of the country this support for the Emperor seemed to be based on religious grounds. The persecution of Protestants which accompanied the 'White Terror' in many southern towns in the months following the return of the Bourbons in 1815 led many British soldiers publicly to declare their hostility to the regime, and to express their belief that Napoleon would return to rule France 'within the next six months'.[131] The police commissioner of Calais drew the appropriate conclusion from all this: it was hardly surprising, he noted, that so many people believed in Bonaparte's comeback if even his traditional enemies seemed so convinced of its imminence.[132]

Protector of the Nation, Bearer of the Apocalypse

In addition to witnessing a harsh military occupation, the early years of the Restoration also saw serious economic hardships and social tensions arising in many parts of France. Alongside the Promethean image of Napoleon as the all-conquering political ruler and patriotic antidote to the Bourbons, the rumours of the Emperor's return also gave rise to another cluster of images: Napoleon the powerful protector of the French nation – the champion of the weak and the oppressed.

As mentioned above, Protestant communities were the victims of royalist oppression in the early months of the Restoration. In the department of the Gard, which was particularly affected, expressions of hope for the Emperor's return among Protestants after 1815 were frequently accompanied by depictions of Napoleon as the promoter of their faith. A woman by the name of Teyssier declared in the spring of 1817 that the Emperor's imminent arrival would be a good thing for Protestants as 'he would build as many temples as we need'. This hope for protection was also mingled with the fantasy of revenge, often expressed in extremely violent terms. A Protestant called François Roman was sentenced to a year's imprisonment for stating in March 1817 that Napoleon would be back 'within three months', following which 'the aristocrats, the priests, and the Catholics would have their heads cut off.'[133]

This duality between protector and avenger appeared even more markedly in Jacobin republican depictions of Napoleon's return. Unlike the Protestants, traditional allies who had embraced Bonapartism throughout his rule under the First Empire, Jacobins had long been implacably hostile to the Emperor, whom they had regarded as a traitor to the republican cause. However, the events of 1815 transformed the image of Napoleon among many republicans, turning him into an emblem of French patriotism, a defender of vulnerable sections of society, and the spearhead of the attack against their oppressors. In March 1817 the new millenarian goal which underlay this republican ideological transformation was outlined by a local official:

'Bonaparte is no longer the ruthless despot who is returning to claim his leaden sceptre, but the hero who will bring forth the liberation of the people. Upon his return he will be appointed Protector of the Republic, and by a remarkable effect on the faithful, this Platonic dream will replace the cult of the true King. At the moment of this sinister metamorphosis, another great sacrifice will be needed, and just as in 1793 it will be necessary to found public felicity upon the extermination of priests, aristocrats, and royalists of all shades. After this deluge of blood and fire, a new light will appear and the first dawn of the new golden age will arise.'[134]

During the Hundred Days, as we saw in Chapter 1, republican expressions of support for Napoleon were frequently accompanied by calls for the physical elimination of aristocrats and priests. These demands continued under the Restoration. In December 1815 a man in Vitry-le-Français declared 'gleefully' that the Emperor's return would get the guillotines working again 'as they had done in 1793'.[135] In January 1816 the mayor of Aurillac received an anonymous letter stating that Napoleon was already back in Paris and that 'lists' of suspect nobles and priests were being drawn up.[136] The nobles and priests of Tonnerre were informed, in an anonymous and barely literate placard, that 'Napoleon would soon return and lead you to the Giliotine' (sic).[137]

These violent visions, however, were not shared by all republican supporters of Napoleon. Some merely hoped his comeback would 'emancipate the people from the yoke of tyranny', as forecast in a republican placard in early 1816.[138] Likewise, a song which announced the return of Napoleon in 1818 preferred to stress the positive values upon which the new-found unity of Jacobin republicans with Bonapartists was based. Celebrating the alliance between 'citizens' (the term which designated the republican community) and 'soldiers' (one of the key Napoleonic constituencies), it asserted that Napoleon had always represented the true national ideals of valour and heroism, both as a republican and as a soldier. The song ended by promising that the Emperor's return would generate civic unity and political concord, as well as social peace.[139]

Protestant and Jacobin republican conceptions of Napoleon as 'protector' were essentially grounded in urban settings. But there were also strong rural dimensions to this paternalist theme. Indeed, many peasants explicitly referred to the Emperor as their 'good father', sometimes adding that his return would contribute to a plentiful harvest.[140] A good father always provided for his children, and Napoleon was occasionally portrayed as a healer, 'travelling from village to village, curing sick peasants with arsenic'.[141] (A somewhat double-edged metaphor . . .) Economic circumstances were also extremely hard in some departments in the early years of the Restoration, with steep rises in the price of wheat and high levels of poverty. The prefect of Saône-et-Loire reported in 1817 that rumours of Napoleon's return were all the more credible in his department because of the 'profound economic misery' of the population.[142] In 1816 a woman named Combe was overheard spreading the story that Marie-Louise and Napoleon were on their way back to France to reclaim their throne, and that 'there would be employment for all'.[143]

This promise of an imperial cornucopia was reflected in the imagery that often accompanied the announcements of the Emperor's comeback. In the Indre it was rumoured that Napoleon was soon returning to France 'with a great deal of wheat';[144] in a similar vein a false imperial proclamation found near Evreux stated that the Emperor was 'ready to land in France with fifty ships laden with wheat'.[145] False proclamations in the Côte d'Or and the Saône-et-Loire, signed by Napoleon and Bertrand, announced that the first measure which would be implemented by the Empire would be the lowering of the price of bread;[146] this was echoed in many placards in the Rhône.[147] In the Bouches-du-Rhône a placard went up in 1820 celebrating the Emperor Napoleon 'who will bring back abundance'.[148] This association of the imperial image with this form of rural providentialism was extremely widespread across France in the 1820s and 1830s.[149] As he was being led away to prison for spreading stories of Napoleon's return, a man of rural origins said simply: 'With him I shall at least have some bread.'[150]

Patriot, protector, avenger, provider: all these images were predicated on 'positive' assumptions that the restoration of the Empire would have beneficial effects for France. But alongside these visions of bliss and restored harmony, Napoleonic-return tales also conjured images of endemic uncertainty and chaos, and of a natural order which was fundamentally shattered.

The cyclical character of the predictions of the Emperor's return brought forth several 'prophetic' accounts. In the autumn of 1815 a man named Perrin, who sold poultry on Fridays at the Marché de la Fromagerie in Lyons, reported that 'a prophet had announced that Bonaparte would soon be back', and that the visionary in question had never failed him.[151] Another self-styled prophet from the Gard was sentenced to three years in prison in 1817 for declaring that France would witness 'a terrible war on the land and on the seas, during which Napoleon would return six times'.[152] In the same year a local 'prophet' was arrested in the Jura for putting up a seditious placard announcing the return of Napoleon. When interrogated by the police he claimed that this message had been dictated to him by a sage who had lived five hundred years before Christ, had described to the local man all the events in Napoleon's life and had predicted that 'there would be a terrible war in 1817.'[153]

Some of the images of the Emperor's return were truly apocalyptic: the complete breakdown of order in all parts of the country, according to one rumour in Chateau Chinon;[154] the burning and pillaging of Paris 'where there were only two houses left standing', as asserted in one tale which went round the Meuse;[155] and the destruction of Gibraltar and the looting of Berlin, according to another.[156] In some cases Napoleon's return was presented as coinciding with the end of the world: in one rural story, this was expected on 8 March 1816, but it had been 'postponed' (presumably by Napoleon) until 27 May.[157]

The Miraculous Emperor

'All is quiet, all is peaceful; the only source of agitation is the imagination.'[158] So spoke the weary police commissioner of Lyons in March 1821, after yet another apocalyptic tale had rocked the city. But this 'imagination' could have devastating social and political consequences, as we have seen throughout this chapter, notably by radically transforming public perceptions of the Emperor.

Indeed, by an inexorable logic, all these positive and negative rumours culminated in the belief that Napoleon possessed miraculous powers. The Emperor held the fate of the world in his hands, but also its origins. An Arab poem in honour of Bonaparte, translated into French in the late Restoration, hailed Napoleon 'as a celestial figure who bears the imprint of divinity'.[159] In many recorded incidents in rural France, his return was announced by the newly born: this was the message conveyed by a baby in Nancy[160] and by a rumour in the Creuse, which also claimed that a 'vision of Bonaparte escorted by angels' had appeared to the mother and child as the fable was narrated.[161] In Auxerre in 1816 it was claimed that a newborn infant had left his mother's womb and cried 'Long Live Emperor' – not just once, but three times.[162]

Napoleon was everywhere, in the skies and beneath the earth: some peasants in the Ardèche claimed that they had seen his portrait

FIGURE 7

The tomb of Napoleon at Saint-Helena

A characteristically romantic representation of Napoleon's burial site on the island. Images of this kind would inspire writers and poets, and also help to propagate the myth of the 'chained Prometheus' which was one of the central elements of the Napoleonic legend. The stormy winds and burst of light also draw upon traditional images of the resurrection of Christ, and thus strongly hint at the Emperor's immortality. In his poem *Napoléon* (1836) Edgar Quinet proclaimed 'He is not dead! He is not dead! From his slumber/ The giant will emerge even stronger at his awakening'.

in the moon, from where he had promised to descend while others placed their ear to the ground to listen out for 'the subterranean army of Bonaparte, which would emerge to conquer the throne'.[163]

A man with such transcendental qualities could defy all the laws of nature, including death (see Figure 7). In 1815 a peasant in the Puy-de-Dôme had declared his belief that Napoleon was 'immortal';[164] and in the 1820s many Napoleonic-return stories crystallized in a rejection of the claim that the Emperor had died. The year of the death of Napoleon (1821) was actually relatively quiet in terms of return stories, but by early 1822 these tales had begun to resurface. In early 1823 placards appeared all over Lyons, denouncing the royal family and the clergy and ending with the statement that 'the one who is desired by us all is Napoleon'.[165] In the same year, the French military intervention in Spain generated a fresh wave of rumours,[166] including claims that Napoleon was still alive; a former soldier asserted that French forces were being very poorly led, and that 'Napoleon was the only warrior who could drive our forces to victory; he was still alive.'[167] From then on, the image of Napoleonic immortality, celebrated in Béranger's song 'He is not Dead',[168] became firmly anchored in the legend.

In the late 1820s, there was a spectacular revival of Bonapartist propaganda in many parts of France, and notably in Alsace, where customs officials seized a pamphlet entitled – a deep breath is needed here – *Yussuf Pacha or history of the Escape of Napoleon from Saint-Helena on the day of his alleged death, of the secret admission of the ex-Emperor into the Court of Constantinople, of his conversion to Islam and of his adventures on land and sea, accompanied by characteristic anecdotes on the present war between Russia and Turkey and important prophecies of Napoleon which will be accomplished.*[169]

Less overtly orientalist accounts of Napoleon's continued existence concentrated on the traditional Bonapartist rejection of the Bourbons, as with the worker from Versailles who stated that: 'The King will not remain long on the throne. Bonaparte will be here in two months. I do not believe in his death.'[170] This faith in Napoleonic immortality was also grounded in a recollection of the past glories and benefits of the First Empire: a man called Rémy, a forest guard in the Yonne, declared that Napoleon had done a lot of good for France: 'He is not dead, I will see him again.'[171] Above all, it was a message of eternal adoration for the Emperor: 'He is still alive and I love him,'[172] declared an agricultural worker in 1824. Appropriately enough, in view of this quasi-divine form of worship, this man's name was Bondieu.

Chapter 3

A Cult of Seditious Objects

Shortly after Napoleon's exile to Saint-Helena, a hen in a village in the Aube laid a flattened egg which was shaped like an effigy of Bonaparte. The entire population crowded around to cheer the miracle and were soon followed by police, who arrested the fowl's proud owner, a local labourer. The hen was also incarcerated. Stendhal concluded this account of the tale in his *Journal*: 'The hen died in prison, but the memory of its egg remained.'[1]

The story symbolized the continuing presence of the Emperor in the collective imagination of the French people after 1815, and also the acute dilemmas faced by the Bourbon authorities in dealing with his legacy. The problem was not one of abstract constitutional rules and lofty theoretical principles: Napoleon was a physical reality, his fate the subject of every conversation, his image lurking in every mind. Indeed, as we saw in the previous chapter, no sooner had he set sail from French shores than rumours of his imminent return began to spread.

Catholic priests and aristocrats trembled at the thought of another 'flight of the eagle', and in some parts of southern France they unleashed a 'White Terror', murdering a considerable number of men who had supported Napoleon during the Hundred Days. These acts of savagery, accompanied by widespread pillaging and looting, created local martyrs, and fortified the determination of workers, peasants and demobilized soldiers to see the return of 'their' Emperor. As the Bourbons struggled to re-establish their hold over the country, a tidal wave of popular Bonapartist agitation swept across France during the summer and early autumn of 1815.

In order to stem this proliferation of support for the 'usurper', as Napoleon was commonly described in royalist writings, the Bourbon authorities took radical measures. All over France, steps were taken to remove from bookshops all the works (books, pamphlets, poems) written and published during the Hundred Days.[2] In 1815 Parliament also adopted a law criminalizing any verbal or written endorsement of Bonaparte. Another bill widened the definition of political crimes to include not only conspiracy and armed rebellion but also any threat against the King and his family, as well as any direct or indirect incitement to alter the line of succession to the French throne. Strict censorship laws also forbade any pictorial representation which could be deemed to libel or threaten the existing government.[3] 'Sedition' was thus defined in extremely broad terms, so as to include any thought, utterance, gesture, or symbolic representation of support for Napoleon.

These juridical measures were followed in the early months of 1816 by a widespread purge of physical objects and symbols of the Napoleonic era. In provincial towns and villages elaborate ceremonies were held in which civic and military emblems of the First Empire were publicly burnt; in Carcassonne a live young eagle was also thrown into the flames. These rituals led to the destruction of many works of art, notably at Orléans, where the pyre included a portrait of Napoleon by Gérard, for which the town had paid 10,000 francs.[4]

However, some artefacts were saved for posterity. In the Maine-et-Loire, the prefecture possessed a magnificent white marble bust of the Emperor by Antonio Canova. In 1816, the local royalists decreed its destruction, but the official ordered to carry out this act of vandalism hid the bust in the attic, where it was rediscovered twenty years later by the poet Mérimée during a visit to Angers in his capacity as Inspector of Historical Monuments.[5]

In many towns, these 'purging' ceremonies were conducted by the hangman – an indication of what some of the more fanatical royalists would have done with the Emperor if they had laid hands on him at the end of the Hundred Days.[6] Although they contained elements of menace, the principal aim of these rituals was cathartic. The page was now being turned: Bonaparte was gone, and his former subjects were being invited to excise all memories of him from their minds.

Unfortunately for the regime, the very opposite occurred. France was soon engulfed in an imperial cult, perpetuated through a plethora of images, symbols, and objects. This imperial legend kept Napoleon alive in the minds of his people and systematically undermined the political legitimacy of the Bourbons. The different manifestations of these seditious objects during the Restoration years will be explored in this chapter.

A Napoleonic deluge

The most striking feature of the Napoleon cult was its sheer scale. In the years between 1815 and 1830 thousands of coins and medals, hundreds of thousands of busts and small statues, and millions of images representing Napoleon were sold, distributed, and exchanged across France. Busts made of plaster were manufactured on a small scale by individuals in their homes and back gardens. The engraver and former marine officer Louis Pillard was arrested in 1818 after police found a plaster mould in his house.[7] Alternatively, such objects, sometimes also made of bronze or copper, were produced in larger quantities in clandestine factories in cities and larger towns, notably in Paris, Lyons, and Grenoble.[8] Despite its best efforts – some of the manufacturers were arrested and prosecuted[9] – the State proved incapable of halting this production line, especially as any shortfall in domestic manufacture was easily compensated for by imports from neighbouring countries – notably from the German and Italian states, as well as from Belgium and Switzerland.[10]

The volume of this foreign trade was impressive: in early 1823 the French police received reports that a French order had been placed in a foundry in Wurtemberg for 12,000 small busts of Napoleon. These objects were smuggled into the country across France's porous eastern border, often with the complicity of local Customs officials.[11] Objects made in France were also exported to other countries – and not only within Europe: in 1826 Customs officials in Nantes seized thirteen crates containing Napoleonic medals, busts, and portraits which were bound for the port of Mahé in India.[12]

A vast 'underground' trade in coins, drawings, portraits, and caricatures portraying the Emperor also flourished during the Restoration period. As with the busts and statues, the production networks were simultaneously local (the works of individual artists), national (Paris was an important centre), and international. Travellers often brought these items into France from other countries and handed them over to Bonapartist agents; sometimes they distributed them directly. In the summer of 1819 a large number of portraits of Napoleon were found in the northern coastal town of Cambrai; police suspicions in this instance were directed at a group of English travellers.[13] Another favoured method was the dispatch of these images by post to innocent-looking addresses. In 1819 the police in Rouen fortuitously stumbled upon a large collection of Napoleonic portraits concealed in a parcel addressed to 'Miss Hower and Madame Mouton, Boarding School, Rue de l'Ecureuil No.7, Rouen.'[14] These ladies clearly had a very broad-minded approach to education.

The images themselves spanned a wide range, showing both old and new motifs in Napoleonic propaganda. The dominant genre were 'dynastic' representations of the Emperor, either alone (in imperial dress) or alongside the Empress Marie-Louise and their son the Duc de Reichstadt. There were also portraits of several 'minor imperials', including most notably Napoleon's first wife Josephine and her son Prince Eugène de Beauharnais. Particularly worthy of note here was the 'prodigious debit' of all images and other paraphernalia associated with Napoleon's son, the heir to the imperial throne. In 1815 local authorities reported that coins bearing the portrait of 'Napoleon II' were in circulation in the Rhône and Isère, in the canton of Vaud and as far afield as Geneva.[15]

Engravings were also extremely popular: in 1818 the police complained that a drawing entitled *The Son of the Regiment* (an evocation of Napoleon and his son during the Hundred Days) had sold out within days of its being printed, and even before its existence had been officially declared to the authorities.[16]

Even in the final years of the Restoration this trade in portraits and coins representing the imperial heir still flourished: they were found in large numbers in Paris[17] and Toulouse[18] but also in rural parts of the Ain[19] and Loiret.[20] These images represented the 'monarchical' aspect of the Napoleonic tradition, which focused above all on the person of the Emperor and his role as the founder of a dynasty.

A second type of image consisted of depictions of Napoleon on Saint-Helena. Here the tone was romantic and often melancholic, and included depictions of the island's bleak and inhospitable terrain.[21] Even before Napoleon's death, there were numerous popular allegories representing him at Saint-Helena in contemplative mood; one image confiscated from a merchant in Toulon even depicted him with one arm cut off, 'with a face expressing the greatest sorrow';[22] another showed a nymph crying over a bust of Napoleon under a weeping willow.[23] After 1821 this mourning theme became very common.

But not all Saint-Helenic images were despondent. The theme of Napoleon's escape from the island, which exercised a powerful appeal in the French public imagination after 1815, was also strongly represented. A drawing entitled *The New Titan*, seized at the home of a painter, showed Napoleon breaking off his Saint-Helena chains and leaping towards Europe;[24] another image showed the Emperor heading away from his prison island under the protection of Turkish troops.[25] This was an illustration of one of the most widespread rumours concerning Napoleon's escape from the island; it was also available in the form of a medallion, which represented Bonaparte with a crescent in the background.[26]

Even in defeat, Napoleon remained all-powerful; and this Promethean strand of the imagery blended naturally into a third variant, which was made up of martial scenes. These represented Napoleon at some of his famous battles, most notably at his camp in Austerlitz[27] and preparing for the engagement at the battle of Eylau.[28] There were also generic images glorifying the feats of arms of the Emperor, as for example in the collection of drawings entitled *Long Live Napoleon, Conqueror and Pacifier*.[29] But the most interesting subset of these Promethean images consisted of representations of the Hundred Days, and notably of the 'flight of the eagle': among these was a drawing of the journey across the sea from Elba, entitled

FIGURE 8

The imperial leap

A representation of Napoleon's flight from Elba (on the right), and his successful march to Paris (on the left). The Emperor's right hand holds a flag with the national colours, bearing the inscription 'Honour and Fatherland'; his left hand clutches a sword and his laurels – a clear statement of Napoleonic strength, although his intentions in March 1815 were peaceful. The group of royalists below are discussing how to react to the news of Napoleon's return to Paris: the man on the right suggests that war should be declared on the Emperor, while the one on the left states: 'Let us pack our bags.' Images of this kind were widely circulated in the early years of the Restoration, and contributed to the glorification of the Hundred Days; they also helped to spread rumours about Napoleon's return.

The imperial leap (see Figure 8); a representation of the landing in Cannes (also available in the form of a medal[30]) and the entry into Grenoble.[31]

Alongside these depictions of key moments in Napoleon's 1815 odyssey there were drawings and caricatures representing his ongoing political battle against the Bourbon royalists. These often took the symbolic form of drawings of imperial emblems 'defeating' their royalist counterparts, most typically the eagle devouring the fleur-de-lys. This image was extremely common in the first decade of the Restoration, and a prisoner in the Var even had his jail sentence extended for adorning the wall of his cell with a large eagle crushing the royal emblem. To avoid all ambiguity he had also scribbled an inscription: 'The eagle will one day come to destroy the fleur-de-lys.'[32] This drawing was made to mark the anniversary of Napoleon's landing in March 1815, celebrated by Bonapartists all over France during the first decade of the Restoration.

An important political element in this subset of images was the preponderance of the theme of anti-clericalism. A colour image found in Laval in 1819 showed Napoleon grabbing his crown back from Louis XVIII, with his soldiers behind him; on the far side of the picture Bourbon soldiers can be seen fleeing, accompanied by aristocrats and priests. The caption of the image ('I am taking back my cap and leaving you with your *calotte*'[33]) illustrated the association of the Catholic religion and the aristocracy with the royalist cause in the middle of Bonapartist devotees (see Figure 9).

These types of drawings also demonstrated the central role of the Hundred Days in the emergence of a new form of Napoleonic politics after 1815, more 'popular' in character and sharing many ideological affinities with Jacobin republicans, the Emperor's new-found allies during the Hundred Days. In contrast with the dynastic and even the martial images, which were not particularly aggressive either visually or in their tone, this 'Jacobin' Napoleonic imagery was extremely threatening. Regicide was commonly advocated and celebrated; placards occasionally recalled the execution of King Louis XVI in 1793, and images and caricatures often showed Napoleon throttling the Bourbon monarchs.

In the winter of 1821–2 a seventy-year-old man called Julien Presté, accompanied, as noted enviously in the police report by 'his

*'I take my bonnet and leave you
with your skullcap'*

Seditious Bonapartist placard

FIGURE 9

A fascinating example of the use of Napoleonic images by Bonapartist propagandists after 1815. The original drawing, produced during the Hundred Days, showed Napoleon and Louis XVIII, with the Emperor grabbing back his crown from the King. The seditious placard incorporates this image into a broader picture (note that Napoleon has become much thinner), which is dominated by an imposing eagle, and also shows Napoleonic soldiers on the right, and royalist supporters fleeing on the left. The placard was clearly the work of a 'popular' Napoleonic group; it contains two spelling mistakes. Also noteworthy is the explicit association of the Bourbons with the Church; this anti-clericalism was a distinct feature of 'popular' Bonapartism after 1815.

33-year-old wife', toured the rural areas of the Ile-et-Vilaine showing peasants a folded drawing which began by looking like a fleur-de-lys. When opened, however, it showed this flower being swallowed by an eagle, and Napoleon emerging to chase away the King and the clergy.[34] And in the aftermath of the assassination of the Duc de Berry by the Bonapartist sympathizer Louvel in 1820, a large number of Napoleonic coins were distributed in the department of the Calvados as a gesture of celebration.[35]

A distinct sub-species of these images represented Napoleon with the emblems of the revolutionary secret society the Carbonari, which was founded in Italy and developed in France in the early 1820s. The police in Grenoble arrested two Italian brothers who were found in possession of a collection of images and medals representing Napoleon with the Carbonaro dagger.[36] These secret societies also used small statues of Bonaparte as signs of recognition, and in some cases affixed their seal (a human skull, bones, and a dagger) at their base.[37]

Symbolic attacks were also aimed directly at the French monarchy: in 1820 five-franc coins were circulating in Lyons, depicting Louis XVIII wearing a religious cape, and with his head covered with a cap.[38] After 1824 his successor Charles X was also lampooned by a series of coins representing him dressed in ecclesiastical costume[39] or as a Jesuit.[40] In the spring of 1827 the authorities were faced with a veritable epidemic of these coins, with large numbers being found in Toulouse, Bordeaux, Carcassonne, Bourg, and Marseille.[41] Many of them also depicted a noose carved around the King's neck.[42]

Sons of Bonaparte

Public demand for these objects was insatiable. In November 1819 a Parisian street trader admitted to the police that he had sold 8,000 busts of Napoleon during the previous four days.[43] Nor was this a phenomenon limited to the early years of the Restoration. In the summer of 1828 the stalls of street hawkers and furniture and antique shops in Paris were littered with images of the Emperor, to the great despair of the local authorities.[44]

The situation in the provinces was no different. Police officers kept a close watch on weekly fairs, confiscating any Napoleonic busts which were on display[45] and often arresting and prosecuting the vendors.[46] But they were powerless to control the principal agents of the distribution of Napoleonic icons in the countryside, the travelling salesmen. As we saw in the previous chapter, these *colporteurs* were the bane of Restoration officials, who often suspected them of spreading Napoleonic rumours. In 1815 the Minister of Police, Decazes, warned all his prefects: 'France is covered with travelling salesmen, who are roaming across the territory in all directions. Through their active industry they are able to reach the smallest villages and even the most remote habitations.'

Describing these hawkers as 'agents of deception and intrigue', Decazes noted in particular the political influence they wielded in rural communities: 'The peasant who has never left his village greets these men as oracles, and finds their stories all the more credible that their dress and forms of speech are familiar to him.'[47] This conclusion was frequently corroborated in local reports from police and justice officials; one salesman travelling in Brittany in 1824 was even arrested because of his physical resemblance to the Emperor, which had led many peasants to ask him whether 'he was the son of Bonaparte'.[48]

In provincial towns a similarly pivotal role in the dissemination of Napoleonic objects (and Bonapartist propaganda) was performed by booksellers, who found all sorts of ingenious ways of circumventing the legislation forbidding the sale of seditious material. The most common method was the removal of all such items from public display; potential customers were alerted to their existence by a gesture or an apparently innocent question ('Would you like to see something interesting?')[49] But in the vast majority of cases – towns were after all relatively small places, where the political affiliations of all figures in the public eye were known – these booksellers were visited *because* they were known supporters of Napoleon.

The example of Frédéric Lemire, a bookseller based in Evreux, offers a good illustration of the characteristics and operating methods of such individuals. A former officer in Napoleon's guard, Lemire sold images and busts of the Emperor in Paris from the early 1820s but also travelled all over the country to ply his trade. He also made frequent visits to Belgium, his principal source of supplies.[50] In 1823 police reports noted that Lemire 'only sold books, images and busts which relate to Bonaparte' and that 'his revolutionary opinions are most ardent.'[51] Emboldened by his success, Lemire even applied for permission to open another bookshop in his native town of Rouen in 1827, though his application was turned down.[52] There were hundreds of men like him all over France between 1815 and 1830.

To what uses were these hundreds of thousands of Napoleonic icons – busts, small statues, images – put both by their distributors and by those who acquired them? The early years of the Napoleonic legend are often seen as essentially apolitical in character: a static and almost timeless celebration of the image of the Emperor, without an accompanying form of political or ideological mobilization.[53]

The archival evidence, however, suggests otherwise. Portraits of Napoleon were generally framed and hidden from view, and were brought out only on special occasions. (Police searches tended to uncover them in wardrobes, carefully wrapped in paper or clothing.)[54] Busts and small statues, however, were generally placed in open view, either over the chimney or outdoors in the garden; on one occasion at least, a man was even seen swallowing his Napoleonic statue as a gesture of celebration after the death of a leading member of the royal family.[55]

But official attitudes towards the public display of such icons varied enormously from one part of France to another, and also from one profession to another. As from late 1815 a private citizen – a doctor or a lawyer, or a peasant or a former soldier in Napoleon's Grande Armée – could feel relatively safe in holding these objects in his homes, as they were effectively regarded by the State authorities as items for private use.[56] For any soldier still serving in the Bourbon Army, however, the mere possession of a Napoleonic bust was grounds for instant detention and court martial; in December 1829 a gunner from the 7th Regiment was arrested in Strasbourg after a bust of the Emperor was found among his personal effects.[57] Yet, despite the threat of such draconian sanctions, large numbers of soldiers (including officers) kept images and busts of Napoleon.

Alongside these manifestations of 'expressive' politics, which were individualistic and private, Napoleonic coins, busts, and images were also deployed as instruments of propaganda and even conspiracy. An official enquiry into the conspiracy of August 1820 in Paris found that the Army officers who had been implicated in the plot used to recognize each other by two means: a special Napoleonic handshake ('representing a double N') and the display of 'small eagles'.[58] Likewise, all the members of a Bonapartist secret society which was active in the Tarn in the early Restoration years wore a brooch featuring a black eagle.[59]

Coins were also used by Bonapartists as a means of mutual recognition, as with a group of imperial veterans in Toulouse who were found in possession of a copper piece bearing the image of the Duc de Reichstadt,[60] or as a way of engaging a political conversation. In Paris in 1820 a police report noted that gold pieces bearing the effigy of Marie-Louise were being handed out to members of the public as a prelude to affirming the superiority of the Napoleonic dynasty over the Bourbon line.[61] After the death of Napoleon coins of his son with the caption 'The Hope of France' were used by Bonapartist agents to underwrite Napoleon II's claims to the French throne;[62] large quantities were also distributed on special occasions, such as the anniversary of the Saint-Napoléon on 15 August.[63] Bonapartists often distributed in cafés portraits and drawings of the Emperor, especially in cities such as Paris where they could carry out these acts and disappear rapidly into the crowd.[64]

Indeed, this effort to disseminate imperial propaganda through images was not limited to towns and cities. In the immediate aftermath of Napoleon's second abdication, rumours of his imminent return were spread in the countryside by men carrying medals of the Emperor, which they often claimed to have received directly from him.[65] In Saint-Lo in 1819 three individuals entered a café and distributed copies of a drawing representing Louis XVIII being strangled by Napoleon, with eagles devouring the fleur-de-lys in the background; the men disappeared before the arrival of the gendarmerie.[66] Most interestingly, there were also examples of Napoleonic objects being used to assist the spreading of rumours: Tuscan-born Jean-Nicolas Dorvichi, a travelling salesman, was arrested in the Yonne for selling eagles and tricolour ribbons and telling his potential customers that 'Napoleon had re-entered France with an Army of 1,800,000 Turks.'[67]

This sort of approach was not always successful, especially as subtlety was not always their perpetrators' strongest suit. For example, in

October 1815 a former Napoleonic soldier was arrested when he tried to force a young man to kiss a portrait of Bonaparte.[68] In February 1820 a man was prosecuted for slipping a tiny bronze statue of Napoleon into the wine of his drinking companion. The unfortunate man swallowed the Emperor, but not all the way – a dramatic illustration of Napoleon's capacity to stick in some people's throats.[69]

A Bourgeois Aesthetic

The proliferation after 1815 of objects and images associated with the Emperor marked the emergence of a veritable Napoleonic aesthetic, which manifested itself in a variety of social settings. This association of the name of Napoleon with a culture of decorative and practical objects was apparent throughout France, transcending age, class, and occupational divisions, and with uses ranging from hedonism, decoration, and entertainment to the overt dissemination of political propaganda. However, among all these aspects of this aesthetic one was most striking: the invocation of Napoleon, as we shall observe, was almost invariably associated with the promotion and celebration of masculine sentiments, male pleasures, and manly virtues.

This cult began almost literally in the cradle. A considerable number of parents from all over France (especially former soldiers of the Grande Armée[70]) named their children after Napoleon – or at least attempted to do so. The risks were high, especially in the early years of the Restoration. In 1816 two artisans from Beauvais were arrested after announcing their intention to name their sons Paul-Joseph-Bonaparte and Louis-Henri-Napoleon; they specified that 'they had wanted their children to bear the names of a warrior'.[71] In Nantes in 1819 the printer Mangin also landed himself in trouble for declaring the names of his newborn son as Victor-Aimé-Eugène-Napoléon; he sought to appease the authorities by claiming that he was fulfilling a promise to his now-deceased brother.[72]

Others were more brazen still; the labourer Le Marec, described as 'barely literate and of ill repute', announced in a tavern in Guinguamp in 1824 that 'he had named his son Napoleon because the Emperor had ruled and would rule again.' (He was clearly a zealous devotee, as Bonaparte had been dead for three years).[73] Even more singular, perhaps, was the case of the doctor in Albi who had been praying for a son upon whom the magical imperial name could be bestowed. Undeterred by the arrival of a daughter instead, he decided to christen her Marie-Louise-Néapoldine; he too was immediately arrested.[74] The Emperor was clearly popular among doctors in the Tarn; another medical officer was arrested in Layrac for naming his new-born 'Marie-Louise-Napoléonide'.[75]

The cult of Napoleon was also intense among the bourgeoisie in the 1820s and 1830s, notably in Alsace, with many instances of children named after the Emperor.[76] It was no doubt this tendency which Flaubert – no friend of Bonapartism – satirized in *Madame Bovary* through the character of the provincial pedant Monsieur Homais, who named one of his sons Napoleon.[77]

Napoleon was also a powerful influence in the pursuits of French children and young men. Throughout the Restoration a large number of schoolteachers secretly celebrated the cult of the Emperor in their classrooms; in the commune of Louhans in 1820 a head-teacher caused an enormous scandal when he paid homage to Napoleon and the principles of the French Revolution at the annual prize-giving ceremony, held in the presence of local religious and secular authorities.[78]

The Napoleonic genie could spring up anywhere. In the Gers, a popular game among children consisted of holding a masquerade in which soldiers dressed in Roman outfits crowned a young boy as their King (an overt allusion to Napoleon's son, the King of Rome).[79] While this elaborate type of ritual tended to find favour among the children of the bourgeoisie, Napoleon was also an instant celebrity among a more working-class clientele; in 1829 an entertainer enjoyed huge success at a carnival in Pontoise with an act which included a mechanical eagle surmounted by a statue of Bonaparte, on whose head two angels deposited the crown of France.[80]

A wide range of 'seditious toys' was also available, including crosses with Napoleonic emblems[81] and statues of Bonaparte specially made for children.[82] The most cunning form of subliminal advertising was the imprinting of Napoleonic forms and images on children's sweets – evidence, to the Restoration authorities, of the ultimate moral callousness of the Bonapartists. Some of these confections were made for special occasions, and were aimed at a more elevated group of consumers – as with the small statues of Bonaparte made in sugar and chocolate by the confectioner Daguillon in Rouen around the time of the Christmas and New Year festivities in 1825.[83] But millions of smaller and cheaper confections were also on offer throughout the year, either with wrappings representing Napoleonic images and symbols[84] or in the form of sweets shaped in the effigy of the Emperor.[85] In some instances the propagandist aspect was not even concealed: in 1817 the confectioner Michaud was arrested in Paris for selling sweets whose wrappings explicitly called for the return of Napoleon.[86]

For adults, the paraphernalia was considerably more extensive, as well as ornate. Bourgeois homes were filled with various objects imprinted with Napoleonic images and signs, ranging from the utilitarian (cups and saucers)[87] to the purely decorative (crystal vases)[88]. Real imperial fetishists could also eat out in restaurants which prided themselves on their use of exclusively Napoleonic crockery – a trade mark which was good for business, less so for relations with the local police.[89] Most notable, however, were the objects specifically designed to be worn or carried – again mostly by men.

There were two distinct versions of this Napoleonic aesthetic: a bourgeois variant, which centred around visible and luxury objects, and a more 'popular' style, which was focused on smaller objects, often practical items for everyday consumption and use. The bourgeois Napoleonic aesthetic knew no shame in its yearning to be seen and admired. It represented not only a projection of the image of the Emperor into the public sphere but also a celebration of the elegance and social refinement of the bourgeois male. Middle-class Bonapartist devotees in cities and towns decked themselves out in items of clothing liberally inscribed with the image of Napoleon: they mopped their brows in affectation with Napoleonic handkerchiefs; made a great show of pointing to their beautiful breeches and silk ties, upon which happened to be imprinted the silhouette of the Emperor; and they kept chills off their delicate necks with finely stitched scarves left dangling across their shoulder just enough for a large imperial 'N' to come into view (or, for those with a modicum of sobriety, an eagle).[90]

Napoleonic apparel for the bourgeoisie was often extremely elaborate, and could even come with a hint of mystery – as with the walking stick whose handle contained a cavity in which a bronze statuette of Bonaparte was concealed. At the touch of a button the Emperor duly popped up, a delightful (or dreaded) reminder of his consistent capacity to appear in unexpected places, and, for the more hopeful, a symbol of the imminence of his return.[91]

When news of the death of the Emperor reached France, hundreds of young men in Lyons went into mourning by fashioning expensive jackets in black silk, with weeping willows imprinted upon them;[92] the city remained one of the centres for the fabrication of this material in the early 1820s.[93] Several incidents involving the public display of these 'jackets of grief' were reported in 1822, notably one case where a retired Army officer proudly showed off his attire to serving military personnel,[94] and material for their manufacture continued to be found in tailors' shops until at least the summer of 1823.[95]

The cult of Napoleon was also a celebration of masculine beauty and grooming. Every part of the bourgeois male body was throroughly prepared for public display, assisted (with remarkable market sensitivity to prevailing cultural fashion) by a range of essential products: for the skin, the fragrance 'Eau du Duc de Reichstadt', and for the hair, a lubricant with miraculously Napoleonic properties, the 'huile libérale'. Both enjoyed extensive circulation in provincial France during the first decade of the Restoration.[96]

Facial hair could also be used directly to express support for the Napoleonic cause; in the Côtes-du-Nord in 1817 there was a spate of moustache-growing among devotees of the imperial cause; these men walked through Saint-Brieuc in groups, provocatively twirling their whiskers.[97] A complex association of Napoleon with a range of flowers also emerged, notably the violet, the carnation, and the camomile; all of these were worn in the buttonhole as a symbol of public identification with the Emperor.

In Paris all the leading Bonapartist *demi-soldes* wore a violet or red carnation on their panama hats.[98] In Niort in 1816 a large number of men celebrated the first anniversary of Napoleon's return by walking the streets of their town with violets in their mouths.[99] Elsewhere in France, such men were arrested, as at Verneuil, where the police incarcerated a group of carnation-bearers who reflected the social diversity of Napoleonic support: a doctor, a weaver, a butcher's assistant, and a beggar.[100] In the following year there was a wide-spread trend towards wearing red carnations in public, especially at the time of the festivity of Saint-Louis; the prefect of the Vosges noted that these flowers were worn by Napoleonic supporters, 'mostly young middle-class men'.[101]

In 1821, police reports from Paris and Lyons noted that 'consider-able numbers of people' were still wearing these subversive symbols in their buttonholes;[102] one account stated that they were placed in prominent view, on the left of the jacket or coat.[103] The pharmacist Barre, although described as 'emphatically liberal', made a hand-some profit during the summer of 1821 by selling violets for five times their market value – evidence, to him at least, of the beneficial effects of the invisible hand.[104] Flowers were also used by Bonapartist political agents during their 'seditious' activities; in the weeks pre-ceding the preparation of the March 1821 insurrection in Grenoble 'a large number of bourgeois men wore carnations on their button-holes';[105] the practice continued until at least the mid-1820s in the Isère.

But being well groomed was not sufficient: it was essential to be noticed, especially by the authorities. And when the police were not looking closely enough, these aesthetes were more than willing to draw attention to themselves, as in Montbéliard where large numbers of townsmen suddenly took to smoking in public places porcelain pipes bearing the effigy of Bonaparte.[106]

The ultimate prize for combining public support for Napoleon with self-infatuation must go to a young man from Lyons called Faure, a store employee who was seen at a production at the Théâtre des Célestins sporting 'a large shining pin with a black hole in the middle, and in his buttonhole two yellow carnations and an enor-mous violet'; the ensemble was worn 'with affectation'.[107] He also provoked the unfortunate local police official, Agent Pointet, by using the interval to accost members of the audience, asking them if they approved of his attire, and especially his floral decoration. However, most of his time was spent admiring himself in the enormous mirror in the foyer.[108]

Popular Objects

The personal effects which made up the material culture of 'popular' Bonapartism were much less elaborate, and their bearers showed little of the aestheticism of the young theatre aficionado from Lyons. There were, admittedly, a small range of personal ornaments, such as black pins and rings bearing Napoleon's effigy; the prefect of Gironde noted (a touch dismissively) that 'these objects are worn only by the lower classes.'[109] Vast quantities of Napoleonic buttons, intended for use on shirts, jackets and coats, were also produced during the Restoration years; in Lyons it was common practice to offer these items as gifts on the anniversary of the birth of Napoleon.[110]

But the 'popular' celebration of Napoleon generally took the form of grafting imperial emblems onto objects and articles meant for everyday (masculine) use. A range of knives with assorted imperial emblems on their handles were designed. Soon these items were so widespread that they became known as 'Napoleon knives'.[111] A police inquiry in 1830 traced one line of production to a factory in Thiers, where the owner declared that he had sold 48,000 such objects over the past four years.[112] One knife found in Paris was described as follows: 'On both sides of the handle are full-length representations of Napoleon, each surmounted by a crown of stars, in the midst of which is a bee; there is also an eagle lying at the foot of the Emperor.'[113]

Tobacco and alcohol were the two favourite sources of everyday pleasure for the common people, and it is not surprising that they occupied a central place in the popular repertoire of the Napoleonic cult. One of the items which effectively defined the concept of the 'seditious object' under the Restoration was the tobacco box (*tabatière*). The cheapest were made of cardboard and sold in their tens of thousands every year all over France; also available were wooden versions, some of them quite ornate. But all shared the common characteristic of being adorned with a variety of Napoleonic representations, most commonly portraits of the Emperor and his family or depiction of battle scenes.[114] Some of the messages conveyed on these boxes were quite intricate. A man travelling through La Rochelle in 1820 was arrested after he was found with a tobacco box on which was a picture showing a group of soldiers engaging in battle. The inscription below the image read as follows: 'The French at Waterloo, 18 June 1815; the Frenchman dies and does not surrender. To French Honour'[115] (see Figure 10).

Waterloo was a powerful image, full of complex and multiple meanings. It was used in this instance to invoke national pride and celebrate military valour, but it was also an excellent inducement for the patriotic French citizen to drown his sorrows. In the Vienne a bottle of liquor bearing a tricolour label and the caption 'Bataille de Waterloo' was all the rage in local inns and taverns in the early 1820s.[116] In Lyons a drink sold as the 'Elixir de Sainte-Hélène' was banned by local police in 1820: this meant that all bottles were seized, their labels torn off and destroyed, and the liquor then returned to the manufacturers.[117]

This 'Elixir' had already been distributed in a dozen departments, and its label offered a fascinating early example of political advertising. On the right, it portrayed Napoleon leaning proudly against a large rock, and on the left a large ship, with a small canoe alongside it. In the centre, towering over the scene, was a large eagle holding a bolt of lightning. This was no placid manifestation of support for the Emperor, but rather an explicit representation of his escape from the island, and (more widely) of the belief that he would one day reclaim his throne in France.[118]

After Napoleon's death the brand name was passed on to his son; in the late 1820s a liquor known as the 'Elixir du Duc de Reichstadt' was on sale in many parts of France but any bottles found on public display were seized.[119] The authorities' political rationale for their zeal in tracking down these 'seditious' beverages was not without credibility. After confiscating a large consignment of forbidden Waterloo liquor in the popular Mouffetard district in Paris, a police report explained: 'In this area the name of the Duc de Reichstadt is too difficult to pronounce for the workers of the lowest class; so instead, when ordering their drinks, they ask for a little drop of Napoleon II, or a smidgeon of the King of Rome. And this is precisely what the faction which seeks to perpetuate our political divisions is seeking.'[120] This was indeed a clever move by Bonapartist agents, transforming routine gestures performed in public houses by hundreds of thousands of drinkers into expressions of support for the Napoleonic dynasty.

FIGURE 10

Cover of tobacco box, representing General Cambronne at the Battle of Waterloo. The caption reads: 'The Guard dies it does not surrender'.

This was an apocryphal saying, attributed to General Pierre Cambronne as he was summoned to surrender by the British cavalry in the final stages of the Battle of Waterloo in June 1815. Heavily outnumbered and knowing that their decision meant a certain death for most of them, Napoleon's Guard refused to lay down their weapons. Cambronne survived, and his phrase became one of the most frequently cited Napoleonic expressions of the 1815–1848 period. The tobacco box was also one of the most widespread sources of 'Napoleonic sedition', often carrying pictures of the Emperor (either on the outside or sometimes in the inside cover).

Over and above their common totemic functions, there were some parallels in the bourgeois and 'popular' uses of their respective cult objects. Items of clothing with Napoleonic buttons were generally worn in private, but occasionally some men could not resist the temptation of showing off their emblems in public: in the Morbihan in 1818 a former member of the National Guard was arrested for appearing at a ball dressed in his uniform, with a set of shining buttons bearing the emblem of the eagle.[121]

Another example was the manifestation of grief. Bourgeois men mourned Napoleon by wearing silk jackets, or by bearing flowers, while for common folk the same function was performed by tobacco boxes representing the death of Napoleon. A common image on these boxes was a mausoleum with the letter N surrounded by an inscription in homage to the Emperor, accompanied by an eagle.[122] These objects were particularly popular among ordinary soldiers and army officers.[123] Some of these tobacco boxes were also designed, like functional equivalents of the Napoleonic walking stick, to pick up on the theme of mystery. Instead of being placed on the inside or outside cover, portraits of Napoleon were sometimes concealed under a false base – to facilitate their use by those working in 'sensitive' professions (notably the military or the police), or simply to represent the common belief in popular Bonapartist folklore that the Emperor was at the bottom of everything.[124]

In general, however, 'popular' objects of the Napoleonic cult were distinctive in being directly employed to wage political battle against the Restoration government. In the early years of the Bourbon regime tobacco boxes were used throughout France to spread rumours of Napoleon's imminent return – and not only by French men and women. In 1818 an Englishman named Fullerton, the captain of a ship which docked at Le Havre, became a local celebrity by waving a gold tobacco box which he claimed to have received from the hands of the Emperor himself in Saint-Helena.[125]

The mere sight of this type of object was enough to provoke fear in some quarters. In Amiens in 1822 two women found a tobacco pouch on the street and stood transfixed, 'not daring to open it'. Eventually one of their acquaintances passed by and lifted the cover, which to the women's horror revealed a portrait of the Emperor. The police were alerted by their screams.[126]

Buttons imprinted with the eagle were commonly used to assist recruitment to the Bonapartist cause: in 1818 a Spanish subject named Carvajol was arrested in Nîmes for using a collection of such buttons to rally support for the Emperor among the Hispanic refugee community in Allais.[127]

Napoleonic-cult objects were also widely used by Jacobin republicans. A group of retired army officers travelling on the coach from Paris to Rouen in March 1821 scandalized the other passengers by exhibiting their collection of tobacco boxes, which all bore a variety of Napoleonic symbols and images, and by announcing 'the imminent restoration of republican government in France'.[128]

One of the reasons why Restoration authorities were so hostile to 'popular' Napoleonic objects was that their bearers often became embroiled in public conflicts. This was the essential contrast between the bourgeois aesthetic, which was decorative and hedonistic, and its lower-class counterpart, where physical violence was never far below the surface. Drunken brawls were frequent in inns and taverns throughout France, either after excessive consumption of one of the many varieties of Napoleonic liquor or when 'seditious objects' were brought out on display in public places. In Toulouse a worker named Tournel was arrested after fighting with two soldiers in a tavern; the cause of the quarrel was his tobacco box bearing assorted imperial designs, which he had pulled out in an attempt to entice his drinking companions to sing Napoleonic songs.[129]

Provocations of this type were accompanied by expressions of devotion often bordering on the foolhardy: a worker named Broux, wearing a coat adorned with imperial buttons, entered a tavern in Lille. After copiously insulting all the patrons who confronted him, he was beaten up and thrown out of the building. However, as he was dragged out he still had the time (or the temerity) to point to the Napoleonic emblems on his coat and declare that 'there is nothing to match such greatness in France today'.[130]

Bearers of these objects were not always the victims of violence – on the contrary. In the Côtes-du-Nord the authorities spent a while chasing a man who had lacerated several portraits of the King with his Napoleonic dagger.[131] In Bléré two men, a baker and a horse-seller, were drinking in a tavern when they caught sight of a plaster representation of King Louis XVIII which was hanging on the wall.

One of the men said: 'This ruler is not for me. If I had my knife on me I would slice his neck open.' His companion immediately produced his Napoleon knife and handed it over, whereupon the royal portrait medallion was pulled down from the wall and beheaded. Both men were still admiring their act of symbolic regicide when the gendarmerie came to arrest them.[132]

The Colours of Patriotism

'These Bonapartist scoundrels will never leave us alone!' screeched the mother-in-law of an inhabitant of Lisieux (in Normandy). She had just stumbled upon a grey paper bag containing some nine hundred tricolour rosettes of various sizes, together with emblems representing the Napoleonic eagle.[133] Of all the seditious objects of 'popular' Bonapartist culture, perhaps the most threatening to the Restoration authorities were those items such as rosettes, caps and banners which were decorated with the 'national' colours of the French Republic and Empire: blue, white, and red.

Over and above the simple fact that they were banned, there were several reasons why public displays of these colours were particularly exasperating to the Bourbons and their supporters. Such manifestations challenged the regime at its most critical symbolic level, the representation of its sovereignty; they highlighted one of the most vulnerable aspects of royalist power, namely its recent re-establishment through the patronage of foreign allies (who furthermore had gone on to conduct a harsh occupation of France until 1818); they could be incorporated into objects that were familiar and easily distributed among the French population and the sight of which could rekindle support for Napoleon or provoke public movements of fear and panic; and above all they evoked memories not only of the Emperor (bad enough in itself) but also of those fateful months in 1815 when Bonapartists and Jacobins had joined forces under the same banner to prevent the return of the Bourbons. Above all, these objects reminded the royalists of the terrible decade of the 1790s, when tricolour objects of all sorts, from banners to items of clothing, had symbolized the fervour of the Revolution.[134]

Bourbon supporters did their level best to discredit the tricolour flag. In the early months of 1816, during the official ceremonies which saw the destruction of Bonapartist emblems, tricolour flags were publicly burnt, ripped into pieces, and on many occasions dragged through the mud.[135] A speech by a local landowner at one of these gatherings, held on the summit of a mountain in the Rhône, sought explicitly to associate the imperial flag with war, conscription, humiliation, and national suffering:

> 'Inhabitants of the countryside, of what do these tricolour banners remind you? They will remind you of your sons, torn from your arms to be led to be massacred after suffering intolerable deprivations; they will remind you of a monster who only ever looked to himself, his own interest, his own life, and who sacrificed millions of men to his vanity. This Bonaparte, accursed by Hell, what reward did he give France for all that blood it sacrificed? He raised the entire universe against us, he buried our glory in the northern ices,[136] and he left our borders, our towns and villages completely without defence. All you honest men who hear me, rally to the white banner, this emblem of honour, of courage, of patriotism! Ask the living and the dead, and they will tell you that we must be absolutely faithful to our King and his God.'[137]

This was a worthy effort, both to associate the tricolour with Napoleon's failings and to invite local populations to rally to the Bourbons. But it failed. French people remained attached to the tricolour, especially in the early years of the Restoration – precisely the time when Napoleonic sentiment was largely associated with national feelings of humiliation, but also when the hopes of his imminent return were at their highest.

In early March 1817 four tricolour flags appeared on the public square of the commune of Vidauban (Var); beneath each flag was a handwritten message: 'You will triumph shortly; so, brave supporters of the Empire, let us always remember and be ready to act at the first signal.'[138] There were also numerous instances of these banners being placed on public fountains,[139] and also on trees on the outskirts of towns and villages, often near a main road or public path – as with the tricolour flag which was found proudly flying on a poplar near the village of Vic-en-Bigorre in late February 1818.[140]

Another common point at which to affix the national colours of the Bonapartists and Jacobins was the church tower – often a gesture not only of commemoration but also of defiance against the Catholic clergy, who were regarded in many parts of France as the most fanatical and contemptible allies of Bourbon despotism.[141] One of Béranger's most famous songs in the early Restoration was 'Le Vieux Drapeau' ('The Old Flag'), which expressed the hope that France would soon be allowed to 'shake off the dust which casts a shadow over its flag's noble colours';[142] an edition of Béranger's songs published in 1821 sold 11,000 copies in a single week.[143]

Smaller and easier than flags to hand out for propaganda purposes, tricolour rosettes were essential instruments of Napoleonic agitation. Police all over France – notably in Lyons – arrested any man or woman seen wearing these objects between August and December 1815[144] but this repression did little to stem the tricolour tide. In Paris these objects became so common in the early years of the Restoration that the police grew demoralized.[145] To the authorities all over France who were seeking to eradicate 'seditious items', rosettes did indeed seem depressingly ubiquitous. They were affixed to hats, caps, and assorted headwear;[146] pinned to small statues of Napoleon and the Duc de Reichstadt;[147] attached to placards, such as the one found in Corbeil in 1819 announcing that 'Napoleon your ruler is about to return, yes, people of France, you will soon wear the national rosette and reclaim your beloved banners';[148] thrown at the door of royalist mayors as a menacing gesture;[149] and distributed in large quantities in inns and taverns,[150] in military garrisons,[151] and in working-class districts.[152] Their essential role in the arsenal of Bonapartist conspirators was highlighted by the house search of the home of a notary clerk called Petit-Jean in early 1822. Hidden in his lavatory were '617 tricolour rosettes, of which seventeen were in silver and destined for military officers; two tricolour flags, sixty packets of ammunition, and 360 bullets.'[153]

Rosettes were not merely distributed as one-off gestures. Bonapartist (and republican) activists often gave them out in the same locality at fixed intervals. In the spring, summer, and autumn of 1826 the town of Sisteron, one of Napoleon's stops in the Basses-Alpes during the 'flight of the eagle', was the scene of a veritable epidemic of rosettes and assorted seditious objects. It began in mid-March with anti-royalist letters deposited in letter boxes, followed by a wave of placards (upon which were pinned tricolour rosettes) which continued to appear regularly until mid-October.

The content of the messages demonstrated that, in this locality at least, republicans and Bonapartists were working in close alliance: the slogans included traditional *carbonaro* references to the destruction of tyranny ('People, take up arms, you will be supported, our daggers are ready; long live Liberty!') but also a wealth of Napoleonic utterances ('Long Live Napoleon, Long Live the Warriors of Waterloo and the tricolour flag'). The placards also repeatedly called for the assassination of the King, and celebrated the memory of Louvel, the Bonapartist assassin of the Duc de Berry.[154]

This omnipresence of tricolour themes, and their increasingly common manifestation as signs of a political alliance between local Bonapartists and republicans, explains why the mere sight of the three colours immediately provoked public attention – and police repression. In March 1817 in the southern village of Bernis a drawing of a revolutionary Phrygian cap was found, with two messages inscribed: below were the words 'French Republic, equality, indivisibility, death' and above was the inscription 'The Emperor or Death'.[155] In Niort in 1819 a gendarme was dismissed from the force for wearing a tricolour hat in a tavern (and for shouting 'Long Live the Emperor!').[156] A woman was arrested and prosecuted in Marseille a year later for decorating her vase with a tricolour feather, and placing this ornament in public view.[157]

More remarkable still was the association of the three 'national' colours with individual and collective movements of delusion and paranoia – often around that fateful time of the year (February to March) when Napoleon's return was on everyone's mind. In some cases this association was genuine; a man caused a stir of panic in March 1823 at a fair in Auxerre when he ambled among the stalls wearing a cap made of tricolour material, with a rosette pinned to the front.[158]

But more often than not the sightings of these colours, and their association with acts of political sedition, were simply delusions. In Paris a policeman forced a peasant who was walking on the rue de l'Echelle to remove his hat (which was not even tricolour but entirely red) and put it in his pocket because it was attracting the attention of passers-by.[159] In the Puy-de-Dôme a young man was arrested for decorating his hat at a local masque with an assortment of ribbons that included the colours blue, white, and red; he was released only after it was established that he had no political opinions, and came from an impeccably royalist family.[160] In April 1830, a few months before the end of the Restoration regime, a sighting of what merely looked like a tricolour flag on the mast of a small boat cruising on the river Saône was sufficient to trigger a frantic exchange of letters between public officials in Paris and Lyons.[161]

Collective delusions involving the tricolour were encouraged in the countryside by Bonapartist agents. In the Dordogne in 1817 agitators went around telling peasants that the three national colours could be seen on the face of the moon at nightfall, and that this vision was a divine sign that Napoleon should rule again; many rural dwellers did indeed gather to try and catch sight of this miraculous portent.[162]

But this type of credulous mistaken belief was not limited to rural dwellers – on the contrary. In Besançon on 21 March 1820, an officer in the local Legion was flying a kite from a high place on the outskirts of the town, from where it could be seen by all its inhabitants. The kite's colours were green, pink, and white, but from a distance they seemed more like blue, red, and white. A persistent rumour began to spread across town that this kite was marking the anniversary of 21 March 1815, when local Bonapartists had marked the return of Napoleon by taking to the streets, tearing down all royalist emblems and hoisting a tricolour flag over the Besançon town hall.[163] Soon many citizens started to believe that the town had fallen into enemy hands; some even thought that Napoleon himself had returned to France again. This movement of panic only subsided when the officer was tracked down and the kite's true colours were revealed.[164]

Many years after his sensational return to France in 1815, Napoleon was still very much of a presence in the recollections (and imaginings) of his compatriots. The woman in Lisieux was right: he just would not leave them alone.

Chapter 4

An Occult Force

On the night of 14 March 1822, seven men assembled in a house in Lyons. It seemed like a normal social gathering, and as each person arrived there were friendly greetings at the front of the building. But anyone watching more closely would also have noted a discreet password being exchanged. Indeed, once the men were all inside, and had moved into a small dark room at the back of the house, the atmosphere changed. A small coffin draped with the tricolour flag and an imperial eagle was brought in and placed upon an improvised platform, and as candles were lit one of the men began to perform funeral rites.

Napoleon had died in May of the previous year, and this group had assembled to pay homage to his memory. The brief ceremony ended with the organizer of the meeting reading out a eulogy to 'Bonaparte the Great'. What was noteworthy about this invocation was how little it dwelled upon the traditional glories of the First Empire. This was a mourning ceremony whose real purpose was not to express nostalgia for what had been, but to affirm the men's faith in the regeneration of the French nation. The Emperor's spirit lived on, inextricably associated with the causes of national liberation and political liberty. Indeed, the speaker was the head of a *Vente* (branch) of the powerful secret society known as the *Carbonari*, a revolutionary organization whose aim was to overthrow monarchical regimes all over Europe. And it was clear that for this French revolutionary activist the Emperor had now become the symbol of his nation's manifold aspirations for liberty – freedom from what was perceived as the despotic and tyrannical rule of the Bourbons, and freedom to establish a new system of government based on 'the sovereign people'.[1]

Secretive activities of this kind were widespread during the Restoration years, and this solemn occasion in Lyons epitomized one of their key characteristics: the symbolic use of Napoleon's image to mobilize groups towards various forms of (subversive) collective action. Given the authoritarian nature of the Restoration regime, political association in early nineteenth-century France was extremely fluid, with small-scale organizations (often extremely informal), loose affiliations, and overlapping memberships. Most 'Napoleonic' political activity took place in these underground settings, providing a new way of life for the individuals and groups who opposed the Bourbon regime – an existence of mystery, adventure, and intrigue, which involved fomenting rebellions and conspiracies to overthrow the government, but also deriding the royalist regime and its laws through public gestures of dissent, and by organizing counter-celebrations.

Indeed, such was its multifarious activity that the 'Bonapartist underground' soon acquired a reputation of ubiquity and omnipotence. Royalists lived in fear of conspiratorial organizations, highlighting their regional, national, and international ramifications, and often dwelling upon their power and social authority among communities and political institutions.[2] The police, too, were constantly on the defensive. Describing the influence of organized Bonapartist supporters in the Parisian area, an internal police memorandum written in 1825 admitted with resignation (and a touch of awe) that 'an occult and admirably organized force is able to move heaven and earth in this department.'[3]

These secretive gatherings, and the political mobilizations to which they gave rise, also showed how much public perceptions of Napoleon had been altered by the events of the Hundred Days. The imperial legacy was dramatically reinvented by many who appropriated Napoleonic images and symbols to define their political goals after 1815. There were already many Bonapartes in the French popular imagination: the Emperor, the intrepid warrior, as well as the lawgiver (see Figure 11); and after his banishment he became a romantic hero too, the defeated but unbroken victim of English perfidiousness at Sainte-Hélène. Through his political resurrection after 1815 an additional, intriguing image was superimposed upon this complex canvas: Napoleon the champion of liberty. How and by whom this image of the 'liberating Emperor' was deployed, and how effective it proved in undermining the legitimacy of the Bourbon order, will be the central questions explored in this chapter and the next.

While it was in part a matter of ideological reinvention, Napoleonic political activity was also indissociable from commemoration. During the Restoration years, Bonapartist campaigning often defined itself through the cult of memories associated with the imperial tradition – especially the celebration of anniversaries of the Hundred Days. Indeed, the date of the Lyons meeting, 14 March, had been commemorated by Napoleonic supporters all over France since 1816, notably among members of the military and several underground associations, as well as the Freemasons. Among the last-mentioned, this ritual had become so widespread that it formed the basis of a stirring Masonic oath:

> 'I swear and solemnly promise, on pain of a secret death and on the most sacred honour, to fight alone and in group, to travel across the seas, whatever journey needs to be made, for whatever expedition which Napoleon the Great may require of me, and to observe the solemnity of his laws. I also promise to meet every year on March 14.'[4]

In all these respects – ideological creativity, institutional force, commemorative endeavour – these gatherings marked the emergence of a new type of social phenomenon in France: the 'anti-fête',[5] the mirror image of the pious, staid, and hierarchical existence promoted by the Restoration authorities in their official festivities. The 'anti-fête' was rumbustious, instinctive, and subversive; it was also remarkably plastic in its form and volatile in its sentiments. In this respect these collective popular mobilizations displayed notable cultural affinities with the republican political celebrations of the 1790s. One of the

FIGURE 11

Glorious reign of 19 years. As he has governed for 15 years.

An image dating from the Hundred Days, offering a stark contrast between Napoleonic and Bourbon rule; it was also used during the Restoration. Louis XVIII is not only shown as a glutton and a *bon viveur*, but also as a ruler who had broken his promises to provide constitutional government and freedom of the press and not to persecute those who had supported the Revolution and Empire (these promises are shown being trampled by the King under the table). The Emperor, in contrast, is shown as a frugal eater (he makes do with a boiled egg), and as a ruler who had brought the Code Napoleon to France, and also established new liberties since his return in 1815, notably a new constitution and freedom of the press. The overall thrust of this image is to underscore Napoleon's achievements as a law-giver.

key characteristics of the festivals of the Revolutionary era was their extreme fluidity, and also their profound ambivalence: as Mona Ozouf put it, festive acts contained elements of menace, and menacing gestures were made with joviality.[6]

This was very much the spirit of the Restoration era's collective Napoleonic mobilizations. The 1822 Lyons meeting was in this sense exemplary: it began as a social gathering, which then turned into a funeral, which was itself transformed into a political conspiracy. This was the essence of the 'anti-fête': all at once joyful and grieving, intensely optimistic and profoundly despairing, offering inclusive visions of a radiant future and blood-curdling threats to the individuals, groups, and social classes which stood in the way of its realization.

Napoleonic Underground Movements

Despite widespread references to 'the Bonapartist party' and 'Bonapartist agents' in Restoration political discourse, the history of these Napoleonic seditious activities has yet to be properly told from the 'inside'. There are several difficulties, all of which raise the wider issue of the identity of 'Bonapartism' between 1815 and 1848.

The degree of organization of Napoleonic supporters varied considerably within France, ranging from informal meetings of small local groups to highly structured organizations. There was also much activity abroad in Europe and America – typified by former Grande Armée officers such as Fabvier, the colonel turned Bordeaux wine merchant after 1818, who played an important role in fomenting anti-monarchist revolts in Spain and Greece[7] and by Charles Lallemand, who devised daring plans to send a flotilla from the United States to liberate Napoleon from Saint-Helena.[8]

A further difficulty in separating out Bonapartist elements lies in the wide range of underground political and associational activity in France between 1815 and 1830. Isolating its distinct 'Napoleonic' element is not always easy – especially as localized groups of self-styled liberals, republicans, and Bonapartists often cooperated across 'ideological' lines. Even when presenting the narratives of particular Restoration conspiracies and revolutionary groups, historians have tended somewhat to undervalue the role played by their 'Napoleonic' components. In his classic account of the Fédérés, for example, Robert Alexander argued that it was these neo-republican organizations that survived after 1815 to constitute the 'hard core' of the political opposition during the Restoration years – an umbrella under which a variety of political forces could coalesce.[9] Other historians have gone even further, presenting Napoleonic activists as a 'sinister' group of men,[10] acting primarily out of spite and personal self-interest, wedded to a 'cluster of half-articulated attitudes' and notable essentially for their backward-looking nostalgia for the Empire and its military glory.[11]

Apart from its caricatural aspects, the problem with this sort of representation of the 'Bonapartist underground' is its one-dimensionality. What was distinctive about Napoleonic conspiratorial activity under the Restoration was precisely the opposite: very much like the 'anti-fête' of which it was a defining expression, it was above all flexible, and this plasticity manifested itself in its organizational forms, in the goals pursued, and above all in the rich and complex lives it afforded the Bonapartist political agitators who were its principal perpetrators.

The groups and institutions whose members embraced the 'Napoleonic' cause varied greatly. At the most informal end of the spectrum, Bonapartists met in small groups after 1815 – often to continue a political association initiated during the Hundred Days, as was the case with the 'ardent' supporters of the Emperor in the town of Gap.[12] Other tasks were to prepare and distribute 'seditious' literature, as at the Tournay home of the pharmacist Nozère who was ably seconded by 'the former teacher Dutilh, author of bad Napoleonic verses';[13] to coordinate activities across a region, as with a group of well-dressed Bonapartists 'speaking several languages' who used to assemble in an abandoned farmhouse in the French Alps;[14] or simply to ruminate, as with a cohort of imperial enthusiasts who regularly got together in the evenings in Grenoble after 1815. Unable to marshal sufficient incriminating evidence against them to justify an arrest, the prefect nonetheless kept a wary eye on this coterie: 'These sorts of dinners are always preceded by small meetings where hopes of great change are held up, and some agitation or other is fomented.'[15] Likewise, a group of around eighty Bonapartists of the Yonne met regularly to coordinate their propaganda activities; their gatherings could not be banned as they were held in honour of 'Nicholas' (one of the many pseudonyms of Napoleon).[16]

Sometimes these gatherings coalesced into more formalized local associations. Perhaps the most well-known was *L'Union*, founded by the lawyer and Freemason Joseph Rey in Grenoble in 1816; its leader and members were directly and indirectly involved in much of the political agitation which shook the town (and the department of the Isère) during the first decade of Bourbon rule. Rey was not himself a Bonapartist, but he could not but recognize that 'in the mountains of the Dauphinois the people nurtured enthusiastic memories for the only man they believed capable of bringing back happiness and glory to France.'[17] His fundamental political aim between 1816 and 1820 was profoundly Napoleonic: to 'forge a link between the civilians and the military'.[18] There were indeed a large number of local military associations, all of which were made up of 'Napoleonic' elements of various kinds. In some parts in southern France, these were offshoots of partisan groups which had sought to continue the resistance to the Allied invasion of 1815.[19]

Elsewhere, these movements were directed by half-pay officers (the famous *demi-soldes*, of whom there were more than 15,000), the blight of the Restoration authorities in many parts of France. Many of these soldiers idolized Napoleon, and became virulent opponents of the Restoration regime. In Pau and across the Basses-Pyrénées, for example, the distribution of Napoleonic images after 1815 was carried out by a secret society led by the local *demi-soldes*; one particular local favourite – no doubt seeking to appeal to popular sensitivities in this Catholic region – was a drawing of the Emperor dressed as a Christian saint.[20]

Secret military associations of this kind were frequently mentioned in official reports: in the Doubs it was believed that around nine hundred serving and former officers were involved in organized subversive activities; in the Calvados, a similar organization existed but the frustrated prefect was unable to penetrate it.[21] In Lyons, a Napoleonic military society met regularly for the first five years of the Restoration in the house of a former member of the Imperial Guard, Jean Baptiste Georges; it was dissolved by the prefect only in February 1821.[22]

In overall terms, however, half-pay officers were by no means systematically hostile to the Bourbon government; a large folder on the political opinions of the *demi-soldes* of the Rhône in 1819–20 showed that only a minority were involved in anti-government agitation;[23] likewise a report on twenty-four *demi-soldes* in the (very Napoleonic) department of the Isère in 1828 showed that fifteen were completely loyal to the regime, and the remainder were either 'reserved' or 'hostile'.[24]

There was also considerable Napoleonic political activity among Freemasons – mostly in the principal Masonic organization, the Grand Orient de France, where the cult of Napoleon flourished under the Restoration.[25] This was in many respects an extension of the practices of the First Empire era, when large numbers of public officials and Army officers were drawn into Freemasonry. A hostile official disposition towards the order had been present from the early years of the Restoration. Several Grand Orient Lodges were closed, for example at Verdun, where all the local Freemasons were deemed 'enemies of the government';[26] and at Rodez, where most of the hundred members were involved in 'conspiring against the royal government', notably by spreading false information about the imminence of Napoleon's return.[27] Other Lodges would be closed for the 'seditious' activities of their members in subsequent years, for example at Les Sables and Fontenay-le-Comte.[28]

Not all Masons were Bonapartists, however. In 1825 the prefect of police, in a detailed report on conspiratorial activity among French Freemasons, even asserted that Masonic endeavour was 'republican in nature'. By this he did not mean that the Lodges were full of republicans (the term did not have a specific meaning at this juncture), but rather that they were places where men could discuss ideas of freedom, independence, constitutionalism, and above all irreligion.[29]

In many departments the authorities were unable – or unwilling – to challenge local Masonic elites, even when they suspected that they had been penetrated by Napoleonic elements. 'The Bonapartists of my department are heavily involved in sedition' wrote the prefect of Ain to his (equally embattled) colleague of the Rhône in 1816, 'and the Masonic lodges are fully implicated in these activities'.[30] A report to the Minister of the Interior in 1822 detailed more evidence of such penetration in many Lodges in 'Napoleonic' departments such as the Yonne, where 'Masonic organizations consist of subversive men, who meet at every political event'; and in the Vendée, where most of the Lodges were in the hands of 'revolutionary elements'.[31] The Lodges of the Calvados were also highly active: the brothers of Falaise were presided over by Lecouturier, an assistant prosecutor who had been dismissed by the Bourbons for his zealous support of Napoleon during the Hundred Days; while those of Caen met regularly and received 'a large number of travellers from Paris' – who were clearly not men who had come merely to savour the atmosphere of the provinces.[32]

In Lyons and its neighbouring areas, the Lodges were dominated by anti-Bourbon elements in the immediate aftermath of Napoleon's fall.[33] In fact, this situation remained unchanged during the 1820s: 'liberals', republicans and Bonapartists mingled freely, and as we noted at the beginning of this chapter, these groups often coordinated their activities and shared a common appreciation of the Napoleonic heritage. The members of the *Philadelphes*, for example, were described as 'revolutionary and republican' in their ideological orientation.[34]

Although informed about the broad purposes of such Lodges, the police seemed powerless to prevent their activities. The Masons of Lyons did not hesitate to provide financial assistance to Napoleonic activists who were being sought by the police.[35] At a Masonic banquet held in the town of Tarare in June 1821 (a month after Napoleon's death), several Masons proposed (to loud cheers) toasts to the 'immortal violet'.[36] Another well-known Napoleonic Lodge was the *Parfait Silence*, which included several men who had been prominent in their support for the Emperor in Lyons during the Hundred Days; an official report noted that 'eagles are embroidered on the Masonic emblems and decorations of this Lodge'.[37] Subsequent investigations of this Lodge by the prefect of Rhône found that only two of the twenty-four active members of the Lodge were royalists; the others were 'more or less resolute liberals, some of whom were ardent revolutionaries'.[38] Some members, it was also noted, wore a variety of non-Masonic emblems representing the imperial eagle.[39]

There was also much covert Napoleonic movement among the Freemasons of the dissident Misraïm Obedience, a breakaway group led by the Bédarride brothers. Confronted by the Grand Orient (which did not like to see its hegemony challenged) and persecuted by the Restoration authorities, many of these Masons were forced to close down their activities in 1822 when the police raided their premises and found the Lodges to be 'exclusively made up of extreme enemies of the Bourbons';[40] many of these were Bonapartist half-pay officers, acting under Masonic cover to pursue their political objectives.[41]

One of the most famous dissident Lodges of the Restoration was the Parisian *Les Amis de la Vérité*, founded around 1818 and linked to several provincial revolutionary associations. In conjunction with Parisian Bonapartist elements, it organized an abortive coup in Paris in August 1820, the 'conspiracy of the French Bazaar'.[42] While many of its key members became leaders in the republican and Saint-Simonist movements (Bazard, Buchez, and Charles Beslay, the veteran of the Paris Commune), philo-Napoleonic sentiments were also in evidence; a police report on a Lodge meeting held in 1823 noted that a pamphlet entitled *Apothéose de Bonaparte* had been distributed to all members.[43]

Also in Paris was the Lodge *Les Amis Bienfaisants*, whose Venerable Jean-Baptiste Brunel was an ardent Napoleonist during the Hundred Days in Carpentras, where he practised law (and presided over the local Lodge). Under the Restoration Brunel moved to Paris, where he was elected to the presidency of *Les Amis Bienfaisants* in December 1819.[44] A police report in 1823 described Brunel's political activities as 'suspect' – hardly surprising, given his apparent membership of all three Masonic obediences.[45]

Freemasonry did not operate only within France; indeed, important parts of its activities were international. In the early 1820s, much of French revolutionary agitation in Spain (in which many former Napoleonic officers were involved) was organized through Masonic Lodges based on the Spanish side of the French border;[46] some of these Lodges had been founded more than a decade earlier by Grande Armée officers during the French occupation.[47] The papers of the Misraïm Lodges seized in 1822 revealed a wide network of contacts outside France, notably with Swiss and American Lodges.[48] The eastern border was particularly porous, as the exposed prefect of the Jura complained in 1824; he particularly noted the 'seditious' activities of Masonic lodges in Geneva and Ferney.[49]

German states, too, were rich in Masonic Napoleonic conspirators; a police report on the arrest of a man named Thannenberg in 1820 noted his numerous contacts with agents of 'the Bonapartist party in France', notably former Army officers. His papers also revealed close ties with several high-ranking members of the French Customs administration[50] – which would perhaps explain how a lot of Napoleonic propaganda managed to find its way into France despite the authorities' 'surveillance'.

In Paris a number of clandestine organizations sought to challenge the Restoration authorities and perpetuate Napoleonic interests, with varying degrees of success – largely depending on their resistance to penetration by the police. In some cases, these associations were well known: with such names as *Le Lion Dormant*, *L'Epingle Noire* and *Les Vautours de Bonaparte* their ideological allegiances were fairly obvious.[51] Some of these groups had powerful networks extending across France and even beyond; the members of the *Epingle Noire*, for example, printed 'seditious' literature in Belgium and distributed it throughout France.[52]

Between the early and mid-1820s, one of the most active transnational Napoleonic secret societies was the *Aigle Noir*, which grew out of Swiss Masonic networks in Geneva and the Vaud region. Its aim was unambiguous: 'to overthrow and execute the Princes of the Bourbon family in order to replace them with the son of Napoleon Bonaparte.'[53] Among its leaders were the Bertex brothers, one of whom had served in the Grande Armée for fourteen years and had accompanied the Emperor to Elba; the association had correspondents in Paris, Grenoble, and Lyons, in several Swiss towns, as well as in Turin, Florence, and Naples.[54] Elements of this organization later continued their activities in collaboration with other (republican) revolutionary groups. A series of meetings involving Masons in Germany, Switzerland, and France, and also including representatives of *Carbonari* and Philhellenic movements, reportedly took place in Wolfberg Castle (Switzerland) between the summer of 1826 and the spring of 1827. Among the papers later uncovered by the police was an image showing a man giving a Masonic handshake to Napoleon, with a caption (in German) reading *Freu bis in den Tod* ('Faithful to the Death').[55]

The most famous underground movement in Restoration France

was the *Carbonari*, which in many ways represented the culmination of all the organized groups previously mentioned. This was the most secretive, militarized, politically wide-ranging and powerful revolutionary society of the period, and at its peak its level of support probably exceeded that of all the other semi-secret and underground organizations put together.[56] Its structure and esoteric rituals also shared many affinities with Freemasonry; indeed, there was considerable overlap in the membership of the two organizations in the early 1820s.[57] In 1825 the Lodge *Les Amis de la Vérité* was described by the prefect of police as the 'antechamber of the *Carbonari*'.[58]

How 'Napoleonic' was this secret society? Its overall aim – the overthrow of the Holy Alliance monarchies – was entirely consistent with Napoleonic objectives, especially during and after 1815. As we saw at the beginning of this chapter, some local branches were made up almost to a man of strong supporters of Bonaparte. But the *Carbonari* also consisted of powerful liberal and republican elements, notably among the Parisian leadership groups. (Part of the strength of the movement lay in its mythical power; there was a widespread belief that the entire organization was run by one single Central Committee, which almost certainly never existed.)

In some localities, such as Lyons and Grenoble, there can be little doubt that local *Carbonari* groups were largely dominated by Bonapartists. In Lyons in 1822, Bonapartist elements in the Carbonari painted daggers and imperial inscriptions on the front doors of royalist officials.[59] In obstinately Napoleonic Grenoble, the prefect noted in 1820 that 'the Carbonari have succeeded in recruiting widely'.[60] A police informant initiated at a meeting on the night of 15 August 1822 – the anniversary of the Emperor's birth – found the *Vente* to be headed by Aymard, a well-known personality among local Bonapartists and a former officer in the Grande Armée: there were believed to be over 150 members of the *Carbonari* in Grenoble alone.[61] A year earlier, Aymard had been one of the leading conspirators in the rebellion of 20 March, which had sought to unseat the prefect in Grenoble.[62]

Portraits of Rebels: Louvel and Berton

Conspiracy was thus central to Napoleonic political activity under the Restoration. Bonapartists praised conspirators and honoured their memory, but they also practised the art themselves by staging plots and organizing insurrections, as well as by other subversive schemes. More than a mere instrument, conspiracy was something of a way of life for the Napoleonic 'people'.

The archetypal figure of the 'popular' Napoleonic conspirator was Louis Pierre Louvel, who fatally stabbed the Duc de Berry in February 1820. An ardent supporter of the Emperor, whom he joined at Elba after working as a saddler in the Grande Armée, Louvel devised the project of killing three leading individuals in the French royal family after 1815.[63] At the time of his arrest he was widely condemned as a 'fanatic';[64] and this view of his gesture as an isolated, pathetic, and almost irrational act is still common.[65] This effective denial of his 'authorship' of his act was further accentuated by the belief that he had been the instrument of some conspiracy (which Louvel always strenuously denied), or that he had been driven to become a killer by the 'revolutionary doctrines' of his time.[66] In the words of a contemporary royalist observer: 'Louvel's only accomplice was the general exaltation of minds, spurred by the press; he had drawn his boldness and his courage from the atmosphere of deleterious opinions.'[67]

Although Louvel's own justification of his act, which he read out at his trial, was censured, his political attitude and motivations can be reconstructed through the numerous police interrogations and judicial enquiries carried out after his arrest.[68] His 'love' of the Emperor was a matter of common knowledge, both to his family and to his work associates; but what also emerged in these investigations was his consistent interest in politics after 1815.[69] His opposition to the Restoration was firmly grounded in 'revolutionary patriotism', which he believed remained embodied in the person of Bonaparte, the only political leader who had stood up against France's 'foreign invasion'.[70]

Louvel was not very literate but he constantly surprised his interrogators by the range of his historical and cultural references. One of Napoleon's most controversial actions in the early years of his rule had been the kidnapping and execution of the Duc d'Enghien, a Bourbon prince accused of conspiring against France. Louvel defended this as a legitimate act of national self-defence in response to an external plot;[71] he also described his own act as similar to the tyrannicides carried out in Roman times by men such as Brutus, expressing pride in his gesture, that of a 'true patriot'.[72] In another session, he compared his action to that of Charlotte Corday, the killer of the Jacobin revolutionary Marat, drawing the conclusion that 'what is a crime in one epoch is seen as a virtuous gesture in another'.[73] Louvel, in sum, was neither weak of mind nor manipulated; his action in 1820 rested upon a coherent set of self-justifications which were characteristic of the views of a wide section of the 'Napoleonic people'.

Louvel's gesture inspired a string of prophecies, apparitions and visions; on the day of the assassination a woman praying in front of de Berry's bust noticed that his features 'offered the image of the most atrocious pain, and there were tears in his eyes'.[74] Bonapartist supporters and sympathizers, in contrast, were triumphant: Jean Rivière, a butcher's boy from Paris, was arrested for shouting that this was a 'festive day' for France because 'that fat pig had bled to death'; and a group of forty former Grande Armée officers gathered in a castle on the outskirts of Paris where they held 'an orgy of rejoicing'.[75]

Many interpreted the event as a premonition of Napoleon's return. An imperialist named Legrand, a merchant from Paris, greeted the news of de Berry's death as a 'happy moment', 'the prelude to the imminent return of Bonaparte'.[76] Former soldier Louis Dumont was even more precise, welcoming de Berry's death and remarking that 'Napoleon had landed at Cadix and was now heading towards Lyons'.[77] Even when they did not echo such 'return' stories, celebratory placards appeared all over France in their hundreds calling for the extermination of the Bourbons.[78] Some were essentially republican in tone, as with the inscription which appeared in Le Vigan (Gard) in early March 1820 stating that 'a hero guided by the hand of Liberty has just struck a mortal blow to Tyranny'.[79] But many other placards carried explicit references to Napoleon. A handwritten note in Beauvais heaped praise upon the Emperor, and warned all royalists to keep their heads down, as they were 'next in line';[80] in Tarascon a placard similarly left little room for ambiguity:

'Berry is dead? O what bliss! One less tyrant in France. Long Live the Emperor!'[81]

When they learnt the news of the Duc's assassination, twelve soldiers in Rouen gave a hearty rendering of the Napoleonic *Marseillaise*, followed by several imperial songs;[82] in Caen, the event was greeted with a distribution of Napoleonic medallions;[83] and at Melun two men were arrested for cheering the annoucement, and beginning a heated discussion about the extent to which Louvel's gesture had been an act of 'popular sovereignty'. (The discussion probably continued behind bars, as they were both arrested.)[84] In another discussion, a Bonapartist member of the National Guard brought Rousseau to the rescue: 'Natural law being the basis of all social order, the princes who violate such laws return their subjects into primitive law.'[85]

In the Ardennes, a former Napoleonic officer took the trouble to attend the mass of remembrance for de Berry, where he shouted 'Long Live the Emperor' at the height of the ceremony[86] and a mason working in Fontenay welcomed the assassination and expressed the hope that it would be followed by many more. As this man's name happened to be 'Empereur', the police no doubt already had him under close observation.[87]

Louvel actually became something of a cult figure. A group of sixty Parisian students defiantly chanted his name in 1821 on the first anniversary of the Duc's death;[88] irreligious Freemasons drank to his health and cited his (alleged) saying that God 'was but a word';[89] and a *Carbonaro* commemorative meeting in Grenoble three years later described Louvel as the man who had shown the greatest morality and made the single largest contribution to the liberation of France since the Restoration.[90] A two-volume fictionalized account of Louvel's plot which appeared in the early years of the July Monarchy presented the aim of the assassination as 'bringing back the Emperor and the republic'.[91]

Louvel represented, in an extreme form, one version of the Bonapartist culture of 'conspiracy': this was symbolized by the loner who carried out his mission both as an act of individual defiance of the authorities and in the hope of inspiring others to follow his example. Another more institutional (and collective) source of Napoleonic 'sedition' during the Restoration was the Army. After their return to power, the Bourbons were hugely suspicious of the French officer corps, which had been the privileged instrument of Napoleonic power and glory throughout the First Empire; many royalist zealots remained convinced that the Emperor's 'flight of the Eagle' had been possible only because of a vast military conspiracy.[92] While evidence for such a scheme was never found, there were plenty of other plots that emerged from the ranks of former Army officers after 1815.

Perhaps the most emblematic of these rebels was General Jean-Baptiste Berton, a former imperial officer who led the ill-fated rebellion in Thouars and Saumur, the failure of which led to his capture and execution in October 1822.[93] Although he had served in the Revolutionary and Napoleonic campaigns with bravery and distinction, Berton was released from active service in 1815; his superiors probably did not forgive his return to active duty during the Hundred Days. Berton's house in Paris became a rallying point for many Napoleonic and Jacobin conspirators. His distinguished record, and his 'talent at peroration'[94] earned him the respect and support of many anti-Bourbon activists, but also the sustained scrutiny of the Bourbon police. He was imprisoned for 'sedition' for five months in 1815–16, and again in June 1820; on both occasions he was eventually released. In September 1820 the State even revoked his military pension, an arbitrary act that led Berton to write a spirited protest to French legislators: 'The sword of persecution is suspended over my head.'[95]

Berton's world-view expressed the bitterness of those elements of the Napoleonic officer corps who had lost all their positions under the Restoration. His writings offered an apologia for the 'glorious art of war', and for many of the campaigns in which he had personally taken part, notably the battles of 1815;[96] he also took up his pen to defend Napoleon's conduct during the battle of Waterloo.[97] He constantly emphasized the value of a permanent Army based on talented and experienced officers and bemoaned the Restoration's removal from the forces of 'good, vigorous, and valiant men, and their replacement by schoolboys and men who were mentally and physically challenged'.[98] He also eloquently articulated the humiliation felt by many of these military men upon their return to their homes after 1815, where they were systematically spied upon by the police and subjected to constant surveillance by mayors and (most ignominiously of all) priests – hardly a way to treat heroes who had defeated the English, Austrian, and Russian armies.[99]

Like many of his military colleagues involved in conspiring against the Restoration (and in contrast with Louvel's simple but acute perceptions of politics) Berton followed Napoleon's celebrated motto about instinct and spontaneity: 'One commits oneself, and then one sees.'[100] He did not have much interest in the political process or in the designation of elites; at the time of the Thouars insurrection, when asked whether the cry should be 'Long Live Napoleon II', he famously replied: 'Shout whatever you like!'[101]

Above all, Berton's discourse played on the theme of 'honour', the cardinal virtue among Napoleonic officers: citing Montesquieu, he lambasted the 'false sense of honour'[102] which underpinned the exercise of monarchical rule and the 'dishonourable' conduct of those men who had cynically betrayed Napoleon after 1815, despite owing him their careers and fortune.[103] After Napoleon's death, he echoed calls for the Bourbons to 'honour the Emperor's memory' by bringing back his remains and burying them below the Vendôme Column in Paris.[104]

This sense of pride was also very much ingrained in Berton's personal ethos; his decision to lead the insurrection in 1822 was undoubtedly the ultimate expression of a philosophy that he had articulated on many occasions, and which could have served as his epitaph: 'For us military men, honour demands that we should never ask a subordinate to do what we would not have the courage or the temerity to undertake ourselves.'[105]

Multiple Lives

For the authorities, another leading source of Napoleonic 'conspiracy' was the Emperor's inner circle – especially his family, and the men who followed him into exile in 1814 and 1815. Leaving nothing to chance, the police kept a close watch on Empress Marie-Louise, on key members of Napoleon's clan such as his brother Lucien, and (upon their return to France) on the Emperor's immediate entourage at Saint-Helena – notably Generals Gourgaud, Bertrand, and Montholon, and his last doctor, Francesco Antommarchi.[106] Even the cook Lepage, who left the island in 1818, was subjected to prolonged interrogation by a French diplomat upon his arrival in Hamburg. He revealed that the atmosphere in Napoleon's house in Saint-Helena had become somewhat rebellious: feuding among the Emperor's associates had increased,[107] all the native servants, dissatisfied with their treatment, had left their posts, and meals were being prepared by Chinese and Indian servants. All of which had put Napoleon in such a foul mood that he had taken to walking around the house with a billiard stick, beating anyone who crossed his path.[108]

Once back on French soil, most of these well-known Bonapartists tried to keep low profiles. But such was the extent of State surveillance that their lives became almost transparent. Some, however, defied the odds to pursue their Napoleonic commitments. The best example of this combination of fortitude and wiliness was given by Jean-Noel Santini, a fellow Corsican who had served as Napoleon's usher, handyman, and hairdresser at Saint-Helena.[109] Sent to London in 1817 on a mission to publicize the Emperor's ill treatment at the hands of his English jailers (which he succeeded in doing; the letters he carried were published, and provoked a debate in the House of Lords about Napoleon's captivity),[110] Santini then travelled to Rome where he was arrested and eventually detained for four years in the Moravian town of Brunn at the behest of the Emperor of Austria.

Released after the death of Napoleon (who left him 25,000 francs in his will), Santini embarked upon a new career as a full-time Bonapartist agent. He repeatedly told the police that he was disconnected from 'public affairs';[111] and the authorities in his native Corsica even had him down as a 'peaceful and tranquil man, who leads a quiet life with his wife'.[112] During his frequent interrogations by the police he also supplied a wealth of false information (a practice cultivated to a fine art by Napoleonic agents), and at one point seemed to have gained sufficient trust to be labelled a 'secret agent of the royal government'.[113] This subterfuge – for such it was – was indirectly confirmed by a report in the late Restoration years, which stated that Santini had remained 'a dangerous courier of the Bonapartist cause'. His travels appeared to have taken him, among other places, to the United States (where he had worked with Joseph

Bonaparte) and Spain (where he had been involved in revolutionary agitation with Murat's son in 1822–3). In France he was closely linked to key leaders in the Napoleonic and liberal opposition in Paris, notably General Foy, the Duc d'Orléans and Lafayette.[114] This 'quiet man', in short, seemed to have led a double life for much of the 1820s.[115]

A capacity to lead multiple existences was an absolute prerequisite for survival in the Napoleonic 'underground'. Police files provide evidence – albeit almost always fragmentary – of extraordinary figures who for years maintained a façade of 'normality' while engaging in covert Bonapartist activity. Examples include men such as Broutat, a senior official at the Ministry of War, who was not only a Napoleonic agent but also a *Carbonaro*, the Venerable of his Masonic Lodge, and a distributor of illicit Bonapartist literature;[116] the priest Jean-Baptiste Gautier, who paid unctuous tributes to the Bourbon monarchy in his church while holding regular gatherings of Napoleonic supporters in his house (where he also concealed imperial propaganda and paraphernalia, including tricolour belts and copies of the Napoleonic catechism);[117] and Le Boucher, a junior public prosecutor at the Angers court, also an active Mason and secret Bonapartist, who used his position to secure low sentences, acquittals and even dismissals of charges against those tried for Napoleonic 'sedition' between 1815 and 1821.[118]

Because their work involved much travel (and therefore exposure to surveillance) Bonapartist couriers were especially vulnerable to police attention. These men and women who carried letters, packages, maps, draft insurrection plans, false proclamations, and large sums of money to various destinations were sometimes followed for periods of time, arrested and subjected to lengthy interrogations; yet the results were invariably frustrating for the police. In 1816, over a period of several months, the police in Chalon-sur-Saône followed a young woman named Jeanne Clerc, a twenty-five-year old musician who regularly travelled to Paris; although she was suspected of carrying Bonapartist correspondence, the authorities never found any incriminating material on her – even though they conceded that they had not always been able to keep track of her movements, as she 'often disguised herself as a man'.[119]

In the same year, the authorities in Abbeville detained Pascal

Sinoquet, a local builder, on 'suspicion of being the agent of some intrigue'. He had been travelling regularly to Paris to deliver packages to well-known Napoleonic addresses, while claiming to be in the capital 'on business'; in his home town he had even developed a reputation as 'an ardent royalist'. He denied any knowledge of the contents of the letters, or of their addressees. Before reluctantly releasing him, the sub-prefect of Abbeville paid this (unintended) homage to the quality of his stonewalling: 'His ambiguous replies; his misleading certificates of good conduct; his false and internally inconsistent declarations; his unsatisfactory accounts of his means of existence; and his erratic lifestyle all seem to suggest that Sinoquet is the agent of a machination.'[120]

What precisely this was, we shall never know; and as Sinoquet wove his way between Paris and Abbeville, hiring builders and conniving with conspirators, socializing with royalists and fraternizing with Bonapartists, ducking away from police officials and hiding his letters from their spies, perhaps this Bonapartist agent was not always quite sure either.

The final type of Napoleonic conspirator was the extrovert, who concealed his Bonapartist activities behind a flurry of movement and a flamboyant lifestyle. To illustrate this form of activism, let us consider the case of Jean Drevon, a clerk in the local court in the Saint-Marcellin district of the Isère. In 1819, he mysteriously gave up this position and went to Paris. He returned a year later a wealthy man, claiming to have inherited a large fortune from an uncle (although there were also rumours that he had married a rich old widow for her money). By the summer of 1821 local authorities in Saint-Marcellin were convinced that Drevon had again become a 'nuisance'; he was in regular contact with Bonapartist elements in the Isère and the Drôme, and upon hearing of the death of Napoleon he had even launched a new fashion: '[Drevon] was the first to wear a violet ribbon pinned to a white hat as a sign of mourning for the demise of Bonaparte; his example was then imitated by many in the locality.'[121]

Unimpressed with his symbolic creativity, the authorities constantly trailed Drevon between 1821 and 1823 – the high water mark of Napoleonic ferment in the Isère, a time of plots, rebellions, and assorted scuffles. (As noted earlier, a group of Napoleonic agitators launched an insurrection in March 1821 and charged into the prefecture building in Grenoble, where they demanded that the tricolour flag be flown.[122]) The police found little to link Drevon to these activities, but much to provoke envy: Drevon entertained 'three or four' people to dinner several nights a week, with a string quartet performing in the background; he travelled regularly to Paris, where he socialized with Bonapartist and liberal notables such as the banker Laffitte; he also visited Lyons with large sums of money, which he lavished on beautiful *objets d'art*, extravagant tips to the postilions, and several (concurrent) mistresses.[123] Very occasionally, the authorities caught glimpses of his parallel life: on one occasion in Lyons he was seen by gendarmes entering a café from which he emerged with a collection of Bonapartist pamphlets.[124]

But such moments of visibility were rare. Indeed, Drevon's skill at managing and circumventing his surveillants was exemplary. His regular trips to neighbouring departments, whose purpose his own authorities knew to be conspiratorial, completely fooled officials in these localities. The prefect of the Drôme wrote that Drevon's numerous visits to the area were connected only with his 'love of music': according to this unsuspecting official, he came 'to play the violin in a chamber ensemble'.[125] (This was a common front among Napoleonic activists in Grenoble, many of whom met in 'musical societies'[126].) Another ploy used by Drevon was his expression of fondness for rural France: asked why he travelled so much, he invariably replied that 'he loved the countryside'.[127] He was also adept at vanishing into thin air: the Parisian police could never quite track his movements in the capital, despite pleading entreaties from the prefect in Grenoble;[128] the Isère gendarmerie fared no better, managing even to lose sight of Drevon for three whole days during a week-long provincial trip in 1823.[129]

When extravagance and cunning no longer sufficed, Drevon also knew how to put his pursuers on the defensive. Stopped and searched by the police on one occasion, Drevon took off all his clothes and threw a tantrum in the police station; he later accused these officers of trying to 'garrotte' him. (It is not unlikely that they did indeed try to strangle him; they must have been quite frustrated with him by now.) He took his complaint directly to the prefect, also throwing in, for good measure, the accusation that officials in the prefecture had 'interfered with his mail'. Drevon's histrionics were so effective on this occasion that the prefect promised not only to investigate his grievances, but also to prosecute any official found to have violated the secrecy of Drevon's correspondence.[130]

In September 1823, the trail finally went cold: Drevon disappeared from the Isère and there were some rumours to the effect that he had gone bankrupt. It was only when the police finally searched his house in Saint-Marcellin that they discovered a crucial clue: among his papers were 'all the decorations of a Rose-Croix'. Drevon had also been, all the while, a high-ranking Freemason.[131]

A Permanent Struggle

Lone workers, military plotters, Freemasons, *Carbonari*, imperial celebrities, ordinary public employees, builders, priests, 'music lovers': Napoleonic conspirators came in almost every conceivable shape and size. Through this variety, these rebels shed a revealing light on the nature of Bonapartism after 1815 – notably on its social heterogeneity, but also on the complex mixture of symbolic, affective, and ideological elements that came together to inspire 'Napoleonic' political activity.

For some, this mobilization was an expression of loyalty to the person of the Emperor. For others, it was a commitment to specific values (patriotism, military glory, etc.). And for others still, Napoleon was 'reinvented' to symbolize new social and political ideals. (More evidence of this transformation will be presented in the following chapter.) Yet across this range there emerged a coherent and stable set of precepts which constituted the 'core' of Bonapartism, identifiable even when its bearers were operating in organizations and groups whose purposes were broader, more diffuse, or more comprehensive.

How far did this 'Napoleonic' identity crystallize through the various 'conspiratorial' movements to which Bonapartists belonged during the Restoration? The relationship between conspiracy and Napoleonic organization was essentially contingent: some (indeed most) conspiracies of the 1816–22 period were organized by groups that were not Bonapartist, and many Bonapartist plotters (most notably Louvel) did not belong to any organization. At the same time, the evidence presented here demonstrates the profound penetration of both the public and conspiratorial spheres by Bonapartist images, aims, and values. Not only the strength but also the fragility of the Napoleonic underground after 1815 lay in this very plasticity: its capacity to operate through existing institutions, whether public or private, 'legitimate' or secretive.

Bonapartism did not need structured organizations to exist and flourish, but rather used them almost indistinctly to pursue its key objectives: destabilizing and undermining the Bourbon order, cherishing the memory of the Emperor, and promoting a Napoleonic political alternative, however vaguely defined. The degree to which these activities were successful will be examined in the next chapter.

Chapter 5

Rebellions in Action

Napoleon's legend clearly inspired an extraordinary range of political activity. But what did all this agitation achieve? History has generally shown little indulgence towards the various forms of Napoleonic political action in the early Restoration – whether plots with a specific Bonapartist purpose (or led by Napoleonic agents), or conspiracies with wider objectives but undertaken with the support of Napoleonic elements. The most successful single act, Louvel's assassination of the Duc de Berry, is typically seen to have resulted in perverse political consequences, causing the Bourbon regime to lurch sharply to the right and strengthening the hand of the 'ultra' royalist elements.[1]

As for the numerous rebellions and insurrections planned by or executed with the help of Napoleonic agitators, they generally seemed to have ended in utter disaster. A conspiracy led by Jean-Paul Didier in Grenoble in May 1816 was easily put down; a plot in Lyons in June 1817 met with a similar fate; the August 1820 'French Bazaar' insurrection in Paris finished before it even started.[2] The climax of *Carbonari* activity in France, which began with a series of revolts in Saumur and Belfort (led, as we saw in the previous chapter, by General Berton), saw the movement eventually spread to large parts of eastern and western France during the spring and summer of

1822. Its defeat sealed the fate of the *Carbonari* as an underground political force.[3]

If these 'national' conspiracies were unsuccessful, things were very different at a local level. In 1815–16, for example, Napoleon's native Corsica witnessed a veritable insurrection (known, after the region in which it was fought, as the 'War of Fiumorbo') between pro-Restoration forces and a local Napoleonic leader, Bernard Poli, who had travelled to Elba in 1814 to meet the Emperor. Poli defined himself as a supporter of Napoleon, rather than of the Empire,[4] and his insurgency was provoked by the attempts of local Restoration authorities to arrest him. Retreating to the Fiumorbo region, he resisted for several months, inflicting several defeats on his adversaries. In early 1816 official reports were describing the region's Bonapartists as fully behind Poli, and manifesting 'much audacity and insolence'; locals in Fiumorbo refused any cooperation with State authorities.[5] In April 1816 Poli's forces, made up of 1,700 combatants (including 500 women) routed a Franco-Corsican army estimated at over 8,000 men.[6] Undefeated, Poli negotiated an amnesty for himself and his troops, after which he left the island with all his possessions (including some valuable jewellery left with him by the former King of Naples, Joachim Murat).

Reading about Poli's exploits in English newspapers in Saint-Helena, Napoleon had followed the actions of his lieutenant with admiration.[7] Committed to Corsica's links with France, Poli defined the rationale for his struggle as follows: 'I promoted this insurgency on the basis of that feeling of independence, which makes all men rush to arms whenever injustice and oppression rear their head'.[8] He returned to the island a few years later, and remained a thorn in the flesh of the Restoration authorities.[9] Indeed, despite its Bonapartist inspirations, and Napoleon's own virulent hostility to any form of self-determination for his native island, the 1815–16 war has been celebrated by some Corsican nationalists as a key moment in the island's struggle for liberty.[10]

These sorts of 'local' actions have received little attention in the historiography of the Restoration. The most charitable view of Bonapartist conspiratorial activity during the decade that followed 1815 was that it was counter-productive (Robert Alexander thus speaks of an opposition which was 'self-defeating'[11]); others have been even harsher, describing the rebellions of this period as 'rather farcical'.[12] However, while it is undeniable that these plots did not bring down the Bourbon regime in the short run, it is a mistake to regard their outcomes as comprehensive failures. These actions kept the Napoleonic flame burning, and harassed the public authorities; in the longer run, there is little doubt that this sustained pressure weakened the regime and contributed to its downfall in 1830.

But the real error here is one of perspective. The plots and rebellions involving Napoleonic groups take on an entirely different complexion if they are seen not as exercises in attempted regime transformation, but rather as wider expressions of the 'anti-fête': a systematic confrontation of the State, whose purpose was constantly to question, unsettle, and drive back official authority. Political and military conspiracy was one of the panoply of instruments of social rebellion against the Restoration – a repertoire which, as we saw earlier, included holding forbidden Napoleonic objects, spreading rumours about the Emperor's return, subverting royalist anniversaries, shouting Napoleon's name, posting seditious placards in public places, singing songs in Bonaparte's honour, and celebrating the moral and political values of individualism that his supporters associated with the Emperor. Napoleonic conspiracy was not so much goal-driven as expressive: it gave its participants an escape from the drab world of Restoration France, and opened up new prospects of adventure, heroism, mystery, and (above all) hope.

The substantive role of this Napoleonic culture in the demise of the Bourbons in 1830 has long been undervalued by French historians, who have tended to regard the July Revolution as the work of liberals and republicans. Although the potency of Bonapartism during the Restoration is generally recognized, this acknowledgement is typically qualified by the claim that it was a force that was both politically and ideologically diffuse, notably lacking 'structure or definition';[13] historians also tend to regard this period as one in which Bonapartist doctrine was somnolent.[14] Yet our evidence will suggest otherwise. In the popular imagination, the Emperor was identified with a clear and coherent cluster of values, at the centre of which was the ideal of freedom, brought to France by the 1789 Revolution. And this 'liberating Emperor' was more than an iconic figure for the Napoleonic tribe: between 1815 and 1830 Bonaparte's image as an emblem of liberty played a crucial federating role among French opposition groups, providing the underlying element of cohesion which unified the 'anti-fête' of the Restoration years.

Subverting Royalist Anniversaries and Symbols

Nothing better captures the sheer exuberance of the 'anti-fête' than the individual and collective gestures of subversion carried out by Napoleonic activists and sympathizers during the official festivities and significant events of the Restoration regime. These gestures effectively stood such occasions on their heads, turning instances of solemn remembrance into moments of gleeful delight. They changed anniversaries intended as religious, socially exclusive, and deferential royalist gatherings into episodes of creative spontaneity, popular participation, and unrestrained Napoleonic enthusiasm.

Derision was one of the central attributes of traditional secular festivities such as the carnival and the *charivari*. It was also one of the principal instruments in the 'anti-fête' repertoire, and it was put to telling use by local supporters of the Emperor. The tradition had already begun during the Hundred Days, when many Bonapartists had expressed their joy at Napoleon's return by publicly desecrating royalist emblems and banners. One of the most colourful incidents of this type was staged by Colonel Verdun, whose regiment was stationed in Toulouse in March 1815. When he heard that Napoleon was back in the Tuileries in Paris, this fervent imperialist displayed his delight by pinning his Saint-Louis military cross to the tail of his dog, and parading it with ostentation around Toulouse. This episode was still part of local folklore in the late years of the Restoration.[15]

After 1815 such mocking gestures were especially targeted against official royalist celebrations, foiling the regime's efforts to promote the image of a dignified, benevolent, and paternalistic King. Pierre Lauré, a stable boy in Béon caused a scandal by naming his dog 'Louis XVIII' and marching him around the commune on 25 August, the day of Saint Louis (the King's patron saint).[16] Celebrations in honour of the King were always vulnerable to these sorts of stunts: in 1824 the municipality of Cartas (Landes) organized a ball for the local population, and a bust of the monarch was prominently placed in the middle of the dancing hall. No doubt in scornful homage to Louis XVIII's legendary appetite, twelve young men emptied a barrel of red wine over the bust, and then proceeded to cover it with cooked vegetables; they were vigorously chanting anti-royalist Napoleonic songs when the gendarmes came to arrest them.[17]

As was characteristic with anti-fête moments, this sort of playfulness frequently traded on grotesque imagery: after describing the king as a 'fat pig and eater of potatoes' a labourer in the commune of Soullans went on to add that he 'regretted that Louis XVIII's tongue and heart were not there on the table where he was seated, as he would have eaten them with vinaigrette.'[18]

Another common way of negating the festive order of the Bourbons was to empty it of all warmth and public fervour. Throughout France, and especially in areas with significant Bonapartist support, local authorities met with waves of sullenness on the day of Saint Louis. One police official in Bordeaux summed up the general situation: 'The fête of 25 August was sad and silent here. The only rejoicing to be seen was that which had been officially ordained.'[19]

Citizens collectively resisted official injunctions to decorate and illuminate their homes on the day of the King's fête, turning darkness into an overt form of civic protest – a tradition which was appropriated by opposition groups throughout the nineteenth century.[20] During the 1822 Saint Louis anniversary in Villeneuve, there were almost no illuminations of private homes, and only three public buildings were (thinly) decorated: the municipality, the gendarmerie, and the Masonic Lodge. This was clearly not the first incident of this sort in the locality, and one official sounded a dire warning: 'There is little doubt that unless the authorities put some order here the festivities of our King will degenerate into insignificance.'[21] This was precisely what happened in many of the larger towns, such as Grenoble; reports on the celebrations in the capital of the Isère routinely bemoaned the 'complete darkness' which shrouded anti-royalist neighbourhoods on the evenings of the day of Saint Louis.[22]

Sometimes unfavourable comparisons were explicitly drawn between the elitism of the Bourbon festivities and the popular character of the First Empire's public anniversaries. After the third successive year in which the king's fête had been gloomily celebrated in Montbrison, with only a private party organized for the local elite and their families, a police official revealed the depth of local resentment (with which he clearly empathized):

'The "popular" classes are grumbling. They remember that during the festivities of the First Empire public dances were organized and refreshments were distributed, and that this was truly a fête for all the French people, unlike this festivity of the King. Accordingly not a single shout was heard, and windows have not been draped with a single banner.'[23]

Derision and negativity undermined the festive order; subversion radically changed its meaning. Enthusiastic Bonapartists transformed the character of official royalist celebrations by bringing an uninvited guest of honour into the proceedings: Napoleon. Between 1816 and 1824, hundreds of men and women were prosecuted for shouting 'Long Live the Emperor' or 'Long Live Napoleon' around the time of 25 August. In case his true feelings were left unclear, François Lescalier accompanied his cry with a threat to remove the royalist banner from the Church tower.[24] In a similar spirit, a fifteen-year-old boy called Deschamps caused a scandal in his school by announcing shortly before the day of Saint Louis in 1824 that the royal flag would be taken down, and that the Empire would soon be restored.[25] This young Napoleonic enthusiast escaped prosecution – because, ironically, his parents' royalist credentials were impeccable.

But others with less useful family connections were not so fortunate. A Bonapartist doctor named Guyomard was sentenced to three months' imprisonment for shouting 'Long Live the Shits' at a Saint Louis's day banquet in his home town of Callac;[26] and Edouard Hardy, a worker in Lille, was sent to jail for two years in 1824 for combining his expression of support for Napoleon with a sonorous cry of 'Fuck the Royal Family.'[27]

The fête of the King also presented an ideal (if risky for the performers) stage for the singing of Napoleonic songs. In 1824 two workers from Caen named Bétourmé and Lecerf were each imprisoned for one month for celebrating the day of Saint Louis with a ditty which began: 'We painfully regret the passing of the greatest monarch of the World' (there were no prizes for guessing who they meant); and Pierre Courtial, a tailor from Nîmes, went to jail for two years for his rendering on 25 August of the Napoleonic version of the *Marseillaise*.[28]

The Bonapartist 'anti-fête' was thus in many ways the perversion of the official order. Instead of tributes to the monarch's life, there were calls for his death; conversely, occasions at which the King and other members of the royal family were meant to be mourned were transformed into moments of gleeful, uninhibited celebration. We saw in the previous chapter in what spirit Bonapartists greeted the news of the assassination of the Duc de Berry; this was no isolated incident. For example, the Restoration instituted a national day of mourning in January to mark the execution of the unfortunate Louis XVI by the Revolutionaries in 1793; this was intended as a day of atonement for France's past sins. In the early years of the regime, there were widespread instances of local rebellion against this official anniversary, with posters announcing the event being defaced, choristers refusing to perform in church, schoolteachers declining to take their pupils to Mass, and seditious notes announcing the return of Napoleon inserted through keyholes.[29]

But the real spirit of the 'anti-fête' was displayed by a group of Bonapartists at Chateauroux in 1816. Their 'commemoration' of the martyred Bourbon monarch took the form of marching through their town with drums beating wildy as they chanted songs 'to the glory of Napoleon the Great'.[30] The same delicate sense of taste was shown by the villager in the Lot-et-Garonne who chose this day to organize a ball to which he invited the entire local population.[31] In Joigny the mayor caused a local scandal by appearing in casual dress at the ceremony, and encouraging the organization of a masquerade in which men 'dressed in imperial uniforms' paraded around town.[32]

Likewise, when Louis XVIII died in 1824, there was rejoicing throughout Napoleonic France. Some locals in the Tarn chose the occasion of the fête of their town's patron saint to sing celebratory songs; they also assaulted the gendarmes who came to arrest them.[33] Perhaps this 'anti-festive' defiance was best exemplified by a woman called Perrimond, who cheekily declared upon hearing of the demise of her obese monarch: 'There will be potatoes for us now that the King is dead, because when he was alive he used to eat them all.'[34]

Napoleon the Liberator

Napoleon's image and the memory of his achievements thus became the linchpin of the 'anti-fêtes' that undermined the Bourbons' commemorative tradition. Indeed, so widespread were these public gestures of defiance under the Restoration that they transformed the Emperor into the emblematic symbol of French liberation. Equated consistently with 'freedom', his name was invoked between 1815 and 1830 in a popular political culture of 'seditious' gestures, proclamations, songs, placards, and cries which challenged the national legitimacy of the Bourbon regime, and helped to prepare the ground for its successful overthrow (see Figure 12).

The freedom that Napoleon came to symbolize in the Restoration years was in part a heritage. The 1789 Revolution had abolished feudal titles, secured civil equality, and distributed land to the peasantry, creating an entire new stratum of smallholding peasants. The First Empire, while asserting its desire to 'end' the Revolution, had guaranteed and reinforced these principles.[35] When the Bourbons returned to power in 1814, and again in 1815, there were widespread popular fears that this heritage would be jeopardized: one of the persistent rumours that haunted the French countryside throughout much of the nineteenth century was 'the restoration of feudalism'.[36] While it promised to preserve this Revolutionary heritage, Napoleonic freedom was also aspirational, representing the varied desires of a range of social groups for greater liberty under the Restoration: here were combined (rather uneasily) the bourgeois wish for greater political rights, the student's desire for more passion and imagination (and less religion), the worker's hopes for 'popular sovereignty' (and cheaper bread), and the military yearning for 'glory'. But for a large number of individuals this freedom was perhaps most centrally about personal self-realization: it expressed the refusal of French men and women to let their horizons be limited by 'fate', or to allow fear and tradition to dictate their behaviour.

It was hardly surprising that Napoleon should have appeared as an icon of individualism – and a somewhat subversive one, at that. Throughout his career he had systematically flouted all the rules, both as a civilian leader and as a military strategist, and his

FIGURE 12

'Is it true, as they say, that things are going so badly?'

The year 1824 saw the death of Louis XVIII; the crowning of his successor Charles X a year later, in the Reims Cathedral, allowed Bourbon traditionalists to recreate the ceremonial of a medieval monarchy – an event which was very coldly received by liberal and popular opinion in France. Nicolas Charlet, one of the most influential propagators of the Napoleonic legend under the Restoration, plays on this sentiment in this representation of a simple, considerate, and caring Emperor, attentive to the people's needs and concerns. In this drawing, first published a few years after the Emperor's death, Charlet also hints at the theme of Napoleonic immortality, and also uses the Emperor to underscore the widespread perception of the Restoration regime as socially exclusive and oppressive.

extraordinary return in March 1815 had defied all the laws of political gravity. This was a man who had cheated death on many a battlefield, and who had seemed to allow nothing to interfere with his destiny: not the Revolution, not the monarchs of Europe, not the French aristocracy and priesthood, not even the Pope. To a large number of his countrymen under the Restoration, Napoleon personified the successful escape from convention, and the aspiration (as he himself put it) to 'live life to the full'.

It is in this light that many of the 'seditious' incidents which took place throughout the Restoration should be interpreted. Men who shouted 'Long Live the Emperor!' after Sunday Mass, for example, as they did in Montbrison in late 1815 and in Chalon in early 1816, were not so much issuing a political challenge to the regime (or even to the clergy) as they were affirming their individuality in a highly formalized setting, in which everyone was expected to 'conform'.[37] Napoleonic freedom, in this sense, rested upon a belief that anything could be done and said: 'The Emperor will soon return, and we will be able to speak our minds.'[38] It was also about spontaneity, and doing something quite out of the ordinary – simple gestures, like carving out the name of the Emperor on the bark of the trees lining a local road;[39] or more ambitious acts, such as travelling up the mountains of the Jura to write the name of Napoleon in large letters in the snow on all the roads leading to the Canton of Vaud;[40] or, as in the case of the farmer Louis Duchesne, going to one's village church at ten in the evening and loudly singing the 'Domine Salvum Fac Imperatorem Nostrum Napoleonem' before frantically ringing the bells.[41]

Alongside these expressions of individualistic freedom, Napoleon's name and image also appeared in popular articulations of a quasi-'republican' form of liberty. At one level this was a continuation of French Revolutionary discourse which defined the absence of freedom as dependence on the arbitrary will of the sovereign – a form of 'slavery'.[42] This was very much the language used by the Corsican rebels led by Poli in 1815–16.[43] After the Didier revolt in Grenoble in 1816, a proclamation was nailed to front door of the municipality of La Mure, where Napoleon had passed a year earlier during his 'flight of the eagle'. It urged the French to break the 'shameful yoke' under which they were held by royalist rule, and referred to the events of

Grenoble as a 'patriotic insurrection' which would lead to the proclamation of Napoleon II. This regime would bring back 'liberty' to the
people of France: 'Long Live the Patrie! Long Live Freedom! Long
Live the Emperor!'[44]

Even when it was not followed by military action, as in Corsica, the
presence of this type of language bore witness to the robustness of
the alliance forged in 1815 between Jacobins and Bonapartists, which
continued throughout the Restoration (and even beyond). The republican imperialist Muret was arrested in 1820 for celebrating this
alliance by shouting 'Long Live the Republic! Long Live the
Emperor! Long Live Napoleon!'[45] Achieving freedom, from this perspective, was intricately bound up in the successful removal of 'the
yoke of tyranny'.[46] A young man from the Nîmes area demonstrated
his perfect understanding of this new dimension of Bonapartist ideology by declaring in 1817 that Napoleon would soon return with his
son 'to liberate the French people from slavery and to restore order'.[47]

This language of 'national liberation' – a strong echo both of the
(early) Revolutionary era and the Hundred Days – was especially
powerful in the initial years of the Restoration, when France was
governed by a Bourbon regime that owed its power to foreign occupation. All the military conspiracies which shook the Boubon regime
were carried out in the name of 'independence' and 'liberty'; at
Thouars in 1822, at the beginning of his ill-fated rebellion, General
Berton issued a proclamation in which he urged French soldiers to
liberate themselves from the 'slavery' to which they were subjected by
the military hierarchy.[48]

Many false Bonapartist proclamations, claiming to be authored by
Napoleon or by members of the imperial family, also strongly played
on this theme. A widely circulated 'Declaration of Empress Marie-
Louise' (a forgery, but an excellent piece of Napoleonic propaganda)
promised the French people who were 'groaning under the terrible
weight of tyranny' that 'the doors of their jails would soon open at
the Emperor's command'.[49] Another proclamation described the
Bourbons as 'a degenerate family better suited to serve the English
than to reign on the throne of France.'[50]

Many imperial songs also drove home the same point; the refrain
of a popular chant of the early Restoration was: 'Let us chase, chase
away slavery, long live, long live Napoleon.'[51] During the Spanish

anti-monarchical insurrection and subsequent French military intervention in 1823, Napoleonic expressions of support for Spanish groups fighting to 'liberate themselves from oppression' used the same neo-republican language and imagery.[52] The Spanish republican leader Mina was frequently celebrated in Napoleonic songs and placards as the 'bearer of freedom', not only for his people but also for the French.[53] And when Louis XVIII died a year later, the imperial enthusiast Vincent Fonseca saluted the 'defeat of slavery' and called on the French people to adopt the slogan 'Napoleon and Liberty'.[54]

This language of liberation encapsulated all the central tensions of Revolutionary ideology. It blended the 1789 ideal of individual self-realization with the inclusive and rallying nationalist language of 1792, when the Republic defended French sovereignty against foreign invasion. More menacingly, it also drew upon the imagery of the 1793 Terror, which focused on the elimination of the 'enemies of the people'.

Napoleon had been seen during his lifetime by many of his enemies as 'Robespierre on horseback', and it seems that this image retained some of its appeal – especially for those Jacobin elements who had rallied to the imperial cause during the Hundred Days. A Napoleonic placard found in 1827 in Bar-le-Duc listed the enemies of France as the monarchy, the aristocracy, and the priests, collectively defined as the 'League of the Execrable'; inviting the French people to 'take up arms' to defend their freedom, the message ended with 'Long Live Napoleon!'[55] The same theme appeared more subtly on the placard found in Agen in 1823, which expressed its support for Napoleon above a drawing representing two daggers (almost certainly a *Carbonaro* message).[56] Threats were also routinely directed at individual elements among the 'enemies of the people'. An anonymous letter sent to a royalist official stated that 'the King will be hanged, and his fat melted to make lanterns to celebrate the return of Napoleon'.[57]

Priests were specifically targeted, too; popular expressions of anti-clericalism frequently assumed a Napoleonic form. In La Guillotière a farmer named Loupa was arrested in March 1816 for attempting to compel his priest to shout 'Long Live the Emperor!' at the end of a Sunday service;[58] likewise, a curé walking past an inn in Voiron in

1819 was greeted with shouts of 'Long Live the Emperor and Down with the *Calotins!*'[59] And nothing could give a former imperial soldier greater pleasure than to walk up to the gates of a large country estate in the Vendée and announce that: 'Soon all these castles will be burnt.'[60]

Local 'collaborators' with the royalists were also censured, at times with extraordinary savagery. A placard found in the Var in 1817 called for the prefect to be executed (for 'failing to serve the people'); for the two lieutenants of the gendarmerie to 'have their ears and noses cut, to be skinned alive, and then to be quartered'; and for the leading royalists 'to be well fed, buried alive up to their head, and then eaten by worms.' This cheerful proclamation ended with the traditional Napoleonic signature: 'Long Live the Emperor!'[61]

Napoleonic freedom was both individualistic and collective, liberating and vengeful; it was also used by 'weaker' groups to celebrate their social identities. Chased and banished by the mighty and powerful in France and Europe, the Emperor became the emblem of the underdog, the proud symbol of the humble man's stubborn resistance against socio-economic exploitation. There is little doubt that a large number of incidents involving 'seditious' expressions of support for Napoleon by peasants should be interpreted in this light. In early 1816, for example, some bourgeois students from the College de Mâcon were chased and stoned by a group of young peasants shouting 'Long Live the Emperor!'. While this may have been a political dispute, it was also a classic manifestation of social rivalry in which one group resented the 'privileges' of the other; Napoleon was here taken as a potent symbol of the principle of 'equality'.[62] Two shepherds on the bank of the Yonne shouted 'Long Live Napoleon' when they saw a well-attired public official passing by; one of them explicitly stated that she had uttered her cry because the man was 'a bourgeois'.[63] Likewise, a group of thirty-eight labourers were heard chanting 'Long Live Napoleon' while working on a field in the Puy-de-Dôme in 1817; among the causes of their dissatisfaction was the inadequate payment provided by the landowner, a prosperous bourgeois merchant.[64]

Inscriptions of 'Long Live the Emperor' on (or above) the front doors of well-off citizens also came under this heading: reports often indicated that the 'victims' of these gestures were men whose wealth was resented locally – either because they displayed it ostentatiously, or because they sought to conceal it.[65] More generally, Restoration authorities readily acknowledged that adverse economic conditions in the countryside played directly into the hands of imperial propagandists.[66]

Whatever the reasons, Napoleon remained the indefatigable companion of the downtrodden throughout the Restoration, here consoling a group of young peasants singing imperial songs outside the village of Néron,[67] there cheering along a corporation of coopers in Lyons,[68] elsewhere reminding prostitute Marie-Françoise Corcelle that 'under the Emperor's reign we were not as unhappy as we are now'[69] and inspiring stable boy Philippe Blottier to cut his arm and defiantly declare that 'his blood ran for the Emperor and he would gladly spill it for him again.'[70]

This metamorphosis of Napoleon into the emblem of French individual and collective liberties was nothing short of remarkable. The Emperor had made no secret of his personal aversion (not to say contempt) for ideas of freedom, and had promoted 'order' and 'glory' as France's supreme political values throughout the years of the First Empire. How, then, is this transformation of his image after 1815 to be explained? To some extent, it reflected the redesign of imperial ideology during the Hundred Days, when Napoleon had introduced the 'Additional Act' guaranteeing a wide range of political liberties. Popular Napoleonic advocacy during the Restoration years occasionally referred positively to 'liberal' principles and values. For example, the 'Declaration of Empress Marie-Louise' promised to bestow upon France 'strong and liberal political institutions', with the rule of law, the election of a National Assembly, and a government which ruled in the interest of the nation as a whole – all very much in line with the demands of the liberal opposition at the time.[71] Freedom, in other words, had been 'grafted' onto imperial political culture.

But the real source of this Napoleonic transformation went deeper. The Emperor could plausibly appear as a champion of French liberties because, in the popular mind, he had become (and perhaps had remained all the time) a powerful symbol of the Revolutionary era. Once the parenthesis of the First Empire was closed, Napoleon was seen by the French people for what he really was: a legitimate heir to the central values of 1789. This explains why so many Jacobin republicans rallied to him in 1815, and indeed remained loyal to his memory throughout the Restoration.

This equation of Napoleon with the Revolution was fortified by much of the anti-Bonapartist literature of the Restoration, which frequently presented the Emperor as the 'son of the Revolution';[72] it also appeared in the spontaneous popular responses to the Bourbons' campaign after 1815 to remove all vestiges of the Revolutionary epoch. In early 1816, local officials declared war on the 'trees of liberty' – which had been planted by the revolutionary authorities in the 1790s to symbolize the emergence of their new political order – and ordered them to be cut down all over France. In some cases, these gestures were prompted by local royalists; in Savigny-sur-Bois (Yonne) the inhabitants petitioned the prefect asking for the local 'tree of liberty' to be cut down 'because the Buonapartists are constantly threatening that we will be hanged on it'.[73]

Although such acts of symbolic vandalism were successfully carried out, they encountered spirited local resistance that often invoked Napoleon's name and spirit. Thus, the prefect of the Creuse's announcement that all the 'trees of liberty' in Guéret would be pulled down was met with a Bonapartist placard denouncing this 'tyrannical order'; it declared that any person who carried it out was 'unworthy of being French'.[74] In Cherbourg, the authorities were so apprehensive about the public's response that they had their 'trees of liberty' removed in the dead of night. In the following few days, the town was covered with placards all carrying the reply, proud and defiant: 'Loyalty to the Emperor'.[75]

Had he known about this spontaneous gesture by his followers, Napoleon would no doubt have savoured the irony. When he had been appointed First Consul and had moved into his official apartments in the Tuileries Palace, he had ordered the trees of liberty which had been planted in the courtyard to be cut down; they were creating 'too much shade'.[76] As they were felled in 1816 all over France, these symbols of republican liberty had now become emblems of Napoleon's political resurrection.

A Local Revolt: the Grand Lemps Affair (1816)

Napoleonic rebellion was thus a much wider and more complex phenomenon than a straightforward series of purely military
conspiracies: it was expressed in a multitude of activities in which
thousands of men and women chose to defy public authority between
1815 and 1830. The occasions for these 'conspiratorial' pratices could
be national, as with the celebrations of royalist anniversaries, but
they could also crystallize around local issues and events.

To appreciate the spirit in which these rebellious gestures were
made, and their complex repercussions on Bourbon authority, let us
consider a specific episode: the 'Grand Lemps affair', a revolt which
took place in the department of the Isère in early 1816. Its main
protagonist was Joseph Emery, the chief military surgeon of the
Imperial Guard – one of Napoleon's most trusted lieutenants at Elba,
and one of the heroic figures of the Hundred Days.[77] Emery had
been sent by the Emperor to prepare his arrival in France in early
March 1815. Despite being twice arrested in Digne and Gap, he had
fulfilled his mission, eventually reaching Grenoble where he had
printed and distributed Napoleon's proclamations shortly before the
Emperor's arrival.[78]

Emery paid a heavy price for his loyalty to Napoleon. He was
expelled from the Army under the Restoration, and the State even
sought to prevent him from practising medicine. Living in the commune of Beaurepaire in early 1816, he continued to be seen as a real
menace by the prefect responsible for the area not only because of his
cult status among the local population, but also because of his insistence on providing free medical aid to the indigent.[79]

Emery was eventually moved by the authorities to the more remote
village of Grand Lemps, where he arrived in late March 1816.
Writing to the prefect, the mayor welcomed Emery's presence, stressing that he had caused no trouble and that the population was
extremely pleased to have such an exemplary citizen in their midst;
the letter ended by urging the prefect to allow the surgeon to remain
in the locality.[80] A week later, clearly fearing the worst, the mayor sent
another effusive testimony, describing Emery's remarkable medical
services to the community. He also added – this was the height of the

season for rumours of Napoleon's return – that Emery had not engaged in political discussions with any of his patients.[81]

Unfortunately, the prefect's pressure on Paris eventually bore fruit: in early April a letter arrived ordering that Emery should be moved forthwith to the department of the Nord. However, when the gendarmes were sent to Grand Lemps to seize the doctor, the village rebelled against this 'arbitrary' decision. Despite Emery's repeated attempts to calm down the local population, and his willingness to accept the deportation order, the crowd refused to allow the law officers to take him away. After prolonged and heated discussions, several times broken off and eventually resumed, the citizens of the village forced Emery's release into the hands of the mayor. There were numerous chants of 'Long Live the Emperor!' throughout the episode, particularly orchestrated by a certain Drevon, one of the ringleaders of the rebellion.[82]

Drevon in many ways stole the show: he was the one responsible for mobilizing the villagers to resist and at the height of the drama he was chased by several gendarmes through the small roads and alleys of the locality. He managed to lose his pursuers, only to reappear a while later with a rifle, which he fired several times in the air 'as a gesture of bravado'; he then disappeared into the surrounding woods.[83] Drevon actually succeeded in evading capture until August, when he was denounced by a royalist informant; he had all the while spent his days in the woods, and had come back into the village at nightfall, 'still armed with his rifle'.[84]

At one level, this resistance proved both futile and costly to the inhabitants of Grand Lemps. Emery eventually went away into his internal exile in mid-April; with the exception of the irrepressible Drevon, many of the key participants in this revolt were immediately arrested and jailed, and the village was declared by the prefect to have 'rebelled against legitimate authority'.[85] In an extraordinary act of retribution, the royalist official ordered the dispatch of a force of 100 men to Grand Lemps (eighty infantrymen and twenty gendarmes); they were to remain in the locality until the mayor and the entire municipal council agreed to travel to Grenoble to pledge their loyalty to the State. Throughout the duration of this occupation, these forces were to be fed and lodged by the village, who were additionally required to pay their occupiers a fixed daily allowance.[86]

But, although the municipal officers rapidly did what was expected of them and fell into line, the 'Grand Lemps affair' was anything but a political victory for the Restoration authorities. Without in any way asking for or encouraging it, Emery had caused a remote village to rebel against the State. This revolt had demonstrated that the general will of a small community, expressed through its municipal elites, was powerful enough to block the execution of an official order – at least in the short run.

In the course of the rebellion, furthermore, the State's conception of 'justice' had been stood on its head: for the citizens of Grand Lemps, the 'outlaw' Emery had appeared as the real hero, and his State tormentors as the true criminals. Indeed, the real outcome of the rebellion was that the Bourbon regime lost whatever little authority it still enjoyed in the locality. This was further compounded by the authorities' crude and brutish display of force in occupying the village, an especially clumsy gesture at a time when Bonapartist propaganda was lamenting the 'occupation' of French territory by foreign troops. This collapse of royalist legitimacy was reflected in the string of local 'Napoleonic' collaborators and sympathizers who enabled the spirited Drevon to elude arrest for more than five months, and above all in the locals' abiding memories of the humble surgeon who had worked for Bonaparte, and whose only crime after 1815 had been his desire to serve his fellow citizens.

The Grand Lemps revolt was of course on a much smaller scale than the Napoleonic rebellions of the 1816–22 period; and unlike many of the major revolts there was no organized political or military force behind it. But it drew together many of the key characteristics of Bonapartist agitation: a blend of national and regional considerations; a strong element of local support for the Napoleonic cause; a deep sense of resentment against Bourbon injustice and 'slavery'; a complex intrigue; and a commitment to action based largely on spontaneity and improvisation. Perhaps most importantly, the Grand Lemps revolt underscored one of the key elements which welded together the agents of the Napoleonic movement under the Restoration: the strength of character of its members. Bonapartist rebels and conspirators were brave, committed, and passionate men, ready to sacrifice their lives for the imperial cause.

The Spirit of Resistance

Far from being all things to all people, Napoleon's image was remarkably coherent: whether inspiring a cult of individual spontaneity and adventure, a wealth of conspiratorial activity, an aspiration towards national liberation, or a popular aversion to the official values of royalism, Bonaparte stood for an instinctively recognizable bedrock of values, which in many senses exemplified the continuing vitality of the Revolutionary tradition of 1789. The Emperor became, in truth, the supreme embodiment of the French people's opposition to the return of the *ancien régime*, and it was very much in this spirit that Bonapartist groups (often in connivance with republicans) celebrated national and local political anniversaries between 1815 and 1830. Napoleonic commemoration, in a context in which the Bourbon State sought to eradicate all memory of the past, was in itself an act of civic defiance; through the effective mobilization of groups all over France, it also became a conspiratorial gesture of political resistance.

The Saint-Napoleon, the Emperor's birthday on 15 August, was the most widely observed 'anti-fête' anniversary of the Restoration years. This occasion, as noted earlier, had been celebrated as France's national day during the First Empire, often with considerable popular enthusiasm. After 1815, men and women all over France manifested their overt opposition to the royalist order (and their continuing commitment to the Emperor) by marking the Saint-Napoleon in a variety of public and private settings. The fête was celebrated by individuals sporting bright red carnations in church;[87] by groups singing imperial songs in taverns[88] (the Napoleonic *Marseillaise* was a particular favourite[89]); and by the distribution in Paris of thousands of medals bearing the Emperor's effigy.[90] In some localities, tradition had it that the fête should be observed in small private meetings;[91] in others, it was an occasion for outdoor gatherings, such as family picnics on the riverside.[92] In Lyons, the day was especially celebrated by the poorer people, 'the secondary classes', as one report put it disdainfully.[93]

But the overriding spirit on this day was one of determination, confrontation even. For supporters of Napoleon, this was an anniversary to be commemmorated at all costs, even if it meant arrest and imprisonment – as in the case of the four labourers who were jailed in Avallon for singing 'revolutionary' songs to the glory of Napoleon.[94] The truly irrepressible ones continued even while incarcerated; in Lyons a group of political prisoners marked the birth of their Emperor by arranging small pieces of candle in the shape of an 'N' on the gates of the cells, an act of creative enthusiasm which earned them several days in solitary confinement.[95] Another prisoner named Camus marked the death of Napoleon in May 1821 by manufacturing a straw tobacco box bearing the effigy of the Emperor ('and several seditious emblems'); his ingenuity left everyone wondering how all this material had been smuggled into the St Joseph prison in Lyons.[96]

Such commemorative determination on the part of Napoleon's partisans often led to violence, especially when republicans joined the fray – as they frequently did. Both groups commonly mounted joint operations during the month of August – either to sabotage the commemoration of royalist anniversaries, especially in Paris,[97] or to stage attacks on royal busts on 15 August.[98] In the village of Vivière in August 1815, there were riots between royalists on the one hand and Bonapartists and Jacobins on the other; the 'revolutionaries', as they were known in this part of the Ardèche, threatened to 'massacre' the mayor for trying to prevent the celebration of the Saint-Napoleon.[99]

The anniversary also elicited the production of 'seditious' placards all over the country; here too the theme of civic and political 'resistance' was preponderant, as in the message posted in Versailles in 1817, which called on France to be 'liberated from the yoke of oppression' by all those men who 'were worthy of calling themselves French and did not wish completely to surrender the nation to foreigners.'[100] It was common for these supporters of Napoleon to blame his French adversaries for selling the country to foreigners: thus Thomas Ballac, a planter from Perreux, declared that it was 'the priests, the royalists, and the aristocrats' who had allowed enemy forces to enter France in 1815; he added that when the Emperor returned these groups would have to be 'destroyed'.[101]

The most remarkable example of this Jacobin-Bonapartist axis on the day of the Saint-Napoleon was a placard posted on the municipal building in a small town in the Lot-et-Garonne in 1823. It was a

Napoleonic poem in nineteen verses, specially written for the occasion. It was all at once a celebration of the three 'national colours', an appeal to 'our friends the liberals', and a tribute to 'all the brave patriots fighting in Spain'. The poem ended by urging the overthrow of the Bourbon regime of 'tyranny' and 'slavery' by appealing explicitly to the Revolutionary traditions of the 1790s: 'Let us arise, all of us French *sans culottes*, and may this day remind us of those joyful times when we celebrated the fête of our friend Napoleon.'[102] Again, this was a compelling example of the fusion of Napoleon into the tradition of 1789.

There was much evidence of 'commemorative cooperation' between republicans and Bonapartists during the Restoration. Many republican artists lent their talents to the glorification of Napoleon, alongside the celebration of their own distinct political lineage. In 1818 the police in Bordeaux arrested a painter named Larroque for creating (and helping to disseminate) 'subversive' material. Two works in progress were found in his house: the first was a representation of the festivity of 14 July 1790, the Fête de la Fédération (one of the mythic moments in republican memory); and the second a portrait of Bonaparte as First Consul (often a preferred image among republicans, as it predated Napoleon's 'imperial' period).[103] In 'revolutionary' strongholds (Paris, Lyons, Grenoble) this alliance of Jacobin and Bonapartist groups extended both ways, with each group helping to mark the other's anniversaries. A republican from Lyons published a pamphlet that sought to make official the reconciliation: 'Bonaparte as General and Consul did too much for France for France not to forgive the Emperor.'[104] On 14 July 1815 a group of around three hundred soldiers had rioted in the centre of Lyons; these men – Jacobins as well as supporters of the Emperor – demanded that France should not capitulate to the Allies and should continue all forms of armed resistance against the invading armies.[105] Opposition to France's military occupation remained a strong source of political unity; when all foreign troops left French territory in 1818, the occasion was greeted by Grenoble students with cries of 'Long Live the Republic! Long Live the Emperor!'[106] Thereafter, the date of 14 July became a landmark in the commemorative calendar; in the Isère, the prefect noted that 14 July was celebrated not only by supporters of the Revolution but also by 'Napoleon's men'.[107]

The force of this link between commemoration and political resistance was especially highlighted in the observation of local anniversaries. Throughout France, and especially on the route followed by Napoleon during his 'flight of the eagle', Bonapartist and republican groups came together to commemorate the first anniversary of Napoleon's passage through their locality. Although local authorities were able to prevent many public demonstrations, the scale of the forces deployed often demonstrated how fearful they were of these Bonapartist 'anti-fêtes'. In Lyons, the prefect ordered no fewer than 6,000 troops from the National Guard to be positioned all over town on the first anniversary of the Emperor's arrival in the capital of the Rhône – a veritable military occupation, albeit one carried out by French forces.[108]

Elsewhere, and despite the intimidating tactics used by the authorities, local groups successfully mobilized to mark key episodes of the Hundred Days. The prize for commemorative determination went (again) to Grenoble (see Figure 13), where groups of citizens assembled each year from 1816 on 6 July to celebrate the town's spirited resistance to the Austrian invasion in 1815, a resistance which under the leadership of General Robert Motte had claimed over 500 enemy lives with very few casualties on the French side.[109] This celebration was simultaneously one of Napoleonic remembrance, local patriotism, and political cooperation among anti-Bourbon groups.

Until the early 1820s, the format for these gatherings remained essentially unchanged. Around a thousand men, mainly from Grenoble and Lyons, divided into 'sections' of twenty, marched through the town in the afternoon, and assembled in an open field. While there were clearly liberals and republicans present, the dominant political colouring was Bonapartist; this could be seen in the covert references to the Emperor (and to the Hundred Days) on the banners and placards that were carried, and also in the large number of Napoleonic symbols worn – notably yellow and red carnations. Once assembled, this 'militia' was inspected by local opposition leaders, in the presence of a crowd of about a thousand onlookers. A brief political rally would then follow, during which memories of the past and hopes for the future were discussed.

The fête typically ended with a fireworks display, after which civic banquets were organized in around a dozen different localities for

FIGURE 13

Entry of Napoleon into Grenoble

During the Restoration years, Grenoble remained a Napoleonic stronghold. This image from the Epinal collection shows the Emperor arriving outside Grenoble soon after the Laffrey incident in March 1815, which is briefly described in the commentary below the drawing. The gates to the town were closed, and the royalist officers commanding the garrison tried to block Napoleon's entry but again (as at Laffrey) the troops disobeyed orders. Popular support for Napoleon had been drummed up by two imperial emissaries, Dumoulin and Emery, sent from Elba, who had arrived a few days earlier and distributed Napoleon's proclamations. The gates were eventually smashed and the fragments brought to the Emperor as a gesture of support; Napoleon then entered Grenoble at ten in the evening.

both participants and spectators; as the wine flowed and the participants evoked the events of recent years, many Napoleonic songs were
performed.[110] 6 July, in short, was a quintessential moment of 'anti-
festive' endeavour: carefully crafted and planned, joyful and
exuberant, nostalgic and mournful (especially after Bonaparte's death
in 1821), but also martial and threatening.[111]

In 1823, this pattern was interrupted by the prefect, the Baron
d'Haussez, who decided to ban all public gatherings on 6 July in the
Grenoble area. It is not clear why, having himself tolerated these
meetings during the previous three years (as had his predecessor
between 1816 and 1819), Haussez had now decided that such a dramatic gesture was necessary. Perhaps the prefect was put under
pressure from his Minister in Paris; perhaps the authorities were wor-
ried about the repercussions of the ongoing war in Spain, or the
resurgence of *Carbonaro* activity after the events of 1821–2.

The prefect's proclamation justified the ban by the 'seditious' character of speeches which were to be given at the commemoration, but
also by claiming that the meeting's true purpose was conspiratorial:
'The real aim of this occasion is to create some kind of federation, to
found a party, and to regroup its members into an organization.'[112]
The response to the ban suggested that this organization not only
existed, but was quite effective; five hundred people appeared in
Grenoble on the day, openly defying the prefect's interdiction. When
asked to disperse by the gendarmes, they disappeared into the woods,
only to regroup later in another location, where they held their commemorative meeting.[113]

To the considerable embarrassment of the authorities, this cat-
and-mouse game continued throughout the decade. In 1824, 1825,
and 1826, proclamations were again issued (using ever more threatening language) banning any public celebrations in Grenoble on 6
July; however, on each occasion the determined organizers successfully circumvented the edict (and the considerable police and troop
presence). The decree announcing the ban in 1825 openly acknowledged that 'in previous years meetings have been held despite the
injunctions of the authorities'.[114] In 1826 the frustrated prefect sent
a copy of his proclamation to all the mayors of the Isère, inviting
them to exercise 'the utmost vigilance' on the day, to ban the sale of
food or drink to 'any gathering of more than twenty people', and to

report any 'suspicious' groups directly to him. One mayor did indeed denounce a group of 6 July commemorators who arrived in his village, but by the time the gendarmes had been sent to the locality the malefactors had all vanished. It later emerged that these festive conspirators had assembled in a mountainous area 'and drunk several toasts to liberty'.[115]

These 'seditious' Napoleonic gatherings continued until the fall of the Bourbon regime in July 1830. And on 6 July 1831, the now-liberated town of Grenoble organized an official ceremony to mark the anniversary of its resistance in 1815. The fête took place in the presence of the entire military garrison 'in full attire'.[116] It was as much a celebration of the town's feisty patriotism in 1815 as a vindication of the resolve shown throughout the previous decade by these hardy activists to remain true to the ideals of their country, their region, and (above all) their Emperor.

Bringing Down the Bourbons

Taken together with its predecessors, this chapter has illustrated the ceaseless nature of the battle that went on throughout the Restoration between the Bourbon regime and the 'Napoleonic' individuals and groups who confronted it. This clash did not take place merely on major 'set-piece' occasions, such as military rebellions and large-scale insurrections; it was a relentless, almost daily activity, in which ordinary men and women expressed their political values through a variety of forms of the 'anti-fête', involving some mixture of rhetoric, practical gesture, political mobilization, and commemoration.

What has emerged is a far cry from the standard view of Napoleonic 'conspiracy' as a catalogue of blunders, failures, and missed opportunities. The conclusion is in fact the very opposite: in a multitude of subtle ways, these 'anti-fêtes' effectively and systematically undermined Bourbon authority. One of their important purposes was to stand the official order on its head, notably by emptying the royalist 'public sphere' of all significance, and demeaning and ridiculing State agents at every opportunity. During the celebrations of royalist, Bonapartist, and local anniversaries, and in a wide range of political gestures, Napoleonic rebels and conspirators turned the tables on their tormentors, subjecting public officials to systematic harassment (and many an embarrassment) throughout the period between 1815 and 1830. At a deeper level, all this Bonapartist agitation served to reveal the contradictions of the Bourbon order, especially its inability to administer the collective life of the French nation in an equitable and impartial manner.

Two examples can illustrate the internal destabilization of the royalist regime through its repeated encounters with Napoleonic rebellion. The first is the pervasive shame experienced by local officials for their failure to eradicate 'sedition'. Successive prefects of the Isère were frequently rebuked by Paris for their incapacity to identify or arrest any of the numerous Napoleonic conspirators in their department.[117] In 1818, after receiving yet another neatly copied text of a false proclamation circulating in the Grenoble area, the Minister of the Interior tartly replied that it was time that the prefect's law officers actually caught someone[118] – and preferably a real culprit, as the police seemed to have a knack of arresting the wrong person.[119] In 1822, after a local incident involving Bonapartists chanting 'Long Live the Emperor!' in the streets of Auch, the Minister fulminated at the prefect of the Gers: 'I am informed that in the capital of your department the police force is entirely without authority, and that its surveillance is completely hopeless.'[120]

But the efficiency of the police was hardly any better in the capital: as we have already seen, there they consistently lost track of key suspects. Spreading chaos and demoralization among State officials, the anti-fête was remarkably successful, as acknowledged in the despairing comment of a prefect: 'The clumsiness, the absolute uselessness of the local police invariably prevent me from taking decisive action against the agents of subversion.'[121]

The second example is arguably more fundamental, and takes us to the heart of the failure of the Restoration order. From the early days of the regime, the royalists sought to use the legal system not only to punish all manifestations of Napoleonic dissent, but also to 'spread terror' among potential rebels.[122] Extraordinarily harsh sentences were meted out to ordinary men and women, often guilty merely of celebrating an imperial anniversary, possessing a Napoleonic object, or shouting 'Long Live the Emperor!' A Bonapartist sympathizer named Jean-Rémi Potillon was given two years for uttering this cry by the tribunal of Dôle,[123] and a man called Noyer was sent to jail for five years for the same offence at Clarensac.[124] A former soldier employed as a labourer in the Saône-et-Loire went to prison for two years for lacking 'sufficient respect for the occupying forces': his crime was naming his horse 'Cossack'.[125] A worker named Taillard was jailed for fifteen months in Lyons because a tobacco box bearing Napoleon's effigy was found in his bed.[126]

Even worse, there was little consistency: in some parts of France, verbal expressions of support for the Emperor could result in sentences of eight days.[127] In December 1824, two men who had shouted 'Long Live the Emperor!' under similar circumstances in Mulhouse and Guingamp were tried by their respective local courts: the first received a six-day sentence, the second three months.[128]

In the long run, this repression was triply ineffective. It did little to stop these 'seditious' expressions and practices throughout the Restoration (if the large number of recidivists is anything to go by, it often had the opposite effect). Furthermore, its exercise was accompanied by such widespread disparities that it gave credence to Napoleonic and republican propaganda, which presented the Restoration as an arbitrary and 'slavish' regime.[129] Finally, its practice was contested from within the judiciary itself, with several notable instances of leniency in cases tried by a prosecutor (or a jury) with Napoleonic sympathies. This clemency shown by some courts which unexpectedly acquitted Bonapartist sympathizers (or refused to uphold their convictions on appeal) often infuriated prefects and even Ministers of the Interior[130] – ultimately these gestures by the courts concerned actually emphasized the disparities in judicial outcomes – and added to the feeling that this was a State whose identity was radically fractured.

What precise role all this political agitation played in bringing down the Bourbon regime in 1830 is of course difficult to specify precisely. On Saint-Helena Napoleon had predicted the downfall of the Restoration, asserting that 'sooner or later a volcanic eruption would engulf the throne, its surroundings and its followers'.[131] But by the time his prediction came true, the Emperor had been dead for nine years. Partly for this reason, and partly in light of the ensuing political conflicts of the 1830s and 1840s, most standard accounts of the events of 1830 have tended to highlight the role played by liberals and republicans in the overthrow of Charles X. The trigger for the

July Revolution was the King's attempt in July 1830 to suppress political opposition to his rule by suspending press freedom, dissolving the
Chamber, and reducing the number of elected representatives. After
three days of fighting in the streets of Paris – the 'Three Glorious
Days' – the Bourbon monarch retreated, and in early August was
forced to abdicate. A few days later the Duc d'Orléans was proclaimed King: thus began the reign of Louis Philippe, which would
last until his overthrow by the republicans in 1848.[132]

How should this political transformation be understood? For the
republican historian Maurice Agulhon, 1830 was a victory of noble
political ideals – in particular, liberty – which would eventually triumph outright in 1848. Not only did Agulhon give no credit to
'Napoleonic' forces for their role in overthrowing the Restoration, he
even argued that the entire period between 1800 and 1830 should be
depicted as 'the era of Counter-Revolution'.[133] For François Furet, the
liberal historian, the Parisian insurrection that brought down Charles
X ultimately demonstrated the vitality of the French revolutionary
tradition, and the tendency of political groups to restage its key
moments throughout the nineteenth century. He also suggested that
1830 was not so much an expression of 'popular', grass-roots politics
(as in the Parisian insurrection of Germinal 1795) but rather a return
to the 'unanimous' spirit that had been manifested in the 1789
Revolution itself, when the French nation had asserted its liberty
against an oppressive regime.[134] This view of the July insurrection as
a victory of 'liberal' values is also advanced by Robert Alexander, who
sees the 'triumph of parliamentary government' as the consequence
of the 'reformist' path taken by the liberal opposition after 1823.[135]

Such interpretations are certainly valuable in setting the events of
1830 in wider contexts. But these approaches are also problematic
insofar as they underplay the fundamental transformation of the
'revolutionary' tradition during the Restoration years, and most
notably its incorporation of the legend of Bonaparte. As we have
seen, Napoleonic images, symbols, and values penetrated French
political culture to such a degree between 1815 and 1830 that it was
often difficult to separate Bonapartism from Jacobinism. This being
the case, to write about the 1830 Revolution without taking into
account the 'Napoleonic' contributions to it makes as much sense as
writing about 1789 without mentioning the influence of Rousseau.

Our evidence certainly suggests a strong Napoleonic contribution to all the long-term factors which led to the collapse of the Restoration order: the regime's inability to establish genuine popular roots, especially in the countryside; the ineptitude of its administrative agents in beating down and eradicating local forms of political resistance; and its failure to make the French people forget the Emperor, and the 'glorious' years of the Napoleonic Empire. Indeed, so passionate was their dislike of their existing condition that they reinvented their own past, turning Napoleon into an emblem of the very Revolution that he had sought to 'end'.

Above all, Bonapartist agitation ruthlessly and systematically exposed the frailties and incoherences of the Bourbon regime, bringing to the fore its repressive and unjust character, and strengthening its reputation among the masses for 'arbitrariness' – a fatal attribute for any French regime after what had happened in 1789. 'Napoleonic' political culture also traded on the people's fears and anxieties, notably through the dissemination of rumours that weakened the government's authority. One of the striking elements here was the persistence of the belief that the Restoration was working to restore feudalism – a factor frequently cited in local explanations of the regime's failure to draw support from peasants.[136]

In view of all the above, it came as no surprise that many of the proletarian elements who took part in the Parisian insurrection of July 1830 did so to accompanying chants of 'Long Live Napoleon!' and 'Long Live Napoleon II!'[137] One detailed account even argues that the course of events was moving in an inexorably Bonapartist direction until the fourth day of the insurrection, when liberal elites succeeded in appropriating the uprising in favour of the House of Orléans.[138] A large number of imperial veterans were on the front line of the barricades, and one doctor reported that two-thirds of the wounded combatants he treated were former soldiers.[139] Several reports cite incidents in which men physically resembling Bonaparte were acclaimed by the Parisian crowd in 1830; one woman fell on her knees and thanked God for allowing her to see the Emperor before her death.[140]

The July Revolution of 1830 was thus not so much a return to 1789, but rather the final act of the persistent confrontation that had pitted Napoleonic and Bourbon factions in France against each other throughout the Restoration years.

Chapter 6

The Prince of Liberal Ideas

In 1840 the July Monarchy, under the prompting of the liberal states-man Adolphe Thiers, organized the repatriation of the Emperor's remains from Saint-Helena. This 'return of the remains' climaxed in a solemn ceremony in the Invalides in Paris, in the presence of a million spectators, and an outpouring of patriotic and emotional national homages to Napoleon.[1] For weeks and indeed months after the event, there was a frenzy of public interest in all things Napoleonic; for instance, a play entitled *The Last Wish of the Emperor*, set in Paris and ending with a grandiose representation of the ceremony, kept audiences captivated.[2] Elsewhere in France, the enthusiasm for the Emperor did not die down either, and many municipalities seized on the atmosphere of Napoleonic fervour to commission public monuments in his honour (see Figure 14).

Like many towns in France with strong imperial memories – it was the site from which Bonaparte had planned to launch his invasion of Britain – the town of Boulogne sought to add its own tribute to the Emperor by commissioning a statue. In the spring of 1841, the town's National Guard invited Victor Hugo, one of France's most esteemed poets and the acclaimed author of *Le Retour de l'Empereur*, to compose an ode for the inauguration of the monument. The ceremony was scheduled for 15 August, the day of the Saint-Napoleon, and several

FIGURE 14

Entry of the procession bearing Napoleon's remains in Paris,
under the Arc de Triomphe, 15 December 1840

In 1840, under the prompting of Adolphe Thiers, King Louis-Philippe arranged for the Emperor's remains to be returned from Saint-Helena. In the French delegation which was sent to bring back the remains of Napoleon were several former members of his entourage, notably Bertrand, Gourgaud, and Marchand. Also accompanying the 1840 expedition was the young Emmanuel Las Cases, the son of the author of the *Mémorial de Sainte-Hélène;* he had been present on the island with his father in 1815–16. The two ships that brought Napoleon's remains back to France reached Cherbourg in late November 1840, and the procession then travelled up the Seine, reaching Paris on 15 December. Despite the bitter cold, more than a million people turned out to pay their respects to the Emperor.

months ahead of the event there was talk of little else in this northern French coastal town.

Hugo, who had witnessed the 1840 ceremonies in Paris,[3] duly obliged with a fiery and martial 'Hymn'. It began by welcoming the 'protection' which the statue would provide to French vessels sailing through the English Channel and by celebrating the idea of 'universal empire' which Napoleon, in the manner of the magnificent Charlemagne, had long pursued so successfully. Lyrical and epic up to this point, the tone of Hugo's poem then became menacing, warning that the current absence of war in Europe was a mere truce, a 'fragile peace resonating with silent struggles'. The ode ended with the hope that France would soon avenge Napoleon by recapturing the Rhine, and pledged an 'eternal hatred' for the criminal English nation, which had 'mutilated' France.[4]

Boulogne was a town that had (and still has) many commercial and cultural dealings with England, and the municipal authorities – local notables who did not like 'trouble' – were greatly alarmed at the thought of such bellicose and Anglophobic sentiments being aired at their official ceremony. Furthermore, these bourgeois leaders also shared the July Monarchy's dislike for the more warlike aspects of the Napoleonic tradition celebrated by the Bonapartists (and many republicans). After some agonizing, these men regretfully decided that Hugo's 'Hymn' was not suitable for their inauguration ceremony. This decision provoked considerable discontent among the National Guard, and much consternation among the local population.

So moved was he by this 'stupid affront' that a schoolteacher named Direy penned a poem to express his indignation. Entitled 'Apology to Monsieur Victor Hugo on the occasion of the apotheosis of Napoleon', this composition lamented the fact that such brave and sublime poetry should have caused the French authorities to 'run scared'. Direy also added his voice to Hugo's attack on England, cursing the 'two odious names of Waterloo and Wellington'. His poem ended with specific words of consolation addressed to Hugo:

> *'Religious hands have restored to Caesar these glorious stanzas*
> *And your verses are now sealed in the plinth of the hero.'*[5]

At the time, this apparent act of restitution was thought to be purely rhetorical. However, these lines were almost literally true. A few nights before the official ceremony, Direy had crept up to the official site with some accomplices and bored a hole in the statue of Napoleon, where he had inserted a copy of Hugo's poem. The verses remained in the Emperor's forearm, encased in a metal tube, for more than a century; they were only found when the monument was taken down for restoration following the damages it suffered during the German bombing of Boulogne in the Second World War.[6]

Thanks to this gesture, Hugo's 'Hymn' was thus reunited with its intended beneficiary, giving a whole new dimension to Direy's final verse: 'The poet and the warrior together muse at the sounds made by the waves.'

The Emperor of the Nation?

After tracking the potency of the imperial cult at the level of popular, grass-roots politics in the earlier parts of the book, this chapter (and the next two) will explore the representations of Napoleon among political and intellectual elites. Here too – as just seen in the Boulogne incident – we shall uncover a great deal of complexity. The Orleanists were the major political beneficiaries of the 1830 Revolution, and their regime sought to embody a sensible compromise between the contradictory aspirations of the French nation: order and reform, authority and liberty, hierarchy and equality. This balancing act was typified in Louis-Philippe, the new sovereign. Unlike his Bourbon predecessors, the King had supported the 1789 Revolution, and he believed that his power to rule came not from God but from the express wishes of the French nation. He also sought to project himself as a benevolent and unpretentious monarch, and was helped in this by his easy manner and portly appearance.

But by 1834 Louis Philippe had already disappointed the more ardent supporters of the 1830 Revolution, and had lost much of his popularity. Popular graffiti all over the walls of Paris represented him as a pear.[7] More fundamentally, even though it constantly asserted its commitment to 'bourgeois' values, his regime had no distinctive moral or political legitimacy: 'As a monarchy, it had betrayed the monarchy; as a revolutionary regime, it had betrayed the revolution'.[8]

Acutely aware of their lack of historical roots in French political culture, Louis Philippe and his Orleanist ministers quickly realized the capital on which they could draw by exploiting the Emperor's extraordinary popularity in France. A high ratio of the public servants who were recruited into the civil and military services after 1830 were men with strong imperial connections.[9] The regime also sought to appropriate the legend for their own 'national' purposes. It was in this spirit that a statue of Napoleon was placed on the Vendôme Column, the Arc de Triomphe was completed, and the return of Napoleon's remains to the Invalides was arranged.

Under the July Monarchy, in short, Bonaparte became part of the 'official memory' of the French State, a symbol of the nation's past grandeur and a reflection of its apparent commitment to the Napoleonic heritage. As Minister of the Interior Rémusat stated in his parliamentary speech proposing the repatriation of the Emperor's remains: 'Henceforth France, and France alone, will possess all the remains of Napoleon. His tomb, as his fame, will belong to no one but to the nation as a whole. The monarchy of 1830 is indeed the sole and legitimate heir of all the memories of which France is proud.'[10]

Yet this official memory was highly ambivalent. Even as he claimed the Napoleonic heritage for the nation, Rémusat also sought to appropriate it exclusively for the Orleanist monarchy. Furthermore, in the parliamentary discussion which followed the Minister's presentation, considerable unease was expressed at the meaning of the Bonapartist heritage – even among liberals. One member regretted that the return of the Emperor's remains would give a fillip to the 'Napoleonic cult', adding that the delegation travelling to Saint-Helena should be asked to leave behind 'all Bonapartist ideas, which are hostile to the independence of peoples and the emancipation of the human spirit, and represent one of the most burning sores of the contemporary social order.' Napoleon, in sum, was acceptable, but without any of the 'subversive' politics of his contemporary followers.[11]

For others, it was the Emperor's historical record that was contentious. These reservations were vehemently articulated in the speech by the republican representative Lamartine, who reminded his colleagues that the Empire had consistently sacrificed liberty at the altar of military glory: 'I do not like these men who have as their official doctrine liberty, equality, and progress, but who adopt as their symbols the sabre and despotism.'[12] This fundamental hostility was essentially shared by Alexis de Tocqueville, who a few years later saluted the Emperor's genius but also regretted his 'despotism', which had enabled the creation of a 'rational and scientific' system of political domination unparalleled in modern history.[13]

Behind the public façade of a nation at one in its communion with its Emperor, therefore, lurked a more troubled reality: Napoleon's ghost continued to provoke controversy, causing passionate debates within the State, across political families and within them. These questions were especially intense and agonized among French liberals. How could a nation aspiring to peace with its European neighbours celebrate the memory of a conquering warrior? And through what intellectual contortions could a French regime which prided itself on governing through the rule of law trumpet the virtues of a ruler who often seemed to care little for the rules of legality or morality? And above all how could a political community which defined itself as 'liberal' uphold as its national symbol an Emperor who had governed France as an absolute despot?

As we look at how they confronted these issues during the first half of the nineteenth century, we shall examine how leading French liberals came to terms with the legacy of Napoleon – a story of conflict and separation, but also one of fascination and reconciliation. A parallel process of intellectual reappraisal occurred within the Napoleonic camp. For Bonapartists, too, the imperial heritage raised serious ideological problems. The producers and disseminators of the imperial cult after 1815 were confronted with the sombre reality of defeat upon which was grafted a powerful 'black legend', which portrayed Bonaparte as a violent and despotic ruler; indeed, through their writings many liberals had contributed to fashioning this negative image. In response, Napoleon and his supporters devised a counter-myth, in which they asserted that the Emperor had been a closet liberal all along, a 'prince of liberal ideas'[14] in the words of Las Cases in the *Mémorial de Sainte-Hélène*. How (and through what literary and ideological devices) this narrative of 'liberal Bonapartism' was constructed will also be one of the central themes of this chapter.

What was at stake in this confrontation between liberalism and France's Napoleonic past went far beyond the question – important though it was – of the 'historical' status of the Emperor. Facing up to the imperial legacy, liberals agonized over the central dilemma faced by their tradition throughout the nineteenth century: could a just and moderate political order be created only through the destruction of the institutions created by the First Empire, or through their adaptation and liberalization?[15] It was the second answer that eventually emerged victorious, cutting across the different strands of French liberalism.

Often told as separate stories, the histories of Bonapartism and liberalism were in fact inexorably intertwined after 1815. Liberal ideas helped to shape the evolving intellectual representation of the Napoleonic heritage; and this legacy, in turn, decisively determined the ideological structure and orientation of French liberalism. In the end, the Emperor enjoyed what was perhaps his greatest posthumous triumph: French liberal traditions effectively incorporated key elements of their nation's Napoleonic past into their own political mythology.

Napoleon and liberalism

After 1789 French liberals aspired to one broad objective: 'finishing' the Revolution by creating a stable political system embedded in a system of laws. Their motto, in effect, was liberty without anarchy, and order without despotism.[16] From this perspective, liberals had broadly (and often enthusiastically) welcomed Bonaparte's emergence and rise to power in the late 1790s, before rapidly becoming disillusioned with his drift towards political authoritarianism and his relentless pursuit of glory through war. Opposition to Napoleonic rule was notably articulated in the exchanges, discussions, and writings of the 'Coppet group', consisting of leading liberal intellectuals united in their hostility to imperial despotism.[17] It was only at the very end of the First Empire, under the extreme circumstances of the Hundred Days, that some liberals began to rally to the Emperor. This separation and reconciliation was in many ways symbolized by Napoleon's contrasting relationship with two of the key figures in the 'Coppet group':

Germaine de Staël, one of the most prominent thinkers of her generation, and her friend and protégé, Benjamin Constant.

De Staël was the daughter of Necker, the great reforming statesman of the *ancien régime*. Exiled from France during the early years of the Revolution, she returned to Paris in 1795, where she set up a prominent *salon* to promote her cherished principles of toleration, conciliation, and justice, and a reconciliation of State power with individual liberty. She first met Bonaparte in December 1797, soon after the General's triumphant return from his Italian campaign. De Staël admired his brilliance and energy, and for a brief while even hoped that he could help to secure for France the liberty which the Revolution had proclaimed but failed to sustain.

By 1800, however, she began to believe that Napoleon's ambitions were leading him in a different direction; in her own words, he was 'a system as much as he was an individual'[18] – and this system did not seem to have much room for liberty. Bonaparte, too, rapidly became defiant. He had begun with an instinctive dislike for de Staël, having little time for anyone with an independent mind (let alone a woman); and this feeling was only accentuated when de Staël's published works began to advocate widespread social and political reform. Napoleon – a voracious reader, who instantly formed strong (and generally negative) views of the printed material that came his way – was irritated by *De la littérature* (1800), a bold and gushing manifesto in favour of the doctrine of perfectibility, which seemed to him a throwback to the Rousseauist sentimentalism which he believed had perverted the course of the Revolution. He was even more riled by de Staël's subsequent work *Delphine* (1802), which he deemed an 'anti-social work' for its attacks on Catholic morality.

A collision was ultimately inevitable between the authoritarian, populist, militarist, and nationalist politician and the tolerant, elitist, reformist and Anglophile woman of letters; in most respects, they belonged to separate universes. To compound these differences, Napoleon took exception to de Staël's increasing interference in the political arena, notably through her *salon* which served as a haven for liberal opponents to his rule. In January 1802 Benjamin Constant was removed from the deliberative Assembly, the Tribunate, for his excessively liberal views, which Napoleon believed (not inaccurately) to have been nurtured in de Staël's *salon*.

A year later Napoleon struck directly at de Staël herself, banning her from Paris, the seat of her political and intellectual influence. Years of intimidation, spying, and harassment followed, with Napoleon also systematically denigrating de Staël, variously calling her a 'rascal', and a 'nasty intriguer', and even asking his officials to spread the word that she was mentally deranged.[19]

In 1810 this clash culminated in the Emperor's furious response to de Staël's *De l'Allemagne*. In this work, she used her celebration of German literary and philosophical achievements to make the case for an 'individualist' liberalism, rejecting all 'utilitarian' calculations in morality and arguing for the supremacy of justice and individual conscience over calculations of State interest. The entire book was in fact a thinly veiled attack on the Napoleonic 'system' of politics and morality, and de Staël further drove home the point by savaging the Emperor for reducing the concept of 'nation' to a coterie of his supporters, friends, and family.[20] Napoleon had a large number of copies of *De l'Allemagne* seized, and its author was sentenced to definitive exile; indeed, she only avoided arrest because Napoleon's officials convinced him that it would probably do more harm than good (an ironic confirmation of de Staël's view that the Emperor was a utilitarian).[21]

The split between Bonaparte and de Staël never healed. The fault was entirely his; she would probably have responded favourably to a serious overture on his part, but it never came. It was therefore left to Benjamin Constant to forge the first decisive link between the Napoleonic system and liberalism. After his exclusion from the Tribunate, Constant wrote a number of works in which he sought to sketch out a liberal politics as an alternative to Napoleon's authoritarian rule. In the *Principes de Politique* (1806) he assailed the imperial system, a mixture of elements drawn from Hobbesian and Rousseauian principles and absolutist practice; and in *De l'esprit de conquête* (1813) he rounded on Napoleon's penchant for war and hegemonic domination, the cornerstone of imperial ideology.[22]

During the First Restoration in 1814, Constant also published several brochures on political and institutional issues, seeking to advance the cause of a liberal monarchy under the Bourbons. When the news of Napoleon's landing in March 1815 reached Paris, Constant (who up to this point had not attacked him personally) published a vitriolic denunciation of the Emperor in the *Journal des Débats*, describing him as 'more terrible and more odious than Attila and Gengis Khan'.[25] There seemed to be no scope for compromise between the two men.

Yet, as we saw in Chapter 1, all of this changed suddenly. On 14 April 1815, a few weeks after Napoleon's triumphant return to Paris, Constant was summoned to the Tuleries by the Emperor. Afterwards he wrote in his diary: 'Long conversation. He is an astonishing man. To-morrow, I shall take to him a project for a new constitution.'[24] Dissatisfied with all the constitutional projects previously submitted to him, Napoleon succeeded in rallying the liberal thinker by asking him to prepare a new draft. Within a few days, Constant was appointed to the Conseil d'Etat, where he wrote what eventually became the 'Additional Act' – an amendment to the imperial constitution which provided for the introduction of key elements of the liberal platform, notably a (qualified) recognition of the principle that sovereignty resided in the nation, ministerial responsibility, freedom of the press, and a greater independence of the judiciary. Despite these proposed changes, as we saw earlier, the 'Additional Act' was a political failure. Both Napoleon and Constant were attacked for this piece of constitutional engineering, the Emperor because many doubted the sincerity of his conversion to liberalism and Constant because of his truly remarkable *volte-face*, which for many smacked of both naivety and opportunism. Liberal Bonapartism seemed either an optimistic illusion or (as some of Constant's enemies alleged) venality dressed up in ideological garb.

Napoleon, as we shall see in the next section, replied to these attacks in the *Mémorial de Sainte-Hélène*. Constant's response preceded the Emperor's by a few years. His *Mémoires sur les Cent-Jours* were first published as a series of separate 'letters' in the *Minerve* in 1819–20, and then gathered together as a two-volume book a few years later. In this work he did much more than defend his own actions: the *Mémoires* also provided a spirited defence of the Hundred Days, and in this sense provided a philosophical justification for the continuation of the alliance between liberalism and Bonapartism after 1815 (see Figure 15).

Constant began by justifying his own decision to serve the Emperor. One of the key arguments of the *Mémoires* was that those who had wondered whether Napoleon could be 'trusted' were in fact

FIGURE 15

Napoleon and Benjamin Constant in the gardens of the
Elysée Palace in June 1815

Constant had been a long and consistent critic of Napoleonic despotism. However, when the Emperor returned in 1815 he rallied to the imperial cause after Napoleon had convinced him that he wished to found his rule on liberal principles. Constant then drafted what was to become the Additional Act to the constitutions of the Empire. This image, which shows Napoleon leading and directing the discussion over the new constitutional amendment, accurately reflects the Emperor's mesmerizing effect on Constant, who wrote after meeting him that Napoleon was 'an extraordinary man'.

posing the wrong question. Constant's decision was based not on faith or considerations of self-interest but on his assessment of the specific circumstances in March 1815. At that moment France was confronted with three terrifying perils: the threat of a restored Napoleonic dictatorship, the possibility of royalist counter-revolution, and the near-certainty of an invasion of its national territory by foreign armies.

Faced with this extreme situation, Constant argued that it was his civic duty to do all in his power to preserve his country's freedom – even if that meant serving Napoleon. In fact, he repeatedly made the point that the reality of foreign invasion alone justified his decision: to abandon the Emperor at such a moment would have been supremely unpatriotic.[25] This proposition, by equating the Napoleonic cause in 1815 with that of national self-defence, implicitly drew an analogy with the revolutionary spirit of '1792', and laid the foundations for one of the key areas of convergence between Bonapartism and liberalism (as well as republicanism) under the Restoration: a common conception of national sovereignty. This was a geographical attribute, expressed in a commitment to the sanctity of France's borders, but sovereignty was above all a philosophical principle about the foundations of legitimate rule: even though he remained the Emperor, Napoleon had now (according to Constant) recognized the 'sovereignty of the people'.[26]

While recognizing that it was driven at least as much by self-preservation as by a genuine change of heart, Constant also noted something of a new political spirit in Napoleon. At their first meeting the Emperor told the author of De l'esprit de conquête that he was 'no longer' interested in expansive wars (he had clearly read Constant's work); he also emphasized his commitment to a more active and participatory political community: 'Public discussions, free elections, responsible ministers, press freedom, I want all of this . . . Press freedom especially; to suppress it is an absurdity.'[27]

Here, as in many other passages in his Mémoires, Constant was also using Napoleon's deeds and utterances to attack the Restoration regime's failings. The liberal thinker was especially critical of these deficiencies with regard to freedom of expression, noting that despite facing the extremity of a foreign invasion the government of the Hundred Days had allowed complete political (and press) freedom –

in stark contrast with the regime that had succeeded it.[28] This too, was an important marker for posterity: by highlighting Napoleon's effective promotion of freedom of expression, Constant tacitly wiped out the entire repressive legacy of the First Empire, and opened up the possibility for liberals and Bonapartists to rally behind the common banner of 'freedom' in later years.

So impressed was Constant by the Emperor's newly found determination here that he even cited Napoleon's claim – fanciful at best – that if Madame de Staël (who was at the time travelling in Italy) were to be arrested by a foreign government he would 'send twenty thousand men to deliver her'.[29]

But perhaps the greatest contribution made by Constant to the 'liberal' rehabilitation of Napoleon was his portrayal of the Emperor in 1815 as a tragic and vulnerable figure, betrayed by all those around him and nobly sacrificing himself after Waterloo to prevent his country from descending into the abyss of a civil war. De Staël (and, come to that, Constant himself in his earlier writings) had dwelled on the oppressive nature of the Napoleonic 'system'. In the *Mémoires*, in contrast, it was the human face of the Emperor that shone through. Recognizing that he was now 'getting older', Napoleon declared that the 'respite provided by a constitutional monarchy' would suit him well;[30] Constant also noted that the Emperor's manner had changed, and that behind his traditional appearance of vigour and determination he had become 'flexible, and even at times lacking in resolve'.[31]

In one of the most vivid and dramatic passages in the book, Constant described his interview with Napoleon immediately after Waterloo. The Emperor was being pressed from all sides to abdicate, notably by the two chambers, but he was resisting on the grounds that his withdrawal from the scene would leave the country open to foreign occupation and domination.[32] There was, however, a clear political alternative: Napoleon could seize absolute power, dissolve the recalcitrant assemblies, and govern as a military dictator with the support of the Army and populations of the towns and countryside. Indeed, as Napoleon was speaking to Constant a small crowd from the Parisian *petit peuple* began chanting 'Long Live the Emperor!' outside his window. But from the very outset the Emperor had told Constant that he 'did not want to be the king of a *jacquerie*';[33] and he concluded that he 'had not returned from Elba only for Paris to be drenched in blood'.[34]

The liberal thinker underscored his admiration for Napoleon's decision: 'He who, still in control of the remains of an army which had been invincible for twenty years, buttressed by a multitude which was electrified by the mere mention of his name, which was terrified by the return of a government which it considered counter-revolutionary, and which needed only a signal to rise against all its enemies, chose to abandon power instead of attempting to hold on to it by massacres and civil strife has, on this occasion, earned the respect of the human race.'[35]

The *Mémoires* were by no means an unqualified apologia for Bonaparte. Throughout his narrative Constant remained true to his liberal principles; he repeated his vehement criticisms of the Napoleonic 'system', especially its yearning for absolute power, its corruption, its contempt for human beings, and the greed and servility it engendered. Yet Napoleon rose above it all; he was the archetype of the tragic hero, 'better than his system, and defeated and fallen for not having been that which he could have become.'[36] In this contrast between the man and the system Constant opened up a crucial gap, which would enable the liberal tradition to begin to worship at the altar of the Napoleonic 'genius' while glossing over some of the seedier aspects of the Emperor's rule. As a historian of Restoration liberalism put it, 'the new Napoleonic myth emerged in order to facilitate, and in some ways to excuse, the fusion of Bonapartists and liberals'.[37]

The Mémorial de Sainte-Hélène

Constant's *Mémoires* took the first critical step in the 'Napoleonization' of French liberalism. A parallel process, that of the 'liberalization' of Bonapartism, was initiated by Napoleon himself, in a book which was to become one of the landmarks of nineteenth-century French literature. Published two years after Napoleon's death, and based on the Emperor's conversations and reflections during his exile, the *Mémorial de Sainte-Hélène* was the first comprehensive articulation of the imperial legend, and despite its length and complexity (and more than occasional repetitiveness) was undoubtedly the most influential work of its kind. The *Mémorial*, as we have already shown, did not create the legend; even if we only consider works on Napoleon published in France in the early 1820s, all of its central themes were already present in popular opinion: the glorification of the Empire, the celebration of Napoleon's military victories, and the lamentations over his exile.[38] What this apologia for Napoleon did, however, was to bring together all these elements into one book. It was the most successful Napoleonic memoir ever written, with its numerous editions enjoying even greater acclaim than the Emperor's own recollections, not to mention the works of his other companions at Sainte-Hélène such as Bertrand, Montholon and Gourgaud.[39]

Little had prepared the author of the *Mémorial* for such fame. Emmanuel de Las Cases, a marquis and naval officer under the *ancien régime*, and a royalist *émigré* during the early years of the Revolution, was something of a late convert to the Napoleonic cause, rallying to the Empire only in 1806. In 1809, he applied for the position of chamberlain, and six months later entered the Council of State. But he emerged as a member of Napoleon's inner circle only during the Hundred Days. Accompanied by his young son, Las Cases followed the Emperor into his exile at Saint-Helena, where he became one of his most trusted companions until his deportation from the island in December 1816.

While the *Mémorial*'s extraordinary and enduring appeal stemmed from the book's multiple literary and philosophical qualities, its immediate success rested upon its one overriding characteristic: its restoration of Napoleon's voice. After years dominated by a dearth of hard information about the imperial exiles, broken only by poor literary fakes, a barrage of rumours, and an outpouring of pro- and anti-Bonapartist propaganda,[40] here at last were the authentic thoughts and feelings of the Emperor during the final years of his life. And despite the strictures of Stendhal, who derided his 'lack of wit', Las Cases was more than a mere scribe. The unique strength of his work lay in its glorification of Napoleon by the effective combination of several types of narration: the *Mémorial* seamlessly blended together the respect of the faithful courtier, the acute perceptiveness of the memorialist, the shrewdness of the investigative journalist, the incisiveness and ideological vigour of the polemicist, and the broad sweep of the political historian.

Written in the form of a diary, the *Mémorial* provided a first-hand account of the first eighteen months of Napoleon's captivity, meticulously detailing the journey from France, first to the coast of England and then across the Atlantic; the topographical details of the barren and inhospitable South Atlantic island; the severe domestic difficulties experienced by the prisoners in their rat-infested home; and the petty deprivations and humiliations inflicted upon the Emperor and his entourage by his jailers, notably the governor of Saint-Helena, the 'hideous' Hudson Lowe.[41]

The documentation of these travails, however, was essentially a device that enabled Las Cases to portray the fortitude of Napoleon's character; as he put it, it was 'a spectacle worthy of the gods to see man doing battle with misfortune'.[42] His account of this struggle – and this was one of the supreme political strengths of the *Mémorial* – revealed a Napoleonic figure heroic in his epic grandeur but also compellingly and often pathetically human.

On many occasions, Las Cases portrayed Napoleon as physically suffering, morally 'beaten down',[43] and prone to bouts of 'melancholy'.[44] There were also frequent allusions to the serious deterioration of the Emperor's health, especially towards the final stages of his sojourn.[45] But having shown Napoleon's vulnerability as a mere mortal, Las Cases then took him back into Elysium, constantly underlining his supreme moral qualities of stoicism, detachment, and lack of interest in all things material. The *Mémorial* uncritically reported Napoleon's assertion that he never had large sums of money at his disposal, even after his triumphant return from the Italian campagin (notorious for its savage French plundering).[46] In a scene from the early days of the Consulate, Bonaparte recalled finding 800,000 francs in a drawer, and handing it over to his fellow consuls Sieyès and Ducos, who then greedily squabbled over it.[47]

Returning from Elba to find letters of denunciation written about him by many State officials whom he himself had appointed, Napoleon remained serene, without any thought of punishment or vengeance.[48] Faced with the unjust and arbitrary English decision to deport him, Bonaparte likewise demonstrated an exemplary 'dignity in adversity':[49] throughout the journey taking him away into exile he appeared 'calm, impassive'.[50] When the English authorities on Saint-Helena tried to demean him by refusing to address him by his imperial title, he responded with equanimity: 'Let them call me what-ever they like, they cannot stop me from being who I am.'[51] Accepting his fate, Napoleon showed no 'rancour, irritation, or hatred', and constantly urged his companions to adopt the same approach.[52] Although unspoken, the analogy with the martyrdom of Christ would not have been lost to most of Las Cases's readers, espe-cially as he also went out of his way to underscore Napoleon's commitment to the Catholic faith.[53]

The *Mémorial* was also a secular moral fable, celebrating the 'Plutarchian' dimension of Napoleon's personality, character, and achievements.[54] Alongside its 'humanization' of the Emperor, the work repeatedly invoked his 'Promethean' qualities, both physical and intellectual. Las Cases offered personal testimony of the Emperor's legendary powers of concentration and capacity for work; he also cited numerous examples of his physical resilience during his military campaigns – notably his wild rides on horseback, with his ret-inue struggling to keep up with his frantic journeys of up to twelve hours. (He delicately omitted to mention that Napoleon often fell.)[55] The work was littered with illustrations of the force of the Emperor's intellect, perhaps nowhere more brilliantly highlighted than in the tight and focused comparisons offered one evening between the English and French Revolutions.[56]

For Las Cases, Napoleon was a born leader, immediately appear-ing to those around him as 'a man made to command others'.[57] He was a ruler who could legitimately be compared with the greatest heroes of antiquity such as Alexander, Caesar and Hannibal;[58] a guardian who had been hailed as the protector of both Christianity and the Islamic faith;[59] and a visionary who could foresee the moment when Europe would be united under one political associa-tion, with a common court, a single currency, and a shared system of weights and measures.[60] Such was Napoleon's capacity for objectiv-ity, noted Las Cases at one point, that he seemed to speak of his own past 'as if it was three hundred years of age; his narratives and obser-vations are cast in a language which literally transcends time.'[61]

Las Cases frequently reported Napoleon's alleged imperviousness to the accusations of his detractors, at one point citing the Emperor explicitly: 'It would be degrading to respond to slander.'[62] None-theless, a considerable number of passages in the *Mémorial* were devoted to defending Napoleon's past actions. Already well furnished with a range of royalist and liberal writings during the Emperor's reign, the 'black legend' was given a new lease of life by his defeat and exile, and it is hardly surprising that Napoleon should have sought to respond to some of these attacks. The *Mémorial* took to task a number of celebrated anti-Napoleonic pamphlets, notably English publications such as the *Anti-Gallican*[63] and Goldsmith's *Secret History*[64] and French 'classics' such as Chateaubriand's *De Buonaparte et des Bourbons*, a vicious tirade perhaps most famous for its allegation that Napoleon had forced the Pope into signing the 1813 Concordat by 'dragging him across Fontainebleau by his white hair'.[65]

Napoleon defended himself concerning both specific events and incidents and the wider set of criticisms about his methods and legitimacy as a ruler. In the first category, he was at pains to deny that he had poisoned any French soldiers suffering from the plague at Jaffa.[66] There was also a long defence of his abduction and execution of the Duc d'Enghien, an admittedly illegal act explained by the natural-law principle of self-protection: 'If it had to be repeated,' reported Las Cases, '[the Emperor] would have done it again.'[67] The matter clearly continued to haunt Napoleon; he repeated the same formula in his Testament[68].

There was also a great deal about Napoleon's more controversial and unsuccessful military campaigns, notably the invasion of Russia in 1812, whose disastrous consequences Las Cases sought to play down[69] and of course his defeat at Waterloo, the real causes of which Napoleon was still at a loss to identify.[70] His *coup d'état* of 18 Brumaire 1799, which had destroyed the Republic and paved the way for the establishment of the Empire, was justified – a familiar argument used by all dictators from Roman times onward – by the 'imperious necessity' of saving the nation: all the arguments about the illegality and immorality of his actions here were nothing but metaphysical verbiage.[71]

Even more important than these specific rebuttals were Napoleon's vigorous responses to the adverse characterizations of his personality and system of rule. His despotism? The Emperor admitted that he had committed many acts which were 'tyrannical', but all had been justified at the time: they were 'necessary evils'.[72] His naked self-interest and ambition? His only concern throughout his career had been to promote the 'empire of reason'.[73] His aspiration to conquer the world, to recreate a 'universal monarchy' in modern form? This was belied by the events of 1815, when he had returned to found a liberal Empire, and (as Constant had also shown) had explicitly refused to save his throne after Waterloo by 'becoming a tyrant'.[74] The Additional Act of 1815 was not, Napoleon stated, a concession to the times; he claimed that if he had succeeded in defeating Russia in 1812, he would have abandoned his dictatorship, created a European confederation and become a constitutional monarch.[75] His sacrifice of the French people to his absolute and unqualified love of war? Napoleon asserted that had no fondness for war, and indeed all the conflicts that he had waged had been imposed upon him, either by his enemies (especially the English) or by the force of cir- cumstances.[76] His destruction of liberty, that most sacred heritage of the 1789 Revolution? Not only did he think this accusation unfounded, but Napoleon also went so far as to affirm that during his reign his countrymen enjoyed more liberty than the citizens of any other European state – including England.[77]

On many a battlefield, Napoleon had mastered the principle that attack was the best form of defence. Interspersed throughout these responses to his critics was a sophisticated (and often creative) 'liberal' reconstruction of the political legacy of the Empire. This was per- haps the greatest single achievement of the *Mémorial*, for which Las Cases should be given equal credit: it hailed Napoleon as the fore- runner of liberalism, locating his reign within the wider framework of the French Revolution, and aligning the Emperor with what were to become the two dominant 'progressive' doctrines of the nineteenth century: liberalism and republicanism.[78] The key element here, repeated on numerous occasions throughout the *Mémorial*, was Napoleon's association with the 'people': the Emperor proudly asserted that he was 'a part of the people'.[79] He recalled travelling incognito around Lyons, where an old lady once told him that 'the Bourbons were the kings of the aristocracy, Napoleon was the king of the people, he is our king'. Even his return in 1815 was justified by the fact he 'had been elected by the people'.[80] Las Cases went to great lengths to underline this point, notably by citing Constant's account of the Hundred Days, in which the liberal writer had also approv- ingly quoted Napoleon's intellectual transformation: 'I am a man of the people; if the people really want freedom, I owe it to them; I have recognized their sovereignty, I must now listen to their wishes.'[81]

In its somewhat tentative liberalism, this statement perhaps more accurately reflected the hesitations in Napoleon's conception of politics during and after 1815, thereby underscoring the importance of the ideological 'twist' orchestrated by Las Cases. For a careful political reading of the *Mémorial* revealed in fact not one, but three distinct Napoleonic voices. In the first, the Emperor spoke the traditional, unreconstructed language of authoritarian Bonapartism (borrowed in many respects from the Revolution). He described the French as an 'old and corrupt' nation concerned only with 'its interests, its pleasures, its vanities';[82] derided the Bourbons for introducing a form of representative government based on an upper and lower Chamber: 'never have assemblies provided prudence and energy, wisdom and vigour';[83] and even impugned the French Revolution, 'one of the greatest evils which could befall any country'.[84] This was the Bonaparte of old, ruthless and triumphant, and entirely oblivious to the concerns of liberalism. In a sense, this was the Napoleon encountered by Madame de Staël.

The second voice – destined to have a much longer career in the history of modern Bonapartism – was that of the 'arbiter', standing above all ideologies. Always choosing his historical role with great care, Napoleon defined himself as the French ruler who had effectively bridged the gap between the *ancien régime* and modernity, 'the natural mediator between the old and the new order'.[85]

The third voice – arguably as much that of Las Cases as of Napoleon himself – was that of the resurgent freethinking officer, imbued with the values of the Enlightenment, resolutely hostile to 'feudalism' and much more attuned to the progressive and 'democratic' spirit of his age.[86] This was how Napoleon had presented himself to Constant in 1815, and it was also in this context that the *Mémorial*, in one of its celebrated passages, cited Napoleon's self-description as the 'Messiah of the Revolution',[87] stressing the Emperor's passion for equality, the 'passion of the century',[88] as well as his belief that 1789 had been 'the true cause of the regeneration of French mores'.[89] In order to bolster this vision of Napoleonic 'liberalism', Las Cases even quoted extensively from a key passage in Constant's letters on the Hundred Days, in which the liberal thinker cited the Emperor: 'I now understand liberty, and have been nour-ished by its thoughts.'[90]

It was this third voice which was most frequently cited and remem-bered and thus came across as dominant in the *Mémorial*; it was to play a vital role in sustaining the legend of Napoleonic liberalism throughout the nineteenth century (see Figure 16). It is also worth noting that this 'humanization' of the Emperor was reinforced by the manner in which successive editions of the work were edited and illustrated. After 1830 the drawings of artists such as Vernet, Raffet and Charlet were used to illustrate several important works on the Napoleonic era; the 1840 edition of the *Mémorial*, illustrated by Charlet, contained no fewer than 500 drawings – most of which dealt with the Saint-Helena period, and depicted Napoleon in 'ordi-nary' poses (and often with considerable humour).[91]

Thiers's History of the Napoleonic Era

The Napoleonic portraits drawn by Las Cases and Constant provided the early building blocks for the construction of a 'liberal legend' of the Emperor. In their different ways, both works drew attention away from the Napoleonic 'system', concentrating instead on 'humanizing' the Emperor by focusing on his magnetic personality and character. They were also distinctive for their focus on the periods of imperial political weakness and vulnerability – the Hundred Days and the early years of exile at Saint-Helena. Indeed, in its infancy this 'liberal Bonapartism' was itself essentially an ideology of opposition, almost of victimhood: for the supporters of Napoleon, it was a lament for the departure of the Emperor, and (after 1821) a homage to his memory, while for the liberals the imperial banner was a convenient device to highlight the failings of the royalist political and civic order after 1815.

The liberal legend of the 'good Emperor' would also be dissemi-nated in popular culture, notably through the songs of Béranger; his *Souvenirs du peuple* (1828) celebrated the memory of a kind, simple, and generous monarch, a friend of the people and defender of French national interests.[92] The next stage in this intellectual evolution would be marked by Louis Napoleon's attempt in the 1830s and 1840s to

FIGURE 16

The man of the people

A central feature of the Napoleonic legend was the association of the Emperor with the 'people'. In the *Mémorial de Sainte-Hélène* Napoleon presented himself as the 'messiah of the Revolution': a monarch who had been chosen by the people, cared for them, and had governed in their best interests; the legend also underscored his simple appearance and manners, which were implicitly contrasted with the pomposity of the kings who had followed him. In the 1830s and 1840s Louis Napoleon would strongly underscore this aspect of the Bonapartist heritage in his own propaganda, notably through his commitment to male universal suffrage.

'modernize' his uncle's legacy by incorporating liberal, socialist, and republican elements into it.[93]

What this vision lacked, however, was an overarching view of the entire history of the Consulate and First Empire, and more specifically a critical intellectual engagement with the cornerstone of Napoleon's system of rule, namely his conception of power. It fell to the liberal statesman, academician, and historian Adolphe Thiers to forge this broader synthesis in his *Histoire du Consulat et de l'Empire* (1845–1862). Begun under the July Monarchy, continued under the Republic, and concluded under the Second Empire, this twenty-volume work sold more than a million copies, and established Thiers's reputation as France's 'national historian' (as well as his fortune).[94] The author was supremely well placed to produce such a work. From his early years at school in Marseilles he had been fascinated by Napoleon, and like many men of his generation his obsession with the Emperor continued well into his adult life. Bringing back Napoleon's remains for burial in Paris had been his idea, eventually adopted and implemented by King Louis Philippe in 1840.[95]

Thiers was also a crafty politician, a key witness of the battles of his time and one of the principal conservative liberal leaders of his generation (and of the next: he played a decisive role in the founding of the Third Republic).[96] His experience of 'the storms of public life' provided a critical backdrop to his account of Napoleonic history.[97] At the same time, he wrote as a professional, drawing systematically upon public sources (he trawled through the thirty thousand pieces which made up Napoleon's archive), travelling across France and Europe to visit the sites of key imperial battles, and using his wide contacts in French elite circles to consult memoirs, many of which were unpublished. In effect his was the first serious history of Napoleonic rule.[98]

Thiers's success was also a reflection of the broad and complementary perspectives from which he approached his subject. He was a great admirer of the bourgeoisie, the class which in his view had made possible the glorious events of 1789, and his *Histoire* essentially narrated the story of the First Empire through its eyes, placing Napoleon's deeds in the broader context of the French Revolution. Above all, what made possible this more rounded

account of the Napoleonic legacy was that Thiers was a fundamentally different kind of liberal from Madame de Staël and
Constant. While they were intellectuals who had remained in opposition for most of their lives, and forged their liberalism in terms of
the protection and nurturing of the individual, Thiers was a liberal
who practised (and enjoyed) statecraft, and valued the preservation
of order as its supreme goal; his liberalism was more conservative
than theirs, and grounded in action and pragmatism rather than
principle or doctrine. He was able to offer a critical perspective on
Napoleon and his system of rule, but one which rested upon an
understanding of the necessity of power rather than an instinctive
defiance of it.

Central to the *Histoire du Consulat et de l'Empire* was Thiers's
aspiration to portray Napoleon with 'fairness' and 'without embellish-
ment';[99] throughout the work he carefully sought to distinguish
between the positive and negative features of imperial power
between 1799 and 1815 – and also between fact and legend. Yet (in
both respects) the boundaries were often blurred. In the very first
volume, for example, Thiers revealed the truth behind General
Bonaparte's crossing of the Alps, one of the decisive moments in the
Italian campaign, which had been immortalized in David's painting
representing him on a magnificent white horse. The truth, it turned
out, was somewhat less lofty: Napoleon had been led across the
difficult mountainous paths on a small grey mule, escorted by a local
guide.

But, having dismantled the legend, Thiers then proceeded to
mythologize the reality by telling of his own encounter with the
peasant who had acted as Napoleon's guide on that occasion. This
humble villager had been assailed with questions by Bonaparte,
and had ended up telling him his entire life story. In the course
of this narration he had discussed all his troubles, in particular
his money problems, which were affecting his marriage prospects. After being led safely across the mountains, Napoleon
had ordered that his guide be given a house, a plot of land, and
a grant to pay for his wedding. This touching gesture by the
man who would become the 'ruler of the world' was evidence,
according to Thiers, of the fundamental goodness of Bonaparte's
heart.[100]

Perhaps the most important line of demarcation in the *Histoire* was between the republican and monarchical phases of Napoleonic rule: the Consulate and the Empire. Thiers saw Bonaparte as a liberator during the consular era, rescuing the French nation from corruption, disorder, and decadence, initiating the reconciliation among different political factions, presiding over the restoration of economic confidence, ending the religious conflicts provoked by the Revolution, and re-establishing 'respect' for France throughout Europe.[101] Thiers underscored his admiration for these grandiose achievements, which eventually led to Bonaparte's (justified) proclamation as Consul for life. In his decision to re-establish a monarchy in 1804, however, Napoleon sowed the seeds of all his later misfortunes: the Empire was in many respects a personal act of vanity, a regime which would be propelled by the relentless drive for conquest and territorial expansion.[102]

By becoming Emperor, Napoleon also made the fatal transition from dictatorship to despotism, turning himself into a ruler who 'took no note either of men or of nature'.[103] From this moment on, he became overwhelmed by 'the disease of ruling', that 'moral plague' which he imparted to all his family and which eventually caused his downfall.[104] (Thiers was also offering here a veiled criticism of Napoleon III's Second Empire, a regime whose political despotism and suppression of 'necessary liberties' he consistently opposed.)

This contrast opened up another powerful distinction which ran through Thiers's work, that between Napoleon's achievements and failings as a civilian ruler and as a warrior. There were spectacular advances in France's system of government under Bonaparte, notably in the creation of the Council of State and prefectorate, the drafting and proclamation of the Civil Code, the reorganization of the judiciary and local administration, and the establishment of the Bank of France. Even under the First Empire, overwhelmed though he was with waging war, Napoleon established the University, aimed at removing education from the hands of the clergy – one of the most remarkable and far-sighted creations of his reign.[105] Yet, for all of these successes, the Emperor's greatest flaw was his obsessive devotion to war, which consumed much more of his time than domestic affairs.

Thiers recognized and saluted Napoleon's 'extraordinary military genius',[106] and devoted the bulk of the middle volumes of the *Histoire* to the narration, with a wealth of detail, of the Emperor's celebrated successes, notably at the battles of Marengo, Austerlitz, Iena, Wagram, and Friedland. While his bourgeois liberal sensitivities were revolted by the carnage of these wars, Thiers nonetheless remained mesmerized by the exploits of the Grande Armée. After describing the thousands of men killed on the battlefield at Iena, he explained that 'these scenes would be horrible, and indeed intolerable, but for the genius and heroism displayed, which compensated for these horrors, and for the glory, this light which embellishes everything, and surrounds it with its dazzling rays!'[107]

And yet, despite his military brilliance, Napoleon proceeded to overreach himself, first in the 'folly' of the dream of universal empire, then in the costly war in Spain, and finally in the catastrophic conflict with Russia, 'the supreme aberration of a genius blinded by despotism.'[108] This image of a ruler warped by his 'insatiable military desires' took Thiers to the heart of his analysis of the Napoleonic *Weltanschauung*, and at the same time brought to the fore his ambivalence about the military aspects of the imperial epic. However hard he tried, Thiers could not find solid ground here. He repeatedly asserted that as a warrior Napoleon remained a 'genius',[109] and yet he also acknowledged that Bonaparte's most egregious mistakes were committed on the battlefield (notably during the Russian campaign, which was nothing but a sequence of blunders and tactical aberrations[110]), and that during his reign the Emperor was responsible for the deaths of more men than even the greatest Asiatic conquerors.[111]

Thiers was also deeply ambivalent about the relationship between war and glory. He constantly celebrated the 'grandeur' that Napoleon brought to France, even though it had come through wars which he condemned as unnecessary, wasteful, and ultimately counter-productive. Perhaps Thiers was simply reflecting the contradictions of his age: at one point, describing the attitude of the bourgeoisie towards the Emperor's return in March 1815, he could not help noting that the citizens of urban France were pleased to see their 'glorious' leader back, even though they were concerned that his return would precipitate war;[112] this ambivalence was no doubt shared by Thiers himself.

To compound the confusion, the *Histoire* also refused to accept any moral difference between the 'glory' produced by defensive and offensive wars: 'The volunteers of 1792 wanted to defend their *patrie* against an unjust invasion; the warlike soldiers of 1805 wished to make France the world's leading power. Let us not seek to make distinctions between such sentiments: it is virtuous to run to the defence of one's country when it is endangered, but it is just as good to devote oneself to making it great and glorious.'[113] In and of itself, this was a perfectly tenable view; however, it did not sit very comfortably with Thiers's censoriousness towards Napoleon's military expansionism (and indeed his later opposition to Napoleon III's suicidal war with Prussia), and his apparent imperviousness to the human costs of warfare.

All these tensions were ultimately reconciled in the *Histoire*'s account of Bonaparte's politics. Here too, Thiers began with an apparently simple distinction: 'Napoleon made war with his genius, and politics with his passions.'[114] At one level, this was a straightforward reference to the Emperor's consistent tendency to allow his political judgement to be swayed by his emotions: the execution of the Duc d'Enghien was provoked by his rage;[115] the rupture of the Amiens peace by his petulance;[116] the Spanish and Russian wars by his vanity,[117] and so on. And yet Thiers's narrative showed that nothing was ever simple with Napoleon. His account of the Hundred Days, for example, highlighted the Emperor's political shrewdness in reading the situation in France accurately in 1814–15, particularly noting the 'simple, open, and skilful' way in which he managed his return to power.[118]

The key point about the events of 1815, in Thiers's view, was that they represented a continuation of the conflict between the *ancien régime* and the Revolution.[119] Seen in this light, Napoleon was thus an agent of the higher historical purpose of 1789, and indeed Thiers often wrote as if the Emperor was its instrument – both for good and for ill. Highlighting the 'intemperance' of the Empire's foreign policy, he noted that it was in many respects a continuation of Revolutionary ambitions, of which Napoleon was the natural heir.[120] Evoking Bonaparte's 'delirium', which was demonstrated by the absence of any sense of continuity, patience, and modesty in his politics, Thiers added that this was not merely a personal character defect: 'It was the French Revolution which was delirious in him, in his vast genius.'[121]

But the Revolution did not only explain Napoleon's political weaknesses; its spirit also shone through his 'liberal' ambitions, achievements, and legacy. In 1815 the Emperor had finally recognized the principle of political freedom: this had come not merely out of calculation or self-interest, but through his understanding that freedom was now 'necessary' – in other words, that the moment had come to provide what the Revolution had promised, and which he had always hoped to crown his rule by delivering.[122] By this subtle move, Thiers accomplished two things: he re-intregrated the Emperor's entire reign into the historical drama of 1789 (just as Las Cases had done in the *Mémorial*), and also incorporated the end of Napoleon's rule into the liberal teleology of nineteenth-century French politics, characterized by the progressive and inevitable emergence of 'necessary liberties'.[123] Bonaparte was also a son of 1789 in respect of its key civic principles: the abolition of feudalism and the establishment of civil equality.[124]

In Thiers's estimation, this was his greatest accomplishment under the Consulate: enabling all French citizens to enjoy equal rights, and to live under the same laws, irrespective of their religion, region, or social class.[125] Napoleon's conception of merit, which flowed from this wider notion of equality, particularly appealed to Thiers's conservative liberalism: '[Bonaparte] thus wished for a hierarchy in society, on the scales of which all men could be ranked following their abilities and talents, independently of their birth.'[126] In this sense, and however paradoxical it sounded, even the crowning of Napoleon as Emperor was a vindication of the revolutionary principle of civil equality, which had made it possible for a mere officer to rise through the ranks to become a monarch.[127]

For Thiers – and here he spoke simultaneously as a bourgeois, a conservative liberal, a statesman, and an historian – Napoleon's supreme achievement and legacy as a son of the Revolution was his creation of a territorial administration that could 'hold France together whenever its head faltered'[128] as it often did during the nineteenth century. The Napoleonic principle of 'centralization'[129] had given rise to an 'admirable hierarchy' of local institutions, through which prefects, representative assemblies and mayors could all work together in the public interest.[130] Napoleon's administrative system was not only 'intelligent and strong', it was also a continuation and application of the true spirit of Revolutionary equality, ensuring that local communities could manage their affairs according to principles which were consistent, fair, just, and enlightened – everything, in short, that could not be achieved were these local communities to be abandoned to their 'capriciousness'.[131]

As an individual, Napoleon may well have been perverted by his passions, but his ultimate inheritance proved to be one of public reason. It was for this reason that all the regimes which had followed the First Empire had kept intact Napoleon's centralized administrative system, and this heritage was for Thiers an absolute blessing; he continued to defend it with implacable vigour throughout his political career.

The Emergence of Napoleonic Liberalism

Liberals began in the early nineteenth century with a wholesale rejection of Napoleon, both as a leader and as a 'system'. The liberal legend began in the 1820s with Constant's humanization of the Emperor, concentrating on the man at the expense of his system while Thiers eventually drew the cycle to a close by forging a positive liberal vision of Napoleon, critical of the individual ruler but awed and inspired by his institutional legacy.

Indeed, it was no accident that the final volume of Thiers's *Histoire* appeared in 1862, just as the French political system was embarking upon an evolution that would culminate in the emergence of a 'liberal Empire', a regime which sought to reconcile imperial rule with notions of democracy, political accountability, and the preservation of individual freedoms. By the early 1860s, the parallel intellectual adaptations of the Napoleonic legacy were edging to a close, both among Bonapartists and liberals. The result was a largely convergent interpretation of Napoleon as a brilliant but flawed ruler who, despite his dictatorial tendencies and his excessive penchant for military glory, successfully restored order in France after the ravages of the Revolution, and thereby paved the way for the triumph of the 'liberal' aspects of the heritage of 1789: bourgeois rule, civil equality, administrative centralization, and national (as distinct from 'popular') sovereignty. The carnage of the battlefields was compensated for by the 'glory' achieved by French arms; in any event, Napoleon's failings as a warrior were superseded by his achievements as a lawmaker. In the words of a popular song written for the Emperor's centenary in 1869:

> *Napoleon was a great captain*
> *But above all a great magistrate*
> *And he composed without difficulty*
> *Great laws for the French State.*[132]

Thiers's liberal synthesis, it should be noted, was not endorsed in its entirety even by his moderate contemporaries. The liberal thinker and statesman François Guizot, while admiring Napoleon's consolidation of the principle of 'capacity' as the basis for political participation, did not share Thiers's enthusiasm for the imperial legend – nor, in general, did the Doctrinaires.[133] Prévost-Paradol, a liberal too (but more progressive politically than Thiers and Guizot) wrote of Napoleon that 'good sense, reason, and even philosophy remain speechless before his reign'.[134] In addition, many objected to Thiers's deliberately flat narrative style, which admittedly in places bordered on the turgid; the prize for cruelty here went to the irrepressible Flaubert, who called his book 'a monument of the most triumphant imbecility' and its author 'a most abject *crouton*'.[135]

While they were generally welcomed by imperial veterans (Pelleport, in his memoirs, expressed his regret that he might die before reading Thiers's volume on the Russian campaign[136]), the measured conclusions of the *Histoire du Consulat et de l'Empire* were deemed unacceptable by the unconditional supporters of Napoleon, who continued to celebrate imperial authoritarianism and rejected any criticism of his rule (generally on the basis of the arguments used by the Emperor and Las Cases in the *Mémorial*).[137] The allegation of imperial despotism was also sometimes countered by the claim that there had been no real liberty in France before 1799; Napoleon could therefore not have destroyed what did not exist.[138]

Thiers's conclusions remained especially controversial among French republicans, who identified with the tradition of 1789 but categorically refused to accept Napoleon (and more generally Bonapartism) as one of its legitimate components. The republican attitude towards the imperial legend became increasingly negative from the 1830s, moving from grudging enthusiasm under the July Monarchy, serious reservations under the Second Republic, to outright and vehement hostility under the Second Empire. After 1851, bitterness towards the uncle became a convenient means to lambast the nephew for his *coup d'état*.[139] Even if it was largely instrumental, and effectively directed at 'Napoléon le Petit', as Victor Hugo contemptuously called France's new Emperor, the republican judgement of the Napoleonic legacy during this period was extremely severe.

In his assessment of Thiers's *Histoire*, Proudhon recognized some positive qualities in Napoleon under the Consulate, but then things turned sombre: 'The eclipse begins at the rupture of the Amiens peace, darkness thickens in Bayonne; in Russia he is merely a false prophet, a hideously egotistical fanatic; at Fontainebleau, he is in desperate straits; at Waterloo, he becomes impotent; and at Sainte-Hélène, a liar. In sum, a FALSE GREAT MAN.'[140]

For the republican philosopher Jules Barni, Thiers's *Histoire* 'sacrificed far too much to Napoleonic idolatry':[141] the Emperor, in reality, had destroyed French liberty, trampled upon morality, and ruined the country through his aggressive and expansionary wars. Indeed – supreme insult – he was not even French. Barni (half Italian himself) offered this damning conclusion not only on the grounds of the Emperor's Corsican origins, but by a wonderful *reductio ad absurdum*: 'This contempt for humanity, this disdain for the opinion of others, this Caesarian vanity, this insensitivity of heart and profound ethical indifference which characterized Napoleon, all this could not have come from a Frenchman.'[142]

For all its intensity, this virulently anti-Napoleonic republican view proved relatively short-lived; it rapidly shifted towards greater emollience after the disappearance of the Second Empire in 1870. Pierre Larousse's *Grand Dictionnaire Universel du XIXe siècle* (1866–1876) re-admitted the Emperor into republican collective memory by incorporating Thiers's distinction between the Consulate and the Empire; the work contained two separate entries, the first a celebration of 'Bonaparte, the greatest, most glorious, most radiant name in history', whose life 'ended' on the day of his *coup d'état* of Brumaire 1799, and the second a condemnation of 'Napoleon I, political and military dictator' whose career as an imitator of the Caesars was launched from that moment.[143] Thiers was thus proved right when he noted, at the end of his *Histoire*, that 'for us French people, Napoleon has claims which we cannot ever forget, whatever our party, birth, convictions, or interests.'[144]

As his overarching conclusions about Napoleon became part of the intellectual and historical mainstream, Thiers had sponsored, accompanied and influenced a series of seismic shifts in nineteenth-century French political culture: the incorporation of the Napoleonic heritage into French national mythology, and the ideological orientation of French liberalism away from 'individualism' (the latter, it might be said, was the price to be paid for the achievement of the former). Above all, the crystallization of this 'Napoleonic liberalism' reflected the emergence of a new and powerful constellation of intellectual forces in France during the 1860s and 1870s, a loose coalition that would hold together – under the political leadership of Thiers and Léon Gambetta – to create the Third Republic, a regime which would unhesitatingly retain Napoleon's administrative and territorial organization.

Thiers's views of the imperial heritage were entirely fitting for this coming era, too. The Emperor's 'remarkable accomplishments' as a lawmaker and creator of administrative centralization would be gratefully received by a nation seeking to recover from the ravages of civil war after 1871; his pursuit of 'glory' (to which Thiers added the judicious qualification 'in moderation') would be remembered by those in the Third Republic's leadership who sought to expand France's colonial empire; and even the negative lesson from his despotic rule would be one which would for ever remain entrenched in republican memory: 'However great the genius of one man, he must never be completely entrusted with the destinies of a nation.'[145]

Chapter 7

Louis Napoleon and the
Imperial Legend

The *Souvenirs* of the Baroness du Montet evoke the presence in the resort town of Baden during the early to mid-1830s of a young and little-known prince. His name was Louis, and he was the only surviving son of Hortense de Beauharnais and Napoleon Bonaparte's younger brother Louis, the former King of Holland. Prince Louis would often be seen walking in town with a pensive expression on his face and his hands behind his back, in the characteristic Napoleonic pose – an affectation that provoked much hilarity among the local aristocracy.

They were even more amused by his repeated invocations of the principle of 'popular sovereignty'. One evening in August, to celebrate the anniversary of Louis's patron saint, a few of his friends held a bucolic party in the ruins of a medieval castle near the Black Forest, with bright illuminations and fiery speeches; the reception ended with one of the guests kneeling down in front of the young Bonaparte and pledging allegiance to the 'future ruler of France'.[1]

While the young Prince clearly thought himself destined to follow in the footsteps of his glorious uncle, this belief was not widely shared among his peers. The Baroness du Montet thought that Louis's ambition to become 'the Emperor of the Republic' was at best eccentric, and at worst delusional; she dismissed it as 'a fairy tale'.[2]

For most of the 1830s and 1840s, even as Louis became better known in France and began methodically to prepare the ground for his rise to power, most observers could not bring themselves to take him seriously as the Napoleonic pretender. He did not resemble the Emperor physically, and entirely lacked his declamatory gifts; what was more, he spoke French with a nasal German accent. His character was even more difficult to fathom. Valérie Masuyer, his mother's lady-in-waiting, who saw him almost every day in the early to mid-1830s, spoke of 'something ineffable, which perhaps exists only in me, which deters me from approaching him, and makes his company awkward'.[3] Hortense Cornu, who knew him from his childhood, could not decide whether he was the most resolute man she had ever met, or the most indecisive.[4]

This impenetrable quality would later become one of Louis Napoleon's hallmarks, and arguably one of his greatest assets: it caused his adversaries consistently to underestimate him. Conservatives and liberals alike regarded him as an ambitious upstart – a 'puerile adventurer' in the words of a public prosecutor in 1840[5] – and even his family frequently thought him an embarrassment; he was often ridiculed as a man of low morals and (in Victor Hugo's amiable analogy) a 'monkey', a pale and worthless imitation of the great Bonaparte. Many even doubted his sanity; de Tocqueville was quite representative of the political and intellectual classes when he commented that all Louis Napoleon's successes after 1848 were the product of his 'folly' rather than his reason.[6]

And yet, some twenty years after the pastoral ceremony in Baden Louis was proclaimed Emperor of France, having first been elected to the Presidency of the Second Republic in 1848. This triumph was not fortuitous (although he did, like Napoleon, enjoy his fair share of luck); nor was it merely the product of naked, self-interested ambition. The key to understanding the Prince's success lay in the dynamic interaction between the imperial legend and his own political destiny. Louis was fashioned and nurtured by the cult of Napoleon, which assumed extraordinary proportions under the July Monarchy; and his own electoral successes in and after 1848 were largely a function of the sheer resonance of the Napoleonic 'name' among the French public.

But although he rode on the Emperor's coat-tails, Louis's political rise also demonstrated a consistent capacity to adapt the Napoleonic legend to his own ends. From the early 1830s until the late 1840s, he almost single-handedly turned a private family tradition and heritage into a public power; transformed what seemed like an impossible burden (the assumption of the Napoleonic mantle) into an inspiration and a source of creative action; redesigned a nostalgic, romantic cult into a forward-looking political doctrine; and above all moulded an external, objectified phenomenon into an internal, creative force, which lived in him and shaped his every political move.

The Emperor's shadow

Louis was born on 20 April 1808; he was the second child of Queen Hortense, Napoleon's stepdaughter. She gave birth in Paris at the Chateau de la Malmaison, the home of her mother Empress Josephine. According to Hortense's memoirs, the baby was initially dangerously weak and had to be wrapped in cotton and fortified by frequent wine baths.[7] Josephine, for her part, commented to the Emperor that the baby was 'beautiful and charming' while praying that he would not grow up to be 'a sulker like his father Louis'.[8]

There was little love lost between Josephine and the Bonaparte clan, whose members had been dismayed by the Emperor's marriage to the widow of General de Beauharnais. They had tried by all conceivable means to prevent the marriage of Louis to Hortense – even to the extent of spreading the rumour that the future bride had been impregnated by the Emperor himself. By the time young Louis was born, the couple, who had enjoyed only fleeting moments of marital happiness, were already estranged. This gave rise to further speculation about whether the King of Holland was indeed Louis's father – an inconclusive debate which would pursue the future Napoleon III for the rest of his life.[9]

After abdicating from the Dutch throne, a kingdom that he had ruled with some considerable eccentricity (Napoleon once wrote to him that he 'did not seem to understand anything about civil administration'[10]), Louis retreated to Italy, well away from his wife. He wrote to her: 'I am consoled by the thought that I am far away from you; we were absolutely not made for each other.'[11] His son was therefore brought up by Hortense, who spoke of her former husband as a 'sick lunatic',[12] a conclusion shared but more charitably expressed by Napoleon himself, who told Las Cases at Sainte-Hélène that 'the mind of Louis was naturally inclined towards the perverse and the bizarre. He was further spoiled by reading too much Jean-Jacques.'[13]

Along with a fondness for the works of Rousseau, the young Louis inherited some paternal character traits (most notably a penchant for melancholy) but his mother Hortense was the primary and most decisive influence on his personality and temperament. She did everything in her power to ensure that the young prince would grow up to be a different man from his father.

The bond between mother and son was passionate and exclusive; his letters to her as a child, as an adolescent, and even as a young man reveal the depth of his filial attachment. 'I love you and kiss you with all my heart' he wrote to Hortense in 1822, adding that he was calling her by the familiar 'tu' instead of the more formal 'vous' because 'to say "vous" to someone that one loves very tenderly is not very appropriate.'[14] Hortense's absences from their residences in Arenenberg and Augsburg were lamented by her son, who on one occasion wrote 'it is already twelve days that you are gone and it seems like an eternity.'[15] In 1833 Louis stated that his feelings for his mother were those of 'complete and utter devotion, nothing could ever replace or resemble them.'[16] Her love for him, too, was absolute; a sentiment reinforced by the fact that her older son Napoléon-Louis had been claimed by his father.

Hortense, however, did not merely dote on Louis. She taught her son from a very early age to think of himself as a man destined for great things; one of Louis's playmates later remembered that he was only twelve years old when he first declared to her that he would one day rule France – an idea the seed of which had clearly been planted by Hortense.[17] Many of his mother's maxims were scrupulously followed by Louis thoughout his political career. This was notably true of her inclusive but somewhat Machiavellian conception of Napoleonic politics: 'The role of the Bonapartes is to appear as the friends of everyone.'[18] In order to achieve this position, it was especially important to avoid being compromised; hence her advice to Louis about his public profile: 'Show yourself a little everywhere, but always be prudent and especially free, and show your hand openly only at the opportune moment'.[19]

Hortense's greatest contribution to Louis's intellectual formation was her choice of Philippe Le Bas as his private tutor in the summer of 1820, a few months after their installation at the castle of Arenenberg, in the Swiss canton of Thurgovia.[20] Le Bas, who was retained for the next seven years, was a former teacher at the Lycée Sainte-Barbe in Paris, and an austere republican, the son of a Robespierrist member of the Convention who committed suicide after the fall of the *incorruptible*. By picking him, Hortense went against the express wishes of her pious and conservative husband, who wanted his children brought up according to 'religious principles'.[21] Following in the wake of the King of Holland, conservative critics of Hortense have often attacked her decision to employ Le Bas as an unconscionable, irresponsible, almost irrational act.[22]

Yet Louis's mother knew exactly what she was doing: she wanted her son to receive not only a broad education in the sciences and the humanities – Le Bas was one of those self-taught republicans who knew everything – but also eagerly to embrace the culture of the modern age. Le Bas, 'cold and reserved in appearance and manner'[23] according to the prefect of Strasbourg who failed to get much out of him in 1825, was a stern tutor, but he established a warm rapport with his pupil, organizing parties for him during Hortense's absences.[24] A letter from Louis to his mother in 1821 stated that he was 'making every effort to work hard; indeed, I have behind me a friend and master, who gives me advice as a friend, and who knows when necessary to use the severity of a master.'[25]

Thanks his tutor, Louis acquired a broad education: he began to learn three languages (German, Italian, and English) and developed a great fondness for classical literature (from Homer and Plutarch to Shakespeare and Corneille) as well as an enduring fascination with mathematics, physics and chemistry. But Le Bas did not feel that his work was an unqualified success; by the mid-1820s – as Louis reached his teens – he was expressing frustration with his pupil's lack of application, at one point even complaining about his 'dissipated' character.[26]

But in overall terms Le Bas's influence was decisive; he not only taught Louis well, but also inculcated in him a sense of commitment to many of his own values, notably fidelity to family traditions, self-reliance, and a concern for the poor and needy. Louis readily gave away his clothes to peasants' children, and frequently interceded with his mother on behalf of servants experiencing material hardship. In 1822 he asked Hortense to give one Napoleonic war veteran, who had served in Arenenberg and was now on the point of retiring, sufficient funds to travel back to his family in Strasbourg. A year later he urged her not to dismiss a cook, who was seasonally employed, as she was the only source of income not only for her family but also for her invalid father.[27]

It was also with Le Bas that young Louis entered his first serious discussions about Napoleon, and more generally the imperial legacy. His tutor, like many republicans of his generation, profoundly admired the Emperor though he criticized his despotism.[28] Le Bas was by his pupil's side when news of the Emperor's death reached Augsburg in May 1821. As we have just seen, Louis was a highly sensitive teenager, and he cried a great deal. Le Bas excused his pupil from formal lessons for three days, but took the opportunity to expound at some length on the lessons – both personal and political – to be learnt from the heritage of the 'Great Man'[29] (Le Bas was intimately familiar with the *Mémorial de Sainte-Hélène*, and there is no doubt that he was the first to introduce Louis to this work).[30]

Throughout the 1820s Louis remained deeply immersed in Napoleonic culture. Many of his drawings represented Napoleonic subjects; one, entitled *The Faithful Eagle*, showed the bird with outstretched wings flying over the tomb of the Emperor.[31] Hortense, too, was a passionate devotee of the imperial cult; she told Valérie Masuyer that she owed everything to the Emperor: 'he has made my life.'[32] The drawing room in Arenenberg was decorated so as to replicate the Malmaison, and all over the castle there were portraits of Napoleon, as well as other members of the Bonaparte and Beauharnais families.[33] The anniversary of Napoleon's death was observed every year; in May 1829 Hortense and her son visited Madame Mère, Napoleon's mother, in Rome. The date was marked on this occasion by a family gathering.[34]

Hortense also regularly received visitors: conspirators against the Restoration (the former Queen was directly linked to several of the Bonapartist plots of the early 1820s in France); general enthusiasts and devotees of the Napoleonic cult (notably Alexandre Dumas); liberal figures such as Juliette Récamier; Italian and Polish patriots, who came to discuss the future of their oppressed nations; and former close associates of Napoleon such as Gourgaud.[35] In 1825, General Bertrand, the Emperor's loyal aide-de-camp, made the journey to Arenenberg, providing the young Louis with the opportunity of meeting the man (already a legend in his own right) who had 'closed the eyes of the Emperor at Sainte-Hélène'.[36]

Louis also read voraciously about Napoleon's life, and (like most young men around him) developed a fascination for Bonaparte's battles – spurred by former Napoleonic officer Denis Parquin, affectionately known because of his booming voice as the 'howling colonel'. After marrying Hortense's *lectrice*, Parquin settled in Switzerland in 1823 and devoted long hours recounting to the young prince the epic engagements in which he had participated (including the conspiracy of 1820); he would later take part in Louis's attempted coups in 1836 and 1840.[37] A letter to his father in 1827 indicated that Louis was perusing several works on the Emperor, notably General Foy's study on the Spanish war.[38] A few years later he was immersed in Napoleon's *Memoirs* (written at Saint-Helena), which inspired in him a sense of awe tinged with sorrow: 'The more I read him, the more I admire his universal genius, and the more I feel sad not only for France but also for the whole of humanity which has failed to appreciate him'.[39] Louis also made pilgrimages to Napoleonic battle sites; during a visit to Waterloo he was 'moved beyond words to see the place where the Emperor's star was for ever extinguished.'[40]

But Louis's real 'bible' was Las Cases's *Mémorial de Sainte-Hélène*. He had begun to read this work while at Arenenberg, and would memorize celebrated passages by heart; during his time at the Thoune military camp in 1829–30 he asked one of Hortense's assistants to send him extracts of 'all the parts relating to the art of war'.[41] Several years later Louis would still read out extracts of the *Mémorial* at Arenenberg; it appears that he had formed the intention of producing a popular edition of the work abridged for a mass audience.[42]

And yet the consequences of this private Napoleonic cult were somewhat double-edged for Louis. True, the Emperor was an inspiration; but the standards he had set as a political ruler, as a lawgiver, and as a military strategist were so high that Louis could not help feeling overwhelmed at times. Already in 1821 he had spoken of the Emperor's 'shadow', which constantly made him strive to be 'worthy of the great name of Napoleon'.[43] But this shadow could be oppressive, especially for a sensitive young man who had yet to make a name for himself. Hortense, exhibiting the prudence of a mother (and more than a slight touch of Bonapartist cynicism) had on one occasion told her son that a great advantage of bearing the name Napoleon was that 'others will break their necks for you'. Louis's response revealed the extent of his self-doubts, but also showed that Le Bas's insistence on the values of self-reliance and autonomy had not been lost upon his pupil:

> 'You speak of my name, unfortunately it is a burden when one cannot merit it through one's own actions, and it is not easy to be worthy of what it demands. It is natural that one should risk one's life to prove oneself but to have an illustrious name without being worthy of it is an obligation, and not a merit, and when one has failed to deserve such recognition then one has all the disagreements of an elevated position without enjoying any of its advantages.'[44]

Such was Louis Napoleon as he entered the age of manhood. Thanks to Hortense, and his tutor Le Bas, he was a cultivated young man who was deeply absorbed in the Napoleon cult; his conception of Bonapartism at this stage was dominated by romanticism.[45] Valérie Masuyer, who first met him upon taking up her position as *lectrice* in the autumn of 1830, when Louis was twenty-two, described him thus: 'He has curly blond hair, regular features, although somewhat strong for his figure, a good, sentimental, melancholic air, which captures attention.'[46] His favourite sport, as was fitting for a good *gentilhomme*, was hunting.[47]

Yet to be an object of passing interest for high society was not sufficient for Louis. He felt that he needed to project himself into the world, and to gain recognition through his deeds rather than merely through his name. 'Not to leave any trace of one's existence,' Napoleon had once said, 'is not to have existed.'[48] Events in France would soon enable Louis to make his mark.

The Making of a Bonapartist Pretender

'The tricolour flag is now flying in France; blessed are they who have restored it to its former glory. Ah, what a joy it is to be French! I hope that after this event we will be allowed to enjoy our rights as French citizens. How happy would I be to see French soldiers with the tricolour cockade!'[49]

News of the overthrow of the Bourbon regime in July 1830 filled Louis with joy, and only increased his yearning to set foot again in his native land, which he had not visited for nearly fifteen years. Ending as it did the rule of Napoleon's inveterate enemies, this political realignment raised hopes that the 1816 law that had banned all members of the Bonaparte clan from France would be repealed. Even more promisingly, the cult of Napoleon began to develop openly in France after 1830, and the energy it unleashed opened up new horizons for Napoleonic politics, most notably the possibility that the imperial pretender the Duc de Reichstadt could advance his claims to the French throne.[50]

Louis hoped that, taken together, all these factors would enable him to find a suitable position in his country. Events in France and elsewhere would have a significant and decisive impact on these hopes, alienating Louis both from the Bonaparte clan and the July Monarchy and setting him on a collision course with the new regime, while at the same time helping to shape his distinct brand of 'Bonapartism'. By 1835 it was clear that he had found his vocation: for better or worse, he would be a Napoleonic conspirator.

First blood was drawn in Italy. Divided into a plethora of states under Papal, Bourbon, and Austrian influence, this was a land rich not only in Napoleonic memories and traditions but also in aspirations for the future: the Emperor had been its ruler in the days of the First Empire. During the reign of Joachim Murat in Naples, Italian revolutionary nationalists had formed the *carbonari*, who had vowed to fight for the liberation of their country from foreign rule, and for its unification; after 1815, many members of the Bonaparte clan who had found refuge in Tuscany strongly sympathized with these views.

The former King of Holland, as we noted earlier, was not one of them, indeed, he was a Papist who brought up his son Napoléon-Louis (Louis's older brother) under strict religious principles. Napoléon-Louis showed his gratitude by becoming a *carbonaro* (and a Freemason), and when nationalist revolts broke out in several Italian towns in February 1831 he joined forces with the revolutionaries.

Although he did not himself join the secret society,[51] Louis also threw himself enthusiastically into battle; since the late 1820s he had considered Italy his 'second homeland', and was deeply committed to its 'national sentiment'.[52] Both brothers fought bravely in the insurrection which broke out in the province of Romagna, with Louis particularly distinguishing himself at the battle of Civita Castellana. However, under both family and international political pressure, the two Bonaparte princes were forced to withdraw from the fray.

Worse was to come: in March 1831, as the Austrian counter-attack swept back across the peninsula, Napoléon-Louis contracted measles and died. The same fate would no doubt have befallen Louis (also struck down by the same disease) had it not been for the providential intervention of Hortense, who arrived to whisk her son away from under the very noses of the Austrians.[53]

Still in disguise, mother and son then made their way into France – from which they were still officially banned – and reached Paris in April 1831. The journey was poignant, not least because although they were delighted to be back in France they were still grieving for Napoléon-Louis. During one stop they were moved to overhear a group of French officers lamenting his death and expressing concern about Louis's health. But although it proved relatively brief, their stay in France was decisive – notably in crystallizing Louis's view that no real compromise could be reached with Louis-Philippe's regime.

Hortense arranged a secret meeting with the King, which was cordial but inconclusive. The cautious monarch did not commit himself to allowing the Bonapartes back into France (indeed, the law banishing them would be repealed only in 1848). Furthermore, when faced with an offer from Louis to join the French army as an ordinary soldier, Louis-Philippe responded that this would only be possible if he were to abandon the name 'Bonaparte' and agree to be called the Duc de Saint-Leu (the title of his father). Informed of this humiliating counter-proposal by his mother, Louis responded vehemently: 'I would rather lie down in my brother's coffin!'[54]

Despite his illness Louis took the opportunity of his presence in Paris to establish his first links with republican political leaders; these ties would be maintained until 1848, both directly and through intermediaries.[55] From the very outset, Louis and the republicans shared a common critique of the principal failing of the July Monarchy: its absence of truly representative institutions. 'As long as universal suffrage is not one of the fundamental laws of the State,' wrote Louis subsequently, 'this so-called "national representation" will only be the representation of particular interests, the deputies will be mandated by only one class, and the Chamber will have neither dignity nor influence, it will merely rubber-stamp the arbitrary actions of a passionate and blind political authority.'[56]

This democratic, neo-republican inspiration, which very much reflected the political philosophy of Louis's tutor Le Bas, was expressed in a publication, *Rêveries politiques* (1832), in which Louis argued that the best system of government was that which combined strong individual leadership with representative institutions, freely chosen by the people.[57] This was to remain Louis's institutional philosophy; it overlapped with republicanism but was nonetheless distinct from it[58] – even though Louis's position was so close to that of the radical left that many Napoleonic (and indeed republican) writers before 1848 spoke of a 'fusion' of the two doctrines.[59]

Even more importantly, Hortense and Louis were able to observe from close quarters the remarkable vibrancy of the Napoleonic cult in France. As they went through Cannes they were shown the house in which the Emperor had spent the night after his landing from the Ile d'Elbe – proof, in their eyes, of the continuing strength of local imperial memories in the area.[60] In their house in Paris on the Rue de la Paix, Hortense and Louis received many Napoleonic associates and agitators; they also witnessed the extraordinary fervour surrounding the celebration of the anniversary of the Emperor's death on 5 May.[61] In front of the Vendôme Column, cohorts of republicans and Bonapartists clashed with the police as the commemoration turned into a demonstration of support for the Emperor's son the Duc de Reichstadt (referred to as Napoleon II by his French supporters).[62] Fearful that the presence of Louis and Hortense might provoke a wave of subversion against his government, Louis-Philippe ordered his 'guests' to be escorted forthwith to the French frontiers.

Louis drew three fundamental conclusions from these events. Firstly, for all his superficial commitment to France's imperial past, Louis-Philippe was fundamentally hostile to any genuine revival of Napoleonic politics. Secondly, the King's regime was highly vulnerable, especially to pressure from the streets. Finally, the name 'Napoleon' still possessed the power to capture the popular imagination in France. A few months after their departure from France Louis told Valérie Masuyer that if he had been well enough on 5 May, he would have joined the demonstrators on Place Vendôme and shouted 'Long Live Napoleon II!'

'What do you think would have happened then?' she asked him.

Louis replied without hesitation: 'Everyone would have followed me'.[63] This belief – laced with many illusions – in the transcendent power of the Napoleonic name would guide Louis's politics for the rest of the 1830s.

Louis's first steps as a French conspirator were taken almost immediately after his visit to Paris. Thanks to his contacts with republican leaders, maintained chiefly through Leonard Chodzko, Lafayette's Polish secretary, Louis was involved in the planning of a Bonapartist-republican insurrection in eastern France. It was to be carried out in November 1831, with the help of sympathetic elements from within the Army, and its aim was to proclaim Napoleon II the ruler of France.[64] Louis helped to fund the preparations, and kept himself ready to enter the conflict from Strasbourg if civil war were to break out. During these months he often cited Napoleon's maxim that 'anything can happen and one should be prepared for anything.'[65]

Unfortunately the French authorities found out about the conspiracy, which had to be aborted. But Louis was already beginning to establish a reputation for himself in liberal and republican circles. When Polish patriots launched an insurrection against Russian rule in late 1830, Louis was asked by leaders of the rebellion to lead an intervention force into the battle zone. The Polish uprising generated a tidal wave of support in France, especially in republican circles,[66] and it was hoped that the name of the 'great Napoleon' would help to galvanize Polish troops in their struggle against the Russians[67] (see

Figure 17). Louis did not feel able to accept (largely because of pressure from Hortense, still reeling in the aftermath of the Italian insurrection which had seen the death of her older son). But he demonstrated his practical support for the Poles by auctioning several Napoleonic objects in his possession, and donating the proceeds for the cause of Polish independence.[68] Like most other French people, Louis remained deeply moved by the plight of the Poles – 'so similar', as he put it 'to our own.'[69]

In the course of the next few years, Louis's standing in French political and intellectual circles continued to grow steadily. Chateaubriand, whose attitude towards Bonapartism had shifted considerably since his scurrilous pamphlet in 1814,[70] wrote to him in 1832 stressing that he was politically committed to the Bourbon pretender, but that if the latter were to fall off his horse he could not think of a more appropriate figure for 'the glory of France' than Louis Napoleon.[71]

A year later Louis met with the celebrated Lafayette, the hero of no fewer than three Revolutions (the American War of Independence, and the French Revolutions of 1789 and 1830). The venerable Marquis regretted the support he had given to the July Monarchy in its early years, and acknowledged that the regime had betrayed the liberal ideals of the 1830 Revolution. Most importantly, he also recognized that the Napoleonic name was the only 'truly popular' one in France, and promised his help to Louis if he were to need it.[72] (This offer must have been welcome, even though Louis knew of Lafayette's reputation as something of a political dilettante, promising assistance to many causes but not always following through.)

Louis also sent an emissary to the charismatic republican leader Armand Carrel, who was known for his great admiration of Napoleon – or, to be more precise, for Bonaparte. As from the early 1830s, and in marked contrast with the attitudes of many of his fellow republicans, Carrel lent his support to petitions calling for the repatriation of Napoleon's remains; his writings celebrated the memory not of the Emperor but of the First Consul: 'the valiant soldier and friend of the Revolution, the man with a passionate belief in the progress of civilization, in hard work and order, and above all in respect for the law.'[73] Carrel's response to the imperial pretender was

FIGURE 17

Faithful as a Pole

Along with Charlet, Denis Raffet was one of the great disseminators of Napoleonic images. This drawing celebrates the multiple links between the Napoleonic tradition and Poland: in 1807 Napoleon created the Duchy of Warsaw, the embryo of what Poles hoped would become a restored sovereign state. Many Poles (especially those in exile) regarded Napoleon as their liberator, and fought in the Grande Armée during the imperial wars. Between 1815 and 1830, many Poles living in France ardently supported the Napoleonic cause, and took part in conspiracies. In 1831, when the Poles launched an insurrection to liberate their nation from Russian rule, there was widespread support for their struggle in France – notably among republicans and Bonapartists. The 'fidelity' which Raffet celebrates is thus mutual: of the Poles for France, and of the French for Poland.

somewhat more guarded, declaring his appreciation for Louis's 'strong figure' and 'noble character', but adding: 'if this young man knows how to understand the new interests of France; if he knows how to leave aside his rights as a member of the imperial dynasty and only remembers the sovereignty of the people, he may well be called upon to play a great role.'[74]

Ironically for Louis, just as his star was rising, it was the Bonaparte clan who remained the greatest single obstacle to the fulfilment of his political ambitions. When the Emperor's son the Duc de Reichstadt died in July 1832, Louis could not help but feel that fate had dealt him a favourable hand; he had now become the most prominent member of the younger 'Napoleon' generation, with freedom to advance the Napoleonic cause in France using all available means (including the recourse to insurrection). But the elders did not see things in the same light. His father periodically warned Louis against any 'compromising' gestures; his letters also complained that his son seemed to be taking little notice of the advice.[75]

Hortense, partly out of fear for her beloved son's well-being, and partly as a matter of political temperament, did not welcome Louis's active involvement in conspiracies either. Already in 1830, after the July Revolution, they had openly disagreed. Louis had argued that 'our aim should be to associate ourselves, in some way, with everything that is happening in France.'[76] Hortense famously replied that he should keep out of 'scuffles', and that their safest bet was to keep their heads down, and hope that such 'responsible' behaviour would be rewarded by the Orleanists.

This conservative, *attentiste* policy was also embraced by Louis's uncles. While in London in 1831 Louis met Joseph, the former King of Naples and Spain, and the most senior member of the Bonaparte clan. A letter from Louis a few years later gave a flavour of how well the meeting had gone: 'You received me like a stranger, and not like your own nephew; with scheming intent, and without any warmth.'[77]

Like Napoleon's other brothers Lucien and Jérôme, Joseph was keen above all not to make waves, hoping (like Hortense) that an emollient approach on their part would be favourably received by Louis-Philippe. Joseph, as the head of the clan, also did not take very kindly to a young upstart intervening in the political arena without his authorization or approval. Louis, however, did not feel in any way obliged to the nominal head of the dynasty; he made his position clear in a letter to his former tutor the abbé Bertrand: 'I have no ties to this family, even though I am part of it.'[78]

In Louis's mind, his relatives' consensual strategy was not only supremely pusillanimous but also doomed to failure, and furthermore was progressively leading to the demise of Napoleonism as a political force. 'How could the French people remember us' he wrote bitterly to Hortense in 1834 'when we ourselves have done our very best for the past fifteen years to make ourselves forgotten! When for fifteen years the only goal of all the members of our family has been to avoid compromising themselves!'[79]

Such craven attitudes were not for him, and Louis thought them unworthy of the illustrious name he bore. In a letter to his father in 1833, it was also clear that his political strategy was being decisively shaped by his Napoleonic readings: 'I am trying to study the actions of the Emperor and to work out his noble intentions.'[80] Above all it revolted him that all those Army officers, politicians, and bureaucrats who owed their careers to Napoleon were now sitting back comfortably, doing nothing to promote the Bonapartist cause. This situation could not be allowed to endure: it was time to act.

The Napoleon Cult After 1830

As we noted earlier, Louis had seen first-hand evidence of the sheer force of the Napoleon cult during his visit to Paris in 1831. Also residing in the French capital at this time, the German poet Heinrich Heine (a liberal monarchist) left a memorable description of the popular adoration of the Emperor that he witnessed:

> 'It is hard for anyone outside France to imagine the extent to which the French people still idolize Napoleon. "Napoleon" is for the French a magical word which electrifies and dazzles them. A thousand cannons lie dormant in this name as much as in the Vendôme Column, and the Tuileries Palace will tremble if these thousand cannons are one day awakened. In the same way as the Jews do not pronounce the name of their God unless necessary, Napoleon is here rarely designated by his name; he is always called 'the man';

but his image is everywhere, in drawings, in plaster, in metal, in wooden shapes and in all situations. On the boulevards and on the crossroads stand a large number of speakers who celebrate the memory of 'the man', and popular singers who recall his exploits. Last night, passing through an obscure little street to return home, I saw a child, barely three years of age, sitting on the ground in front of a small illuminated tallow candle; he was mumbling a song to the glory of the great Emperor.'[81]

In the years that followed, this popular cult if anything intensified; now that the Restoration regime's injunctions had been lifted, Napoleon's image appeared everywhere. To the busts and small statues, drawings, plates, tobacco pouches, and smaller items of clothing of the 1815–30 period, which we encountered in Chapter 3, were now added Napoleonic wallpaper, clocks, watches, lamps, pottery, biscuits, cider bottles, glasses, fans, writing paper and envelopes, calendars, inkwells, and much else.[82] Memoirs of the First Empire, works of historical fiction such as Marco de Saint-Hilaire's *Souvenirs*, the drawings of Denis Raffet and Nicolas Charlet, and the images d'Epinal all popularized decisive episodes of the Napoleonic saga[83] (see Figure 18).

In many respects the Emperor became the object of a quasi-religious cult. This was illustrated in Bellangé's famous lithograph that shows a peasant gazing adoringly at a portrait of Napoleon above his mantelpiece, and telling his priest that the Emperor was 'the Eternal Father'. Intellectuals too shared in this messianism, with the Polish national poet Mickiewicz officiating as its high priest from the Collège de France.[84] In the artistic and literary spheres, Napoleon was no less ubiquitous: there were ninety plays glorifying the Emperor performed in Paris between 1830 and 1840,[85] while the writings of Balzac, Stendhal and Hugo, and the songs of Béranger all celebrated the memory of Napoleon the Great.[86] The main character in Stendhal's *Le rouge et le noir*, Julien Sorel, typified the young men of his generation who became devotees of the Napoleonic cult; all his thoughts, feelings, gestures, and ambitions developed under the shadow of the Emperor, and the *Mémorial de Sainte-Hélène* was 'the book he loved most of all'.[87]

It was also during the early 1830s that local 'sites of memory'

FIGURE 18

Reflection

Napoleon is shown here in pensive mood, on the eve of a battle (as suggested by the map on the table). In this drawing by Raffet, the candlelight symbolizes the Emperor's military genius, another common theme in the legend. Napoleon's extraordinary intellectual power is conveyed here, but also his solitude.

began to emerge all over France. All along the route of the 'flight of the eagle', locations where the Emperor had stopped were marked, remembered, and visited. In Grenoble the gates through which Napoleon had entered the town became a site of pilgrimage; in his memoirs Persat recalled spending his meagre savings on organizing a trip to the sacred location with a dozen elderly *grognards* (imperial veterans), all of whom 'wept as they touched with their hands these august relics'.[88] The inn at Golfe-Juan where Napoleon had stopped after his landing in March 1815, owned by a man named Jacomin, put up a bold sign: 'At my inn Napoleon had a rest; come here to drink and celebrate his name.' In 1838, Chateaubriand stopped by, soon to be followed by Victor Hugo. Pilgrimages of this kind became common.[89]

Private individuals too participated in these 'monumental' commemorations, which often took the form of Napoleonic inscriptions on the fronts of their homes.[90] A former imperial soldier named Louis Petit, who had joined the Grande Armée in 1812 and had been wounded at the battle of Ligny in June 1815, went one step further in his village of Saint-Riquier (Somme): he built his entire house in the shape of Napoleon's legendary hat.[91]

Strasbourg and Boulogne

As Louis observed and read about all this popular imperial fervour, and saw the July Monarchy's shameless attempts to ride on its coat-tails, he could not fail to notice that the cult lacked an organized political dimension. Balzac and Stendhal's novels and Béranger's songs undeniably helped to maintain the Napoleonic cult, but after 1830 these artistic creations did not automatically turn people into advocates of an imperial regime. Indeed, the major conspiracies of the early 1830s were all carried out by republicans; in 1834 Louis even began the journey to Lyons to take part in the insurrection which broke out there.[92]

In many respects, the republicans had assumed – or, to be more precise, had recaptured – the mantle of the Revolution which had been borne by the Bonapartists for much of the period between 1815 and 1830. In June 1832, at the funeral of the former Napoleonic General Lamarque in Paris, republicans and Bonapartists joined forces to demand greater political and social justice; the ensuing riots, which lasted two days, were brutally suppressed by the police.[93] In this general 'efflorescence of Napoleonism', the name of the Emperor was constantly invoked by all shades of republicanism.[94]

But the alliance was tactical, and not grounded in absolute trust on either side: many republicans – it was part of their political heritage – were instinctively defiant of 'the cult of superior men'.[95] As for Louis, he noted that for all their qualities of idealism and 'virility' the republicans were fatally divided and often undisciplined. And, as he remarked to Valérie Masuyer, they did not have two key constituencies with them, the Army and the people: 'both were Bonapartist'.[96]

From these perspectives, the rationale behind the Strasbourg and Boulogne *coups de force* was clear: to fire the 'thousand cannons' to which Heine had referred, in order to give a political expression to the widespread popular identification with the imperial past and to make the French people recognize Louis as the legitimate heir to the Napoleonic tradition.[97] For, in Louis's mind, the personal and the political were closely linked. In its law of April 1832, the July Monarchy had confirmed the proscription which banned the Bonaparte clan from France, and Louis realized that he could not promote the imperial cause in his native land without some form of political organization; and this, in turn, required his presence on French soil. Louis's attempts to overthrow the Orleanist regime were also direct challenges to his uncles, who had sought to appease the French government and thwart his political ambitions; his *coups de force* were almost as much directed at the supine and cravenly Napoleonic elders as against the Orleanist regime of Louis Philippe. Louis also sought to exploit the political vacuum created by the crushing of the republican movement, especially after the defeat of the 1834 insurrections and the ensuing 'monster trial' which effectively destroyed the republican networks in France's major cities and towns.

Above all, Louis's conspiracies were acts of faith; as he put it in a letter written in 1835, 'It is precisely because I appreciate full well all the obstacles my first steps in any career would encounter that I have taken as my principle only to follow the inspirations of my heart, of my reason, of my conscience.'[98] These 'inspirations' all pointed him towards one goal: the overthrow of the July Monarchy. Louis made two attempts at this, taking as his explicit model the 'flight of the eagle'.

The conspiracies were broadly similar in their design: Louis assembled a group of followers and attempted to take control of a garrison town with strong imperial traditions and memories (Strasbourg in October 1836, and Boulogne in August 1840). The plan was simple: to establish local control with the help of the military, to generate a wave of Bonapartist support within the Army and the wider public, and thereby to instigate a general movement which would rapidly lead to the fall of the government in Paris.

However, neither attempt even got off the ground. On both occasions the conspirators were arrested within hours: in Boulogne Louis shot a grenadier in the face, at which point all the conspirators panicked and fled, and were eventually fished out of the sea;[99] and at Strasbourg the extent of the debacle was summed up in the following exchange between Louis and a sergeant.

'Rally to me! I am the son of the Emperor!' shouted the imperial pretender excitedly as he accosted the junior officer.

'The Emperor's son is dead,' replied the sergeant stiffly, 'and I only know the King.'[100]

In the short run, the Strasbourg and Boulogne affairs brought nothing but disaster for Louis. Initially treated with leniency by Louis-Philippe, who put him on a ship to the United States, Louis was not so fortunate the second time: he was tried by the Cour des Pairs and sentenced to life imprisonment. The 1836 events took a serious toll on Hortense's health, and she died the following year – an 'irreparable loss' for Louis.[101] And, far from showing sympathy for his efforts to raise the family banner, the Bonaparte clan reacted with fury; the prize for familial rage went, not untypically, to Louis's father, who cut off his son's allowance and for a while refused to open his letters. After 1836 the French government even threatened the peaceful Swiss with war if they allowed Louis to remain on their territory, thereby forcing the prince into exile in London.

Above all, the conspiracies struck a blow at Louis's prestige within France; in the words of Maxime du Camp, a sardonic observer of the political vicissitudes of these years, the two plots were greeted with 'considerable hilarity'.[102] The French government added to Louis's humiliation by putting out the (false) claim that he had sobbed uncontrollably after his arrest in 1836; the general impression it sought to convey was that these Bonapartist plots had been poorly planned, inadequately executed, and completely lacking in popular sympathy.

It was of course beyond dispute that the conspiracies were carried out with (at times staggering) ineptitude. But the evidence with respect to organization and local support is far less incontrovertible. The July Monarchy had every incentive to play down the Strasbourg and Boulogne affairs, most notably for fear that the real extent of French military involvement in Louis's plans might be uncovered. It is now generally agreed that the Strasbourg coup was actually extremely well planned, enjoying deep and wide-ranging support among local military, civic, and political groups (including the republicans).[103] We also now know, thanks to the memoirs of the then Minister of the Interior, Rémusat, that the French government had successfully penetrated Louis's inner circle in London, and had found out about his plans to launch a second attempt in 1840.[104]

The full truth behind these stories will probably never be known; Louis had all the official files sent to him in 1848, after he became President of the Republic, and almost certainly destroyed some of the evidence.[105] But enough material has survived to indicate that both the Strasbourg and Boulogne affairs were serious conspiracies – much more so than believed by contemporaries.

Another key dimension of the conspiracies of 1836 and 1840 was their profound entrenchment in the Napoleonic legend. Both plots coincided with the zenith of the cult of Bonaparte in France, and their genesis and execution have much to reveal about the complex relationship which was being forged in Louis's mind between his own political destiny and the mythology of the imperial past.

The preparation and execution of both conspiracies revealed the extraordinary extent of Louis's faith – almost mimetic in its character – in the imperial legend. True, he did not present himself as an unreconstructed zealot for all things imperial. At his trial in 1840 Louis claimed that his intention in attempting to overthrow the July Monarchy was not to restore the Empire by authoritarian means but to organize a democratic consultation so that the French people could 'freely decide' whether they wished to be governed by a monarchy, a republic, or an Empire.[106] Indeed, his consistent emphasis on the principle of 'popular sovereignty' during the 1830s highlighted his rejection of both the despotic politics and the 'conquests' and 'universal wars' associated with the First Empire.

At the same time, though, Napoleonic institutions clearly remained his panacea: they provided the only form of government that could restore the 'majesty' of power, and bring to the people the 'dignity, order and prosperity' which they yearned for.[107] Louis also expressed the essence of this backward-looking vision in his declaration to his judges in 1840: 'I represent before you a principle, a cause, and a defeat: the principle is the sovereignty of the people; the cause is that of the Empire, the defeat, Waterloo.'[108]

It is therefore clear that, despite Louis's claims about turning away from the warlike traditions of the Napoleonic era, avenging the military humiliation of 1815 was a central underpinning of the conspiracies of 1836 and 1840. Indeed, there was a militarist flavour to both operations, with the Army being the privileged focus of Louis's attentions and utterances. He sought support and encouragement from military officers, not without success; during his preparations for the 1836 coup, Louis visited Baden, and slipped across the border into Strasbourg, where he met a group of French officers. He declared to them that the cause he was fighting for was the eagle, 'which represents, as in 1815, the rights of the people which have been ignored and the principle of national glory.' The speech, it appears, was enthusiastically received.[109]

The very choice of Strasbourg was also determined in part by the memories of the Napoleonic era: the 4th Artillery Regiment which was stationed there had been the one that had welcomed the Emperor back into Grenoble during the 'flight of the eagle'.[110] In the proclamations that Louis prepared for distribution in Strasbourg (another direct imitation of Napoleon's approach in 1815) he used an explicitly martial tone to appeal to the generation which had been shaped by the Hundred Days. In his message to the French people, he presented himself as a bearer of the 'sword of Austerlitz' in one hand and 'the testament of Napoleon' in the other. The July Monarchy's betrayal of the ideals of the 1830 Revolution were illustrated by its diplomatic capitulation to the Holy Alliance, most notably its abandonment of the causes of Polish and Italian independence.[111] In another message, Louis urged French soldiers to help deliver France from the 'traitors' who were governing it; he also promised to reintegrate the Army into the nation, wiping away the consequences of the affront of 1815.[112]

Past and Future

For the moment, Louis's grandiose messages failed to reach, let alone move, their intended audiences. In 1836, and again in 1840, his conspiracies fell miserably short of their aims, leaving him isolated and embittered. The Parisian Prefect of Police Delessert, who had already incarcerated the Napoleonic pretender after Strasbourg, found himself feeling sorry for the dishevelled Prince who was brought to him again in 1840: 'This unfortunate young man hardly looks like a conqueror, indeed he seems completely deprived of energy, and realizes that his presumption has led him into an absolute impasse.'[113]

'What have I done,' Louis somewhat disingenuously asked his father, 'to be the pariah of Europe and of my own family?'[114] The short answer was that he had failed. In 1840, as the whole of France solemnly greeted the return of the Emperor's remains, Louis was ignominiously holed up in the fortress of Ham – an austere fifteenth-century fortification situated in the Somme. Most of his countrymen seemed to have forgotten him; those who still remembered were beginning to be suspicious of a prince who, as one group of republicans noted, seemed to be 'nourished by the same thirst for ruling as our old tyrant'.[115] He consoled himself by composing some bad verses invoking the spirit of Napoleon, in which the Emperor was made to reply soothingly: 'You suffer for me, my friend, I am pleased with you.'[116]

The French people still worshipped Napoleon, but they did not want to return to the past; this much Louis understood. What he had underestimated, however, were the key differences between 1815 and the circumstances more than twenty years later. In 1840, there was no threat of a foreign invasion; public dissatisfaction with the Orleanists was nowhere near as great as it had been with the Bourbons; and the French Army was no longer ready to roll over at the mere mention of Napoleon's name.

Yet at another level things were not completely bleak for Louis. His endeavours had established his name in the public eye – a precious achievement, which he would build upon and consolidate during the 1840s. Police archives also suggest the existence of sympathizers, notably in Paris, where there was some conspiratorial activity of

'Buonapartist' groups during the summer months of 1840.[117] In September 1840, a mob waving a tricolour flag marched from the Rue Saint-Denis to the Place du Chatelet, chanting 'Long Live Reform! Long Live the Emperor Napoleon!'[118]

But incidents of this sort did not lead to very much, and they appear to have died down by the end of 1840. Most fundamentally, one of the lessons of Louis's failed coups had been that the existence of the cult of Napoleon was a necessary but not sufficient condition for the restoration of Bonapartist rule; the French people were not prepared to hand themselves over to a complete stranger. Thanks to his challenges to the Orleanist regime at Strasbourg and Boulogne, however, Louis had begun to establish himself as the principal living Napoleonic personage. Even his imprisonment in the fortress of Ham – which would last nearly six years – was beneficial; he too, like the Emperor, would be a martyr for the sacred cause.

Chapter 8

The Making of an Emperor

Among the conspirators sentenced for their role in the unsuccessful coup at Boulogne was Jean Gilbert Victor Fialin. Out of affectation, he had added the title 'de Persigny' to his name, and was thus known as Fialin de Persigny. In the summer of 1835 he had arrived at Arenenberg to offer his services to Louis, declaring grandly that he was 'not a member of the Bonapartist party but of the napoleonic religion'.[1] The son of a Napoleonic officer killed in action in 1812, Fialin had become an apostle of young Louis's cause, after a military career during which he had embraced *carbonaro* revolutionism under the influence of the republican leader Kersausie.

After his 'Napoleonic' conversion Fialin launched a new publication in 1834, *L'Occident Français*. It only had one issue. However, it compensated for the brevity of its existence by the sheer exaltation of the sentiments displayed by its editor. Echoing the discourse of the Saint-Simonians, the religious and philosophical cult which celebrated the advent of a new society based on progress and industry, the review's tone was millenarian:

'It seems that the great voice which came from the Orient to announce the arrival of the Messiah now proclaims to the Western world the vast political synthesis towards which we are each day advancing. Let us then grasp the Napoleonic Idea, put to the rack and executed on the rocks of Saint-Helena! In this imperial idea resides the tradition which has been sought after by the nineteenth century, the real social law of the modern world.'[2]

Immediately admitted into Louis's inner circle, Fialin de Persigny was to play a decisive role in the prince's life. More than any other single individual – more so, without doubt, than Louis himself – Persigny believed that France's redemption lay in the restoration of a Napoleonic regime, and he worked feverishly to achieve it; the restoration of the Second Empire in December 1852 was largely his work. He was, before that, one of the key organizers of the conspiracies of 1836 and 1840 (and later, as we shall see, of the 1851 *coup d'état*). He managed to escape after the Strasbourg debacle; however, he was captured at Boulogne, and his role in the conspiracy earned him a jail sentence of twenty years, from which he was delivered only by the 1848 Revolution.[3]

But arguably Fialin de Persigny's most important contribution was to impress upon Louis the need to develop and systematize his political thinking – to make, in short, the critical transition from 'Napoleonism' (the sentimental identification with the Emperor) to 'Bonapartism' (the belief in a political system governed by Napoleonic ideas and institutions). This chapter will explore how the prince successfully carried out this shift, which led to his election as President and eventually to his proclamation as the Emperor of France.

Napoleonic Ideas Revisited

De Persigny's conception of the imperial tradition came straight out of the *Mémorial de Sainte-Hélène*, which he read obsessively during the 1830s, as well as during his eight years of imprisonment between 1840 and 1848.[4] In the manner of Las Cases, he saw the Emperor as a lover of peace, a democrat, an emancipator of peoples, and above all a faithful embodiment of the principles of 1789.[5] As mentioned in the previous chapter, this was very much the orientation of Louis's own thinking in the 1830s, and this convergent appreciation of the

Napoleonic legacy no doubt helped to cement the rapport between the two men. At the same time, Fialin was (and would remain throughout his life) a strong devotee of the principle of 'authority', and he undoubtedly stiffened Louis's resolve in this respect. In addition to his passion for the First Empire, Fialin modelled his vision on the political and cultural achievements of the Romans; he often presented the Emperor Napoleon as a ruler who had been 'entirely Roman in his heart and in his mind'. Sharing with Louis his passion for the history of Julius Caesar and the reconstruction of the imperial heritage, he also imparted to the prince his loathing of Orleanist rule, which had turned France into a 'small, petit bourgeois society, lacking in ambition and in grandeur'.[6]

Fialin de Persigny's intellectual influence shone through the major work published by Louis Napoleon, *Des Idées Napoléoniennes*, written in London and first published in 1839. The book was a vigorous defence of the Napoleonic heritage, very much in the spirit of the *Mémorial*: it praised the Emperor as 'the messiah of new ideas'[7] (an echo of Napoleon's now famous self-description as the 'Messiah of the Revolution'[8]) and celebrated the First Empire as the regime that had prepared the ground for the enjoyment of liberty and equality in France.[9] Napoleon's power had rested upon the 'unlimited confidence' he enjoyed from his people; this bond with the masses would always remain at the heart of any Napoleonic political system.[10] There was a long section on Napoleon's political and administrative organization (another of Persigny's strong interests), whose foundation was democratic but whose apex was the principle of authority – an excellent synthesis which had stimulated 'capacities' and promoted merit on the basis of talent.[11]

What of Napoleon's wars? Louis repeated the Emperor's claim at Sainte-Hélène that he had never been the 'aggressor';[12] yet he also added that the wars of the Empire had been beneficial in the long run, provoking liberal and nationalist sentiments among the peoples of Europe – like the terrible floods of the Nile, which were initially devastating but left stretches of fertile land in their wake.[13] But the key message was that modern Napoleonic politics was not about war. In a passage which would be frequently repeated in later decades, *Des Idées Napoléoniennes* stated (again, the influence of de Persigny's Saint-Simonist readings was apparent here) that 'the Napoleonic idea is not one of war, but a social, industrial, commercial, and humanitarian idea'.[14] However great Napoleon's successes on the battlefield had been, they were not for the present age: indeed, the real ambition of Bonapartism was to achieve 'civil glory', which was both 'more lasting and more durable'.[15]

The central conclusion of the book, in sum, was that a future Napoleonic State would be democratic and progressive but not republican. This was arguably the strongest element of influence wielded by Persigny: unlike Louis's other writings of the 1830s, which praised the concept of liberty and had a strong 'republican' flavour, *Des Idées Napoléoniennes* had relatively little to say about political freedom and representative institutions. Liberty was actually defined from the outset as a personal disposition: Louis portrayed himself as a 'free man' precisely because he was not dependent upon any political organization or sect.[16] Likewise the evidence that the Emperor had not been an 'autocrat' was presented in individual, not collective terms: it was false to accuse Napoleon of despotism because he had never removed anyone from his post without first ordering an inquiry, and indeed had listened a great deal to the opinions of others.[17]

Alongside his contributions to *Des Idées Napoléoniennes*, which laid down the general principles of a democratic but authoritarian Bonapartism, Fialin also played an important role in fashioning the public image of the new Napoleonic pretender. In his *Lettres de Londres*, written in 1839 and published in France a year later, he drew an idealized portrait of the Prince, based on conversations with him and his inner circle during their London exile. The *Lettres* in many ways constituted a seminal work, marking a decisive shift towards an openly 'imperial' presentation of the Bonapartist project: the voice of the author was that of an 'old soldier of the Empire',[18] and the book launched Louis's very own 'imperial legend'. Copies of the *Lettres* were mailed to French officers, and distributed by Bonapartist agents in towns and military barracks, and many of its apocryphal tales would later be repeated and further embellished by Napoleonic propagandists.

France, Fialin de Persigny argued, was weary of sterile conflicts and contending political utopias: she was in search of 'practical ideas and a new faith, a new creed'. Louis Napoleon was the apostle of this millennium.[19] In the 1830s, Louis had often dwelled on his 'popular' characteristics; when he had spoken to French army officers during his furtive visit to Strasbourg, for example, he had stated that 'he had a name which could be of service, it was a plebeian name, as plebeian as France's past glory.'[20] In the *Lettres*, in contrast, the language was diametrically different: every effort was made to underscore the princely dimension of Louis's personality. His heart was 'noble',[21] and his demeanour 'dignified and composed';[22] he cherished the politics of honour,[23] and in his private life he was 'gallant' and 'chivalrous', throwing himself into a river to retrieve a flower which had blown out of the hair of a princess.[24] Above all, according to his physician Dr Conneau, Louis was 'a man who appreciated only the serious side of life';[25] this was a prince who – again, an obvious allusion to the great Bonaparte – had no time for the 'idle chatter' of politicians and parliamentarians.[26]

If his portrait of the individual was more than slightly touched up, Fialin de Persigny's account of Louis's place in the Napoleonic tradition was completely mythologized. The Bonaparte family, he asserted without blinking, 'has always been perfectly united'[27] (at the time this was written, Louis was barely on speaking terms with his father, and had effectively been repudiated by his uncles). Although Louis freely admitted in private to having no memories of Napoleon or his childhood in Paris prior to 1815, de Persigny constructed several Aesopian fables about the encounters between the uncle and his young nephew. The one which would be most frequently cited in later years was his account of a discussion before the Emperor's departure for Waterloo in 1815, when Louis (then an eight-year-old) apparently urged Napoleon to be allowed to accompany him to the battlefield.[28] Louis even claimed to 'remember' that, as he sat on the Emperor's knee on that occasion, he had 'felt one of his tears land on his forehead'.[29]

The point here, of course, was to present and legitimize Louis as the exclusive heir to the Napoleonic throne. Such was de Persigny's artistic creativity that he even managed to find physical resemblances between the nephew and his uncle: the similarity was remarkable 'to any soldier of the Old Guard', and indeed to any observer: 'It is impossible not to be struck, as before the bust of the emperor, by the imposing dignity of this Roman profile, whose lines are so pure and solemn.'[30] The prince also shared many of Napoleon's personal qualities: 'tireless physically as well as morally, austere, hard-working, the nephew of the Emperor is a real Roman of the Republic.'[31] And if Napoleon had been a modern Julius Caesar, his nephew would fully assume his heritage and become an 'Augustus', the unifier of his nation and the scourge of its corruption and decay. More than a decade before its advent, de Persigny predicted that Louis would restore the Empire.[32]

Thanks to the active help of his accomplice, Louis had largely initiated the intellectual transition from Napoleonism to Bonapartism by the time he entered the fortress of Ham to serve his life sentence in 1840. He assumed much of the legacy of the First Empire, while reneging on the bellicosity and political despotism (which he tended to dismiss anyway). A Bonapartist State would be 'democratic' at its base in that its institutions would be legitimized by mass suffrage; at its summit, however, it would be governed by the principle of 'authority' – a concept whose salience was if anything reinforced through the influence of de Persigny.

This was as far as Louis's political thinking extended, and it is interesting that in all the time he spent incarcerated (nearly six years) he devoted no further attention to major political questions. He proffered bland generalities in occasional articles he wrote in local newspapers such as the *Progrès du Pas-de-Calais*; the two major publications during his time at Ham were a three-volume study of artillery[33] and the short pamphlet entitled *L'extinction du paupérisme* (1844), in which the Prince developed a series of proposals for advancing the economic conditions of workers, most notably through the formation of associations and the creation of military-style agricultural colonies. Although the major underlying influence of the pamphlet was Saint-Simonian, this work earned Louis much attention among socialists and republicans, many of whom believed that the prince had converted to their cause; the pamphlet was to prove especially helpful in 1848 in helping to attract Louis's working-class support.[34]

The only occasion on which Louis returned to the political fray was in 1843, when he vigorously defended Napoleon's legacy against a fierce attack by Lamartine. It was almost as if Louis was rehearsing his central arguments for his own seizure of power in 1851. A dictatorship, he replied to the republican leader (who had denounced

Napoleon's seizure of power in 1799), was a 'necessity not an example which can be converted into a principle';[35] such a dictatorship was justified when the regime it replaced was corrupt and decadent (as had been the case with the republican Directory). Napoleon's rule had brought back order and economic prosperity to France, and healed the wounds opened by the 1789 Revolution.[36]

The Emperor had made mistakes, Louis conceded, but 'what would always distinguish him in the eyes of the masses was that he was the king of the people, while the others were monarchs of the aristocracy and the privileged classes'.[37] As he languished in his cell in Ham, Louis could only hope that one day he too would become the king of the people; his only consolation, as he wrote to his cousin, was that he could still feel 'the shadow of the Emperor protecting me and giving me his blessing'.[38]

From Representative of the People to President

On May 26 1846 the prefects of all French departments received an urgent memorandum from the Minister of the Interior concerning the escape from prison of an important detainee; the 'strictest orders' to find and arrest the fugitive were to be given. His physical description was as follows: '37 years old, height 1m. 66, light brown hair and eyebrows, small grey eyes, big nose, average mouth, brown beard, blond moustache, pointed chin, oval face, pale complexion, head pressed into his shoulders, wide shoulders, stooped back, thick lips.'[39]

By the time local officials received this message, Louis – for it was he – was already well on his way to London. His colourful escape from the fortress, carrying a plank on his shoulder and disguised as a worker (he had also shaved off his moustache) set the stage for the events of 1848, the *annus mirabilis* in the Prince's life.[40] It would start with his election as a French deputy, and then as the first President of the newly founded Second Republic in December 1848.

Neither outcome was even remotely predictable at the time. A police report from Paris in May 1846 noted that Louis's escape from Ham 'had provoked no effect whatsoever on the population'.[41] And, in contrast with the 1830 Revolution, there was no significant

'Napoleonic' contribution to the overthrow of the Orleanist monarchy in 1848.[42] Louis was still in exile in London, and there was no organized 'Bonapartist' political force in France at the time – even though police reports indicated that Louis had established close links with republican exiles in the British capital.[43]

The prince rushed to Paris at the end of February 1848 to volunteer his services to the new republican government, which politely but firmly declined the offer.[44] But the magic of his name still worked wonders. In May he announced his candidature for the new Legislative Assembly, which (under the new system agreed by the Republic) was to be elected by male universal suffrage. Although he campaigned very little in person he was triumphantly elected in four constituencies. His political platform began by referring to his attempts at Strasbourg and Boulogne, for which he took full responsibility. His ideological pitch was decidedly inclusive: he expressed support for the Republic and its principle of popular sovereignty, and stressed his commitment to social justice and economic prosperity: his six specific pledges included the 'amelioration of the fate of working people', the 'extinction of poverty through work' (a reference to his 1844 pamphlet), and the 'respect for people and property'; he also pressed for greater French support for the peoples of Italy and Poland.[45]

After the republican Assembly threatened to invalidate his election, Louis was forced to resign his seat almost immediately. However, he stood again in September and this time was returned by five constituencies (and he topped the list in the Seine). Soon after Louis had taken his seat, the Assembly decided that Presidential elections would be held in December: after a relatively brief campaign, Louis was elected, trouncing his main opponent, the conservative republican leader Cavaignac. The newly elected President could now savour his victory over the political elites who had earlier ridiculed him: Louis had been endorsed by 5.4 million voters, as against the 1.4 million who had supported Cavaignac. The left-wing republican Ledru-Rollin, who had famously called Louis an 'imbecile', had received 370,000 votes.[46]

How had a man who had been back in France for barely three months, and who had been politically unknown in February 1848, achieved such a staggering victory over his rivals? Louis's triumph was typically explained in one of two ways. Firstly, it was seen as an expression of the 'political irrationality' of the masses: credulous and uneducated, and faced with a list of candidates they knew little or nothing about, the peasants – the majority of the French population – voted massively for Louis because of his name, and the glorious memories that it evoked.[47]

According to another line of interpretation, the electorate voted for a conservative saviour, a man who would protect their property and prevent France from falling into anarchy and chaos; this fear was heightened by the workers' insurrection of June 1848, which was savagely repressed.[48]

The two explanations were somewhat inconsistent with each other: the first implied that peasants were dim-witted and gullible, while the second suggested that they were driven by self-interest and fear. Karl Marx, who closely followed the events in France during these years, later sought to square the circle when he represented the Bonaparte dynasty as the embodiment of 'the peasant's superstition, not his enlightenment; his prejudice, not his judgement; his past, not his future'.[49]

These approaches were oversimplistic. There were, it is true, many instances of rural Frenchmen voting for Louis because they thought he was the Emperor resurrected. ('There is a good reason' a peasant told a dumbfounded Mérimée 'why we called HIM Malmort.'[50]). And there is little doubt that the workers' revolt of the summer of 1848, during the terrible 'June Days', created real apprehension among the more conservative and traditional sections of French society.

But Louis's appeal to the peasantry expressed something much more fundamental: like Napoleon before him, he symbolized the Revolutionary principle of equality, and the proletarian defiance of the old aristocracy. There were many instances of the local aristocracy being caught completely unawares by the strength of this sentiment. In the autumn of 1848 the Duc de Luynes, a wealthy landowner, called an electoral meeting in his locality before the presidential contest to promote the candidacy of Cavaignac. The peasant audience cheered politely, and the local notable believed the result was a foregone conclusion. When the votes were declared, Cavaignac had received only one ballot: the Duc's. Everyone else had voted for Louis.[51]

The Prince's success in December 1848 was also a function of his superiority and strategic advantage in three overlapping areas: the effectiveness of his propaganda, the breadth of his ideological appeal, and above all his capacity to tap into the Napoleonic legend while at the same time offering a renewed and 'modern' version of Bonapartism. Between May and December 1848, drawing from the traditions of the 1820s and 1830s, Napoleonic supporters all over France inundated the country with propaganda objects. Boxes of matches, portraits, medals bearing Louis's image, figures of imperial eagles with red ribbons, brochures, songs and almanacs were distributed in French towns and villages, drawing voters' attention to Louis's name and celebrating his contribution to the defence of the Republic. A popular Napoleonic song stated that 'I am a firm republican, and I give it to you for sure: we need a Napoleon to support the nation.'[52]

This oral political culture was especially successful in disseminating the Bonapartist message in the deep countryside – precisely those parts of France to which the republicans made little effort to reach out. A popular lithograph released in November 1848 entitled *The Universal Vote* represented the French people gathered around a statue of Bonaparte: a clever play on the meaning of 'universal suffrage', here represented as the general will of the French people for a return to the Napoleonic tradition.[53]

But Louis Napoleon's name was also very popular in the towns in 1848; contemporary observers stressed his support among veterans and soldiers, domestic servants, workers and artisans.[54] An electoral proclamation urging the Parisian electorate to support Louis was signed by a man describing himself as 'an old republican of 1792, a soldier at Waterloo and a worker who fought on the barricades in February [1848]'.[55] In these urban areas, in addition to the propaganda objects mentioned above, the Prince was able to rely on a range of newspapers. These publications were aimed at a mass audience, and were extremely cheap. (In fact, they were often distributed free.) But the role of the press was not decisive; in 1848 Cavaignac had nearly twice as many newspapers supporting him as did Louis Napoleon, and yet he still lost heavily.[56] However, Bonapartist newspapers offer significant evidence of the ideological range and diversity of Louis's political support in 1848. In his summer legislative campaign the Prince had newspapers which were conservative (notably *La*

Constitution, whose motto was 'Liberty, Order, Union, Force), republican (*Le Napoléon Républicain*, whose programme was the 'abolition of poverty') and socialist (*L'Organisation du Travail*, which sought to rally Louis's working-class support).[57]

Perhaps the most important publication was *Le Petit Caporal*, which remained in print throughout the summer and autumn of 1848, and supported Louis both in his legislative and presidential campaigns. This paper had a large readership (30,000) and was edited by Marco de Sainte-Hilaire, the author of several classic works on the Napoleon cult. Its political message was simple: 'Napoleon without despotism.' It supported Louis because he was the candidate who sought to transcend political and partisan divisions and work for 'the good of France'.[58] It rejected class and occupational divisions between bourgeois and worker, soldier and citizen, and took as its model Bonaparte the consul, rather than Napoleon the Emperor.[59]

While *Le Petit Caporal* celebrated French national glory, its tone consciously eschewed any form of 'militarism', which it regarded as ridiculous and counter-productive.[60] Endorsing Louis's candidature for the Presidency, Marco de Sainte-Hilaire redefined the 'sword of Austerlitz', which Louis had brandished during his conspiracies, to mean social peace, civil equality, and order.[61] Arguably, it was this revised version of 'popular' Bonapartism – democratic, middle-of-the-road, progressive, and non-partisan – which played most strongly among the literate classes during Louis's campaigns of 1848.

Through oral and written material, and through propaganda objects, the Napoleon cult too played a significant – in all probability, decisive – role throughout the period leading up to Louis's Presidential victory in December. *Le Petit Caporal* provided a good example of this process. Alongside its political and informative functions, it also devoted much space to the celebration of the imperial legend, running stories about key episodes in Napoleon's political and military career, and celebrating the anniversary of 15 August. Its slogan ('The Newspaper of the Young and Old Guard') also appealed directly to the Napoleonic veterans – an enormous political constituency in 1848. Many issues also offered famous Napoleon quotations, such as 'the first casualty of every revolution is individual happiness' – an apposite motto for the troubled times of 1848.[62]

But the emphasis in most of this propagandistic literature was again on the 'liberal' legend: newspapers repeatedly referred to Napoleon as 'the Emperor of Peace', committed to social order, civil harmony, and economic prosperity rather than war and military expansion. This re-creation of the imperial image was stretched to its absolute limits by the *Napoléon Républicain*, which declared that the Emperor's only dream had been that 'the worker be happy and earn six francs a day'.[63]

A booklet aimed at a popular audience, published shortly after Louis declared his candidature for the presidency, dwelled on the heritage of the First Empire at length. Written up in the form of citations from the *Mémorial*, it celebrated Napoleon as a 'popular' Emperor, committed to France's glory and prosperity, but hostile to war; his real and lasting achievements were his Civil Code and especially the 'vast administrative and financial system' he had created, which still provided the foundations of the modern French State.[64] Although Louis was not mentioned explicitly the book was clearly published under his auspices; indeed it was suffused with the messianism of de Persigny, notably in its conclusion that the Empire was not merely something from the past, but also a model for the future.[65]

But the Napoleon cult was not the exclusive preserve of Bonapartists, nor of republicans, nor indeed of any particular class or social group; in 1848 'a majority of the French population partook in it'.[66] Between 1841 and 1848, alongside the flourishing secular cult, there had been a marked revival in the association of Napoleon's name and image with Christianity.[67] The presidential outcome was, if anything, overdetermined; with his cold analytical lucidity Guizot expressed the point succinctly: 'It is much' he said of Louis's victory of December 1848, 'to be all at once a national glory, a revolutionary guarantee, and a principle of authority.'[68] The issue was whether, and on what terms, the 'Prince-President' would be able to reconcile these different principles, and the varying political constituencies they represented.

From Prince-President to Emperor

Even to his allies and sympathizers, Louis remained something of a mystery after his election to the Presidency. Victor Hugo, still an energetic Bonapartist in 1848, emerged in late December from a dinner at the Elysée Palace wondering about the sheer plasticity of France's new ruler:

'As I left the Palace I started to reflect. I thought about the sudden installation, the improvised protocol, the mixture of bourgeois, republican and imperial motifs, the appearance of this profound thing which we now call the President of the Republic, his entourage, his personality, and the whole train of events. It is not one of the least curious aspects of the situation that we have here a man who can be variously addressed, at the same time and from all sides, as prince, highness, monsieur, monsignor, and citizen. Every event is leaving its mark, in a higgledy-piggledy way, on this all-purpose personality.'[69]

Louis's opaqueness (which was deliberate; he had remembered his mother's advice) was variously interpreted (see Figure 19). His opponents tended to dismiss it as an obvious sign of his intellectual mediocrity. Thiers called him a 'cretin', and the Comte d'Haussonville a 'Bonaparte of the funfairs'.[70] Others regarded him from the outset as a scheming conspirator, who was simply biding his time to prepare for the violent overthrow of the Second Republic; this Machiavellianism was seen as an inevitable consequence of his perverse 'Napoleonic' heritage. On the day of his installation as President, National Assembly President Armand Marrast told a colleague: 'We are all screwed! He knows the extraordinary power of his name. He understands his potential, and everything that he can achieve, he will.'[71]

The prediction would be realized, but things were not so simple. Louis's Presidency would be marked by growing social tensions and political conflict, notably between the new President and the National Assembly, both elected by male universal suffrage, and would end with his infamous anti-republican *coup d'état* of December 1851, the prelude to the restoration of the Empire a year later. But there was no linear relationship between his intentions in 1848 and the outcome of 1852. The political context changed rapidly in France during this period, requiring Louis to adjust his strategy and tactics. And as we have already noted, the prince was much more politically sophisticated

FIGURE 19

Prince Louis Napoleon Bonaparte

In this drawing, probably made shortly before the Prince's return to France in 1848, Louis Napoleon projects the image that many people would take away after meeting him: an alert and intellectually able man, yet also one who did not fully reveal himself. He had remembered his mother Hortense's advice: 'Show your hand openly only at the opportune moment.' This enigmatic side to his appearance and character would become further accentuated with time, and would soon lead to his nickname of 'the Sphinx'.

than his opponents gave him credit for, and he had skilfully amended his image (and the Napoleonic heritage) in crucial areas in order to develop and maintain his popular support across the country.

But all of this notwithstanding, Bonapartism was deservedly pilloried by posterity for the violent and illegal means that it deployed to achieve Louis's political goals in 1851–2. In his defence, it could only be said that he carried out his coup with some reluctance; and that the recourse to political violence was a widespread feature of mid-nineteenth-century French political culture, and by no means the exclusive preserve of the 'Napoleonic' tradition.

The basic political objectives of the 'Prince-President' after December 1848 were relatively straightforward: 'Security first, then improvements. Bring together all the old parties, reunite and reconcile them, such must be the goal of our efforts.'[72] In a message to the National Assembly in 1849 Louis declared that 'the name of Napoleon is itself a programme: it signifies, domestically, order, authority, religion, popular welfare; externally, national dignity.'[73] This was a quintessentially Napoleonic approach, seeking to transcend political differences through the personal appeal of the ruler. The key constituency to be won over were the republicans, the most active and dynamic political force in France, whose national leaders had vehemently opposed Louis's Presidential candidacy (even though a significant proportion of republican voters had supported him); indeed, Louis at this stage considered himself much closer politically to the republican forces of 'movement' than to the conservative forces of 'order'. He asked the republican leader Lamartine to form a government, but the poet – heavily defeated in the presidential elections – did not respond to the overture, a defiant posture shared by all his republican colleagues.[74]

Rebuffed by the left, the Prince-President had no option except to turn to the forces of 'order'; but while the conservatives were happy to work with him it became rapidly clear that they regarded him as a purely decorative figure, to be used and eventually discarded when he had served his purpose. Louis's problems were compounded by the provisions enacted by the Assembly when it established the Presidency: the incumbent's term of office was limited to four years, and he was not allowed to stand for re-election. (see Figure 20).

From the outset, then, Louis was constrained both by political and constitutional factors, and the issue of his re-election weighed especially heavily on his relationship with the national political elites. The President's assertion and projection of his power was a slow and uneven process, mediated by the shifting balance of forces in France between 1849 and 1851. In Paris, he was at first completely isolated: he had no political party of his own, and relied heavily on his inner circle (dominated by the loyal, hyperactive, and ever-scheming de Persigny). The President initially exercised little control even over the government, except in respect of the appointment of the Prime Minister. However, by October 1849 Louis was able to form a ministry made up largely of his own nominees; it included the likes of Rouher, Fould, and Magne, all of whom were to play a leading role under the Second Empire.

Equally difficult was Louis's relationship with the Army. The Republic had relied on the military to suppress the insurrection of June 1848, and in the presidential elections a majority of officers had voted for Cavaignac. The Army elite was by no means Napoleonic, and its political influence was not negligible; by the summer of 1850 Louis's relationship with Changarnier, the head of the National Guard had seriously deteriorated, and there was even talk of Changarnier leading a military coup against the President. Louis resolved the crisis in January 1851 by dismissing the conspirator.[75] But the major conflict opposed the President to the National Assembly. Louis tried to negotiate a constitutional revision that would allow him to stand for re-election in 1852, but the conservative majority returned in the May 1849 elections was not willing to compromise. In July 1851 a vote to amend the Constitution was carried by a significant majority (446 to 278), but not by the three-quarters needed: a moral victory for Louis, but a political defeat.[76]

A *coup d'état* now seemed the only way out of the impasse. Plots and threats of the use of force were common among all mainstream political forces under the Second Republic, especially in the increasingly polarized atmosphere that followed the 1849 elections: the Orleanists, the leading conservative group in the Assembly, fearful of what their leader Thiers described as the 'vile multitude' carried out a 'legal' coup in 1850 by voting for a new electoral law which excluded more than a third of the voters (mostly workers) from the franchise, and their leaders frequently spoke of overthrowing the President.[77]

FIGURE 20

Manifesto of Louis-Napoleon Bonaparte to the electors

A proclamation of Louis Napoleon before the Presidential elections of December 1848, which would see his triumphant election. The message here plays on the themes of continuity and change. On the one hand, Louis celebrates his Napoleonic lineage: the poem in the centre of the manifesto is entitled 'The shadow of the Emperor presents him to the people of France'. But his proclamation also makes clear that, if elected, his policies would be very different from those of Napoleon: he would respect the wishes of the people, and defend the institutions of the Republic; he also committed himself to a peaceful foreign policy.

One promise made here would come back to haunt Louis Napoleon. According to the Constitution, the President was to be elected for a single four-year term, and could not be reappointed. Louis gave a solemn undertaking: 'I hereby pledge my word of honour that I will, after four years, relinquish power to my successor, and leave in his hands a stronger State, and all public liberties intact.' This was not quite how things turned out in 1851–2 . . .

By 1851, another critical factor was pushing the Prince-President towards confrontation: the increasing political strength of the radical republicans, the 'démoc-soc'. Their vote increased dramatically in 1849, and many of these republicans were also members of secret societies which openly threatened the country with civil strife in 1852.

Largely to break out from his political isolation in Paris, Louis developed the practice of touring the provinces, where he carefully pitched his messages to suit local temperaments. (On 30 July 1849 he denounced the 'cult of war' in royalist and Catholic Nantes; the very next day at republican and Napoleonic Saumur he celebrated France's 'military spirit'[78].) During these provincial tours Louis sounded out public opinion, and generally cultivated his image as a national leader transcending partisan divisions. He also used his speeches to appeal directly for political support against the Paris elites – a strategy which proved extremely fruitful; by the summer of 1851 it was clear that his political support among the traditional Napoleonic constituency, the peasantry, had hardened.[79] Indeed, whenever he visited the provinces, the cry was rarely 'Long Live the President!' but rather 'Long Live Napoleon!'[80] (see Figure 21).

Louis seems to have reached his final decision to carry out his coup in the summer of 1851. Among the key instigators was de Persigny, still the arch-conspirator, who had been pushing in this direction for some time, as well as the clever, hedonistic and amoral Morny, an off-spring of Hortense's relationship with Flahaut; Louis only discovered that he had this half-brother after his mother's death.[81] The date was carefully chosen by Louis himself: 2 December, the anniversary of both the crowning of Napoleon in 1804 and the battle of Austerlitz a year later. On that morning, the people in the capital awoke to discover new decrees announcing the dissolution of the Assembly, the institution of a state of siege in the Parisian military region, and the restoration of universal suffrage. The last measure demonstrated the extent to which the coup was initially directed primarily against the conservative majority in the Assembly – a fact which perhaps explains the relatively limited popular resistance in Paris.

However, the character of 2 December was fundamentally trans-formed by the vigorous fight put up by the republicans in the provinces. Serious revolts broke out in twenty-seven departments of the centre and the Midi, and the repression was savage: around

FIGURE 21

Louis Napoleon receiving deputies from the provinces

This image, representing the 'Prince-President' in animated discussion with elected representatives, draws attention to one of the major power bases of Louis Napoleon during the Second Republic: provincial (and especially rural) voters. The President is portrayed inspiring respect (and even deference) among the deputies, and the image symbolizes his capacity for leadership and his sense of purpose. Louis's left hand, pointing to the Vendôme Column, the monument to the triumphs of the imperial wars, represents the political continuity with France's Napoleonic past.

27,000 people were arrested and swiftly sentenced by *Commissions Mixtes* instituted by the regime.[82] The atmosphere of terror unleashed by the authorities had certainly not been planned by Louis (although we do not know for sure; there is almost no record of what he said or did at the Elysée during the days immediately following the coup). But its effects were to prove lasting – not least in the enduring hatred that his actions would nurture in republican memory. The provincial violence, and the manner of its containment, also had an important political consequence. By the time these popular rebellions were put down, the nature of Louis's coup had been fundamentally transformed: it had now become a conservative exercise in 'order' restoration.[83]

The restoration of the Empire came a year later in November 1852, in a plebiscite which was enthusiastically supported by 7.8 million voters, with only 253,000 negative votes (and two million abstentions).[84] But even this crowning of the Napoleonic legend was not a foregone conclusion after the *coup d'état*; the early signs were that Louis wanted to keep the republican form of government, which was 'reassuring' to the public.[85] Several factors pushed him to take the final plunge: the pressure of de Persigny, now his Minister of the Interior, who complained of the President's 'timidity'[86] and used his position systematically to mobilize national and local opinion in favour of the return of a Napoleonic State;[87] the spontaneous and increasingly insistent calls from the Bonapartist grass roots, which urged the President to revert to the Empire and celebrated its return triumphantly;[88] and also Louis's own observations during his trips to the provinces in the summer and autumn of 1852, where he saw that there was genuine public support for this change.[89]

But perhaps Louis's deepest reason for the restoration of the Empire was personal. He had been dismayed by the violence that had accompanied his coup, and he remained haunted by it for the rest of his life. In a telling proclamation after the December 1851 plebiscite, which overwhelmingly endorsed his coup, he had declared that this popular vote had 'absolved' him of his earlier actions – a clear public acknowledgement of his inner torment. The Empire, with its glorious memories, ceremonial trappings, and festive endeavours was a way for the people, but above all for their ruler, to exorcise those terrible memories of December 1851.

The Nephew and his Uncle

By the end of 1852, Louis had achieved what he had first set out to accomplish sixteen years earlier in the Strasbourg 'scuffle': a Napoleonic regime properly and comprehensively endorsed by universal suffrage. As one of his admirers later recognized, his early life had been 'stranger than fiction';[90] his route to power had been long and arduous, and as late as the summer of 1846, as he languished in his cell in the fortress of Ham, it must all have seemed hopeless. But he had remained unbending in his commitment, and his letters between 1840 and 1846 demonstrate that he never lost his underlying belief in his *fortuna*.

From an individual perspective, it is hard not be impressed by his resilience. Lesser men would have been broken, but Louis kept the faith – thanks to his extraordinary determination, largely inherited from his mother Hortense and also nurtured by his tutor Le Bas (who nonetheless strongly disapproved of the 1851 coup).[91] He did so despite repeated failure, despite years of imprisonment and political isolation, and despite his almost complete repudiation by the Bonaparte clan. Like Napoleon, though, Louis was never one to bear grudges, and with the restoration of the Empire he installed the good-timer Jérôme, now aged seventy-eight, as Senator, Marshal of France, and Governor of the Invalides, with an official residence in the Palais-Royal and a large annual public endowment. This deluge of luxuries gave such a fillip to Napoleon's youngest brother that he lived on until 1860. After 1848 Louis maintained his popularity in the country and survived further obstacles and ambushes: the institutional hostility of the Assembly; categorical political rejection by the republicans; attempts by the forces of 'order' to sideline him; and even an assortment of civilian and military conspiracies.

Louis was of course fortunate in many respects. By establishing an institution directly elected by universal suffrage in a country whose political culture was still predominantly oral and deeply committed to the memory of the great Napoleon, his opponents handed him the Presidency on a platter, enabling Louis to re-emerge from the political wilderness in 1848. In the election of December that year his name was universally known, unlike those of all of his opponents;

many voters, for example, thought that the moderate republican candidate Lamartine was a woman ('La Martine').[92]

Perhaps Louis's greatest piece of luck was that throughout the years of the Second Republic his conservative and republican adversaries hated each other more than they disliked, let alone feared, him. But it is undeniable that none of his successes would have been possible if the portrait painted by his adversaries of a weak and indecisive mediocrity had been even remotely accurate. In fact, with the benefit of hindsight, one might argue that he played an almost flawless hand: the Strasbourg and Boulogne conspiracies of 1836 and 1840, while they were setbacks in the short run, enabled Louis to establish himself as the legitimate imperial pretender; his political writings further developed this image while at the same time distancing Bonapartism from the more bellicose aspects of the Napoleonic tradition; and even his carefully cultivated ambivalences after 1848 allowed Louis to present himself to the electorate as a leader who stood above parties and worked for 'the good of France'.

However admirable his qualities and achievements, though, Louis's political reputation remained bedevilled by the December 1851 coup, which hung around his neck like an albatross. He tried to explain it away, blaming others for using excessive force, invoking the Napoleonic principle of 'necessity', and coining artful formulae such as 'I abandoned legality only in order to restore what was right.'[93] He also did his best to mitigate the terrible effects of the repression, notably by sending officials to review the sentences passed on the hoof by the *Commissions Mixtes*, by granting hundreds of amnesties and pardons, and even by entertaining individual requests from his former republican acquaintances; George Sand memorably described a visit to the Elysée in January 1852 when the President tearfully held her hands and promised to free anyone she wanted.[94]

Louis remained defensive about 2 December throughout the Second Empire, and it is significant that the regime never celebrated this date as its political anniversary, preferring instead to honour the birth of Napoleon on 15 August, the 'Saint-Napoleon'; a saint is always useful when a mortal sin needs covering up. In truth, however, even though it offended his sensitive nature as an individual, the coup was entirely congruent with Louis's political trajectory and indeed with the Napoleonic tradition as it developed after 1815.

Fighting alongside the *carbonari* in Italy, and repeatedly plotting to overthrow Louis-Philippe, Louis was simply following the path taken by Napoleonic conspirators of the Restoration, who had relentlessly struggled against the Bourbons and contributed to their downfall.

Louis was a 'child of political romanticism';[95] he belonged to a progressive political generation which had been shaped and fortified by the political struggles of the 1820s and 1830s, and was immersed in what might be called its 'culture of the underground'. It was a brave, noble-spirited, and idealistic generation, but also one that regarded 'bourgeois' rule and the trappings of parliamentary democracy with considerable contempt – a sentiment which was often even more pronounced on the republican left and among the Saint-Simonians.[96]

It should not be forgotten, in this context, that these republican groups were also deeply involved in conspiratorial activity between 1830 and 1851. Perhaps the only major difference between these radical conspirators and their Bonapartist counterparts (and more than occasional comrades) was that the latter were more successful in consolidating their gains. If the December 1851 coup, carried out initially against a conservative and reactionary Assembly and with the promise of restoring universal suffrage, had failed in Paris, and Louis and his accomplices had been massacred in the Elysée courtyard, who can doubt that France would today be full of monuments honouring the 'Prince-President' as one of the fallen soldiers in the battle to establish the modern democratic Republic?

What, finally, of Louis's relationship with the history of his uncle the Emperor and with the Napoleonic legend in a wider context? A comparison of the paths to power taken by Bonaparte and his nephew before they acceded to their imperial thrones suggests some similarities. 'The people recognized as sovereign, here is the key to the enigma, the secret of imperial power': so spoke the republican Félix Pyat, a resolute enemy of Bonapartism who nonetheless recognized its success in hunting on republican lands.[97] Like Napoleon, Louis sought to cultivate the image of a national leader and 'popular sovereign' who transcended partisan differences – this was, and indeed remains to this day, the defining political principle of Bonapartism. Both men also had a broadly similar philosophical outlook: they believed in the Revolutionary principles of civil equality, progress,

and social change, in the instrumental value of religion, in the necessity of State power to transform society, and above all in the value
of the 'nation', that supreme political community in whose name
every political action had to be justified and legitimized. Both men
also seized power under similar circumstances, pushing aside a decay-
ing Republic in order to rally the French people to a new vision of
'order' that would seek to reconcile antagonistic groups, classes, and
factions.

And yet this is perhaps where real differences between the two
men begin to emerge. Napoleon, without doubt, was welcomed as a
genuine saviour, as a solution to a problem that was not of his own
making. Even his worst enemies could not hold General Bonaparte
accountable for the catastrophic state of France in the late 1790s,
whereas Louis, as President of the Republic between 1848 and 1851,
was fundamentally implicated in, and therefore at least partly responsible for, the 'anarchy' his coup sought to redress. This perhaps
explains the very different historical 'memories' of 1799 and 1851:
Napoleon's legend never really suffered much damage because of
his coup, whereas the reverse was the case for Louis. His image in
France remains associated, even today, with the *coup d'état* that
brought down the Second Republic.

Overall, the differences between Napoleon and Louis outweighed
the similarities. While he was an intelligent man, and arguably more
politically astute than his impetuous uncle, Louis obviously lacked
Napoleon's sheer, radiant, overpowering brilliance. (In fairness, the
Prince only ever claimed to be the follower of the Emperor, not his
successor.) Furthermore, the Bonaparte family played a crucial role in
Napoleon's rise to power: without Lucien's steadying hand on the 18
Brumaire, the coup would almost certainly have failed; whereas the
clan did nothing but impede Louis's ascent during the 1830s and
1840s. Napoleon's reputation, based largely on his military prowess,
was already established by the time he took power, whereas Louis had
yet to achieve anything in the political domain in 1848 – and this was
still essentially true in 1851.

Napoleon, it could be argued, achieved most of his truly great
political and institutional transformations before he became
Emperor; Louis, in contrast, had to wait to assume the imperial
mantle before truly making his mark as a political leader, notably by

fundamentally changing his country's social and economic landscape. The Empire, in short, was Napoleon's reward for what he had already done; for Louis, it was an incentive to act.

Most crucially, Napoleon had already begun to create his own legend in 1799 – notably by creatively rewriting key episodes of his life and military career; Louis, in contrast, was largely the beneficiary of his uncle's reputation. As Furet put it, Louis was the 'child of the Napoleonic legend'.[98] He did, of course, amend this heritage in significant ways, particularly by insisting that his version of Bonapartism was not despotic and warlike. The ends were the same, but the means were to be different. The Emperor had flattened any opposition that lay in his path, both on the battle-field and in the political arena; Louis had wanted to do things differently, to take the people along with him, *all* the people, and to unite them despite their partisan differences. He especially hoped to take the republicans along with him, as had Napoleon; after all (in contrast with the Emperor) did Louis not share much of their political philosophy?

And yet this was where circumstances, and the irony of life, dealt Louis the most cruel blow. He did eventually achieve supreme and absolute power in 1852, but only at the cost of alienating the republicans, and by using those very Napoleonic methods – deceit, violence, the recourse to illegality – that he had hoped to leave behind for ever. His uncle's legend carried him to power, but with a vicious sting in its tail.

Chapter 9

Warriors of Peace

In September 1852 Prince-President Louis Napoleon paid an official visit to the department of the Isère. Hardened Napoleonic enthusiasts since the beginning of the Hundred Days, the people in this region had overwhelmingly supported his *coup d'état* in December 1851, and they were about to vote for the restoration of the Empire with similar gusto. As he arrived in the Saint-Marcellin area, throngs of well-wishers turned out to greet the nephew of Napoleon. Streets and homes were decorated with flags, banners, and arcs-de-triomphe, and some citizens even erected small chapels in his honour, as if for a religious celebration. Evidently, the cult of the imperial tradition was flourishing here.[1]

To mark the occasion, a popular rally was organized in Grenoble, where municipal delegations from each commune were invited to meet the President. In his desire to prepare public opinion for the restoration of the Empire, the head of State had specifically asked that all survivors of the Grande Armée (Napoleon's legendary fighting force) should be invited to join the processions; and to symbolize the 'Napoleonic' character of the event, the banner of each commune should be borne (wherever possible) by the most robust veteran of his locality.[2]

On the day of the rally there was indeed a large turnout of

Napoleonic veterans, who came from all over the department. In many senses these old warriors effectively stole the show. The crowds could easily pick them out, since they wore the distinctive insignia of the Society of the Old Army of which they were all members – a small medal of the Emperor Napoleon hanging on a tricolour ribbon. Some were carrying imperial memorabilia, such as small plaster statues of Bonaparte and wooden replicas of the Vendôme column. Many had also brought out their old uniforms, somewhat tattered but all the more evocative of the epic battles that they had waged.

Especially striking were the enthusiastic reactions of the public to the presence of these veterans. There was a powerful sense of national patriotism generated by these living symbols of the great imperial wars, which had brought so much 'glory' to the French nation. But the sight of these men and their uniforms also produced strong sentiments of more local pride. The military regiments based in Grenoble had fought bravely in 1814, and again in 1815, to resist the Allied invasion of France; these episodes, whose commemoration had been a central feature of popular opposition to the Bourbons under the Restoration, were still vivid in the collective memory of the local populations.[3] Most remarkable of all was the extent to which individual veterans were known to their peers: as he stood watching the procession, the sub-prefect of Saint-Marcellin was shown a former captain of artillery, 'more than seventy years old, but marching with an almost juvenile gait, who had been with the Emperor Napoleon during the Egyptian campaign'.[4] This officer was Captain Faure, one of the eminent citizens of Vienne and something of a local celebrity.[5]

On the eve of the establishment of the Second Empire, this moment captured the depth and potency of Napoleonic political culture in mid-nineteenth-century France, with its popular cult of the Emperor and his nephew, its rich memories of the imperial wars, and their complex historical connotations at local levels. This three-cornered relationship between State authorities, Napoleonic veterans, and the French people will be the subject of this chapter. Its central argument is that (contrary to received wisdom)[6] the Napoleonic legend remained a potent force in France after 1851, principally through the vigorous public roles played by the veterans of the imperial wars.

These old combatants performed important political functions. As Louis Napoleon sought to consolidate his power after his *coup d'état*, he consciously drew upon elements of the imperial myth to legitimize his rule. Already strong in 1852, his relationship with the surviving warriors of the Grande Armée would be further developed in subsequent years, culminating in the establishment of a new State decoration, the Médaille de Sainte-Hélène. This award helped the regime to mobilize public support, especially in rural parts of France.

Lastly, the narratives of the imperial veterans will shed a revealing light upon their retrospective characterization of the Napoleonic era, and in particular their cult of the Emperor. Why did these soldiers, 'the obscure, the small men, the rank-and-file' in the words of Edmond Rostand, the very men who experienced nothing but hardship during the Napoleonic campaigns, nonetheless continue to celebrate the Emperor's memory? And to what extent did their representations of their commander change over time? Here, among the very soldiers who had accompanied him across Europe, will be underscored one of the key transformations of Napoleon's 'legendary' image in the course of the nineteenth century: from warrior and conqueror to lawmaker and bearer of peace.

Creators of the Legend

At the end of the Napoleonic wars it is estimated that around 1.1 million soldiers returned to their homes in France.[7] Discharged in large numbers in 1815, and often persecuted when they sought to re-enter civilian life, the former soldiers and officers of the Grande Armée were generally treated as pariahs by the Restoration authorities. During the 'White Terror' of the summer and autumn of 1815, Napoleonic veterans were persecuted, humiliated, and in some instances murdered.[8] And as the royalist regime sought to consolidate its authority, its hostility to these former imperial elements hardened. The reason was simple: as a local official put it in 1821, the strongest support for the Napoleonic cause came from 'rural inhabitants and former soldiers'[9] – two groups which of course often overlapped.

After 1815, Napoleonic veterans were the primary contributors to the imperial 'legend'; and they were also at the vanguard of the political battle against the Restoration. They were invariably the first in line on all the major 'fronts' mentioned in earlier chapters: the production and dissemination of 'seditious' objects, the propagation of rumours, and the organization of national conspiracies and local rebellions. Ritually denounced in official reports of the Restoration era, their participation in dissident activities was extensive, including most notably spreading false information; engaging in intimidating behaviour; distributing Napoleonic songs; celebrating imperial anniversaries; and expressing public support for the Emperor (or, in the later years of the Restoration, his son the Duc de Reichstadt). Former soldiers (and their wives) also participated actively in these anti-royalist manifestations; they were disproportionately represented among those fined and imprisoned by the Restoration for shouting 'Long Live the Emperor!'[10]

Taken as a group, the imperial veterans of the Restoration era stood out in four particular respects: in their absolute and unqualified loyalty to the cause and memory of Napoleon, whom they venerated as a god (so much so that they often recited prayers in his honour, drawn from the imperial catechism);[11] in their repeated and vehement proclamations of nationalism, expressed in their support for the 'three national colours' which had been spurned by the Bourbons; in the precariousness of their material conditions (reports often highlighted the extreme poverty in which they lived, a condition shared by former officers and soldiers alike[12]); and in the culture of violence in which they revelled – symbolic and verbal violence against the supporters of the royalist order, particularly the aristocracy and the clergy, and commemorative pride in the most bellicose aspects of the Napoleonic era. For these men, the Napoleonic legend was almost exclusively concerned with military glory: the Emperor, as a popular imperial song put it, was a 'messiah' who had successfully 'set fire to the Danube and ignited the Rhine'.[13]

After 1830, the public image of the imperial veterans underwent something of a transformation. Although their material conditions did not change substantially, their active role in the propagation of the Napoleonic 'legend' earned them a privileged position in artistic and literary representations of the Napoleonic cult. Notable examples include the paintings of Horace Vernet and the lithography of Fesneau, *Souvenirs et reconnaissance*, which showed an old soldier seated at his table gazing at a small statue of the Emperor by his window.[14] The drawings of Raffet idealized the Napoleonic fighter, endowing him with the qualities of stoicism and bravery that were so central to the legend; these images also celebrated Napoleon's popularity among ordinary soldiers (see Figure 22).

The other key sentiment attributed to the veterans in these artistic representations was sorrow – bitterness, even – at their callous treatment by their fellow citizens. The imperial war veteran Goguelat, one of the leading characters in Balzac's *Médecin de Campagne* (which saw seven editions between 1833 and 1846), commented wistfully on the fate of all his comrades after 1815: 'France is crushed, the soldier is nothing, he is robbed of his just deserts, and packed off home to be replaced by aristocrats who cannot even walk.'[15]

With this 'cultural' rehabilitation of the former soldiers came the first stage of their return into the public sphere through the establishment of Napoleonic veterans' societies, which began to flourish in Paris and in many parts of provincial France – notably, as we have seen, in the Isère – during the 1840s.[16] The voices of these soldiers were also relayed in the *Revue de l'Empire* (1842–8), which was edited in Paris by Charles Temblaire and often carried short pieces by eyewitnesses and participants in various Napoleonic campaigns. The first issue also noted more soberly that time was already beginning to run out for many veterans: 'the old soldiers of the former army are disappearing every day before us.'[17]

For all these men, the climax of this period was marked by the ceremonies of December 1840, which saw the return of their beloved Emperor's remains to France. Veterans were the largest single contributors to a subscription to raise funds for a monument to Bonaparte, launched by the newspaper *Le Siècle*.[18] When Napoleon's remains were brought back, veterans appeared at every stage of the journey from Normandy to Paris, often wearing their old uniforms. This was a particularly poignant moment for them, kindling sentiments of patriotism and pride and also intense emotion at the sight of the procession which brought back the 'ruler of the universe'.[19] And although the imperial veterans were present at the Invalides, they were refused the right to be represented in the official procession – an exclusion which typified the July Monarchy's ambivalences towards the Napoleonic cult.[20]

FIGURE 22

'Sire, you can rely on us as much as on the Old Guard.'

A characteristic representation by Raffet of Napoleon on his way to the battlefield. Here the Emperor is riding alongside the Young Guard, made up largely of younger conscripts who express their loyalty and devotion to the imperial cause. Images of this kind celebrated Napoleon's closeness to his soldiers, as well as the patriotism and bravery of the Grande Armée; they also appealed to the nationalistic sentiments of many French men and women who longed for 'revenge' after Napoleon's defeat in 1815. Especially during the period between 1815 and 1848, this sentiment was an important component of the mindset of the veterans.

In the years that followed the 1840 ceremonies, relations between the Orleanist authorities and the imperial warriors deteriorated still further; many local veterans' associations were (rightly) suspected of providing a cover for anti-government activity. A Saint-Napoléon society, based in Lille, was dissolved in 1841 for 'subversion'.[21] After several clashes with the government (partly provoked by their support for the plight of Louis Napoleon), the members of the main veterans' association in Paris, the *Société Philanthropique des Débris de l'Armée Impériale*, were even banned in 1845 by the Prefect of Police from wearing their military uniforms in public. This decision provoked strong criticism in the liberal and republican press[22] (see Figure 23).

At the time of the 1848 Revolution, this veneration of the Napoleonic soldier had become deeply entrenched in the collective French consciousness, strengthened by the contributions of writers and artists but above all by the 'oral traditions' of the numerous families who numbered in their midst one or more members of the Grande Armée. There were numerous examples of the social and political importance of what might be called this 'veteran culture' within French families: the celebration of specific imperial battles, the naming of children (not only men; a generation of women were called 'Napoléonie'), and the singing of songs about imperial soldiers. Nor was this merely a 'private' culture: in the 1848 elections, many candidates drew attention, in their manifestos, to the military service of their fathers in the Napoleonic wars, and the persecutions suffered by their families in 1815.[23]

In the late 1840s and early 1850s, veterans remained the most active disseminators of the Napoleonic legend.[24] Perhaps the most celebrated memoir produced by an imperial veteran, Captain Jean-Roch Coignet's *Cahiers*, was first published in Auxerre in 1851. Coignet, who joined the French Army in 1779, had borne arms with Napoleon in Italy, been incorporated in the Guard, and had then accompanied the Emperor at Austerlitz, Iena, Friedland, Eylau, and Wagram. Later he had campaigned in Russia and Saxony, and finally had fought at Waterloo. This remarkable survivor played a major role in propagating the Napoleonic myth in his native Yonne between 1815 and 1848.

Like Coignet, a significant number of former imperial soldiers all over France kept the Napoleonic flame burning in their localities,

FIGURE 23

*The veterans of the First Empire gathered before the Vendôme Column,
on the occasion of the anniversary of the death of Napoleon.*

After the Revolution of July 1830, veterans of Napoleon's Grande Armée developed
the habit of gathering every year at the foot of the Vendôme Column in Paris on 5
May – especially after 1832, when a statue of Napoleon was placed above the
column. After 1840, these gatherings gave rise to increasing tensions with the
Orleanist government, which eventually banned the veterans from wearing their old
uniforms in public – a decision that caused great resentment among Napoleon's old
soldiers.

notably through formal and informal societies.[25] Many campaigned actively for Louis Napoleon's election to the Presidency, and celebrated him as the worthy inheritor of the imperial political tradition.[26] Yet the political values of these former participants in the imperial epic were essentially rooted in the past. A proclamation from a group of veterans expressly called on all former soldiers to vote for Louis Napoleon 'as a gesture of protest against the treaties of 1815, against Waterloo, against the prison of Sainte-Hélène, and against all the injustices and persecutions which have befallen the brave soldiers of the Grande Armée.'[27]

It could be argued that Louis Napoleon's victory, in this context, was little more than a specific instance of a wider cultural trait, which gave civic recognition and political affirmation to any individual whose close relative had served the imperial cause on the battlefields between 1799 and 1815. In this sense, even though they were not directly honoured by French governments after 1830, the veterans had become objects of quasi-universal communal admiration and social respect; the stage was set for their public recognition by the Second Empire.

A New Imperial Decoration

By the late 1840s and early 1850s, there were still over four hundred thousand survivors of the imperial wars in France. They were scattered all over the national territory, and their social and economic conditions varied enormously, with some living in absolute poverty. But a considerable number had successfully returned into civilian life, becoming – for example – schoolteachers, artisans, innkeepers, and smallholders.[28] Invariably, these men were known and respected figures in their local communities, and these positions would be further enhanced by the Second Empire's decision to award them an official decoration.

Emperor Louis Napoleon (or, as he became known after 1852, Napoleon III) created the distinction of the Médaille de Sainte-Hélène in August 1857.[29] It was to be awarded to all those, of both French and foreign nationality, who had fought under the French national flag during the Revolutionary and imperial wars. The commemorative medal was made of bronze, and was to be worn at the buttonhole, suspended by a green and red ribbon. One side depicted the likeness of the Emperor, and the other carried the inscription 'Campaigns from 1792 to 1815 – To His Companions of Glory, His Final Thought, 9 May 1821.'[30] This was a reference to Napoleon's testament, in which he had bequeathed half his private estate to the surviving soldiers who had served under the Revolution and Empire; this clause had never been executed.[31] It has been estimated that 390,000 veterans were still alive in 1857 to receive their medals[32] – a remarkably high figure, which is partly explained by the relative youth of the recruits of the Grande Armée in the final campaigns of the First Empire.[33]

Why did Napoleon III establish the award? Its ostensible purpose was to honour the many surviving veterans of the French Armies of the Napoleonic era, to help identify those among them who were in need of material assistance and support, and (in the words of a poem written to celebrate the new medal) to 'console these warriors for decades of suffering'.[34]

But there were also deeper symbolic and political dimensions at work. Louis Napoleon was obsessed with the legitimation of his lineage: with the Médaille de Sainte-Hélène the Second Empire sought, by celebrating its links with the founder of the imperial dynasty, to exorcize the regime's 'illegitimate' origins in the 1851 *coup d'état*. Napoleon III also hoped to use these awards to create a 'popular aristocracy', and demonstrate that his regime remained true to the Bonapartist ideal of a society in which talent and merit could be recognized irrespective of wealth or social origin. The Second Empire had already initiated the practice of awarding the Legion of Honour to mayors of small rural communes; the Médaille de Sainte-Hélène was from this point of view an extension of the process of 'democratizing' the honours system.[35]

The processing of individual claims, the verification of entitlements, and the issuing of the medals began in earnest in the autumn of 1857.[36] It was a huge operation, involving the entire French state bureaucracy at the national, departmental, and communal levels. On the whole, the operation proceeded very satisfactorily, with officials making every effort to track down those former combatants who were living in their localities.[37] The longevity of some of these survivors was literally miraculous: few would have held up much

hope for the soldier who was discharged in 1802 after being diag-
nosed with 'general weakness and chronic chest pains, with manifest
symptoms of pulmonary phtisis.'[38] Yet this gallant veteran was still
there in 1857 to receive his medal; there were many others like him
all over France.

But it should not be imagined that all the former servicemen were
in a state of physical decrepitude. The records held in departmental
archives across France attest to the remarkable experiences and continuing vitality of many recipients of the Médailles. Consider the
example of Pierre Nollet, who came from the village of Saudrupt in
the Meuse. In April 1813 he joined the Army and was immediately
assigned to serve as courier for Napoleon. He performed this task for
over a year, during which he was on the front line of several key battles in the French campaign.[39] Although in his early seventies by
1858, Nollet was still in good health and received his medal enthusiastically. And what of former corporal Augustin Aubertin, born in
1778, who saw active service between 1798 and 1812, during which
he fought for over twelve years? Aubertin did battle in the Italian and
Spanish campaigns, and sustained two injuries, one at a skirmish in
the Tyrol in April 1798 and the other at the battle of Albuéra in May
1811. In his eightieth year in 1858, he was still in excellent health and
greatly looked forward to receiving his medal.[40] These individual
stories reflected the remarkable odds which these former military
servicemen had overcome in order to receive these awards, four or
five decades after the conclusion of the Napoleonic wars[41] (see
Figures 24, 25, and 26).

The bureaucratic procedures involved did not go smoothly everywhere. The process of vetting candidates and delivering the medals
also give rise to problems, especially among those imperial veterans
who had no documents to confirm their years of service. Take the
case of André Poupon, a textile worker from Lyons. Poupon's was a
tale of fortitude and misery in equal measure. Having enlisted as a
volunteer in June 1807, he had fought in the campaigns of Wagram
(1809), Holland (1810), Russia (1812), and Belfort (1815). During the
Russian campaign he was captured and sent to Siberia, where he was
interned for eighteen months; he developed rheumatic pains that
plagued him for the rest of his life. Sent back to France through an
exchange of prisoners in 1814, Poupon was discharged, but – being

Last survivors of the Grande Armée

Blind survivor of the Grande Armée 1858

FIGURES 24, 25 AND 26

These three drawings vividly capture the physical appearance of Napoleonic veterans under the Second Empire, at the time of the establishment of the Médaille de Sainte-Hélène (each veteran is here shown wearing his medal). It is estimated that around 390,000 survivors of the Grande Armée received their decorations from the imperial State in 1858, during the celebrations of the national festivity of 15 August, the Saint-Napoleon. Through their central role in these ceremonies, the veterans helped not only to broaden the popular appeal of the Second Empire but also to perpetuate the Napoleonic legend.

a passionate Bonapartist – he enlisted again during the Hundred Days. His body took a severe battering during his eight years of active service: his right arm was pierced by a Cossack lance at Smolensk, his feet froze during the retreat from Moscow, and a Prussian sabre cracked open his head at Belfort.

And yet this was not the end of André Poupon's troubles. Destitute and miserable, he spent the entire Restoration period in abject poverty. The Bourbons, as noted earlier, had nothing to offer the veterans of an army whose commander-in-chief they had so bitterly opposed. All attempts by local officials in the 1820s to draw attention to the plight of former soldiers of Napoleon's forces fell on deaf ears in Paris.[42] After the change of regime in 1830, Poupon sent a petition to the Duc d'Orléans asking him for a state pension, attaching all his military-service documents. His request found no favour, and his papers were never returned. Two further decades of deprivation followed. Louis Philippe's regime was eager to exploit the Bonapartist legend to its own advantage, as we have seen, but it showed little interest in the fate of the Emperor's loyal foot soldiers.

In 1850, under the Second Republic, Poupon again petitioned the prefect of the Rhône for help, stressing his old age, material destitution and poor health. Still he received no reply. Three years later – by now the Second Empire had been proclaimed, and Poupon's hopes were high – he tried the Ministry of War. This time he received a letter back, informing him that he was not eligible for any state support as he had been officially classified as a deserter. This bureaucratic mistake (for it was one – his was an extremely common name) caused Poupon to fall seriously ill. Finally, still lacking any documents to prove his membership of the Grande Armée, he appealed in 1857 directly to Napoleon III. Moved by his plight, the Emperor seems to have ruled in his favour.[43]

Similar dramas unfolded all across France, not always with the eventually positive result that Poupon's repeated and impassioned pleas received. Thomas Aubert, a prison warden, found his application turned down because his discharge papers were issued collectively to a group of around thirty soldiers at the chaotic end of the 1815 campaign. Despite the award of the medal to many of his companions in the same regiment, several of whom vouched for him, his pleas remained unanswered.[44] Others, such as Marie-Antoine

Lardet, a textile worker, could not produce their discharge papers because they were destroyed in the 'wretched invasion of 1815'[45] – a reminder that many servicemen returned to their villages at the end of the Napoleonic wars only to face more hardship and misery.

Local officials sometimes weighed in on behalf of disappointed applicants. The mayor of St Lager was 'painfully affected' to learn that none of the ten applicants from his commune had been granted their medals. He appealed to the sub-prefect to have their cases re-examined, stressing that it was of 'public notoriety' in his commune that all these men had served in the Grande Armée.[46]

The Award Ceremonies

The continuing vitality of the Napoleonic legend came into clear focus in the 1850s and 1860s during the official festivities of the Bonapartist regime. The imperial veterans were officially incorporated into the ceremonial order of the Second Empire from the very outset. The old soldiers notably performed a central role in the national festivity of the Saint-Napoléon, celebrated on 15 August.[47] This was already the case well before the institution of the Médaille de Sainte-Hélène – for example, in Paris, where the former soldiers were assembled outside the Madeleine Church in 1852 and provided a guard of honour for the head of State;[48] and also at Sainte-Claude in 1852,[49] La Châtre in 1853,[50] and Carcassonne in 1854.[51]

What were the political allegiances of the veterans? Were they all enthusiastic devotees of the Bonapartist regime after 1851, as the official propaganda of the Second Empire implied? In a very small number of cases, there is evidence of imperial veterans refusing to take part in the festivities because of their 'opposition to the government'[52] – a reminder that many of those who had fought for Napoleon (especially during the Hundred Days) were not necessarily Bonapartists. Furthermore, many former soldiers did not necessarily remain committed to the Napoleonic cause in subsequent decades.[53]

Local monographs occasionally provide glimpses of individual rebels. In the Cher, after the 1851 *coup d'état*, former imperial soldier Claude Vilain reaffirmed his faith in the principles of republican socialism, and his admiration for the philosopher Pierre-Joseph

Proudhon; he publicly declared that he 'was very fond of the uncle, but after what he has done, not of the nephew.'[54] In a similar vein, another veteran of the Napoleonic Guard warned Louis at the time of the Presidential election that '1848 is not 1804'; in other words, Louis was to be elected as the guardian of the Republic, and not as the founder of a new Empire. It is unlikely that this veteran would have greeted the *coup d'état* (not to mention the advent of the Second Empire) with any enthusiasm.[55]

At the same time, these expressions of dissent were relatively limited; there is little sign that opposition to the Empire was widespread among Napoleon's former soldiers and officers. And even if they were present, these critical voices would have been drowned out by the enthusiasm shown by the overwhelming majority, and the extraordinary popular acclaim which greeted the veterans during the Saint-Napoléon ceremonies. These festivities were especially joyful in the year 1858, when the veterans were issued with their medals and certificates. In some localities the celebrations were even extended by several days in order to provide a fitting tribute to the *Médaillés*. In the town of Pertuis, for example, a local official noted that the festivities had taken place 'under conditions which had not been witnessed up till that point'. There were three days of rejoicing: Napoleon III was feted on 15 August, with all the traditional religious and civic manifestations; a large agricultural fair was held on the following day, with public amusements and distributions of prizes to farmers; and the festivities culminated on 17 August with a ceremony in honour of the commune's Médaillés de Sainte-Hélène.

This event took place in the afternoon, in the presence of most of the inhabitants of Pertuis. A large banquet then followed, and in the evening there was a spectacular display of fireworks. There was little doubt that, for the local population, the third day had represented the climax of the festivities.[56]

Forms of Honour

From the very outset – and long before the advent of the Second Empire – the notion of 'honour' was foremost in the minds of the veterans. Already under the Restoration, despite their difficult material conditions, the former soldiers of Napoleon had stood out from this perspective; as one historian put it, '[the veteran] would always remain one of a kind, obeying a spiritual discipline ignored by those around him: a certain rigidity, an acute, demanding sense of honour which struck many as old-fashioned, if not a relic of the middle ages.'[57] It was clear that, for these men, the celebration of the imperial cult was inextricably bound with a commitment to 'honourable' behaviour.

In the later years of their lives, as they were rewarded with the Médaille de Sainte-Hélène, the veterans' attachment to this notion of 'honour' became even more marked. The concept appeared repeatedly in the internal discourse and practices of the associations of imperial veterans that mushroomed all over France after 1858. One such organization, at La Chapelle Saint-Denis, brought together a hundred veterans living in this Parisian neighbourhood. At its founding meeting in May 1858 the association approved a constitution of thirty articles, and elected an executive bureau of six members, presided over by Hébert, the mayor of La Chapelle.[58] The association's definition of the decoration was striking:

'The medal of Sainte-Hélène is an eminently honourable distinction for all those who have the right to wear it, as for those who do not have the honour of being decorated by it, but who know how to understand and appreciate its meaning.'[59]

The aim of the Corporation was to foster solidarity among its members and to engender 'respect and honour' of the medal,[60] to ensure that it was always worn 'decently' and never 'dishonoured' by any action or insult.[61] Individual members who were in material need and who wished to plead with Napoleon III for assistance were required to have their appeals vetted by the Corporation first; again, the point was clearly to preserve the reputation of the membership as a whole.[62]

Transgressions of this code of honour were severely punished. Any member who brought the Corporation's good name into disrepute by his 'scandalous conduct and depraved morals' was liable to be permanently expelled.[63] All members were also under an obligation, when one of their colleagues died, to attend his funeral; failure to pay their respects to the last remains of a veteran was also grounds for dismissal from the Corporation.[64] The behaviour of all *Médaillés* towards each other had at all times to be marked by the 'decency which always has to be shown by men who respect one another.'[65] Elsewhere in France some associations, such as the Médaillés de Sainte-Hélène of Maine-et-Loire, adopted even more stringent criteria, reserving the right to deny membership to any imperial veterans who did not enjoy a 'social position, which alone can guarantee them the respect which they enjoy as individuals.'[66]

As a group, the imperial veterans were also extremely sensitive to their status, and reacted with appropriate emotion to any impropriety displayed by public institutions towards them. The main culprits here tended to be the municipalities. At Tours in 1859 the veterans were placed at the back of the civic procession; its leaders marched so rapidly that the *Médaillés* were left behind and eventually cut off by the crowd; the mayor ackowledged that the old soldiers had been 'offended'.[67] At Aix in 1859 the municipality had also tried to get away with the strict minimum in terms of the organization of public festivities. There was no civic procession from the *mairie* to the church, and only the mayor and his deputy attended the religious service. Even worse, the municipal posters which traditionally announced the national festivity to the population were not printed that year. Apart from providing details of the day's events, these posters also served as the official summons, notably to all veterans, to attend the *Te Deum* in the cathedral. The sub-prefect noted that the *Médaillés* were 'deeply offended by this oversight'.[68]

Often this sort of behaviour rallied the entire local population in gestures of solidarity with the veterans, and against the municipality; in November 1852 many inhabitants of the eastern village of Landersheim signed a petitition to the Minister of the Interior demanding the dismissal of their mayor on the grounds that he was 'persecuting the old veterans of the Empire.'[69] In the same year, the behaviour of the curé of the parish of Vritz, who refused to allow the delegation of Médaillés de Sainte-Hélène to enter his Church bearing the tricolour flag they had flown during the procession, proved even more offensive.[70] Similarly a priest caused a scandal when he described the *Médaillés*, who were slowly shuffling into the Church along with the rest of the municipal procession, as 'old goats'.[71]

But these were relatively isolated incidents. The overwhelming majority of administrative reports of the national festivities spoke not only of the warmth and respect shown by local populations towards the veterans, but also of the extraordinary effects their presence at times inspired. In the village of Sacy in 1859 the official procession was made up of a strong contingent of imperial veterans; the mayor noted that 'everywhere on its passage the procession was greeted with great fervour'. Indeed, that year's celebrations in the commune – the first in which the *Médaillés* had taken a full part – had proved the most memorable and festive to date.[72] At Cousancelles the firemen elected to honour the imperial veterans in a special way. The enthusiastic scenes that followed were described by the mayor:

'The firemen in an impeccable outfit wished not only to escort the local authorities [to church], but insisted on the honour of fetching the Médaillés de Sainte-Hélène from their homes and accompanying them together with the municipal council to the ceremonies of the day, after which they again escorted the veterans back to their homes, where they presented their arms and gave a roll of honour. These old and brave relics of our glorious armies responded to these military honours with energetic cries of 'Long Live the Emperor!', repeated a thousand times by the inhabitants who had spontaneously accompanied the escort.'[73]

The Napoleonic legend was still alive and well in this locality, as in so many other parts of France where the old warriors were greeted with enthusiasm. It is not surprising, then, that official reports typically dwelled on the contentment of the imperial veterans. The Police Commissioner of Avignon noted in 1861: 'Everyone yesterday saw with pleasure the old Médaillés de Sainte-Hélène in the civic procession. The faces of these brave old folk were radiant with happiness.'[74]

This special place of the veterans in the hearts and minds of the French public was noted by State officials across France. The *procureur-général* of Colmar wrote in 1858 that 'the institution of the Médaille is very popular, especially in the countryside where there are still a substantially large number of relics of our old troops.'[75] This was echoed by the sub-prefect of Béziers: 'The presence and the enthusiasm of the Médaillés of Sainte-Hélène have produced a happy effect on public consciousness. By honouring them, the Empire has conquered the sympathies of even the most indifferent and rallied many hearts.'[76]

Entertaining the Veterans

The pivotal position of the imperial veterans in the propagation of the Napoleonic legend under the Second Empire received joyful confirmation during the various forms of entertainment laid on in their honour by local officials. The strength of communal sociability, the vigorous dissemination of Bonapartist ideology, and the physical resilience of the *Médaillés* themselves shine through the surviving accounts of these festivities.

In the majority of localities the festivities in honour of the veterans took the classic form of nineteenth-century French celebrations: the banquet. In the larger towns these occasions were patronized by the entire administrative elite: at Toulouse in 1858 sixty imperial veterans were guests of honour at a banquet at the prefecture[77] and at Rouen in 1859 the banquet in honour of the *Médaillés* was organized by the mayor, with the prefect of the Seine-Inférieure and the top military brass in attendance.[78] No banquet would have been complete without a proliferation of toasts. In these cases they were typically made to the health and good fortune of the Emperor Napoleon, his nephew Napoleon III (and the imperial family), and the former soldiers of the Grande Armée. At Marsillargues in 1858 a banquet for thirty-six guests was laid out by the communal authorities in honour of the imperial veterans. After the dinner the mayor invited all those present to drink to Napoleon III and his family. The Police Commissioner then stood up:

'Gentlemen, allow me in turn to offer a toast to the memory of the great man whose glorious memories still resonate powerfully in our hearts; to the glory and prosperity of his illustrious descendant, the founder of the noble legion of Sainte-Hélène; and to these veterans who by adorning their scarred breasts revive in the hearts of our little children feelings of enthusiasm and patriotism, and make heroes of all those humble conscripts who fought memorable battles in order to make France the queen of civilized nations.'[79]

The distinctive appeal of the Bonapartist legend shone through here. This was not merely an invocation of patriotism and nationalism through the great figures of the Napoleonic dynasty. It was also a reminder of the powerful role of the 'people' in sustaining the Bonapartist myth – a collectivity symbolized here by the Médaillés de Sainte-Hélène, and invested with the qualities of simplicity and martyrdom, and at the same time fortitude and pride. The notion of 'nobility' was also essential, conveying both an elevation based on honour and virtue and a sublimation of social differences through effort and achievement. In the Bonapartist scheme of things, nobility was not merely a matter of birth: it could be acquired, and indeed acquired by the most humble *grognard* fighting for his country – as reflected in the saying that every soldier in Napoleon's army carried a field marshal's baton in his knapsack.

The festive atmosphere also gave new lease of life to the veterans. Most remarkable, in this respect, was the vitality shown by the forty *Médaillés* of the commune of Chateaudouble in 1861. The day before the festivities they felled a pine tree and carried it to the main square of the town, where they chopped it into small logs to be used for the bonfire. On 15 August they took a full part in two processions, one in the morning and the other in the early evening, after which they gathered again at a banquet given in their honour by the municipality. After the dinner the imperial veterans led the guests out again into the town in a torchlight procession, which rapidly attracted a large following. At midnight this merry band could still be heard singing the refrain of Béranger's Napoleonic ditty: '*Parlez-nous de lui, grand-mère, grand-mère, parlez-nous de lui.*'[80] The festivities carried on until the early hours of the following morning, when the *Médaillés* 'somewhat inebriated, if truth be told, concluded this great national festivity by a breakfast paid for from their own funds.'[81]

Bearers of the Legend

Imperial veterans, as we have noted throughout this book, played a critical role in the establishment and propagation of the Napoleonic legend after 1815 – often at a very high personal cost to themselves. What has also emerged in this chapter, however, is that those distinguished warriors who were still alive during the 1850s and 1860s continued to have a significant impact on French public consciousness. Their prominence during the Second Empire's festivities bore witness to the respect and admiration they enjoyed among large sections of society, and (more generally) to the deep entrenchment of the Napoleonic legend in local communities throughout the nineteenth century. Above all, these veterans demonstrated the powerful connection between the Napoleonic legend and Bonapartist politics under the Second Empire; contrary to the received wisdom that the *coup d'état* dealt it a severe blow, the legend was forcefully revived after 1852, helping (through the *Médaillés*) to cement the political foundations of the imperial regime.

One of the most striking features to emerge is the sheer resilience of the veterans, especially the ordinary soldiers. It is true that the institution of the decoration of the Médaille de Sainte-Hélène by the Second Empire came too late for many of them; already in 1857 – the year the Médaille was established – many communes had only one or two surviving veterans from the Napoleonic era.[82] But even though the process of natural attrition led to a gradual decline in their numbers during the 1860s there were still enough of them for the veterans' presence to be noticeable at public events. Indeed, the last Napoleonic soldier to receive his decoration in the department of the Vosges did so in February 1870 – only a few months before the downfall of the Second Empire.[83] The deaths of imperial combatants continued to be recorded in Bonapartist publications throughout the 1860s,[84] and funerals of *Médaillés* continued to be held well into the following decade.[85] In 1887 a Saint-Napoléon banquet was held in Paris at the Salon des Familles; among the 750 guests was a nonagenarian *Médaillé*.[86] And according to the newspaper *Le Gaulois*, there were still four surviving French *Médaillés* in 1894, all aged over a hundred; the eldest was Jean-Jacques Sabattier, born on 15 April 1792 in Vernoux-l'Ardèche.[87]

Resilience, therefore; and also robustness. These men, generally aged between the late sixties and the mid-eighties, took a full and active part in the civic ceremonies of the Second Empire, most particularly the Saint-Napoléon. In provincial and rural communes the veterans typically participated in two processions, one in the morning and the other in the afternoon. In towns with statues of Napoleon, as in Bordeaux, the *Médaillés* also often held a special procession to lay a wreath at the feet of their Emperor.[88] In many instances they also, as we have seen, continued the celebrations well into the night. Their stamina not only put to shame guests of significantly lower age, but also inspired a local poet from Rouen in 1865:

> *Malgré tant de souffrance*
> *Malgré tant de revers*
> *Lauriers de notre France*
> *Vous êtes toujours verts!*[89]

The theme of honour has appeared as a *leitmotif* throughout this account. The *Médaillés* often spoke of themselves as 'veterans of honour'[90] and administrative reports from all over France stressed the 'pride' with which the imperial veterans wore their medals.[91] This dignity manifested itself in the conduct which the veterans displayed in their social interactions with each other and in the models of civic behaviour and heroic emulation which they sought to personify within their own communities.

The evidence uncovered in this chapter suggests that they were more than successful in this respect: during the celebrations of the Saint-Napoléon the depth of the public feelings of esteem and admiration for the war veterans was constantly in evidence. The institution of the Médaille de Sainte-Hélène was welcomed, and poems and pamphlets were written in its honour;[92] inhabitants of towns and villages turned out in large numbers to witness the award of the decorations to the meritorious citizens of their commune; the presence of the imperial veterans in the processions of 15 August was greeted with acclaim; and individuals, groups, and institutions all over France gave generously to help those *Médaillés* who were experiencing material hardship.

And what is more, the veterans seemed to appeal to all sections of society – young and old, rich and poor, bourgeois, worker, and peasant, agnostic and believer. Particularly noteworthy was the appeal of the veterans in rural France, as highlighted by numerous administrative reports throughout the period. In 1869 the sub-prefect of Vitry-le-François (Marne) pointed out that the awards to the imperial veterans had given rise to sentiments of enthusiasm 'everywhere in our countryside'.[93] In the Aveyron, reports from 1857 onwards stress the 'touching' and 'effusive' character of the awards ceremonies, and the large public turnout.[94] Likewise in the Puy-de-Dôme, where there were around 4,000 *Médaillés* in 1857: the imperial veterans played a central role in the festivities of the Saint-Napoléon, and largely contributed to their popular success between 1858 and 1869.[95]

So, why this universal respect? Not, it is clear, because the veterans had been decorated by the regime; as noted earlier, the former soldiers were already objects of widespread public admiration and esteem in the 1840s, a full decade before their official 'recognition' by the French State. Indeed, the remarkable status enjoyed by the *Médaillés* was a tribute to something more complex: the glorious 'memory' of France's Napoleonic past, which they personified; the physical qualities of bravery, endurance, and resilience, which they had demonstrated throughout their lives; their sense of 'discipline', and the 'honourable' social behaviour which they insisted upon in their interactions with each other and with their fellow citizens.[96] Perhaps most important of all was the reconciliation, in the festive landscape of the Saint-Napoleon, of the dichotomy between the notables and the people – a transcendence that was often stressed in poems written in honour of the decoration,[97] in statements by leaders of veterans' associations,[98] and which remained throughout the nineteenth century one of the key facets of the Bonapartist conception of military honour. The veterans were the ordinary heroes of the Napoleonic tradition, models of civic virtue and social emulation.[99]

What, then, of the veterans' political values? Their dominant sentiment, of course, was their passionate, overriding, unqualified adoration of their Emperor. Raffet's celebrated print of Napoleonic soldiers, with the caption 'They complained but they always followed him',[100] continued to hold true even more intensely after 1815. For the extraordinary adventures he had brought them, from the burning sands of Gaza to the frozen ice of the Berezina, for the social promotion through merit, for the glories of victory and (perhaps especially) for those poignant moments of defeat and desolation, Napoleon continued to be loved by them all – despite the sufferings he had made them endure, despite the broken lives that they had led for thirty, forty years after the end of the imperial wars, despite everything. As a former officer explained:

'We hated his despotism but we could not but recognize in Napoleon an extraordinary genius, which ultimately gave him the right to command and to be obeyed. In our eyes he was one of those giants who emerged once in every thousand years to accomplish a mission or execute a sentence, to regenerate or to punish. This man had in him something which even the most intelligent, the most gifted of his contemporaries lacked, something which made him a leader before whom one would tremble, a seducer who charmed and was adored. With one look he would make you want to crawl beneath the earth, and with another he would conquer you.'[101]

The *Médaillés'* repeated references to the theme of 'conquest', and their invocations of Bonaparte's exploits across Europe might invite the rather simplistic conclusion that the veterans were mere instruments of French 'chauvinism', the lowest and most debased expression of French national sentiment in the nineteenth century.[102] There is no doubt that the martial theme of Napoleonic domination and conquest was present, and reverberated powerfully through the songs, poems and dramas of the period.[103] A veteran of the Russian campaign of 1812 warned 'foreigners' that Frenchmen would 'soon come to avenge what was done to them in 1815'.[104] But here too things were much more complex. Many of the *Médaillés* of the 1850s and 1860s were strong supporters of Italian and Polish national independence, and often expressed publicly their identification with these causes.[105]

Furthermore, despite the imperial veterans' fondness for celebrating 'some of their military feats',[106] their bellicosity was often tempered, notably by an emphasis on the restraint (real and alleged) shown by the Emperor during his campaigns. One *Médaillé* even described the Emperor as a supreme advocate of the *temperamenta belli*: 'If only it was known how many acts of devotion to humanity [Napoleon] showed in the midst of the horrors of war, how many victims he pulled away from the fury of his own soldiers, too often carried away by the perfidiousness of the enemy or the necessity of self-preservation; and if only it was understood that the motto of this excellent man, before and after battle, was "respect for women, children, and old people", he would be universally appreciated and respected.'[107]

So: in the eyes of many veterans, Napoleon has been a generous and humane ruler, even on the battlefield. Most interestingly, a noticeable ideological shift developed in the perspectives of the former soldiers. In the early years of the Restoration, as we noted at the beginning of this chapter, Napoleonic military exploits were seen as the exclusive component of the imperial legend. Even in 1848, 'veteran' culture was essentially a backward-looking nostalgia for war, interlaced with cries for revenge.

During the 1850s and 1860s, however, the feats of the Napoleonic armies were typically celebrated alongside the civic and political aspects of the Bonapartist epic. Indeed, in the Napoleonic tradition of the Second Empire reference was more often made to the pre-eminence of civic virtues over martial ones: 'Military qualities, as the Emperor used to say, are necessary only in some circumstances and some moments. Civic virtues, which are characteristic of the real lawmaker, can at all times influence public happiness.'[108] This was the kind of language typically used by Bonapartist elites during the Saint-Napoléon festivities of the 1850s and 1860s – even by old soldiers. Speaking at the ceremony in 1858 at which the imperial veterans of Albi received their medals, the local deputy (a General and a Médaillé de Sainte-Hélène, as well as the mayor of Albi and President of the *Conseil Général* of the Tarn) spoke of 'the immortal glory of our great Emperor, who, *all at once*, was a man of genius, a warrior, a lawgiver, and a profound political strategist.'[109]

In fact, the militarist theme was overshadowed by two other motifs. The first was the age-old notion of 'France as the bearer of civilized values' – a progressive civilization which had disseminated the values of 1789 to Europe under Napoleon Bonaparte, and was continuing to spread the message of Christianity to France's colonies (a theme which would be seamlessly picked up by the Third Republic). A popular Napoleonic song composed by a veteran celebrated the Second Empire's wars as 'struggles for justice, for peace, and for the restoration of security among oppressed peoples.'[110]

The second theme, of course, was peace. 'The Empire brings peace' was one of Louis Napoleon's slogans from the earliest days of the regime, and it built upon the legend created by the *Mémorial*, according to which Napoleon had not sought or provoked conflicts; these had been imposed upon him by his adversaries. This 'pacific' theme assumed a strong place in the imagery and rhetoric of the veterans. A former soldier of the First Empire stressed the irenic character of the Napoleonic tradition in a song that he composed in 1852, urging the foreign powers to 'deal with Louis and have trust in him; he does not want wars.'[111] In 1859 a poem entitled 'The French Echo', written by a Napoleonic veteran, was sent to the prefect of Gironde; it ended with a tribute to the Bonapartist diplomacy, 'for which peace was another name.'[112]

By the 1850s and 1860s, the image of Napoleon and the Napoleonic tradition among former imperial soldiers was softer and less warlike. It was even by no means uncommon to see the Emperor presented as a champion of liberalism. During the inauguration of the statue of Bonaparte in Grenoble in 1868, the main speech was delivered by Monsieur Point, the mayor of Vourey; he too was a former officer of the Grande Armée who had been decorated with both the Légion d'Honneur and the Médaille de Sainte-Hélène. Point's remarks about Napoleon came straight out of the 'liberal legend': the Emperor, in his estimation, had not been a lover of wars; it was his perfidious enemies who had consistently drawn him into combat. His true legacy was the Code Civil, 'a monument which is as honourable as all his victories on the battlefield' (Thiers's influence was manifest here). And what of the Emperor's political views, and his excessive penchant for despotism? Monsieur Point firmly rebutted this accusation, noting that Napoleon had 'protected equality, which is nothing but liberty in action'; he concluded, in an emphatic echo of the words of the *Mémorial*, that 'at heart the Emperor was a liberal.'[113]

Through this blending of past and present, authoritarianism and progress, memory and ideology, the imperial veterans thus helped not only to keep alive but also to reinvent France's Napoleonic past. In so doing, they prepared the ground for the reappropriation of the imperial epic by republican pedagogues such as Ernest Lavisse, a great admirer of Napoleon. As was the case for hundreds of thousands of French men and women during the first half of the nineteenth century, the young Lavisse first learned about the history of France through members of his family, and from the imperial veterans of his locality. Like so many of his countrymen, Lavisse had a relative who had followed the Emperor to some remote part of Europe, with burning feet and aching limbs, but also with a joyful spirit. Such men would recall, with intense pride mingled with sorrow, the triumphs and disasters of the Napoleonic era, and that fleeting but sublime moment seared for ever in their memories: 'All of a sudden, 'twas the emperor who passed by'.[114]

Conclusion

The Legend Lives On

In 1901, a French journalist travelled to Warsaw to meet the last known soldier of Napoleon. Lieutenant Vincent Markiewicz had served in the Emperor's Polish regiment, and then in his Guard, and at the ripe old age of 106 he had survived every single one of his French comrades.[1]

Markiewicz had joined Napoleon's Army when it had been stationed in Warsaw in 1811, and had followed the Emperor to Russia, where he took part in the battle of Borodino and the occupation of Moscow, and survived the terrible, savage retreat which followed, in which most of Napoleon's forces were destroyed. He then fought in the Spanish campaign and again at Leipzig, where he had four horses killed under him. He was awarded the Legion of Honour in 1813, and promoted into Napoleon's Guard; he then remained at the Emperor's side, fighting at Waterloo and accompanying Napoleon to Saint-Helena. After returning to Europe, he served in the Russian Army in Poland in the 1820s, then went to live in France for a decade, where he dabbled in Bonapartist conspiratorial activities. Thereafter he fought in Hungary and in the Ottoman Empire in the 1840s and 1850s, and ended his military career in the 1860s in Garibaldi's Army, battling for Italian independence.[2]

It was fitting that the last survivor of the Napoleonic military epic was a Pole, a member of a nation that had loyally supported Napoleon, and was still awaiting to recover its own freedom and sovereignty – a predicament which continued to give the imperial myth a powerful political edge among Poles.[3] In France, the status of the legend was undergoing something of a change at the turn of the century. After a brief hiatus in the early years of the Third Republic, public interest in all things Napoleonic had revived: Edmond Rostand's play *L'Aiglon*, a sweeping evocation of the imperial saga, had opened to enormous critical acclaim.[4] The tale of Lieutenant Markiewicz provoked a great deal of curiosity, and much indignation, too, as the officer seemed to be living in particularly impoverished circumstances. But French interest in the story was essentially folkloric. It stemmed from a conception of the legend as romantic nostalgia, a longing for an era of adventure which was understood to have ended, at least in its 'classical' sense; for some, it was also becoming the privileged expression of an individualistic, nationalist cult of transcendental heroism. It was in this spirit that the writer Maurice Barrès celebrated Napoleon as a 'professor of energy' in his novel *Les Déracinés*.[5]

Yet the Napoleonic myth was no longer, as it had been for so long in the nineteenth century, part of an overarching political project. Bonapartism never recovered from the collapse of the Second Empire: after 1871 its electoral and political challenges to the Republic (notably during the campaign mounted by General Boulanger) consistently foundered.[6] Fragmented into different factions, and bitterly divided among themselves, Bonapartists in the late nineteenth century were reduced to commemorating the anniversary of the Saint-Napoléon in small groups.[7]

Things had been very different before 1870. The legend, as it has been portrayed in this book, was a broad and complex phenomenon, but our central argument is that for much of the nineteenth century it represented much more than romantic nostalgia for the imperial past. Through its idealized view of the legacy of the 1799–1815 period, and its heroic images of the Emperor himself, the legend supported a powerful cluster of political ideas and values. It celebrated French military glory and national pride – an aspect of the Napoleonic heritage which was especially highlighted in the writings of French novelists and poets, and in the yearnings of those who

sought to avenge the humiliation of 1815. But the legend also captivated and mobilized millions of men and women in wider and more
creative ways, and it is in these respects that it decisively shaped
modern French political culture. In the course of the nineteenth century, the Napoleonic myth both expressed and helped to mould
popular attitudes towards the legitimacy of mass intervention in
public life; it celebrated the 'liberal Emperor' of 1815, the champion
of French sovereignty and promoter of progressive reforms; and it
helped to crystallize a distinct style of populist political action – the
'anti-fête' – which challenged the 'national' legitimacy of monarchical rule, and eventually helped to bring down a regime that offended
the principles of French 'patriotism' in 1830.

Seen in this light, and despite its fixation on the image of the
Emperor, the legend represented something that was larger than
Napoleon and, indeed, that transcended him. It used the image of
the Emperor – the 1815 Napoleon of the people, as stated previously,
not the despotic ruler or conquering warrior – to uphold the central
myths of the 1789 Revolution: civil equality, democracy, modernization, and popular sovereignty. These were the very same values that
were later adopted by the triumphant Republic. In the words of
François Furet, Bonapartism and the Napoleonic legend were 'the
simplest and the most widespread forms through which the spirit of
the Revolution continued to haunt the nation.'[8] A popular brochure
published in the first half of the nineteenth century (by an author
describing himself as a 'proletarian') underscored the point:
'Napoleon has descended into his tomb but Bonapartism is not dead;
it has become republican'.[9]

We saw in Chapter 6 how this intellectual transformation was initiated by Napoleon himself, and then later how Louis Napoleon both
developed and exploited this ideological mélange – full of ambigui-
ties, of course, but all the more potent for that – in order to propel
himself into office in 1848. Finally, it was the imperial veterans, by
effectively rallying behind the restored imperial regime after 1852,
who enabled popular imperial traditions and memories to be perpetuated for two further decades. In other words, what distinguished
the Napoleonic legend in nineteenth-century France from its subsequent formulations was that it was a predominantly 'popular'
phenomenon.

It was popular first in a literal sense: from the very outset the legend defined Napoleon as a ruler chosen by the people. In the words of a stage actor in Lyons in August 1815: 'The throne was much better suited to Napoleon than to Louis XVIII, because Napoleon had been elected by the people, and the French people well appreciate that an elective government is better than a hereditary one.'[10] That the French people never enjoyed an 'elective government' under Napoleon is of course a moot point; this sort of statement reflected the depth (and the rapidity) of the transformation of the Emperor's political image after the Hundred Days. From despotic monarch and lover of war Napoleon instantly became, in Julien Sorel's words, 'the only king remembered by the people'.[11]

The legend was also popular in that it reached an extraordinarily broad audience: there were more biographies of Napoleon written between 1815 and 1914 than of any other figure.[12] It was popular, above all, in that the legend developed in a manner which was largely spontaneous and unregulated, without the active intercession of the State – and often, especially in the period 1815–48, against its express wishes. Even under the Second Empire, the mass appeal of the imperial veterans was grounded in factors that operated independently of the regime.

This 'popular' legend died out by the end of the nineteenth century with the demise of the last imperial veterans – not coincidentally. From this moment, Napoleon was essentially co-opted into the official culture of the French State. After securing their hold over national power after 1880, even the republicans jumped on the bandwagon. At regular intervals the Republic organized official ceremonies to commemorate the imperial era, always adapting the message to the particular needs of the moment. In 1921, the centenary of Napoleon's death provided an opportunity to celebrate the triumph of French arms in the Great War; in 1969, the bicentenary of his birth allowed President Pompidou to dwell on Napoleon's restoration of the dignity of the State and the construction of European unity – both of which mirrored the recent achievements of his own Gaullist party.[13]

In modern France, Napoleon continues to enjoy a unique status. The Emperor remains a popular 'historical' figure, regularly portrayed in films and documentaries; and the production of literary material about the Empire continues to burgeon, with dozens of new titles each year. It is worth mentioning that hagiographic works on the life of the Emperor still enjoy noteworthy successes – Max Gallo's effusive and melodramatic study being a case in point.[14] More remarkably, men not hitherto known for their Napoleonic interests suddenly discover the need to go in search of his life, to explore its mysteries and contradictions, and to cross their own destinies with his.[15]

The cult is also maintained by specialized organizations, one of which works to preserve Napoleonic monuments in France, and by institutions such as the Fondation Napoleon, which promotes research into the history of the two Empires and celebrates key events in the imperial commemorative calendar.[16] It is true, though, that the more cynical *Zeitgeist* of the present times has affected even Napoleon. One of the great literary successes of recent years was Patrick Rambaud's novel *La Bataille*, which was awarded both the Goncourt and the Académie Française prizes; it depicted the Emperor as a coarse tyrant, indifferent to the fate of his soldiers, barely capable even of speaking French, and fatally self-obsessed.[17]

This type of depiction of the Emperor seems to mark a return to the 'black legend'. Indeed, the old French divide between a 'republican' memory and a 'Napoleonic' tradition remains real. In 1850, Michelet expressed the traditional, nuanced view of early-nineteenth-century republicans: 'Let us not rely on a legend which has been so baneful for the world, that of Napoleon; for a long time he was nothing but a deceitful ruler. He only became the 'great' Napoleon at Saint-Helena [. . .] Let us insist instead on the pure and saintly legends of the *Revolution*. The *Grande Armée* also accomplished miracles, its soldiers were examples of heroic patience'.[18]

After Louis Napoleon's 1851 coup, however, even such qualified endorsements disappeared from republican discourse; all forms of Bonapartism were decried as antithetical to French political culture, and ruinous to the nation's prosperity and territorial integrity. In 1871 one of the first actions carried out by local republicans in Golfe-Juan was to bring down the column that had been erected to mark the landing of Napoleon in this coastal village in March 1815 – the prelude to the Emperor's spectacular 'flight of the eagle' and the Hundred Days.[19] A pamphlet written a few years later sought to remind the French people that both Napoleonic Emperors had been responsible for the dismemberment of the nation – Bonaparte in 1815, and Napoleon III in 1871.[20] Republicans had their own 'great men' (in the nineteenth century, Voltaire, Hoche, Lamartine, and Gambetta)[21] through whom were celebrated the principles of reason, secularism, and universalism; while Napoleon was seen as the embodiment of something very different – 'glory', individualism, and the cult of force.[22] This divide between the two camps also became a physical one: since its reinauguration in 1885, the republicans have buried their heroes in the Panthéon – the 'Ecole Normale of the Dead', in Mona Ozouf's wonderful expression[23] – while Napoleon has remained in the splendour and relative isolation of the Invalides.

And yet the gap between these two 'cults', and between their respective forms of institutionalized 'memory', is rather less significant than it would appear at first glance.[24] As noted at the end of the previous chapter, the pedagogues of the Third Republic did not hesitate to draw upon the imperial heritage: Napoleon, like Joan of Arc and Charlemagne, was a useful icon for a regime that sought to reconstruct the nation's collective identity on the ruins of the 1870–1871 defeat.[25] Adults too were fed a literature that glorified the achievements of Napoleon: a collection of short works devoted to 'Great Men' published by Pierre Lafitte included one contribution on Bonaparte.[26]

But the association between republicanism and Bonapartism ran much deeper. As we have seen throughout the book, the political values associated with the 'imagined' Napoleon – the Emperor of the legend – were intertwined with republican principles from the very outset. Through their core principles of order, nationalism, centralization, unity around a charismatic leader, and a plebiscitary conception of democracy, Bonapartists represented (along with republicans) one of the dominant forms of French democratic politics in the nineteenth century. Since 1945 the same neo-Napoleonic principles have inspired Gaullism, the leading political force on the French right. Indeed, the nation's most popular 'historical' figure is now General Charles de Gaulle, the leader of the French Resistance during the Second World War and later the founder of the Fifth Republic.[27] His iconic status in contemporary France illustrates the extent to which the 'republican' tradition has internalized and even absorbed key elements of the Napoleonic heritage.

The Gaullist saga has many similarities to the Napoleonic legend. For a long time, very much like the literature on Napoleon, French writings on de Gaulle have been dominated by memoirs and hagiography. In a wonderfully subtle book, Maurice Agulhon has argued that the structure of the Napoleonic and Gaullist legends are in fact identical. In both cases, they begin with an 'admirable' act, in which an individual charismatic leader saves the French nation (1799, 1940). Both men then dissipate their heritages (Napoleon by his senseless wars, de Gaulle by his petulant withdrawal from politics in 1946 and his 'authoritarian' return to power in 1958). Then, finally, after their deaths, they both bask in retrospective glory, idolized even by those who once detested them.[28] Régis Debray, the former Marxist revolutionary turned Gaullophile,[29] is in this sense a successor to nineteenth-century Napoleonic turncoats such as Edgar Quinet and Chateaubriand (but without, alas, the literary talent of either).

Most fundamentally, de Gaulle represents a modern version of the 'liberal legend' of 1815. In him, as in the Emperor before him, France celebrates a saviour who united its people against foreign invasion and occupation; a patriot who remained inflexibly attached to the nation's sovereignty, and sought to uphold its universal mission; and a lawgiver who saved France from 'anarchy' and created a stable system of rule. French political elites continue to subscribe to the idealized Gaullist vision of a France which is both republican and 'monarchical', authoritarian and prestigious, sovereign and influential, determined and prophetic, imperious and irascible, realistic and visionary, demanding and respected, bold and ambitious.[30] How else is this myth to be described, except as an updated formulation of the Napoleonic legend?

This remarkable continuity of values and ideals – from the 1789 Revolution through Napoleon to de Gaulle – tells us a great deal about the elements that metaphorically 'hold France together'. In the first instance, it reveals the enduring appeal of a certain type of myth in the nation's collective consciousness. Napoleon, de Gaulle: it is difficult not to observe that, for all their differences as individuals, these two giants of the modern French historical experience shared several common features. They were both prophets, accurately predicting the shape of things to come for their people. They were also outsiders who transcended the limitations of their respective situations – for the one, his Corsican origins; for the other, his absence of political connections – to achieve 'greatness'. Both experienced their finest hours in circumstances of extreme conflict – a reflection of the absolute centrality of warfare in shaping French collective memory, even though Napoleonic military greatness was distinctive for its sheer prowess in the art of war, and for the Emperor's consistent achievement of 'glory'. Both men, finally, were able (at particular historical junctures) to symbolize a distinct ideal of the French *patrie*: Napoleon in 1815 and de Gaulle during the Second World War defied foreign domination and occupation to represent the political sovereignty of their people; 'the *patrie* conceived as a quasi-religious ideal'.[31]

Napoleon and de Gaulle are not the only French historical figures whose memory and ideological lineages have been mythologized. If we consider that other great favourite of the nation's historical memory, Joan of Arc, we find a similar process at work. (The difference in the case of *La Pucelle* is perhaps that her memory has remained vigorously 'disputed' among Catholics, republicans, and nationalists.)[32] The republican tradition, too, is full of myths – myths based on memory and historical experience, but also on invention and 'forgetting'. It was through this capacity for creative redesign that the republicans managed, in the second half of the nineteenth century, to transform a series of failed political experiments and murderous episodes (the Terror, the killings of June 1848 and the massacres of the Paris Commune) into a new dawn for humankind (or, more modestly, for the French people).[33]

Critics of French political culture have occasionally wondered whether such a reliance on 'mythology' is a healthy phenomenon for a modern society, especially one that prides itself in its Cartesian rationalism. These attempts to appropriate the past for ideological purposes can undoubtedly lead to the misrepresentation of history – such was the case, indeed, with the Napoleonic legend for most of the nineteenth century. Nearer our time, the Gaullist 'myth' of a French nation united in resisting German occupation arguably perverted later generations' understanding of what happened in their country between 1940 and 1944; it is only over the past decade that France has truly begun to face up to the legacies of this sombre period.

Myths can also distort the present: by providing the concepts and images through which events are perceived, 'mythical' discourse can misrepresent reality and thereby prevent necessary change. This is often held to be the case with the principle of 'unity', one of the sacrosanct values celebrated by the Napoleonic tradition (and the Jacobins): so powerfully has this ideal been entrenched in French elite thinking that it has blocked badly needed reforms to the country's system of territorial administration.[34] The combined force of the Jacobin and Napoleonic myths has also been held responsible for some particularly aberrant characteristics of the French polity – notably its consistent yearning for State intervention, its incapacity to develop a genuine liberal tradition, and the continuing weaknesses in its practice of political representation and democracy.[35]

Yet it is somewhat excessive to lay all of this at the Emperor's door. Napoleonic myths that developed in France after 1815 were also positive forces, which at various moments performed constructive, creative, and healing functions. To what remains, in cultural terms at least, a Catholic nation, Napoleon's exile and death at Saint-Helena continues to represent a modern tale of martyrdom. To all those individuals who felt trapped by the accidents of birth, the weight of social convention, or the constraints of economic circumstances, the Emperor provided a galvanizing ideal of ambition, emancipation, and achievement through personal effort. To schoolteachers trying to construct an idea of 'France' as a collectivity created through a harmonious blend of different ethnic and territorial groups, the Corsican *petit caporal* represented the quintessence of the provincial boy made good. To a country constantly disturbed by political volatility, economic modernization, and social transformation, Napoleon remained a shining star in the nation's firmament, a fixed point which could be recognized by the French people, and which would remind them who they were. And to a nation traumatized by military decline, the fear of 'decadence', and the threat of physical annihilation, the Emperor's legend responded with the enduring hope of that most sacred of ideals: the achievement of immortality.

Notes

Introduction: Rethinking the Legend

1 'Cet espèce de bonnaparte'. Letter dated 19 September 1815. Archives Nationales, Paris, BB3—151.

2 Cited in Daniel Fabre, 'L'atelier des héros', in P. Centlivres, D. Fabre and F. Zonabend (eds.), *La fabrique des héros* (Paris: Editions de la Maison des Sciences de l'Homme, 1998), 299.

3 On the so-called 'black legend' of Napoleon, see Jean Tulard, *L'Anti-Napoléon: la légende noire de l'Empereur* (Paris: Julliard, 1965).

4 For a bibliography of recent works on the Napoleonic legend, see Gérard Gengembre, *Napoléon: la vie, la légende* (Paris: Larousse, 2001), 121–125. See also the various contributions in the conference proceedings, *Napoléon de l'histoire à la légende* (Paris : In Forma, 2000).

5 'scélérat illustre'.

6 Pierre-Maxime Schuhl, *Le culte des grands hommes* (Paris : Institut de France, 1974), 3–4.

7 Steven Englund, *Napoleon: a political life* (New York and London: Scribner, 2004), 459.

8 The classic statement of this view is Philippe Gonnard, *Les origines de la légende napoléonienne: l'œuvre historique de Napoléon à Sainte-Hélène*, first published in 1906; it was re-edited in Geneva by Slatkine in 1976.

9 Natalie Petiteau, *Napoléon de la mythologie à l'histoire* (Paris: Seuil, 1999), 37.

10 See the entry by François Monnier, 'Propagande', in Jean Tulard (ed.), *Dictionnaire Napoléon* (Paris: Fayard, 1999 ed.), 586–592; also Alan Forrest, *Napoleon's men: the soldiers of the Revolution and Empire* (London: Hambledon, 2002), 75–76.

11 This is the thesis in Jean Tulard's classic work, *Le mythe de Napoléon* (Paris: Armand Colin, 1971); more recently, Tulard has even argued that Napoleon was 'the inventor of the propaganda used by totalitarian regimes'. See Jean Tulard, *Le temps des passions* (Paris, Bartillat, 1996), 175.

12 Jacques-Olivier Boudon, *Histoire du Consulat et de l'Empire* (Paris : Perrin, 2000), 442–443.

13 See Jacques-Olivier Boudon, 'Grand homme ou demi-dieu? La mise en place d'une religion napoléonienne', in *Romantisme* 100 (1998), 131–141.

14 'Mentir comme un bulletin'.

15 Sylvain Venayre, *La gloire de l'aventure. Genèse d'une mystique moderne* (Paris: Aubier, 2002), 196.

16 For this distinction between myth and legend, see Frédéric Bluche, *Le Bonapartisme: aux origines de la droite autoritaire (1800–1850)* (Paris: Nouvelles Editions Latines, 1980), 168–169.

17 Georges Lefebvre, *Napoléon* (Paris: Presses Universitaires de France, 1953), 574.

18 Bluche, *Le Bonapartisme* (op.cit.), 169.

19 In May 1816, a group of schoolboys from the villages of Thury and Lainsecq were publicly denounced by the prefect of Yonne for organizing a fight between their schools, in which one side was labelled 'royalist' and the other 'Bonapartist'. AD Yonne III M^1 70.

20 For example, Bluche, *Le Bonapartisme* (op.cit.), 172.

21 See for example the pamphlet by Ganneau, a cult leader who was also known as 'Le Mapah'; his title was in itself a philosophical statement: *Waterloo. A vous beaux fils de France morts pour l'honneur, Salut et Glorification! Qu'est-ce que l'honneur? L'honneur c'est l'unité* (Paris: Bureau des Publications Evadiennes, 1843).

22 See Henry Houssaye, *La Garde meurt et ne se rend pas. Histoire d'un mot historique* (Paris: Perrin, 1907). Houssaye demonstrates conclusively that Cambronne did not utter these legendary words when asked by the English to surrender at Waterloo; he probably did, however, say 'Merde.'

23 See Edgar Quinet, *1815 et 1840* (Paris, 1840).

24 This was the theme in Louis Veuillot, *Waterloo* (Paris: Gaume, 1861); on the representations of Waterloo in nineteenth-century France see Jean-Marc Largeaud, 'Mémoire et identité: Waterloo et la genèse de la défaite glo-rieuse', in Natalie Petiteau (ed.), *Voies nouvelles pour l'histoire du Premier Empire* (Paris: La Boutique de l'Histoire, 2003), 283–302.

25 See most notably A. Dayot, *Napoléon raconté par l'image, d'après les sculpteurs, les graveurs, et les peintres* (Paris: Hachette, 1895); Maurice Descotes, *La légende de Napoléon et les écrivains français du XIXe siècle* (Paris: Minard, 1967), which looks at a group of writers, both sympathetic and hostile; for more specific studies see D. Page, *Edmond Rostand et la légende napoléonienne dans* l'Aiglon (Paris: Champion, 1928); Del Litto Vittorio, 'Stendhal et Napoléon', *Cahiers d'Histoire* XVI (1971); Saint-Paulien, *Napoléon, Balzac et l'Empire de la Comédie Humaine* (Paris: Albin Michel, 1979).

26 See Saint-Mathurin, 'Le culte de Napoléon en Allemagne de 1815 à 1848', *Revue des Etudes Napoléoniennes*, January–June 1917, 48–87; and L. de Guillebon, 'Les vétérans napoléoniens dans les pays rhénans', *Revue des Etudes Napoléoniennes*, July–December 1931, 309–315.

27 Jules Deschamps, 'La légende de Napoléon à travers le monde', *Revue des Etudes Napoléoniennes* July–August 1926, 33–36.

28 Quoted from a Spanish religious text of 1808; Pilar Martinez-Vasseur, 'Le catéchisme patriotique de 1808', in *L'enfance et les ouvrages d'éducation* (University of Nantes Press, 1985), Vol.II, 76.

29 See Jules Deschamps, 'Les défenseurs de Napoléon en Grande-Bretagne de 1815 à 1830', *Revue des Etudes Napoléoniennes*, October 1958, 129–140; Stuart Semmel, *Napoleon in the British Imagination* (New Haven: Yale University Press, 2004).

30 Lee Kennett, 'Le culte de Napoléon aux Etats-Unis jusqu'à la guerre de sécéssion', *Revue de l'Institut Napoléon*, October-December 1972, 152.

31 G. F. Pardo de Leygonier, 'Napoléon et les libérateurs de l'Amérique Latine', *Revue de l'Institut Napoléon*, January 1962, 29–33.

32 Minas Tchéraz, 'La vie de Napoléon d'après une légende Arménienne', *Revue des Etudes Napoléoniennes*, January–June 1935, 181–182.

33 P. Chalmin, 'Les variations de la légende napoléonienne', *Revue Historique de l'Armée* (1961), 40.

34 Jean-Pierre Royer, Renée Martinage, and Pierre Lecocq, *Juges et notables au XIXe siècle* (Paris: Presses Universitaires de France, 1982), 50–52.

35 For a local study, see Daniel Bernard, 'Surveillance des itinérants et ambulants dans le département de l'Indre au XIXe siècle', in Philippe Vigier *et al.* (eds), *Maintien de l'ordre et polices en France et en Europe au XIXe siècle* (Paris: Créaphis, 1987), 235–250.

36 Report of sub-prefect of Sens to prefect of Yonne, 18 March 1816. AD Yonne III M[1] 78.

37 As the prefect of Vendée put it in 1821: 'The gendarmes and the chief of police are all known to the locals, and as soon as they appear their presence causes the topic of conversation to change'; quoted in Pierre Carila-Cohen, 'Une "bonne" surveillance? La gendarmerie et la collecte du renseignement politique en province sous la monarchie censitaire', in Jean-Noël Luc (ed.), *Gendarmerie, état et société au XIXe siècle* (Paris: Publications de la Sorbonne, 2002), 230.

38 Arlette Farge, *Le goût de l'archive* (Paris: Seuil, 1989), 21–22.

39 Police report, Lyons, 24 April 1821. AD Rhône 4 M 241.

40 For another illustration of the vibrancy of French popular culture during the first half of the nineteenth century, see Sheryl Kroen, *Politics and theater: the crisis of legitimacy in Restoration France 1815–1830* (Berkeley: University of California Press, 2000).

41 This theme of the 'anti-fête' is further explored in Sudhir Hazareesingh, *The Saint-Napoleon: celebrations of sovereignty in nineteenth-century France* (Cambridge, Mass.: Harvard University Press, 2004).

42 See our earlier work, co-written with Vincent Wright, *Francs-maçons sous le Second Empire* (Rennes: Presses Universitaires de Rennes, 2001).

1: The Flight of the Eagle

1 *Mémoires de Marchand* (Paris: Tallandier, 2003), 169.
2 Guy Godlewski, *Napoléon à l'Ile d'Elbe* (Paris: Nouveau Monde Editions, 2003), 182.
3 François Furet, *La Révolution Française* (Paris: Hachette, 1988), Vol.II, 31.
4 *Mémoires de Marchand* (op. cit.).
5 'A l'Armée'. Proclamation of Napoleon, Golfe-Juan, March 1, 1815.
6 The expression caught on after being first used by Chabrol, the prefect of the Seine department, as he welcomed the King back to Paris in early July 1815.
7 Cited in S. and A. Troussier, *Napoléon, la chevauchée héroïque de l'Ile d'Elbe* (Lausanne, 1965), 27.
8 Notably the regiment based in Marseille, which was fiercely royalist. See Jean Thiry, *Le vol de l'aigle* (Paris: Berger-Levrault, 1942), 20.
9 Ch. Florange, *Le vol de l'aigle* (Paris: Margraff, 1932), 50.
10 Thiry, *Le vol de l'aigle* (op. cit.), 33.
11 Florange, *Le vol de l'aigle*, 51.
12 Troussier, *Napoléon* (op. cit.), 67–68.
13 Ibid., 110–11.
14 Ibid., 74.
15 Ibid., 118.
16 For an account of these incidents by Napoleon's secretary during the Hundred Days – he joined the Emperor at Lyons – see Fleury de Chaboulon, *Mémoires pour servir à l'histoire de la vie privée, du retour, et du règne de Napoléon en 1815* (London: John Murray, 1819), Vol.I, 177–178; 198–226; 242–244.
17 [Alexandre de Laborde], *Quarante-huit heures de garde au Chateau des Tuileries pendant les journées des 19 et 20 mars 1815, par un grenadier de la garde nationale* (Paris, 1815).
18 Thiébault, quoted in Henry Houssaye, *1815* (Paris: Perrin, 1909), Vol.I, 368, fn.1.
19 See for example *Histoire du cabinet des Tuileries depuis le 20 mars 1815 et de la conspiration qui a ramené Buonaparte en France* (Paris: Delaunay, 1815); M. Lamartelière, *Conspiration de Buonaparte contre Louis XVIII* (Paris: Dentu, 1815); and Helena Williams, *Relation des évènements qui se sont passés en France depuis le débarquement de Napoléon Buonaparte au 1er mars 1815 jusqu'au traité du 20 novembre* (Paris: Dentu, 1816).
20 [Fenouillot], *Le cri de vérité sur les causes de la Révolution de 1815* (Besançon, 1815), 5.
21 Ch.Tremblaire, 'Le parti Bonapartiste 1815–1840', *Revue de l'Empire* Vol. II (1844), 201.
22 See Emile Le Gallo, *Les Cent Jours. Essai sur l'histoire intérieure de la France*

depuis le retour de l'Ile d'Elbe jusqu'à la nouvelle de Waterloo (Paris: Félix Alcan, 1924), 29–38.

23 See Albert Espitalier, *Deux artisans du retour de l'Ile d'Elbe: le chirurgien Emery et le gantier Dumoulin* (Paris, 1934).

24 Françoise-René de Chateaubriand, *De Buonaparte, des Bourbons, et de la nécéssité de se rallier à nos princes légitimes* (Paris, 1814), 35; emphasis in text.

25 Castellane, *Mémoires*, cited in Philip Mansel, *Paris between the Empires 1814–1852* (London: Phoenix, 2003), 71.

26 Cited in Le Gallo, *Les Cent Jours* (op. cit.), 17.

27 See Godlweski, *Napoléon à l'Ile d'Elbe* (op. cit.).

28 'Au peuple français'. Proclamation of Napoleon, Golfe-Juan, 1 March 1815.

29 Ibid.

30 'Les généraux, officiers, et soldats de la Garde impériale, aux généraux, officiers, et soldats de l'armée.' Proclamation, Golfe-Juan, 1 March 1815.

31 'A l'Armée' (op. cit.).

32 'Au peuple français' (op. cit.).

33 Cited in Le Gallo, *Les Cent Jours* (op. cit.), 57.

34 *Mémoires de la Reine Hortense* (Paris: Plon, 1927), Vol.III, 2.

35 Houssaye, *1815* (op. cit.), Vol.I, 248.

36 One of the royalist officers, Captain Randon (who later became a Marshal under Napoleon III) left a detailed account of the episode; see 'Retour de l'Ile d'Elbe', *Revue de l'Empire* Vol.V (1847), 329–341.

37 Thiry, *Le vol de l'aigle* (op. cit.), 89.

38 Police report, Paris, 19 March 1815, cited in Houssaye, *1815* (op. cit.), Vol.I, 327.

39 Napoleon cited this figure in a conversation with Raudot, the mayor of Avallon, in March 1815. See Claude-Marie Raudot, *Mes oisivetés* (Avallon, 1862). For a selection of Napoleonic songs, see Pierre Barbier and France Vernillat, *Histoire de la France par les chansons: Napoléon et sa légende* (Paris: Gallimard, 1958).

40 Declaration of Vienna Congress, 13 March 1815. AD Isère 52 M 6.

41 *Le Moniteur*, 27 March 1815.

42 Benjamin Constant, *Mémoires sur les Cent-Jours* (Tübingen, 1993), 198–201.

43 Le Gallo, *Les Cent Jours* (op. cit.), 211.

44 Chateaubriand called it 'an ameliorated version of the royal Charter.' Houssaye, *1815* (op. cit.), Vol.I, 546.

45 Stéphane Rials, 'Acte Additionel', Jean Tulard (ed.), *Dictionnaire Napoléon* (Paris: Fayard, 1999 ed.), Vol.I, 34–36.

46 Constant, *Mémoires sur les Cent-Jours* (op. cit.), 216.

47 Lafayette, *Mémoires* Vol.V, 417–418.

48 Joseph Rey, *Des bases d'une constitution ou De la balance des pouvoirs dans un Etat* (Grenoble, 1815). Rey argued that workers and labourers should not be given the vote, as they lacked education.

49 Charles de Rémusat, *Mémoires de ma vie* (Paris: Plon, 1958), Vol.I, 209.

50 See police reports for late April and May 1815 in Archives Nationales F7 3734 (rapports de police, 1815).

51 Le Gallo, *Les Cent Jours* (op. cit.), 229.

52 I am grateful to Malcolm Crook for drawing this point to my attention.

53 For further details see Frédéric Bluche, *Le plébiscite des Cent-Jours* (Geneva: Droz, 1974).

54 For a republican critique of the Additional Act, see the pamphlet *Le Printemps sacré de 1815. Aux hommes libres* (Paris, 1815).

55 Fleury de Chaboulon, *Mémoires* (op. cit.), Vol.II, 107–108.

56 Marie-Victorine Perrier, *Adresse de Marie-Victorine aux français* (Paris, 1815), 1–7.

57 Police report, 19 May 1815. AN F7 3734.

58 Le Gallo, *Les Cent Jours* (op. cit.), 379–426.

59 Prefect of Gironde report, 22 April 1815. AN F7 3734.

60 Prefect of Seine-Inférieure, Rouen, 21 April 1815. AN F7 3734.

61 In this instance, a police search found nothing. 'Rapport sur l'esprit des écclésiastiques', Grenoble, 29 May 1815. AD Isère 52 M 6.

62 Police report, Chartres, 8 April 1815. AN F7 3734.

63 Police report, Toulon, 26 May 1815. AN F7 3734.

64 Le Gallo, *Les Cent Jours* (op. cit.), 182.

65 Prefect of Corsica report, Ajaccio, 23 April 1815. AN BB3—152.

66 Emile Labretonnière, *Macédoine: Souvenirs du Quartier Latin* (Paris: Marpon, 1863), 165.

67 Police report, Paris, 7 April 1815. AN F7 3734.

68 Jean-Claude Caron, *Générations romantiques: les étudiants de Paris et le Quartier Latin (1814–1851)* (Paris: Armand Colin, 1991), 227.

69 Cited in Le Gallo, *Les Cent Jours* (op. cit.), 102.

70 Agricol Perdiguier, *Mémoires d'un compagnon* (Paris: Imprimerie Nationale, 1992 ed.), 73.

71 Police report, Avignon, 24 April 1815. AN F7 3734.

72 Houssaye, *1815* (op. cit.), Vol.I, 488.

73 Police report, Paris, 31 March 1815, quoting a coach driver returning from a journey between Clermont-Ferrand and Brioudé. AN F7 3734.

74 For an excellent study, see Robert Alexander, *Bonapartism and revolutionary tradition in France: the Fédérés of 1815* (Cambridge: Cambridge University Press, 1991).

75 Prefect of Mont Blanc report, 5 June 1815. AN F7 3734.

76 Police report, Toulouse, 30 May 1815. AN F7 3734.

77 Le Gallo, *Les Cent Jours* (op. cit.), 307.

78 *Mémoires de la Reine Hortense* (op. cit.), Vol.III, 4.

79 Houssaye sums up the dismal situation: 'The prefects were poor, and the mayors were even worse.' *1815* (op. cit.), Vol.I, 506.

80 Police report, Compiègne, 8 April 1815. AN F7 3734.

81 Robert Margerit, *Waterloo* (Paris: Gallimard, 1964), 208.
82 Annie Jourdan, *L'Empire de Napoléon* (Paris: Flammarion, 2000), 301–302.
83 Houssaye, *1815* (op. cit.), Vol.III, 518–520.
84 Louis Madelin, *Histoire du Consulat et de l'Empire* (Paris: Tallandier, 1976), Vol. XVI, 190.
85 Margerit, *Waterloo* (op. cit.), 290.
86 Ibid., 337.
87 Ibid., 379.
88 On this theme, see the conference proceedings edited by Marcel Watelet and Pierre Couvreur, *Waterloo lieu de mémoire européenne (1815–2000)* (Louvain, 2000).
89 See Chapter 6.
90 See, for example, the account of General Gaspard Gourgaud, *Campagne de dix-huit cent quinze, ou relation des opérations militaires qui ont eu lieu en France et en Belgique pendant les Cent Jours* (Paris: Plancher, 1818).
91 See notably Z.-J.Piérart, *Le drame de Waterloo: Grande reconstitution historique* (Paris: Revue Spiritualiste, 1868).
92 Colonel Charras, *Histoire de la campagne de 1815: Waterloo* (Brussels: Meline, 1858), 417.
93 Adolphe Thiers, *Histoire du Consulat et de l'Empire* (Paris: Paulin, 1860), Vol.XX.
94 Englund, *Napoleon* (op. cit.), 444.
95 Louise Cochelet, *Napoléon et la Reine Hortense* (Paris: Tallandier, 1910), 190–191.
96 Jean Tulard, *Joseph Fouché* (Paris: Fayard, 1998), 332–340.
97 Jean Lucas-Dubreton, *Le culte de Napoléon* (Paris: Albin Michel, 1960), 9–26.
98 Le Gallo, *Les Cent Jours* (op. cit.), 481.
99 Frédéric Bluche, 'Les pamphlets royalistes des Cent-Jours', *Revue de l'Institut Napoléon* (131), 1975.
100 Hippolyte Carnot, *Mémoires sur Lazare Carnot* (Paris: Hachette, 1907), Vol.II, 459.
101 Lucien Bonaparte, *La vérité sur les Cent-Jours* (Paris: Ladvocat, 1835), 102–103.
102 General Bertrand, *Cahiers de Sainte-Hélène 1818–1819* (Paris: Albin Michel, 1959), 96.
103 Le Gallo, *Les Cent Jours* (op. cit.), 485.
104 Marquis de Coriolis d'Espinouse, *Le tyran, les alliés et le roi* (Paris, 1814), 5–6.

2: Birth of a Legend

1 He had been appointed in February 1820. See *Mémoires du Baron d'Haussez* (Paris: Calmann-Lévy, 1896), Vol.I, 312.
2 Prefect of Isère report, Grenoble, 23 May 1820. AN F7 6650.
3 Furet, *La Révolution Française* (op. cit.), Vol. II, 42.

4   Ibid., 46–47.

5   Figure for the year 1820, cited in Roger Magraw, *France 1800–1914: a social history* (London: Pearson, 2002), 205.

6   See Chapter 6.

7   Reports of prefect of Bouches-du-Rhône, Marseille, and *procureur*, Aix, 9 February 1815. AN BB3—152.

8   On this episode see Jean Tulard, *Murat* (Paris: Fayard, 1999), 374–383.

9   Prefect of Hautes Pyrénées report, Tarbes, 20 February 1816. AN F7 3736.

10   Police reports on incidents in the Haute-Saone and Yonne, 4 March 1817. AN F7 3788.

11   Police report, Lyons, 23 March 1820. AN F7 6910.

12   Prefect of Nord report, Lille, 1820, on the songwriter Ausaldi, overheard performing his ode to Napoleon. The bard was arrested. AN F7 6909.

13   Account of former soldiers' meeting held in Marseilles, police report, 10 March 1819. AN F7 3791.

14   Prefect of Rhône report, 11 March 1816. AN F7 3736.

15   Police report, Grenoble, 15 February 1817. AN F7 3788.

16   Even after the belief in Napoleon's return had subsided, March continued to be associated with extraordinary events. In March 1829 there were reports from Lyons that the King had died, which caused some commotion in the Drôme and neighbouring departments. See prefect report, Valence, 3 March 1829. AN F7 6769.

17   Police report, Paris, 1 March 1817. AN F7 3788.

18   Police report, Lyons, 3 March 1817. AN F7 3788.

19   Police report, Metz, 7 March 1817. AN F7 3788.

20   See François Ploux, *De bouche à oreille: naissance et propagation des rumeurs dans la France du XIXe siècle* (Paris: Aubier, 2003), 75.

21   Report of subprefect, Chateausalins, 8 March 1818. AN F7 6866.

22   Prefect of Drôme report, 17 March 1817. AN F7 3788.

23   Police report, Lyons, 20 July 1821. AD Rhône 4 M 229.

24   For example the prefect of the Gard (report, Nimes, 3 January 1822): 'The situation in the department continues to be as calm as could possibly be desired.' AN F7 6769.

25   Reports from Nîmes, Strasbourg, Toulouse, Bourbon-Vendée, Clermont-Ferrand, Nevers, Etampes, and Lyons, March 1822. AN F7 3795.

26   Mayor of Belleville report, 17 November 1815. AD Rhône 4 M 237.

27   Police report, Lyons, 15 January 1816. AN F7 3736.

28   See for example the police report, Rodez, 1 April 1819, on the rumours which had spread at a fair in the town. AN F7 3791.

29   Police report, Pau, 4 January 1817. AN F7 3788.

30   Police report, Toulouse, 30 December 1816. AN F7 3788.

31   Police report, Corsica, undated [1817]. AN F7 3788.

32   Prefect of Corsica reports, 23 October 1820; 1 January 1821; 15 February 1821. AN F7 6906.

33 Gendarmerie report, Nancy, 23 February 1818. AN F7 6866.
34 'Chanson Nouvelle', circulating in the Rhône in the early Restoration years. AD Rhône 4 M 238.
35 Folder on 'Ulysses et Télémaque', AN F7 6839 (Libelles, chansons, placards séditieux).
36 One of the many stories circulating in Sens (Yonne) in the early months of 1818. Police report, Paris, 24 February 1818. AN F7 6866.
37 Police report, Grenoble, 13–14 January 1817. AN F7 3788.
38 Prefect of Rhône report, Lyons, 15 March 1816. AN F7 3736.
39 Prefect of Meurthe report, Nancy, 24 February 1818. F7 6866.
40 Prefect of Loire Atlantique report, Nantes, 29 December 1815. AN F7 3736.
41 Police report, Lyons, 20 September 1816. AD Rhône 4 M 227.
42 Procureur report, Fontainebleau, 7 January 1816. AN F7 3736.
43 Sub-prefect of Sens report, 18 March 1816. AD Yonne III M¹ 78.
44 Police report, Bourg, 29 February 1816. AN F7 3736.
45 Prefect of Doubs report, Besançon, 30 March 1816. AN F7 3736.
46 Prefect of Basses-Pyrénées report, Pau, 4 January 1817. AN F7 3788.
47 Prefect of Dordogne report, Périgueux, 18 January 1817. AN F7 3788.
48 Police report, Paris, 18 April 1816. AN F7 6729 (colporteurs).
49 Prefect of Isère to prefect of Rhône, 3 December 1817. AD Rhône 4 M 239.
50 Report to Minister of Justice, 14 February 1827. AN F7 6729.
51 Circular to all prefects, Paris, 20 March 1823. AN F7 6729.
52 Report to Minister of War, Bourges, 3 June 1822. AN F7 6729.
53 Report of mayor of Chamoux, 16 September 1815. AD Yonne III M¹ 87.
54 Prefect of Seine-Inférieure report, Rouen, 3 May 1818. AN F7 6866.
55 Confidential report, Chateau Thierry (Aisne), September 1820. AN F7 6866.
56 Undated report. AD Yonne III M¹ 67.
57 Prefect of Gironde report, Bordeaux, 24 February 1818. AN F7 6866.
58 Prefect of Indre report, Chateauroux, 4 February 1816. AN F7 3736.
59 Prefect of Somme report, Amiens, 4 March 1818. AN F7 6866.
60 Minister of Interior, Paris, report of 3 March 1823. AN F7 6729.
61 Anonymous denunciation to Minister of Interior, dated 18 June 1820. AN F7 6906.
62 Report of prefectoral councillor, Bourg (Ain), 15 March 1820. AN F7 6906.
63 Report of sub-prefect, Chateausalins (Meurthe), 8 March 1818. AN F7 6866.
64 Gendarmerie report, Metz, 21 September 1820. AN F7 6909.
65 Mayor of Avallon report, 20 March 1817. AD Yonne III M¹ 89.
66 Prefect of the Somme report, Amiens, 4 March 1818. AN F7 6866.
67 Prefect of Meuse report, Bar-le-Duc, 28 February 1816. AN F7 3736.

68 Prefect of Hautes-Pyrénées report, Tarbes, 28 January 1816. AN F7 3736.
69 Police report, Nantes, 5 March 1819. AN F7 3791.
70 Police report, Toulouse, 19 January 1816. AN F7 3736.
71 See for example the circular letter to the prefects of these departments from the prefect of Rhône, Lyons, 3 October 1815. AD Rhône 4 M 227.
72 Prefect of Seine-et-Marne report, Melun, 12 February 1816. AN F7 3736.
73 Prefect of Aube report, Troyes, 16 April 1821. AN F7 6913.
74 Prefect of Deux-Sèvres report, Niort, 23 January 1816. AN F7 3736.
75 Police report, Troyes, 10 January 1816. AN F7 3736.
76 Police report, Nevers, 29 January 1816. AN F7 3736.
77 Police report, Tulle, 13 March 1816. AN F7 3736.
78 Police report, Draguignan, 13 March 1817. AN F7 3788.
79 Gendarmerie report, Bastia, 11 November 1816. AN F7 3788. The men were arrested but – a sign of the precarious political conditions on the island – none were prosecuted.
80 Police report, Angers, 11 January 1817. AN F7 3788. The source of this information was a letter written by one of the deserters to his mother, who lived in the Maine et Loire.
81 Report of sub-prefect of Montbéliard, 2 March 1818. AN F7 6869.
82 Prefect of Doubs report, Besançon, 19 March 1818. AN F7 6869.
83 Police report, Avallon, 31 January 1816. AN F7 3736.
84 Prefect of Meuse report, Bar-le-Duc, 26 January 1816. AN F7 3736.
85 Police report, Lyons, 3 March 1817. AN F7 3788.
86 Procureur report, Lyons, 15 March 1820. AD Rhône 4 M 281.
87 'Aux habitants de Lyons', 19 March 1821. AD Rhône 4 M 229.
88 Prefect of Rhône, Lyons, 22 March 1821. AD Rhône 4 M 229.
89 Ploux, *De bouche à oreille* (op. cit.), 154–155.
90 This is argued, notably, by Bernard Ménager; see *Les Napoléon du peuple* (op. cit.), 21.
91 Claude Brelot, 'Terreur et contre-terreur dans le département du Jura de 1816 à 1818', *Travaux de la Société d'Emulation du Jura* (1977), 225.
92 Georges Lefebvre, *La Grande Peur de 1789* (Paris: Armand Colin, 1932).
93 Robert Tombs, *France 1814–1914* (London: Longman, 1999), 337.
94 Robert Alexander, *Rewriting the French revolutionary tradition: liberal opposition and the fall of the Bourbon monarchy* (Cambridge: Cambridge University Press, 2003), 230.
95 Prefect of Deux-Sèvres report, Niort, 26 February 1818. AN F7 6866.
96 Ménager, *Les Napoléon du Peuple* (op. cit.), 24.
97 Prefect of Ain report, Bourg, 10 January 1816. AN F7 3736.
98 Prefect of Maine et Loire report, Angers, 3 January 1816. AN F7 3736.
99 Prefect of Lot-et-Garonne, Agen, 26 March 1817. AN F7 3788.
100 Prefect of Rhône report, 15 March 1816. AN F7 3736.
101 Prefect of Gers report, Auch, 8 January 1816. AN F7 3736.
102 Ploux, *De bouche à oreille* (op. cit), 141.

103 Gendarmerie report, Auxerre, 9 July 1816. AD Yonne 3U1 1776.

104 Prefect of Morbihan report, Vannes, 14 January 1817. AN F7 3788.

105 Reports of prefect of Basses-Pyrénées, Pau, 23 February 1818, AN F7 6866; and prefect of Meuse, Bar-le-Duc, 17 June 1818; AN F7 6869. This particular story resurfaced periodically in the following years; it appeared again in Lyons in 1820. See police report, 15 February 1820; AD Rhône 4 M 229.

106 'Au peuple du Nouveau Monde', cited by prefect of Deux-Sèvres, Niort, 31 July 1819. AN F7 6866.

107 Police report, Perpignan, 9 January 1816. AN F7 3736.

108 Police report, Lille, 19 January 1816. AN F7 3736.

109 Police report, Chateauroux, 23 January 1816. AN F7 3736.

110 Special report, police commissioner, Bourg, 3 January 1816. AN F7 3736.

111 Prefect of Hautes-Pyrénées report, Tarbes, 28 January 1816. AN F7 3736.

112 *Procureur* report, Aix, 20 March 1817; AN BB18—1017; reports from Prefects of Bouches-du-Rhône, Marseille, 18 March 1817; Var, Draguignan, 20 March 1817; and Gard, Nîmes, 6 April 1817. AN F7 6668.

113 See Chapter 6.

114 Prefect of Meuse report, Bar-le-Duc, 13 March 1816. AN F7 3736.

115 Police report, Lyons, 15 January 1816. AN F7 3736.

116 Prefect of Côte d'Or report, Dijon, 18 January 1816. AN F7 3736.

117 For examples of these 'Austrian illusions', see Le Gallo, *Les Cent Jours* (op. cit.), 136–138.

118 Police report, Richelieu, 1 April 1817. AN F7 3788.

119 Police report, Lyons, 14 July 1815. AN F7 3734.

120 Report of mayor of Saint-Chaumond, 26 July 1815. AN F7 3734.

121 See for example the report of prefect of the Meurthe, Nancy, 13 March 1818. AN F7 6866.

122 Police report, Grenoble, 22 August 1822. AD Rhône 4 M 229.

123 Report of prefect of Loire, Montbrison, 27 June 1828. AN F7 6993.

124 Report of prefect of Marne, Chalon, 30 December 1815. AN F7 3736.

125 Minister of Interior report, Paris, 6 November 1815. AD Yonne III M¹ 87.

126 Report, Arras, 6 January 1816. AN F7 3736.

127 Police report, Lyons, 20 March 1819. AD Rhône 4 M 245.

128 Prefect of Seine-et-Marne report, Melun, 11 January 1816. AN F7 3736.

129 Prefect of Nord report, Lille, 11 January 1816.

130 Prefect of Calvados report, Caen, 14 January 1816. AN F7 3736.

131 Prefect of Vaucluse report, Avignon, 11 January 1816. AN F7 3736.

132 Report, Calais, 12 February 1816. AN F7 3736.

133 Both cases quoted in 'Tableau de délits, de cris, discours et actes séditieux ou de nouvelles alarmantes commis dans le département du Gard depuis le 15 février jusqu'au 15 mai de l'année 1817'; Nîmes, 26 May 1817. AN BB18—1017.

134 Report of sub-prefect of Melle, 30 March 1817. AN BB30—190.

135 Report of sub-prefect, Vitry-le-Français, 27 December 1815. AN F7 3736.

136 Prefect of Cantal report, Aurillac, 12 January 1816. AN F7 3736.

137 Report of sub-prefect of Tonnerre, n.d. [1816]. AD Yonne III M¹ 89.

138 Prefect of Mayenne report, Laval, 5 January 1816. AN F7 3736.

139 Report of gendarmerie of Ariège, Foix, 7 August 1818. AN F7 6839.

140 Prefect of Doubs report, Besançon, 30 March 1816, on statements made by rural inhabitants in the area. AN F7 3736.

141 Prefect of Meuse report, Bar-le-Duc, 13 March 1816. AN F7 3736.

142 Prefect of Saône-et-Loire report, Mâcon, 21 March 1817. AN F7 3788.

143 Gendarmerie report, Lyons, 6 October 1816. AD Rhône 4 M 238.

144 Prefect of Indre report, Chateauroux, 10 January 1817. AN F7 3788.

145 Prefect of Eure report, Evreux, 15 February 1816. AN F7 3788.

146 Prefectoral reports, 10 February 1817. AN F7 3788.

147 'Take courage, Napoleon is returning, and we will have bread at 4 sols.' Police report, Lyons, 24 December 1816. AD Rhône 4 M 238.

148 Gendarmerie report, Marseille, 7 March 1820. AN F7 6906.

149 For the example of Alsace, see Chalmin, 'Les variations de la légende' (op. cit.), 51.

150 Police report, Cambrai, 18 March 1816. AN F7 3736.

151 Police report, Lyons, 15 October 1815. AD Rhône 4 M 237.

152 'Tableau de délits, de cris, discours et actes séditieux ou de nouvelles alarmantes commis dans le département du Gard depuis le 15 février jusqu'au 15 mai de l'année 1817'; Nîmes, 26 May 1817. AN BB18—1017.

153 Prefect of Jura report, Lons-le-Saunier, 20 January 1817. AN F7 3788.

154 Report of sub-prefect, Chateau Chinon, 8 January 1816. AN F7 3736.

155 Prefect of Meuse report, Bar-le-Duc, 13 March 1816. AN F7 3736.

156 Report of subprefect, Pithiviers, 9 February 1816. AN F7 3736.

157 Prefect of Meuse report, Bar-le-Duc, 13 March 1816. AN F7 3736.

158 Report, Lyons, 20 March 1821. AD Rhône 4 M 241.

159 *Apothéose de Napoléon, poème traduit de l'arabe par Victor Lavagne* (Paris: Roy-Terry, 1829), 24.

160 Prefect of Meuse report, Bar-le-Duc, 13 March 1816. AN F7 3736.

161 Prefect of Creuse report, Guéret, 3 January 1816. AN F7 3736.

162 Report, Auxerre, 1816. AD Yonne III M¹ 74.

163 Prefect of Ardèche report, Privas, 1 March 1816. AN F7 3736.

164 Quoted in Ménager, *Les Napoléon du Peuple* (op. cit.), 32–33.

165 Report of mayor of Lyons, 23 February 1823. AD Rhône 4 M 242.

166 Notably a range of stories about the unfavourable fate met by French soldiers; a rumour in the Haute-Loire thus spread considerable alarm among the local population by claiming that the town of Bayonne had fallen into Spanish hands and that French troops in Spain were 'cornered'. Prefect of Haute-Loire report, Le Puy, 29 April 1823. AN F7 6729.

167 *Procureur-général* report, Agen, 1 May 1823. AN BB30—193.

168 Jules Garsou, *Les créateurs de la légende napoléonienne* (Brussels, 1899), 18.
169 Cited in Paul Leuilliot, *L'Alsace au début du XIXe siècle* (Paris: SEVPEN, 1959), Vol.I, 494–495.
170 *Procureur* report, Versailles, 12 November 1824. AN BB18—1117.
171 Police reports, Paris, 11 March and 26 April 1825. AN BB18—1121.
172 Procureur report, Aix, 7 September 1824. AN BB18—1114.

3: A Cult of Seditious Objects

1 Stendhal, *Journal* (Paris: Le Divan, 1937), Vol.V, 171.
2 In Lyons, the operation was completed by August 1815. Police report, 12 August 1815. AD Rhône 4 M 237.
3 Ménager, *Les Napoléon du peuple* (op. cit.), 16.
4 Jean Lucas-Dubreton, *Le culte de Napoléon 1815–48* (Paris, 1960), 51.
5 Prosper Mérimée, *Notes de voyage* (Paris: Biro, 2003), 166.
6 Police report, Lille, 18 January 1816. AN F7 3736.
7 Prefect of Isère report, Grenoble, 15 April 1818. AN F7 6704.
8 Prefect of Isère report, Grenoble, 25 August 1819. AN F7 6704.
9 See, for example, the police report, Lyons, 7 May 1818, on the arrest of four men involved in the manufacture and distribution of copper statues of Napoleon; three were former soldiers of the Grande Armée, and had also been ardent Bonapartists during the Hundred Days. AD Rhône 4 M 245.
10 Police report, Lyons, 28 December 1815. AN F7 3736.
11 Police report, Paris, 1823. AN F7 6706.
12 Customs report, Nantes, 6 September 1826. AN F7 6706.
13 Gendarmerie report, Lille, 31 July 1819. AN F7 6705.
14 Prefect of Seine-Inférieure report, Rouen, 9 December 1818. AN F7 6866.
15 Prefect of Rhône report, Lyons, 30 December 1815. AD Rhône 4 M 227.
16 Police report, Paris, 28 March 1818. AN F7 6869. One of the ways in which the authorities sought to control and regulate the dissemination of images was by requiring hawkers to deposit a copy of all their images with the local administration – an injunction which was frequently ignored.
17 Police reports 18 May, 12 June, and 15 October 1828. AN F7 6706.
18 See the report of the mayor of Toulouse, 27 March 1827. AN F7 6705.
19 Police report, Bourg, 18 April 1827. F7 6704.
20 Gendarmerie report, Blois, 9 February 1830. AN F7 6704.
21 Prefect of Seine-Inférieure, Rouen, report of 22 October 1823 on a collection of images confiscated at a local fair. AN F7 6704.
22 Sub-prefect of Toulon, report, 24 November 1818. AN F7 6706.
23 Prefect of Moselle report, Metz, 7 June 1819. AN F7 6705.
24 Prefect of Tarn report, Albi, 31 August 1820. AN F7 6910.
25 Image seized at a bookseller's in Lons-le-Saunier; prefect of Jura report, 23 January 1821. AN F7 6705.
26 Prefect of Bouches-du-Rhône report, Marseille, 26 January 1816. F7 3736.

27 Gendarmerie report, Chateaudun (Eure et Loir), 12 August 1827. AN F7 6704.
28 Image found on sale at Saint-Lo (Manche); gendarmerie report, 23 October 1822. AN F7 6705.
29 Images confiscated at Draguignan (Var); prefect report, 1 February 1819. AN F7 6706.
30 Prefect of Bouches-du-Rhône report, Marseille, 26 January 1816. AN F7 3736.
31 For comments on images depicting the return journey, see reports of gendarmerie, Chateaudun, 12 August 1827, AN F7 6704; on the landing in Cannes, prefect of Gironde report, Bordeaux, 29 July 1819, AN F7 6704; and on Grenoble, prefect of Seine-Inférieure report, Rouen, 27 October 1829, AN F7 6706.
32 Prefect of Var report, Draguignan, 19 March 1820. AN F7 6910.
33 Prefect of Mayenne reports, Laval, 30 August and 5 October 1819. AN F7 6705.
34 Gendarmerie report, Angers, 12 January 1822. AN F7 6704.
35 Prefect of Calvados report, Caen, 23 February 1820. AN F7 3792.
36 Prefect of Isère report, 18 March 1823. AN F7 6704.
37 Police report, Paris, 3 March 1823. AN F7 6706.
38 Police report, Lyons, 13 September 1820. AD Rhône 4 M 245.
39 Prefect of Bouches-du-Rhône report, Marseille, 16 January 1826. AN F7 6704.
40 Prefect of Vienne report, Poitiers, 23 April 1827. AN F7 6706.
41 Various police and prefectoral reports, AN F7 6706.
42 Prefect of Somme report, Amiens, 5 January 1830. AN F7 6706.
43 Police report, Paris, 13 November 1819. AN F7 6706.
44 Police report, Paris, 12 July 1828. AN F7 6706. For a list of Parisian shops where Napoleonic memorabilia could be purchased (discreetly) between 1815 and 1830, see Henri d'Alméras, *La vie Parisienne sous la Restauration* (Paris: Albin Michel, 1909), 369–370.
45 Prefect of Ardennes report, Mézières, 31 August 1827. AN F7 6704.
46 Police report, Paris, 19 November 1827. AN F7 6706.
47 Letter of Minister of Police, Paris, 19 December 1815. AD Tarn IV M IV/3.
48 Report of *procureur*, Ploermel, 13 May 1824. BB18—1113.
49 Prefect of Oise report, Beauvais, 15 July 1819. AN F7 6705.
50 Reports of prefect of Eure (Evreux), 10 July 1822, and prefect of Seine-Inférieure (Rouen), 19 October 1822. AN F7 6704 (dossier Lemire).
51 Prefect of police reports, Paris, 21 April and 20 May 1823. AN F7 6704 (dossier Lemire).
52 Prefect of Seine-Inférieure report, July 1827. AN F7 6704 (dossier Lemire).
53 Bluche, *Le Bonapartisme* (op. cit.).
54 See, for example, the report of the prefect of the Ardennes, Mézières, 22

September 1822, on the discovery of a collection of Napoleonic objects in a house in Charleville. AN F7 6704.

55 Incident cited in Jean Lucas-Dubreton, *Louvel le régicide* (Monaco: Lep, 1965), 22.
56 'Bustes et portraits de Bonaparte'. Prefect of Yonne circular, Auxerre, 1 December 1815. AD Yonne III M¹ 82.
57 Prefect of Bas-Rhin report, Strasbourg, 3 December 1829. AN F7 6705.
58 Report by Marquis de Pastoret, in *Cour des Pairs. Réquisitoire sur la conspiration du 19 Août 1820* (Paris: Imprimerie Royale, 1821), 35–37.
59 Lucienne Curie-Seimbres, 'Joseph-Léonard Decazes et les derniers bona-partistes Tarnais (1815–1819)', *Revue du Tarn*, Spring 1976, 77.
60 Report of mayor of Toulouse, 27 March 1827. AN F7 6705.
61 Police report, Paris, 26 January 1820. AN F7 6705.
62 Prefect of Ardennes report, Mézières, 15 February 1823. AN F7 6704.
63 Police report, Paris, 29 April 1821. AN F7 6706.
64 Police report, Paris, 12 December 1818. AN F7 6706.
65 Report of police, Toulouse, 19 January 1816. AN F7 3736.
66 Gendarmerie report, Saint-Lo (Manche), 29 July 1819. AN F7 6705.
67 Undated report [1815]. AD Yonne III M¹ 68.
68 Report, Ministry of Justice, Paris, 26 October 1815. AN BB3—152.
69 Police report, Paris, 19 February 1820. Archives de la Préfecture de Police, Aa 343.
70 See the examples cited in Natalie Petiteau, *Lendemains d'Empire: les soldats de Napoléon dans la France du XIXe siècle* (Paris: La Boutique de l'Histoire, 2003), 132.
71 Police report, Beauvais, 28 December 1816. AN F7 3788.
72 Police report, Nantes, 20 February 1819. AN F7 3791.
73 *Procureur* report, Guingamp, 1 December 1824. AN BB18—1118.
74 Police report, Albi, 21 February 1816. AN F7 3736.
75 Curie-Seimbres, 'Joseph-Léonard Decazes et les derniers bonapartistes' (op. cit.), 77.
76 Chalmin, 'Les variations de la légende' (op. cit.), 49.
77 Gustave Flaubert, *Madame Bovary* (1856).
78 Prefect of Saône-et-Loire report, Mâcon, 2 September 1820. AN F7 6910.
79 Gendarmerie report, Auch, 3 March 1820. AN F7 3792.
80 Prefect of Seine et Oise report, Pontoise, 14 October 1829. AN F7 6706.
81 Police report, Paris, 13–14 July 1817. AN F7 3788.
82 Customs report, Paris, 12 September 1828. AN F7 6706.
83 Prefect of Seine-Inférieure, Rouen, 7 January 1826. AN F7 6706.
84 Police report, Paris, 3 October 1825. AN F7 6705.
85 Prefect of Var report, 7 January 1828. AN F7 6706.
86 Police report, Paris, 3–4 January 1817. AN F7 3788.
87 Prefect of Ardennes report, Mézières, 30 April 1822. AN F7 6704.
88 Police report, Paris, 5 May 1823. AN F7 6706.

89 Prefect of Seine-Inférieure report on confiscation of twenty-four Napoleonic plates from a local restaurant, Rouen, 9 November 1822. AN F7 6706.

90 There are numerous accounts referring to the production, distribution, and consumption of all these items throughout the Restoration years in AN F7 6704, 6705 and 6706.

91 Prefect of police reports, Paris, 23 July and 9 August 1819. AN F7 6704.

92 Prefect of Rhône report, Lyons, 10 August 1821. AN F7 6916.

93 See police reports, Lyons, 16 November 1821 and 29 May 1822. AD Rhône 4 M 245.

94 For reports on the affair, see prefect of Lot-et-Garonne, Agen, 4 March 1822, AN F7 6705; and police report, Paris, 30 April 1822, BB30—193.

95 See report of prefect of Meurthe, Nancy, 25 July 1823. AN F7 6705.

96 On perfume, see prefect of police, Paris, 19 November 1819, AN F7 6706; on *huile des libéraux*, reports of prefects of Ardennes and Vienne, 11 June 1820 and 28 February 1821, AN F7 6705.

97 Prefect of Côtes-du-Nord report, Saint-Brieuc, 29 August 1817. AN F7 6848.

98 Edouard Guillon, *Les complots militaires sous la Restauration* (Paris: Plon, 1895), 47.

99 Prefect of Deux-Sèvres report, Niort, 16 March 1816. AN F7 3736.

100 Incident cited in Jean Vidalenc, *Le département de l'Eure sous la Monarchie constitutionnelle* (Paris: Marcel Rivière, 1952), 155.

101 Prefect of Vosges report, Epinal, 8 September 1817. AN F7 6848.

102 Police reports, 3 July 1821 (Lyons) and 31 July 1821 (Paris). AD Rhône 4 M 245.

103 Police report, Lyons, 14 July 1821. AD Rhône 4 M 229.

104 Police report, Lyons, 25 July 1821. AD Rhône 4 M 229.

105 Prefect of Isère report, 14 January 1822. AN F7 6650.

106 Prefect of Doubs report, Besançon, 27 May 1826. AN F7 6704.

107 Police report, Lyons, 30 July 1821. AD Rhône 4 M 229.

108 Prefect of Rhône report, Lyons, 30 July 1821. AN F7 6848.

109 Prefect of Gironde report, 4 January 1827. AN F7 6704.

110 Prefect of Rhône report, Lyons, 18 August 1820. AN F7 6705.

111 'Couteau Napoléon.'

112 Prefect of Vienne report, Montmorillon, 21 March 1830. AN F7 6706.

113 Prefect of Cher report, Bourges, 2 November 1829. AN F7 6704.

114 Prefect of Allier report, Moulins, 12 December 1819. AN F7 6704.

115 Prefect of Charente-Inférieure, La Rochelle, 12 October 1820. AN F7 6906.

116 Prefect of Vienne report, Poitiers, 28 February 1821. AN F7 6705.

117 Police report, Paris, 20 April 1820. AD Rhône 4 M 245.

118 The description of the label is in a report from the prefect of the Doubs, Besançon, 15 March 1820. AD Rhône 4 M 245.

119 Police report, Paris, 11 September 1829. AN F7 6706.

120 Internal police memorandum, Paris, 27 August 1829. AN F7 6706.

121 Gendarmerie report, Malestroit, 18 February 1818. AN F7 6866.

122 Prefect of Hautes-Alpes report, Gap, 17 September 1822. AN F7 6704.

123 Prefect of Isère report, Grenoble, 14 January 1822. AN F7 6650.

124 Prefect of Ardennes report, Mézières, 11 May 1822. AN F7 6704.

125 Police report, Paris, December 1818. AN F7 6889.

126 Prefect of Somme report, Amiens, 5 April 1822. AN F7 6706.

127 Police report, Nîmes, 31 March 1818. AN F7 6869.

128 Tax-collector letter, Dieppe, 16 March 1821. AN F7 6913.

129 Prefect of Haute-Garonne report, Toulouse, 9 December 1822. AN F7 6705.

130 Police report, Lille, 2 October 1820. AN F7 6909.

131 Police report, Paris, 31 July 1824. BB18—1111.

132 Prefect of Indre-et-Loire report, Tours, 4 March 1818. AN F7 6866.

133 *Procureur* report, Lisieux, 1 June 1817. AN F7 6704.

134 See Nicole Pellegrin, *Les vêtements de la liberté: abécédaire des pratiques vestimentaires en France de 1780 à 1800* (Paris: Alinea, 1989).

135 Report of mayor of St Lager, 24 March 1816. AD Rhône 4 M 227.

136 A reference to Napoleon's disastrous Russian campaign of 1812.

137 Speech of Monsieur Brai, 24 March 1816, reported by mayor of St Lager; AD Rhône 4 M 227.

138 *Procureur* report, Draguignan, 12 March 1817. AN BB18—1017.

139 For example in Caumont (Vaucluse) on the night of 24 September 1818; prefect of Vaucluse report, Avignon, 1 October 1818. AN F7 6706.

140 Prefect of Hautes-Pyrénées report, Tarbes, 23 February 1818.

141 For examples of tricolour banners found on church towers, see police report, Vesoul, 5 January 1816, AN F7 3736; and Laon, 26 December 1817, AN F7 3788.

142 Cited in Guillon, *Les complots militaires sous la Restauration* (op. cit.), 58.

143 David Pinkney, *The French Revolution of 1830* (Princeton, NJ: Princeton University Press, 1972), 49–50.

144 For a list of people arrested and prosecuted in Lyons between August and December 1815, see AD Rhône 4 M 245 (*emblèmes et enseignes séditieux*).

145 Various reports, Seine folder, AN F7 6910.

146 Prefect of Aube report, Troyes, 15 May 1823, on a variety of such articles confiscated at a fair. AN F7 6704.

147 Police report, Paris, 6 August 1827. AN F7 6705.

148 Prefect of Seine et Oise report, Versailles, 27 November 1819. AN F7 6706.

149 Report of *procureur-général*, Nîmes, 11 March 1817, on incident at Beauvoisin (Gard). AN BB30—1017.

150 Prefect of Hérault report, 3 June 1818. AN F7 6704.

151 Gendarmerie of Hautes-Alpes report, Gap, 21 February 1818. AN F7 6866.

152 Sub-prefect of Corbeil report, 23 March 1827. AN F7 6706.
153 Gendarmerie report, 11 January 1822. AN F7 3795.
154 Prefectoral and police reports, Sisteron, March–October 1826. AN F7 6704.
155 'Tableau de délits, de cris discours et actes séditieux ou de nouvelles alarmantes commis dans le département du Gard depuis le 15 février jusqu'au 15 mai de l'année 1817' Nîmes, 26 May 1817. AN BB18—1017.
156 Gendarmerie report, Niort, 27 April 1819. AN F7 3791.
157 Prefect of Bouches-du-Rhône report, Marseille, 6 July 1820. F7 6906.
158 Prefect of Yonne report, 24 March 1823. AN F7 6704.
159 Police report, Paris, 3 March 1820. AN F7 6706.
160 Prefect of Puy-de-Dôme report, Clermont-Ferrand, 10 February 1821. AN F7 6916.
161 See, most notably, the letter of the mayor of Lyons, 1 April 1830. AD Rhône 4 M 242.
162 Prefect of Dordogne report, Périgueux, 3 January 1817. AN F7 3788.
163 Le Gallo, *Les Cent Jours* (op. cit.), 130.
164 Prefect of Doubs report, Besançon, 22 March 1820. AN F7 3792.

4: An Occult Force

1 Police reports, Lyons, 8 and 17 August 1822. AN F7 3795.
2 See for example the anonymous pamphlet, *Des conspirateurs et des conspirations* (Paris, 1822).
3 Police memorandum, undated [1825]. AN F7 6772.
4 Document found on travelling salesman in Evreux. Report of prefect of Eure, Evreux, 17 February 1816. AN F7 3736.
5 See Sudhir Hazareesingh, 'L'opposition républicaine aux fêtes civiques du Second Empire: Fête, anti-fête, et souveraineté', *Revue d'Histoire du 19e siècle*, No. 26–27 (2003), 149–171.
6 Mona Ozouf, *La fête révolutionnaire* (Paris: Gallimard, 1988 ed.).
7 On the colourful life and career of this officer, who lived until 1855, see Antonin Debidour, *Le Général Fabvier, sa vie militaire et politique* (Paris: Plon, 1904).
8 On the activities of Lallemand in the United States, Spain, Belgium, and France, see Frédéric Bluche, *Le bonapartisme: aux origines de la droite autoritaire (1800–1850)* (Paris: Nouvelles Editions Latines, 1980), 138–139.
9 Alexander, *Bonapartism and revolutionary tradition* (op. cit.), 257–274; 285.
10 Alan Spitzer, *Old hatreds and new hopes: the French Carbonari against the Bourbon Restoration* (Cambridge, Massachusetts: Harvard University Press, 1971), 19.
11 Ibid., 278–279.
12 Police report, Gap (Hautes-Alpes), 4 February 1817. AN F7 3788.
13 Procureur report, Tarbes, 16 May 1817. AN BB30—190.

14 Prefect of Hautes-Alpes report, Gap, 12 March 1821. AN F7 6913.

15 *Procureur-général* report, Grenoble, 8 July 1818. AN BB30—190.

16 Report of sub-prefect of Sens, 18 March 1816. AD Yonne III M¹ 78.

17 Joseph Rey, *Histoire de la conspiration de Grenoble en 1816* (Grenoble: Barnel, 1847), 221.

18 Cited in Pierre-Arnaud Lambert, *La Charbonnerie Française 1821–1823* (Lyons: Presses Universitaire de Lyons, 1995), 78. Rey was in exile in England between 1820 and 1826; he returned to France after being amnestied.

19 There were reports of such activities in the Drôme, Basses-Alpes, and Isère in late 1815; see the correspondence among local prefects in AD Isère, 52 M 8.

20 Police report, Pau, 4 January 1817. AN F7 3788.

21 Reports of prefect of Doubs, Besançon, 1 March 1816; and prefect of Calvados, Caen, 28 February 1816. AN F7 3736.

22 Petiteau, *Lendemains d'Empire* (op. cit.), 273.

23 'Demi-soldes, 1819–1820'. AD Rhône 4 M 281.

24 Police report, Grenoble, 15 February 1828. AD Isère 52 M 6. For a re-assessment of the 'myth' of the *demi-soldes*, see Jean Vidalenc, *Les demi-soldes, étude d'une catégorie sociale* (Paris: Marcel Rivière, 1955).

25 See Joseph Kiener, *Berceau historique des mystères de la Franc-Maçonnerie* (Paris, 1860); Kiener was a Mason and a bookseller who served as one of the dig-nitaries in the Bonaparte Lodge in Paris during the 1850s; he believed (as did many of his comrades) that Napoleon had been a Freemason.

26 Prefect of Meuse report, Bar-le-Duc, 28 February 1816. AN F7 3736.

27 Prefect of Aveyron report, Rodez, 5 February 1816. AN F7 3736.

28 André Combes, *Histoire de la Franc-Maçonnerie au XIXe siècle* (Paris: Editions du Rocher, 1998), Vol. I, 137.

29 Report of prefect of police to Minister of Interior, Paris, June 1825. AN F7 6689.

30 Bourg, letter dated 23 January 1816. AD Rhône 4 M 227.

31 Various reports, dated January 1822; AN F7 6684 (sociétés secrètes).

32 Prefect of Calvados report, Caen, 23 February 1820. AN F7 3792.

33 See the report of mayor of Vaise, 23 August 1816. AD Rhône 4 M 227.

34 Police report, Lyons, 18 September 1822. AD Rhône 4 M 263 (*loges maçon-niques*).

35 Georges Ribe, *L'opinion publique et la vie politique à Lyon lors des premières années de la Seconde Restauration* (Paris: Sirey, 1957), 156–157.

36 Police report, Lyons, 21 June 1821. AD Rhône 4 M 263.

37 Information contained in letter of prefect of Isère to prefect of Rhône, Grenoble, 21 August 1822. AD Rhône 4 M 263.

38 Undated police report [1822] on activities of six Masonic Lodges of Lyons. AD Rhône 4 M 263.

39 Prefect of Rhône report to Minister of Interior, Lyons, 11 September 1822. AD Rhône 4 M 263.

40 Police report on Amboise Lodge, 27 August 1822. AN F7 6684.

41 Combes, *Histoire de la Franc-Maçonnerie* (op. cit.), 75.

42 Bluche, *Le Bonapartisme* (op. cit.), 144.

43 Police report, Paris, 26 June 1823. AN F7 3795.

44 Combes, *Histoire de la Franc-Maçonnerie* (op. cit.), 113.

45 Police report, Paris, 13 May 1823. AN F7 6685.

46 Police report, Bayonne, 15 March 1822. AN F7 3795.

47 Edouard Guillon, *Les complots militaires sous la Restauration* (Paris: Plon, 1895), 256.

48 Report of prefect, Metz, 18 September 1822. AN F7 6685.

49 Prefect of Jura report, Lons-le-Saunier, 11 June 1824. AN F7 6684.

50 Reports of prefect of Moselle, 13 and 22 September 1820; AN F7 6909.

51 d'Alméras, *La vie Parisienne sous la Restauration* (op. cit.), 367–368.

52 Edmond Biré, *L'Année 1817* (Paris: Champion, 1895), 123.

53 Report of police informer Achard, 20 July 1824. AN F7 6685.

54 Police note to Minister of Interior, 29 August 1824. AN F7 6685.

55 Police report, Paris, 31 July 1826. AN F7 6668.

56 A note from the War Ministry dated 8 April 1822 estimated that the membership of the *Carbonari* in France exceeded 800,000. AN F7 6684.

57 Dossier 'Carbonari en Italie, en Suisse; Charbonniers Bons Cousins en Franche-Comté' [1821–22]. AN F7 6684.

58 Report of prefect of police, Paris, June 1825. AN F7 6689.

59 Police report, Lyons, 19 February 1822. AD Rhône 4 M 245.

60 Prefect of Isère report, 6 August 1820. AN F7 6650.

61 Prefect of Isère report, 17 August 1822. AN F7 6650.

62 Prefect of Isère report, 3 July 1823. AN F7 6650.

63 In addition to the Duc de Berry, Louvel planned to assassinate the Duc d'Angoulême and the Comte d'Artois.

64 See Guillaume de Bertier de Sauvigny, *La Restauration* (Paris: Flammarion, 1974), 163.

65 Spitzer, for example, refers to 'poor mad Louvel' ; *Old hatreds and new hopes* (op. cit.), 36.

66 See, for example, *Conjuration permanente contre la Maison de Bourbon et les rois de l'Europe* (Paris: le Normand, 1820).

67 *Mémoires du Baron d'Haussez* (op. cit.), Vol.I, 317.

68 This painstaking work forms the basis of Gilles Malandain's article, 'La conspiration solitaire d'un ouvrier théophilanthrope: Louvel et l'assassinat du Duc de Berry en 1820', *Revue Historique* Vol. CCCII/2 (2000).

69 Ibid., 380.

70 Ibid., 390.

71 Ibid., 391.

72 Ibid., 386.

73 Ibid., 388.

74 Marquise de W***, *Pressentimens, rêves, visions, apparitions et singularités qui ont précédé la mort de S.A.R.Mgr. le Duc de Berry* (Paris: Moreau, 1820), 13–14.

75 Reports in Archives de la Préfecture de police, Paris, Aa 343 (Affaire Louvel, 1820).

76 Report of *procureur*, Nogent-sur-Marne, 23 February 1820 (Legrand was passing through Nogent when he made these comments). AN F7 6745.

77 Report of prefect of Allier, Moulins, 19 February 1820. AN F7 6745.

78 There are two weighty folders on public reactions to the assassination in the Archives Nationales (F7 6745 and 6746); for Paris, see the series held in the Prefecture de Police archives in the Aa collection (folders 343 to 352).

79 'Mort aux tyrans du monde'. Placard, Le Vigan, early March 1820. AN F7 6745.

80 Gendarmerie report, Beauvais, 26 February 1820. AN F7 6909.

81 Gendarmerie report, Tarascon, 5 March 1820. AN F7 6906.

82 Prefect of Seine-Inférieure report, 18 February 1820. AN F7 3792. The original version of the *Marseillaise* was composed by Rouget de l'Isle, a young captain of the French Revolutionary Army; in 1792 it became the official anthem of the French Republic.

83 Prefect of Calvados report, 23 February 1820. AN F7 3792.

84 Gendarmerie report, Melun, 23 February 1820. AN F7 3792.

85 Cited in Lucas-Dubreton, *Louvel le régicide* (op. cit.), 22.

86 Prefect of Ardennes report, Mézières, 1 April 1820. AN F7 3792.

87 Prefect of Seine-et-Oise report, 12 March 1820. AN F7 3792; see also gendarmerie report, 11 March 1820; AN F7 6910.

88 Prefect of police report, Paris, 19 February 1821. AN F7 6916.

89 Report of prefect of police, Paris, June 1825. AN F7 6689.

90 Anonymous letter to prefect of Isère, 15 February 1824. AN F7 6650.

91 Etienne Lamothe-Langon, *Louvel et l'inconnu* (Paris: Dentu, 1834), Vol. I, 316.

92 Guillon, *Les complots militaires sous la Restauration* (op. cit.), 10.

93 For a detailed account, see Honoré Pontois, *La conspiration du Général Berton* (Paris: Dentu, 1877).

94 From a police report, 1822, cited in Guillon, *Les complots militaires sous la Restauration* (op. cit.), 179, fn.1.

95 Jean-Baptiste Berton, *A MM. Les Membres de la Chambre des Pairs, et à MM. Les Députés des Départemens, au Corps Législatif* (Paris, 1821), 5.

96 Jean-Baptiste Berton, *Précis historique, militaire et critique des batailles de Fleurus et de Waterloo* (Paris: Delaunay, 1818), v.

97 For an account of this controversy, see Ephraim Harpaz, *L'école libérale sous la Restauration* (Geneva: Droz, 1968), 225 fn.12.

98 'Des hommes caducs de corps et d'esprit'. Jean-Baptiste Berton, *Commentaire sur l'ouvrage en dix-huit chapitres de M. le Lieutenant-Général J.-J. Tarayre, intitulé De la force des gouvernements* (Paris: Delaunay, 1819), 14; see also 178 and 179.

99 Jean-Baptiste Berton, *Considérations sur la police* (Paris, 1820), 27 and 41.

100 'On s'engage et puis on voit.'

101 Cited in Eugène Bonnemère, *Etudes historiques saumuroises* (Saumur: Roland, 1868), 20.

102 Berton, *Considérations sur la police* (op. cit.), 15.

103 Jean-Baptiste Berton, *Lettre à M. le Baron Mounier, Directeur-Général de la Police du Royaume, sur la mort de Napoléon* (Paris, 1821), 6.

104 Ibid., 10.

105 Berton, *Considérations sur la police* (op. cit.), 9.

106 The various reports are in F7 6668 and 6669 (famille Bonaparte).

107 There were a number of petty jealousies among the imperial entourage; the main conflict was between Bertrand, Montholon, and Gourgaud and Las Cases, who was resented because he was the most recent convert to the Napoleonic cause, and also the one whose company Napoleon seemed to appreciate most.

108 Report of French consul on his interrogation of Lepage, Hamburg, 26 August 1818. AN F7 6668.

109 The best account of his life is in Alberic Cahuet's chapter, 'Noel Santini, "la bête noire" de la Sainte-Alliance', in *Après la mort de l'Empereur* (Paris: Emile-Paul, 1913), 127–198.

110 The pamphlet, published in London by Ridgways in 1817, was entitled *An appeal to the British Nation on the treatment experienced by Napoleon Buonaparte in the island of St Helena by M. Santine* (sic), *huissier du cabinet de l'Empereur.*

111 Police report, Lyons, 13 February 1824. AN F7 6926 (dossier Santini).

112 Sub-prefect of Bastia letter, 29 March 1824. AN F7 6929.

113 Prefect of Rhône report, Lyons, 26 March 1825. AN F7 6926.

114 Prefect of Bouches-du-Rhône report, Marseille, January 1828. AN F7 6926.

115 Santini lived to see the restoration of the Empire under Napoleon III, who appointed him to the post of keeper of the Invalides; he died in July 1862. He published his memoirs, which unfortunately offer few insights into his underground activities. See *De Sainte-Hélène aux Invalides. Souvenirs de Santini, gardien du Tombeau de l'Empereur* (Paris: Lacombe, 1854).

116 Note from War Ministry on the activities of Monsieur Broutat, Paris, 3 October 1822. AN F7 6685.

117 Gautier was eventually arrested in the spring of 1818. Prefect of Manche report, Saint-Lo, 5 April 1818. AN F7 6869.

118 Report on Le Boucher, *procureur-général*, Angers, 31 October 1821. AN F7 6684. His activities were uncovered by a somewhat circuitous route: a young man who attended one of the Masonic meetings at which Le Boucher was present told his mother about the political activities which went on there; the mother unburdened herself of this information to her priest, who passed it on to the police on condition that the anonymity of the family was preserved.

119 Mayor of Chalon report, 21 October 1816. AD Yonne III M^1 87.

120 Prefect of police report, Paris, 16 February 1816. AN F7 6869.
121 Prefect of Isère report, Grenoble, 1 September 1821. AN F7 6650.
122 For a full account of this insurrection as seen by the royalist officer who had to deal with it, see *Mémoires du Baron d'Haussez* (op. cit.), Vol. I, 354–366.
123 Report of sub-prefect of Marcellin, 16 September 1821. AN F7 6650.
124 Ibid.
125 Prefect of Drôme report, Valence, 11 March 1823. AN F7 6650.
126 Police report, Grenoble, 11 January 1822. AN F7 3795.
127 Prefect of Isère report, Grenoble, 1 September 1821. AN F7 6650.
128 Ibid.
129 Prefect of Isère report, Grenoble, 16 April 1823. AN F7 6650.
130 Prefect of Isère report, Grenoble, 17 April 1823. AN F7 6650.
131 Prefect of Isère report, Grenoble, 9 September 1823. AN F7 6650.

5: Rebellions in Action

1 G. de Bertier de Sauvigny, *La Restauration* (Paris: Flammarion, 1955), 164–168.
2 See Biré, *L'Année 1817* (op. cit.), 110–118.
3 For an account of all these conspiracies, see Spitzer, *Old hatreds and new hopes* (op. cit.), 77–141.
4 'Mémoires du Commandant Bernard Poli'. The original manuscript of Poli's memoirs is held in the Corsican departmental archives. The full text was published in *Etudes Corses* in 1954–55; this distinction between Napoleonism and imperialism appears in no. 3 (July 1954), 13.
5 Prefect reports, Ajaccio, 11 and 19 February 1816. AN F7 3736.
6 'Mémoires du Commandant Bernard Poli'. *Etudes Corses*, nos. 7–8 (1955), 44–51.
7 Pierre Antonetti, *Histoire de la Corse* (Paris: Robert Laffont, 1973), 443–44.
8 'Mémoires du Commandant Bernard Poli'. *Etudes Corses* nos. 7–8 (1955), 64.
9 See for example the report of the Prefect of Police, Paris, 24 June 1822 on a visit by Poli to the capital, during which he had lost the agents who were responsible for trailing him – much to this official's frustration. AN F7 6916.
10 See, for example, the poem by Ghiacumu Simonpoli, *Fiumorbu in guerra 1815–1816. Poema in ottu canti* (Bastia: Edizioni Di 'U Montese'), 1963.
11 Alexander, *Rewriting the French revolutionary tradition* (op. cit.), 135–186.
12 Sharif Gemie, *French revolutions 1815–1914* (Edinburgh: Edinburgh University Press, 1999), 30.
13 Pamela Pilbeam, 'Upheaval and continuity, 1814–1880', in Malcolm Crook (ed.), *Revolutionary France* (Oxford: Oxford University Press, 2002), 38.
14 Bluche, *Le Bonapartisme* (op. cit.), 158.

15 Prefect of Haute Garonne report, Toulouse, 14 December 1827. AN F7 6913.

16 Undated report. AD Yonne III M^1 71.

17 Minister of Interior report, Paris, 7 September 1824. AN BB18—1114.

18 *Procureur* report, Les Sables, 10 September 1824. AN BB18—1114.

19 Police report, Bordeaux, 27 August 1819. AN F7 3744.

20 Hazareesingh, *The Saint-Napoleon* (op. cit.).

21 Gendarmerie report, Villeneuve (Lot-et-Garonne), 26 August 1822. AN BB30—193.

22 Prefect of Isère report, Grenoble, 26 August 1822. AN F7 6650.

23 Police report, Montbrison (Loire), 26 August 1819. AN F7 3744.

24 Report of *procureur-général*, Riom, 17 October 1815. AN BB3—151.

25 Report of *procureur*, Nancy, 19 August 1824. AN BB18—1113.

26 Report of *procureur*, Rennes, 14 September 1824. AN BB18—1114.

27 Report of *procureur*, Lille, 1 September 1824. AN BB18—1114.

28 Reports of *procureur*, Caen, 12 September 1824; and *procureur-général*, Nîmes, 4 September 1824. AN BB18—1114.

29 Reports of prefects of Manche, Meuse, Lot-et-Garonne, and Nièvre, January 1816; AN F7 3736.

30 Police report, Chateauroux (Indre), 22 January 1816. AN F7 3736.

31 The event was closed down by the police, and the organizer prosecuted. See police report, 10 February 1816. AN F7 3736.

32 Report of sub-prefect of Joigny, 30 May 1816. AD Yonne III M^1 88.

33 Procureur-général report, Toulouse, 18 November 1824. AN BB18—1116.

34 Procureur report, Draguignan, 4 October 1824. AN BB18—1116.

35 See Jacques-Olivier Boudon, *Le Consulat et l'Empire* (op. cit.).

36 Ploux, *De bouche à oreille* (op. cit.).

37 On these incidents, see reports by prefects of Loire (December 1815) and Marne (February 1816), AN F7 3736.

38 Declaration of Etienne Grenier, 1817. *Tableau de délits*, Nîmes, 26 May 1817. AN BB18—1017.

39 The trees were on the road between the villages of Romilly and Marailly. Gendarmerie report to prefect of Aube, 31 July 1826. AN F7 6704.

40 Police report, Besançon, 3 March 1816. AN F7 3736.

41 Gendarmerie report, Beauvais, 8 November 1820. AN F7 6909.

42 For an elaboration of this neo-Roman conception of republican freedom, see Quentin Skinner, *Liberty before liberalism* (Cambridge: Cambridge University Press, 1998).

43 See the beginning of this chapter.

44 'Aux habitants de La Mure'. Undated proclamation, AD Rhône 4 M 227.

45 Prefect of Cher report, Bourges, 10 October 1820. AN F7 6906.

46 Napoleonic placard, Laval, 1816. Report of prefect of Mayenne, 5 January 1816. AN F7 3736.

47 *Tableau de délits*, Nîmes, 26 May 1817. AN BB18—1017.

48 Guillon, *Les complots militaires sous la Restauration* (op. cit.), 185.
49 Proclamation of Marie-Louise, dated 15 February 1817. AN F7 6706.
50 Proclamation of Eugène de Beauharnais, dated October 1817. AN F7 6705.
51 Prefect of Nièvre report, Nevers, 27 October 1819. AN F7 6909.
52 'Placards séditieux affichés à Lyons, 1819–1823'. AN F7 6910.
53 See the many reports on the Spanish war in AN BB30—193 (*procureurs*, Agen division).
54 *Procureur* report, Aix, 4 October 1824. AN BB18—1116.
55 Prefect of Meuse report, 3 January 1827. AN F7 6705.
56 *Procureur* report, Agen, August 1823. AN BB30—193.
57 Placard [undated], AN F7 6839.
58 Mayor of La Guillotière report, 23 March 1816. AD Rhône 4 M 227.
59 Police report, Grenoble, 21 August 1819. AD Isère 52 M 23. 'Calotin' was a popular nineteenth-century term of abuse for priests. For examples of the use of the term (and its derivatives), see Jacqueline Lalouette, 'Expressions de l'anti-cléricalisme', in *La République anticléricale* (Paris: Seuil, 2002), 311–313.
60 Report of prefect of Bourbon-Vendée, 15 May 1829. AN F7 6772.
61 Placard [undated]. AN BB18—1017.
62 Police report, Macon, 15 January 1816. AN F7 3736.
63 Report of sub-prefect of Joigny, 8 March 1816. AD Yonne III M^1 87.
64 Report of *procureur-général*, Riom, 13 March 1817. AN BB18—1017.
65 See, for example, the report of the sub-prefect of Joigny, 30 May 1816. AD Yonne III M^1 88.
66 See, for example, the report of the prefect of the Allier, Moulins, 22 May 1820. AN F7 6909.
67 Gendarmerie report, Méribel (Ain), 29 April 1820. AN F7 6906.
68 Police report, Lyons, 28 July 1820. AN F7 6910.
69 Police report, Paris, 21 April 1819. AN F7 6910.
70 Ibid.
71 Proclamation of Marie-Louise, dated 15 February 1817. AN F7 6706.
72 For a colourful example, see *Apothéose de Napoleone Buonaparte ou signalement de l'antechrist, manifesté à tout l'Univers par l'esprit de vérité* (Paris, 1821), 13.
73 Petition to prefect of Yonne, dated 30 November 1815. AD Yonne III M^1 84.
74 Prefect of Creuse report, Guéret, 26 March 1816. AN F7 3736.
75 Prefect of Manche report, Saint-Lo, 5 January 1816. AN F7 3736.
76 José Cabanis, *Le sacre de Napoléon* (Paris: Gallimard, 1970), 44.
77 See Chapter 1.
78 See Godlewski, *Napoléon à l'Ile d'Elbe* (op. cit.), 42.
79 Prefect of Isère report, 3 January 1816. AN F7 3736.
80 Letter of mayor of Grand Lemps to prefect of Isère, 30 March 1816. AD Isère 54 M 14 (dossier Emery).

81 Letter of mayor of Grand Lemps to prefect of Isère, 11 April 1816. AD Isère 54 M 14.

82 This man bears no apparent relation to the Drevon mentioned in the previous chapter.

83 Report of justice of the peace, Grand Lemps, n.d. AD Isère 52 M 14.

84 Police report, Grenoble, 14 October 1816. AD Isère 52 M 14.

85 Proclamation of prefect of Isère, n.d. AD Isère 52 M 14.

86 Ibid.

87 Army report on Church ceremony in Epinal (Vosges), 15 August 1817. AN F7 6848.

88 Incident in Morbihan in 1818, cited in letter of prefect of police, Paris, 3 September 1818. AN F7 6869.

89 Police report on incident in cabaret, Lyons, 16 August 1819. AD Isère 52 M 23.

90 Army report on interrogation of soldier, Paris, 29 April 1821. AN F7 6706.

91 Prefect of Côtes-du-Nord report, Saint-Brieuc, 31 August 1819. AN F7 3744.

92 Gendarmerie report, Tulle (Corrèze), 18 August 1820. AN F7 6906.

93 Police report, Lyon, 11 August 1820. AD Rhône 4 M 229.

94 Report of sub-prefect of Avallon, 14 August 1815. AD Yonne III M^1 66.

95 Report from Saint-Joseph penitentiary, Lyons, 17 August 1822. AN F7 6705.

96 Ministry of Interior letter to prefect of Rhône, Paris, 18 June 1821. AD Rhône 4 M 245.

97 Police report, Paris, August 23, 1822. 'There is among the liberals, Buonapartists and old Jacobins of the Faubourg St-Antoine a considerable agitation, aimed at creating trouble on the occasion of the King's Fête' [the Saint-Louis].

98 Gendarmerie report (Lot), 18 August 1820. AN F7 6909.

99 Procureur report, Privas, 19 August 1815. AN BB3—151.

100 Prefect of Seine-et-Oise report, 26 August 1817. AN F7 6706.

101 Report dated 2 September 1815. AD Yonne III M^1 65.

102 Procureur of Nérac report, 16 August 1823. AN BB30-193.

103 Prefect of Gironde report, Bordeaux, 4 December 1818. AN F7 6889.

104 Cited in Adrien Dansette, 'Légende et transfiguration', in Sainte-Hélène terre d'exil (Paris: Hachette, 1971), 312.

105 Police report, Lyons, 14 July 1815. AN F7 3734.

106 Police report, Grenoble, 2 December 1818. AD Isère 52 M 22.

107 Prefect of Isère report, Grenoble, 16 July 1820. AN F7 6669.

108 Prefect of Rhône report, 11 March 1816. AN F7 3736.

109 Albin Gras, Grenoble en 1814 et 1815 (Grenoble: Maisonville, 1854), 60.

110 Prefect of Isère report, Grenoble, 3 July 1823. AN F7 6650.

111 For accounts of these gatherings in 1818 and 1820, see Alexander, Rewriting the French revolutionary tradition (op. cit.), 123.

112 Proclamation of prefect of Isère, Grenoble, 4 July 1823. AD Isère 52 M 26.

113 Prefect of Isère report, n.d. [1823]. AN F7 6650.

114 Proclamation of prefect Jules de Calvière, 2 July 1825. AD Isère 52 M 26.

115 Draft prefectoral report, n.d. [1826]. AD Isère 52 M 26.

116 Proclamation, Grenoble, 9 July 1831. AD Isère 54 M 6.

117 See for example the letter from the Minister of the Interior to the prefect, 29 November 1815. AD Isère 52 M 14.

118 Minister of Interior letter to prefect, 24 February 1818. AD Isère 52 M 22.

119 See, for example, the report on the escape of the Bonapartist suspect Galant, after the police raided his home and arrested his brother. Police report, Grenoble, 30 April 1816. AD Isère 52 M 9.

120 Minister of Interior letter to prefect, 23 October 1822. AN F7 6769.

121 Prefect of Isère report, Grenoble, 16 July 1820. AN F7 6669.

122 Expression used by prefect of Marne, Rheims, 31 August 1817; his report applauded the severe verdict of the local court against Anne-Marie Simonard, who had been sentenced to deportation for 'threatening violence against the royal family'.

123 Report of *procureur*, Dôle, 11 August 1824. AN BB18—1113.

124 Report of *procureur-général*, Nîmes, 11 March 1817. AN BB18—1017.

125 Cited in Lucas-Dubreton, *Le culte de Napoléon* (op. cit.), 80.

126 Police report, Lyons, 6 November 1817. AD Rhône 4 M 245.

127 Verdict on case of Pierre René Talec, arrested for shouting 'Vive l'Empereur!' in 1825; *procureur* report, Vannes, 7 April 1825. AN BB18— 1120.

128 Reports of *procureur*, Altkirch, 11 December 1824; and procureur, Guingamp, 1 December 1824; AN BB18—1118.

129 This conclusion is shared by Jean Vidalenc, 'La Cour prévôtale de Seine-Inférieure, 1816–1818', *Revue d'Histoire Moderne et Contemporaine* Vol. XIX October–December 1972, 533–556. See also Brelot, 'Terreur et contre-terreur dans le département du Jura', (op. cit.), 206.

130 See, for example, the scandalized letter of the Minister of the Interior, Paris, 21 March 1824 on the verdict of the tribunal in Arbois in the case against Louis Mouret, who had sung a 'seditious song'; he had been sentenced to a fine of five francs, and this verdict had been upheld by the appeal court. AN BB18—1113.

131 Las Cases, *Mémorial* (op. cit.), Vol.I, 393.

132 For an account of the events of July 1830, see Mansel, *Paris between Empires* (op. cit.), 226–267.

133 Maurice Agulhon, '1830 dans l'histoire du XIXe siècle français', in *Histoire vagabonde* (Paris: Gallimard, 1988) Vol.II, 32.

134 Furet, *La Révolution* (op. cit.) Vol.II, 107–112.

135 Alexander, *Rewriting the French revolutionary tradition* (op. cit.), 333.

136 See, for example, the report of the mayor of Charny, 24 February 1820,

which addresses the failure of the Restoration to make much political headway in his locality since 1815; he cites rumours about the restoration of the *dîme* as one of the main reasons. AD Yonne III M[1] 86.

137 H. Thirria, *Napoléon III avant l'Empire* (Paris: Plon, 1895), Vol. I, 17.

138 Pinkney, *The French Revolution of 1830* (op. cit.), 293.

139 Petiteau, *Lendemains d'Empire* (op. cit.), 285.

140 Ménager, *Les Napoléon du peuple* (op. cit.), 71.

6: The Prince of Liberal Ideas

1 See Jean Tulard, 'Le retour des cendres', in Pierre Nora (ed.), *Les lieux de mémoire* (Paris: Gallimard, 1986), Vol.II (2), 81–110.

2 Gilbert Martineau, *Le retour des cendres* (Paris: Tallandier, 1990), 137.

3 See his wonderful description of the day's events in his entry 'Funérailles de l'Empereur', dated 15 December 1840, in Victor Hugo, *Choses Vues 1830–1848* (Paris: Gallimard, 1972), 148–165.

4 Victor Hugo, *Hymne* (Boulogne, 1841). This poem does not appear in his collected works – perhaps unsurprisingly in the light of Hugo's subsequent loss of enthusiasm for Bonapartism after 1851, not to mention the welcome he received from the 'hateful' English during his years in exile under the Second Empire.

5 Louis Direy, *A l'occasion de l'apothéose de Napoléon. A Monsieur Victor Hugo: Apologie* (Boulogne, 1841).

6 Letter of Director of Archives du Nord to Director-General of Archives de France, Lille, 5 October 1959. I am grateful to Mrs Estelle Dietrich of the Musée de l'Histoire de France in Paris for showing me this document, which also contains a full account of the 1841 incident.

7 Guillaume de Bertier de Sauvigny, 'Louis-Philippe et Guizot vus par des voyageurs américains', in *La France au XIXe siècle. Etudes historiques* (Paris: Publications de la Sorbonne, 1973), 202.

8 Furet, *La Révolution* (op. cit.), Vol.II, 161.

9 Pinkney, *The French Revolution of 1830* (op. cit.), 290–291.

10 Speech of May 12, 1840, in *Procès-verbaux des séances de la Chambre des députés* (Paris: Henri, 1840), Vol.V, 338.

11 'Discussion du projet de loi concernant la translation des cendres de l'Empereur', May 26 1840; in *Procès-verbaux des séances de la Chambre des députés* (Paris: Henri, 1840), Vol. VII, 11–12.

12 'Translation des cendres de Napoléon', in *La politique de Lamartine. Choix de discours et écrits politiques* (Paris: Hachette, 1878), Vol.I, 294.

13 Alexis de Tocqueville, speech at the Académie Française, 21 April 1842, in *Oeuvres complètes* (ed. F. Mélonio) (Paris: Gallimard, 1989), Vol. XVI, 264–265.

14 Emmanuel de Las Cases, *Mémorial de Sainte-Hélène* (ed. Marcel Dunan) (Paris: Flammarion, 1951), Vol. I, 311.

15 Lucien Jaume, *L'individu éffacé* (Paris: Fayard, 1997), 11.

16 See Sudhir Hazareesingh, *From subject to citizen* (Princeton, NJ: Princeton University Press, 1998).

17 On the political thought of this group, see the proceedings of the 1998 conference edited by Lucien Jaume, *Coppet, creuset de l'esprit libéral* (Paris: Economica, 2000).

18 Madame de Staël, *Dix années d'exil* (Paris: Fayard, 1996), 49.

19 *Lettres inédites de Napoléon Ier* (Paris: Plon, 1897), Vol. I, 84, 88, and 210.

20 Jaume, *L'individu éffacé* (op. cit.), 46–47.

21 For Napoleon's views of the book, see his letter to his Minister of Police Savary in September 1810. *Lettres inédites* (op. cit.) Vol.II, 74.

22 The *Principes* of 1806 remained unpublished during Constant's lifetime (and indeed throughout the nineteenth century).

23 *Journal des Débats*, 19 March 1815.

24 Benjamin Constant, *Journaux intimes* (Paris: Gallimard, 1952), 438.

25 Benjamin Constant, *Mémoires sur les Cent-Jours* (Tübingen: Niemayer, 1993), 63 and 200.

26 Ibid., 211.

27 Ibid., 211.

28 Ibid., 259–260.

29 Ibid., 298.

30 Ibid., 212.

31 Ibid., 213.

32 Ibid., 284.

33 A old French term, dating from the Middle Ages, denoting a peasant revolt. Ibid., 211.

34 Ibid., 285.

35 Ibid., 285–286.

36 Ibid., 291.

37 Paul Thureau-Dangin, *Le parti libéral sous la Restauration* (Paris: Plon, 1888), 154.

38 See the analysis of popular pamphlets published immediately after Napoleon's death by Georges Lote, 'La mort de Napoléon et l'opinion bonapartiste en 1821', *Revue des Etudes Napoléoniennes*, July–December 1830.

39 There were four subsequent editions: in 1824, 1830, 1835, and 1840. At least 40,000 copies had been sold by 1850; see Martin Lyons, *Le triomphe du livre. Une histoire sociologique de la lecture dans la France du XIXe siècle* (Paris: Promodis, 1987), 93.

40 For an analysis of some of this literature, as published in the collections of the 'Bibliothèque Historique' in the early years of the Restoration, see Philippe Gonnard, 'La légende napoléonienne et la presse libérale (1817–1820), *Revue des Etudes Napoléoniennes* (January–June 1912), 235–258.

41 Las Cases, *Mémorial de Sainte-Hélène* (op. cit.), Vol.I, 515.

42 Ibid., Vol. I, 51.

43 Ibid., Vol. I, 262.

44 Ibid., Vol. II, 16.

45 See, for example, Vol. II, 359, 428, 478.

46 Ibid., Vol.I , 128–129.

47 Ibid., Vol. II, 9–11. Sieyès ended up with the lion's share (600,000 francs), to the great dissatisfaction of Ducos.

48 Ibid., Vol. I, 195–196.

49 Ibid., Vol. I, 66.

50 Ibid., Vol. I, 15, 21.

51 Ibid., Vol. I, 62.

52 Ibid., Vol. I, 465.

53 'Idées religieuses de Napoléon', ibid., Vol. II, 194–208.

54 The text cites Pascal Paoli's characterization of Napoleon as 'a young man cut from the cloth of antiquity, a man from Plutarch.' Las Cases, *Mémorial de Sainte-Hélène* (op. cit.), Vol. I, 98; see also Vol. II, 648.

55 Ibid., Vol. I, 263–64. On the equestrian representations of Napoleon, see L. Guillot, 'Napoléon à cheval', *Revue de l'Institut Napoléon* (Vol. 3, 1939), 133–147.

56 Ibid., Vol. I, 559–563.

57 Ibid., Vol. I, 127.

58 Ibid., Vol. II, 575–76.

59 Ibid., Vol. I, 160, 179.

60 Ibid., Vol. II, 233 and 583.

61 Ibid., Vol. I, 245.

62 Ibid., Vol. I, 117–118.

63 Ibid., Vol. I, 146–47.

64 Ibid., Vol. I, 349.

65 Ibid., Vol. II, 205, fn.1; see also Chapter 1.

66 Ibid., Vol. I, 150–152.

67 Ibid., Vol. II, 628.

68 'Testament de Napoléon', ibid., Vol. II, 881.

69 Ibid., Vol. II, 458–468.

70 Ibid., Vol. I, 761–762; Vol. II, 244–258.

71 Ibid., Vol. II, 8.

72 Ibid., Vol. I, 534.

73 Ibid., Vol. I, 554–555.

74 Ibid., Vol. I, 492–93.

75 Ibid., Vol. II, 233 and 583.

76 Ibid., Vol. II, 543.

77 Ibid., Vol. II, 60.

78 Ibid., Vol. I, 311.

79 Ibid., Vol. I, 252.

80 Ibid., Vol. I, 384; also Vol. II, 132: 'a monarch elected by the people'.
81 Ibid., Vol. I, 446.
82 Ibid., Vol. II, 44.
83 Ibid., Vol. II, 348; see also 393.
84 Ibid., Vol. II, 300.
85 Ibid., Vol. II, 233.
86 Antoine Casanova, *Napoléon et la pensée de son temps* (Paris: La Boutique de l'Histoire, 2000), 301.
87 Las Cases, *Mémorial de Sainte-Hélène* (op. cit.), Vol. I, 496.
88 Ibid., Vol. II, 609.
89 Ibid., Vol. II, 469.
90 Ibid., Vol. I, 446.
91 Julia Schnitker, 'La Révolution Française et le Premier Empire dans les livres illustrés en France de 1815 à 1870'. Ph. D. thesis, University of Paris-IV, 1999, Vol. I, 117–119.
92 On the political evolution of Béranger's Napoleonic songs during the 1820s, see Jean Touchard, *La gloire de Béranger* (Paris: Armand Colin, 1968), Vol. I, 258–265.
93 See Chapter 8.
94 Pierre Guiral, *Adolphe Thiers* (Paris: Fayard, 1986), 287.
95 Ibid., 163.
96 See Sudhir Hazareesingh, *Intellectual founders of the Republic* (Oxford: Oxford University Press, 2001).
97 Adolphe Thiers, *Histoire du Consulat et de l'Empire* (Leipzig: Meline, 1845), Vol. I, 4.
98 Jean Tulard, *Le mythe de Napoléon* (Paris: Fayard, 1977), 20.
99 Thiers, *Histoire* (op. cit.), Vol.XII, xi.
100 Ibid., Vol. I, 291.
101 Ibid., Vol. III, 429–433.
102 Ibid., Vol. V, 45–46.
103 Ibid, Vol. XX, 606.
104 Ibid., Vol. XIX, 42.
105 Ibid., Vol. VI, 401.
106 Ibid., Vol. XVII, 742–743.
107 Ibid., Vol. VII, 101.
108 Ibid., Vol. XIV, 547.
109 On the characterization of Napoleon's military genius, see for example Vol. X, 374; and Vol. XX, 614–615.
110 Ibid., Vol. XIV, 542–546.
111 Ibid., Vol. XX, 610–611.
112 Ibid., Vol. XIX, 193.
113 Ibid., Vol. VI, 17–18.
114 Ibid., Vol. VII, 538.
115 Ibid., Vol. IV, 444 and 464.

116 Ibid., Vol. XVII, 716.

117 Ibid., Vol. XVII, 736, 740, and 744.

118 Ibid., Vol. XIX, 92–93.

119 Ibid., Vol. XIX, 191.

120 Ibid., Vol. XVII, 758.

121 Ibid., Vol. XX, 613.

122 Ibid., Vol. I, 43–44.

123 Ibid., Vol. XIX, 344–345; 377.

124 Ibid., Vol. II, 133.

125 Ibid., Vol. III, 355.

126 Ibid., Vol. III, 356.

127 Ibid., Vol. V, 204–205.

128 Ibid., Vol. XX, 621.

129 Ibid., Vol. XX, 620.

130 Ibid., Vol. I, 119–120.

131 Ibid., Vol. I, 116.

132 *Le centenaire de Napoléon Ier. Chanson patriotique* (1869).

133 Pierre Rosanvallon, 'Guizot et la question du suffrage', in Marina Valensise (ed.), *François Guizot et la culture politique de son temps* (Paris: Seuil, 1991), 131.

134 Lucien Prévost-Paradol, *La France Nouvelle* (Paris: Michel Lévy, 1868), 309.

135 Quoted in Jean Lucas-Dubreton, *Aspects de Monsieur Thiers* (Paris: Editions Rencontre, 1966), 238.

136 Jean Lucas-Dubreton, *Soldats de Napoléon* (Paris: Tallandier, 1977 ed.), 14.

137 For an example of this line of thinking, see the anonymous pamphlet *Le centenaire de Napoléon Ier. Notice historique sur la vie de l'Empereur par un ami de la vérité* (Metz, 1869), 48.

138 A point made by Théodore Fadeville, *Histoire populaire de Napoléon Ier* (Paris: Giraud, 1853), 52–53.

139 Petiteau, *Napoléon de la mythologie à l'histoire* (op. cit.), 115–120, 230–231.

140 Pierre-Joseph Proudhon, *Napoleon Ier, manuscrit inédits* (Paris: Montgredien, 1898), 251; emphasis in text.

141 Jules Barni, *Napoléon et son historien M. Thiers* (Geneva, 1865), 386. The same conclusion is offered in his shorter book *Napoléon Ier* (Paris: Germer Baillière, 1870), 185–186: the Emperor was a 'nefarious man'.

142 Barni, *Napoléon et son historien M. Thiers* (op. cit.), 365. From Chateaubriand to Taine, this emphasis on Napoleon's 'foreign' blood was an important element in the 'black legend'; Madame de Staël also spoke of Bonaparte as a 'fatal foreigner'.

143 *Grand Dictionnaire Universel du XIXeme siècle* (Paris, 1874 ed.), Vol.II, 920; Vol.XI, 804.

144 Thiers, *Histoire* (op. cit.), Vol.XX, 674–675.

145 Ibid., Vol. XX, 675.

7: Louis Napoleon and the Imperial Legend

1   *Souvenirs de la Baronne du Montet*, 485; quoted in André Lebey, *Les trois coups d'état de Louis-Napoléon Bonaparte. Strasbourg et Boulogne* (Paris: Didier, 1906), 136.

2   Ibid., 202.

3   Entry for 15 November 1830, in Valérie Masuyer, *Mémoires de Valérie Masuyer, dame d'honneur de la Reine Hortense* (Paris: Plon, 1937), 58.

4   Marcel Emerit, *Madame Cornu et Napoléon III* (Paris: Editions des Presses Modernes, 1937), 150.

5   *Cour des Pairs. Attentat du 6 Août 1840. Réquisitoires et répliques de M. Franck Carré, procureur général du Roi* (Paris: Imprimerie Royale, 1840), 21.

6   Alexis de Tocqueville, *Souvenirs* (Paris: Gallimard, 1964).

7   *Mémoires de la Reine Hortense* (Paris: Plon, 1927), Vol.II, 3.

8   Lebey, *Les trois coups d'état* (op. cit.), 2.

9   The general view among dispassionate observers is that the King of Holland probably was, after all, Louis's father; see Lebey, *Les trois coups d'état* (op. cit.), 11; see also Adrien Dansette, *Louis-Napoléon à la conquête du pouvoir* (Paris: Hachette, 1961), 35.

10 Letter of Napoleon to Louis Bonaparte, Berlin, 6 November 1806, in *Lettres inédites de Napoléon Ier* (Paris: Plon, 1897), Vol.I, 79.

11 José Cabanis, *Le sacre de Napoléon* (Paris: Gallimard, 1970), 184.

12 *Mémoires de Valérie Masuyer* (op. cit.), 62.

13 Las Cases, *Mémorial de Sainte-Hélène* (op. cit.), II, 375.

14 Letter of Louis to Hortense, Augsburg, 26 September and 2 November 1822. Archives Nationales (Paris) 400 AP 39; emphasis in text.

15 Letter of Louis to Hortense, Augsburg, 11 June 1823. AN 400 AP 39.

16 Letter of Louis to Hortense, 4 January 1833. AN 400 AP 39.

17 Mme. Cornu, cited in Lebey, *Les trois coups d'état* (op. cit.), 18.

18 Ibid., 21.

19 Cited in Dansette, *Louis-Napoléon à la conquête du pouvoir* (op. cit.), 48.

20 The castle is still standing today, and hosts an excellent Napoleonic museum.

21 Ibid., 38.

22 See, for example, André Damien, 'La jeunesse suisse de Napoléon III', *Souvenir Napoléonien* (September 1976), 18: 'One cannot reasonably explain how Hortense, who had a religious upbringing, who was brought up in the purest traditions of the old monarchy, and in absolute respect of the Church and Royalty, could have accepted in her intimacy such a resolute enemy of these traditions, an opponent of any form of spiritual education, and a notorious atheist.'

23 Prefect report, 25 August 1825. AN F7 6669.

24 Letter of Louis to Hortense, 27 August 1823, AN 400 AP 39.

25 Letter of Louis to Hortense, 15 June 1821. AN 400 AP 39.

26 Letter of Le Bas to his family, Rome, 9 March 1826, cited in Stéfane-Pol, *La jeunesse de Napoléon III. Correspondence inédite de son précepteur Philippe Le Bas* (Paris: Juven, 1901), 323.

27 Letters of 19 June 1822 and 23 June 1823; AN 400 AP 39.

28 Letter of Le Bas to his family, Arenenberg, 5 August 1821, cited in Stéfane-Pol, *La jeunesse de Napoléon III* (op. cit.), 94.

29 Letter of Louis to Hortense, Augsburg, 24 July 1821; AN 400 AP 39.

30 Le Bas discusses the *Mémorial* in a letter to his family, Augsburg, 24 March 1823, cited in Stéfane-Pol, *La jeunesse de Napoléon III* (op. cit.), 167.

31 Reproduced in Stéphane-Pol, *La jeunesse de Napoléon III* (op. cit.), 241.

32 Entry for 13 May 1831, *Mémoires de Valérie Masuyer* (op. cit.), 212. Napoleon, with perhaps a slight touch of exaggeration, had once described Hortense as 'the most virtuous of women'. *Lettres inédites de Napoléon Ier* (op. cit.), Vol.I, 232.

33 Entry for 4 October 1830, ibid., 14.

34 Letter of Louis to his father, Rome, 5 May 1829. AN 400 AP 40.

35 Jacob Hugentobler, 'La famille Bonaparte à Arenenberg', *Revue des Etudes Napoléoniennes*, September 1932, 113.

36 Report of prefect of Haut-Rhin, Colmar, 1 October 1825. AN F7 6668.

37 See Jacques Jourquin, *Souvenirs et biographie du Commandant Parquin* (Paris: Tallandier, 2003), 403–404.

38 Letter of Louis to his father, Rome, 17 November 1827. AN 400 AP 40.

39 Letter of Louis to his father, Rome, 13 April 1830. AN 400 AP 40.

40 Letter of Louis to Hortense, Brussels, 14 November 1832. AN 400 AP 39.

41 Letter of Louis to Hortense, Florence, 21 December 1830. AN 400 AP 39.

42 Entry for June 1836; *Mémoires de Valérie Masuyer* (op. cit.), 330.

43 Letter of Louis to Hortense, Augsburg, 24 July 1821; AN 400 AP 39.

44 Letter of Louis to Hortense, London, 7 December 1832. AN 400 AP 39.

45 Dansette, *Louis-Napoléon à la conquête du pouvoir* (op. cit.), 45.

46 Entry for September 1830; *Mémoires de Valérie Masuyer* (op. cit.), 9.

47 Hugentobler, 'La famille Bonaparte à Arenenberg' (op. cit.), 118.

48 Letter of the Emperor to his brother Jérôme, Paris, 6 August 1802, in *Lettres inédites de Napoléon Ier* (op. cit.), Vol.I, 389.

49 Letter of Louis to Hortense, 12 August 1830. AN 400 AP 39.

50 See Lucas-Dubreton, *Le culte de Napoléon* (op. cit.), 298–328.

51 H. Thirria, *Napoléon III carbonaro* (Paris: De Soye, 1899), 7. The author argues that Louis sympathized with *carbonari* goals but was not initiated into the organization, contrary to the subsequent legend.

52 Entry for 26 October 1830; *Mémoires de Valérie Masuyer* (op. cit.), 40.

53 She was disguised as an English lady, and Louis as her lackey. Lebey, *Les trois coups d'état* (op. cit.), 49.

54 *Mémoires de Valérie Masuyer* (op. cit.), 197.

55 Maxime du Camp, *Souvenirs d'un demi-siècle* (Paris: Hachette, 1949), 26.

56 Letter of Louis to Hortense, Baden, 4 July 1834; AN 400 AP 39.

57 Lebey, *Les trois coups d'état* (op. cit.), 77.

58 See Julien Boudon, 'Louis-Napoléon Bonaparte: du "jacobinisme" au "socialisme"?', in Frédéric Bluche (ed.), *Le Prince, le peuple, et le droit. Autour des plébiscites de 1851 et 1852* (Paris: Presses Universitaires de France, 2000), 191–198.

59 For example, see 'Notice sur les écrits du Prince Napoléon-Louis Bonaparte', *Revue de l'Empire* Vol. III (1845), 2–3.

60 *Mémoires de Valérie Masuyer* (op. cit.), 176.

61 *Mémoires de la Reine Hortense* (Paris: Plon, 1927), Vol. III, 305.

62 Lebey, *Les trois coups d'état* (op. cit.), 66.

63 *Mémoires de Valérie Masuyer* (op. cit.), 253.

64 Lebey, *Les trois coups d'état* (op. cit.), 61.

65 Entry for July 1831; *Mémoires de Valérie Masuyer* (op. cit.), 251.

66 See Philippe Darriulat, *Les patriotes. La gauche républicaine et la nation 1830–1870* (Paris: Seuil, 2001), 38–44.

67 Thirria, *Napoléon III avant l'Empire* (op. cit.), Vol. I, 8–9.

68 The auction raised 20,000 francs. Dansette, *Louis-Napoléon à la conquête du pouvoir* (op. cit.), 73–74.

69 Letter of Louis to his father, 10 May 1833; AN 400 AP 40.

70 See Chapters 1 and 6.

71 Cited in Armand Laity, *Le Prince Napoléon à Strasbourg, ou relation historique des évènements du 30 octobre 1836* (Paris, 1838), 17.

72 Ibid., 18.

73 Armand Carrel, 'Sur le Retour des Cendres', *Le National*, 4 October 1830; cited in Edouard Driault, 'Un républicain napoléonien: Armand Carrel', *Revue des Etudes Napoléoniennes*, July–December 1936, 38–39.

74 Laity, *Le Prince Napoléon à Strasbourg* (op. cit.), 20.

75 Dansette, *Louis-Napoléon à la conquête du pouvoir* (op. cit.), 99.

76 Letter of Louis to Hortense, 15 August 1830. AN 400 AP 39.

77 Cited in Dansette, *Louis-Napoléon à la conquête du pouvoir* (op. cit.), 101.

78 Ibid., 99.

79 Letter of Louis to Hortense, Baden, 10 July 1834. AN 400 AP 39.

80 Letter of Louis to his father, Arenenberg, 9 July 1833. AN 400 AP 39.

81 Article dated 19 January 1832, in Heinrich Heine, *De la France* (Paris: Gallimard, 1994 ed.), 54.

82 John Grand-Carteret, 'La légende napoléonienne par l'image vue sous un jour nouveau', *Revue des Etudes Napoléoniennes* (January–June 1923), 30.

83 Lucas-Dubreton, *Le culte de Napoléon* (op. cit.), 403–405.

84 Ibid., 415.

85 Sylvie Vieilledent, 'Le retour du 'petit chapeau' en 1830', in *Napoléon de l'histoire à la légende. Actes du colloque, 30 novembre–1 décembre 1999* (Paris: In Forma, 2000), 367.

86 Dansette, *Louis-Napoléon à la conquête du pouvoir* (op. cit.), 84–86.

87 Stendhal, *Le rouge et le noir* (Paris: Gallimard, 1972 ed.), 33. Stendhal himself owned three editions of the *Mémorial*, which he read several times. See Louis Rozelaar, '*Le Mémorial de Sainte-Hélène* et le romantisme', *Revue des Etudes Napoléoniennes* (July–December 1929), 204.

88 Persat, *Mémoires*; cited in Lucas-Dubreton, *Le culte de Napoléon* (op. cit.), 327.

89 Florange, *Le vol de l'aigle* (op. cit.), 17.

90 See J. Sattler, 'Une curieuse inscription Napoléonienne', *Le Vieux Papier* (January 1964).

91 F. Beaucour, 'La maison de l'Empereur à Saint-Riquier', *Le Vieux Papier* (July 1962).

92 By the time he reached Geneva the uprising had been defeated.

93 Martineau, *Le retour des cendres* (op. cit.), 66.

94 Paul Thureau-Dangin, *Histoire de la Monarchie de Juillet* (Paris: Plon, 1888) Vol. I, 595.

95 Louis Blanc, *Histoire de Dix Ans 1830–1840* (Paris: Germer Baillière, 1877), Vol. II, 330–331.

96 Entry for July 1831; *Mémoires de Valérie Masuyer* (op. cit.), 252. This was perhaps more an expression of bravado than an appreciation based on hard evidence; a police report in 1836 claimed that 'there is absolutely no influence of the Bonapartists in the Army' – but then this too may have been wishful thinking, this time on the part of the Orleanist authorities. Report of 1 November 1836, Paris. AN F7 3888.

97 Lebey, *Les trois coups d'état* (op. cit.), 92.

98 On the 1834 events and the ensuing 'monster trial,' see Jeanne Gilmore, *La République Clandestine 1818–1848* (Paris: Aubier, 1997), 189–246. Letter of 30 January 1835, Arenenberg, cited in Thirria, *Napoléon III avant l'Empire* (op. cit.), 10.

99 Gabriel Perreux, *Les conspirations de Louis-Napoléon Bonaparte. Strasbourg, Boulogne* (Paris: Hachette, 1936), 77.

100 Lebey, *Les trois coups d'état* (op. cit.), 155–156.

101 Letter of Louis to his father, Arenenberg, 5 October 1837. AN 400 AP 40.

102 Du Camp, *Souvenirs d'un demi-siècle* (op. cit.), 48.

103 See the chapter on the 1836 conspiracy in Félix Ponteil, *L'opposition politique à Strasbourg sous la Monarchie de Juillet (1830–1848)* (Paris: Hartmann, 1932), which is largely based on Archives Nationales papers, notably CC 767 and 768.

104 Charles de Rémusat, *Mémoires de ma vie* (Paris: Plon, 1960), Vol.III, 404; Rémusat received a letter from London three days before the Boulogne landing warning him that the attempt was imminent.

105 Dansette [*Louis-Napoléon à la conquête du pouvoir* (op. cit.), 190] believes that the traitor was General Montholon, Napoleon's former companion-in-exile at Saint-Helena, but this has not been proved beyond doubt.

106 *Discours du Prince Napoléon-Louis devant la Cour des Pairs, prononcé dans la séance du 28 septembre 1840* (Paris, 1840), 2.

107 Laity, *Le Prince Napoléon à Strasbourg* (op. cit.), 25.

108 *Discours du Prince Napoléon-Louis* (op. cit.), 3.

109 Quoted in Lebey, *Les trois coups d'état* (op. cit.), 122.

110 Laity, *Le Prince Napoléon à Strasbourg* (op. cit.), 41.

111 Ibid., 62.

112 Ibid., 65.

113 Prefect of Police report, Paris, 11 August 1840. AN F7 3890.

114 Letter of Louis to his father, London, 12 July 1837. AN 400 AP 40.

115 Cited in Iouda Tchernoff, *Le parti républicain sous la Monarchie de Juillet* (Paris: Pedone, 1901), 385.

116 Lucas-Dubreton, *Le culte de Napoléon* (op. cit.), 386.

117 See notably the police report of 30 July 1840, Paris, on the arrest of a man named Jean-Louis Hart for 'uttering seditious cries and carrying munitions'. Hart claimed that he had been hired by Napoleonic activists in Paris who were planning a coup which was to lead to the proclamation of 'the Constitution of 1793'. Arch. Pref. Police, Paris, Aa 426 (*évènements divers* 1840–1847).

118 Report, Paris, 2 September 1840. Arch. Pref. Police, Paris, Aa 426.

8: The Making of an Emperor

1 Cited in Marcel de Baillehache, *Grands bonapartistes* (Paris: Tallandier, 1899), 92.

2 Cited in Honoré Farat, *Persigny, un ministre de Napoléon III* (Paris: Hachette, 1957), 21.

3 Ibid., 76.

4 Georges Goyau, *Un roman d'amitié entre deux adversaires politiques: Falloux et Persigny* (Paris: Flammarion, 1928), 95.

5 Farat, *Persigny* (op. cit.), 22.

6 Letter from Doullens detention centre, November 28 1841, quoted in André Lebey (ed.) *Dix lettres inédites de Persigny* (Paris: Cornély, 1909).

7 Louis Napoléon, *Des idées napoléoniennes* (Bruxelles: Société Typographique Belge, 1839), 17.

8 See Chapter 6, page 170.

9 Ibid., 28.

10 Ibid., 125–126.

11 Ibid., 86.

12 Ibid., 100.

13 Ibid., 116–117.

14 Ibid., 136.

15 Ibid.

16 Ibid., Preface, vi.

17 Ibid., 87–88.

18 Jean-Gilbert-Victor Fialin, Duc de Persigny, *Lettres de Londres* (Paris: Levavasseur, 1840), 53.

19 Ibid., 37–38.
20 Laity, *Le Prince Napoléon à Strasbourg* (op. cit.), 29.
21 Persigny, *Lettres de Londres* (op. cit.), 107.
22 Ibid., 3.
23 Ibid., 60.
24 Ibid., 17.
25 Ibid., 73.
26 Ibid., 60.
27 Ibid., 30.
28 Ibid., 41–46.
29 Ibid., 57.
30 Ibid., 55.
31 Ibid., 75.
32 Ibid., 111.
33 *Le passé et l'avenir de l'artillerie* (Paris, 1846).
34 Lucas-Dubreton, *Le culte de Napoléon* (op. cit.), 390–391.
35 *Réponse de Louis-Napoléon Bonaparte à M. Lamartine* (Paris: Librairie Napoléonienne, 1848), 4.
36 Ibid., 5.
37 Ibid., 8.
38 Letter of Louis to Prince Napoleon, Ham, January 22 1842; in *Napoléon III et le Prince Napoléon. Correspondance inédite* (Paris: Calmann-Lévy, 1925) (ed. Ernest d'Hauterive), 9.
39 Minister of the Interior: circular to all prefects, Paris. AD Isère 52 M 27.
40 On Louis's escape, see Pierre Hachet-Souplet, *Louis-Napoléon prisonnier au fort de Ham. La vérité sur l'évasion de 1846* (Paris: Dentu, 1894).
41 Prefecture de Police, Paris; report dated 27 May 1846. AN F7 3839.
42 On the events leading to the overthrow of Louis Philippe, see Mansel, *Paris between Empires* (op. cit.), 398–404.
43 Prefecture de Police, Paris; report of June 1846. AN F7 3839.
44 Lucas-Dubreton, *Le culte de Napoléon* (op. cit.), 424.
45 'Citoyens électeurs de la Seine' (London, 30 May 1848). Electoral proclamation of Louis-Napoléon Bonaparte. Bib. Nat. LB54-283.
46 Louis Girard, *Napoléon III* (Paris: Fayard, 1986), 95.
47 Maurice Agulhon, *Les quarante-huitards* (Paris: Gallimard, 1992), 200–201.
48 Furet, *La Révolution* (op. cit.), II, 401.
49 'The Eighteenth Brumaire of Louis Bonaparte', in Karl Marx, *Political writings* (London : Penguin, 1973), Vol. II, 240.
50 Lucas-Dubreton, *Le culte de Napoléon* (op. cit.), 428; emphasis in text.
51 Ibid., 463.
52 Cited in Robert Pimienta, *La propagande bonapartiste en 1848* (Paris: Cornély, 1911), 43.
53 Image reproduced in Grand-Carteret, 'La légende napoléonienne par l'image' (op. cit.), 34.

54 Dansette, *Louis-Napoléon à la conquête du pouvoir* (op. cit.), 279.
55 Quoted in Petiteau, *Lendemains d'Empire* (op. cit.), 291–292.
56 Dansette, *Louis-Napoléon à la conquête du pouvoir* (op. cit.), 277.
57 Pimienta, *La propagande bonapartiste* (op. cit.), 44–45, 49.
58 *Le Petit Caporal* No. 1 (June 15–18, 1848). Bib. Nat. LC2-1887.
59 *Le Petit Caporal* No .2 (June 18–20, 1848).
60 *Le Petit Caporal* No.11 (August 27–31, 1848).
61 *Le Petit Caporal* No. 18 (October 9–13, 1848).
62 *Le Petit Caporal* No. 10 (August 24–27, 1848).
63 Cited in Pimienta, *La propagande bonapartiste* (op. cit.), 52.
64 *Paroles impériales prononcées à Sainte-Hélène et réunies par un croyant* (Paris: Bonaventure, 1848).
65 Ibid., 11.
66 A. J. Tudesq, 'La légende napoléonienne en France en 1848', *Revue Historique* July–September 1957, 84.
67 The key work here was Beauterne's *Les sentiments de Napoléon sur le christianisme* (Paris: Waille, 1841); it had had nine editions by 1848.
68 Dansette, *Louis-Napoléon à la conquête du pouvoir* (op. cit.), 280.
69 Entry for 24 December 1848, in Victor Hugo, *Choses vues* (Paris: Gallimard, 1972), 761–762.
70 Cited in Dansette, *Louis-Napoléon à la conquête du pouvoir* (op. cit.), 261 and 263.
71 Cited in Lucas-Dubreton, *Le culte de Napoléon* (op. cit.), 466.
72 Letter to Prince Napoleon, 10 April 1849; in *Napoléon III et le Prince Napoléon. Correspondance inédite* (op. cit.).
73 Message of the President of the Republic, 31 October 1849, in *Discours et messages de Louis-Napoléon Bonaparte* (Paris: Plon, 1853), 65.
74 Girard, *Napoléon III* (op. cit.), 101–102.
75 Ibid., 130.
76 Dansette, *Louis-Napoléon à la conquête du pouvoir* (op. cit.), 360.
77 Ibid., 341.
78 *Discours et messages* (op. cit.), 51–53.
79 Girard, *Napoléon III* (op. cit.), 126.
80 Thirria, *Napoléon III avant l'Empire* (Paris: Plon, 1896), Vol. II, 268–269.
81 Farat, *Persigny* (op. cit.), 114–120.
82 On the rural resistance to the coup, see Ted Margadant, *French peasants in revolt. The insurrection of 1851* (Princeton, NJ: Princeton University Press, 1979).
83 Ménager, *Les Napoléon du Peuple* (op. cit.), 110.
84 Girard, *Napoléon III* (op. cit.), 183.
85 Ibid., 180.
86 Quoted in Alfred de Falloux, *Mémoires d'un royaliste* (Paris: Perrin, 1888), Vol. II, 223.
87 Farat, *Persigny* (op. cit.), 133–136.

88 Ménager, *Les Napoléon du Peuple* (op. cit.), 116–117.
89 See notably his speech at Bordeaux on 9 October 1851: 'France seems to wish to return to the Empire'; *Discours et messages* (op. cit.), 240–241.
90 *The early life of Louis Napoleon, by an Englishwoman* (London: Bosworth, 1860), 1.
91 Stéfane-Pol, *La jeunesse de Napoléon III* (op. cit.), 368.
92 Eugen Weber, *Peasants into Frenchmen* (Stanford: Stanford University Press, 1976), 248.
93 'Je suis sorti de la légalité pour rentrer dans le droit'.
94 Girard, *Napoléon III* (op. cit.), 157–158.
95 André Lebey, *Louis-Napoléon Bonaparte et la Révolution de 1848* (Paris: Juven, 1907), Vol. I, 130.
96 Thureau-Dangin, *Histoire de la Monarchie de Juillet* (op. cit.), Vol. I, 269.
97 Cited in Lucas-Dubreton, *Le culte de Napoléon* (op. cit.), 462.
98 Furet, *La Révolution* (op. cit.), II, 266.

9: Warriors of Peace

1 Report of sub-prefect of Vienne, 18 October 1852. AD Isère 54 M 7 ('Voyage du Prince Louis Napoléon', 1852).
2 Prefect of Isère to all mayors, 10 September 1852. AD Isère 54 M 7.
3 Report of sub-prefect of Saint-Marcellin, 21 September 1852. AD Isère 54 M 7.
4 Ibid.
5 Report of sub-prefect of Vienne, 18 October 1852. AD Isère 54 M 7.
6 See notably Bluche, *Le Bonapartisme* (op. cit.), 172.
7 Natalie Petiteau, 'Les vétérans du Premier Empire : un groupe socio-professionnel oublié', *Cahiers d'Histoire* Vol. 43, No. 1, 1988, 27–28.
8 See Petiteau, *Lendemains d'Empire* (op. cit.), 254–255 ; 270–271.
9 Report of prefect of the Rhône, Lyons, 21 July 1821. AN F7 6916.
10 See various reports in AN BB18—1118; 1119; 1120; 1123; and BB30—190 and 193.
11 For more on the veterans' devotion to the memory of Napoleon, see Petiteau, *Lendemains d'Empire* (op. cit.), 134.
12 For examples of the grinding poverty of former officers, see Lucas-Dubreton, *Le culte de Napoléon* (op. cit.), 80–90.
13 'Aux mânes d'un grand homme'; cited in police report, Epinal, 14 January 1822. AN F7 3795.
14 For more examples of this imagery see Day-Hickman, *Napoleonic art* (op. cit.).
15 Honoré de Balzac, *Le médecin de campagne* (Paris: Gallimard, 1974 ed.), 239–240. The passage in which Goguelat narrated his recollections of his imperial campaigns became so famous that it was published as a separate pamphlet entitled *Histoire de l'Empereur racontée dans une grange par un vieux soldat et recueillie par M. de Balzac* (Paris: Dubochet, 1842).

16 Lucas-Dubreton, *Le culte de Napoléon* (op. cit), 401.

17 'Le soldat de la vieille garde', *Revue de l'Empire* I (1842), 78.

18 Petiteau, *Lendemains d'Empire* (op. cit.), 133.

19 Jean Vidalenc, 'L'opinion publique en Normandie et le retour des restes de Napoléon en Décembre 1840', in *La France au XIXe siècle* (op. cit.), 212–224.

20 E. M. Laumann, *L'épopée Napoléonienne. Le retour des cendres* (Paris: Daragon, 1904), 153–154.

21 Marie-Christine de Bouët du Portal, 'A propos de la Saint-Napoléon: la solennité du 15 août sous le Premier et le Second Empire', *Revue de l'Institut Napoléon* (158–159) , 1992, 162.

22 Maurice Bottet, *Vétérans frères d'Armes de l'Empire Français, débris et Médaillés de Sainte-Hélène 1792–1815* (Paris: Leroy, 1906), 36–37.

23 A. J. Tudesq, 'La légende napoléonienne en 1848', *Revue Historique* CCXVIII, July–September 1957, 69 and fn.3; 75–76.

24 See chapter 3 in Garnier-Pagès, 'Le Gouvernement Provisoire', in *Histoire de la Révolution de 1848* (Paris: Degorce-Cadot, 1848), esp. 118–119.

25 A number of cases are cited in Petiteau, *Lendemains d'Empire* (op. cit.), 306–308.

26 See for example the pamphlet by former Napoleonic officer Commandant Leblanc, *Histoire politique, militaire, et privée du Prince Napoléon-Louis Bonaparte* (Paris: Giroux et Vialat, 1848).

27 *A nos anciens camarades de l'Armée, électeurs du département de la Seine* (1848). Bib. Nat. LB54—1873.

28 See Petiteau, *Lendemains d'Empire* (op. cit.), 189–248.

29 The idea was floating around in Bonapartist circles from the early 1850s. See, for example, *Relation historique de l'institution de la Médaille de Sainte-Hélène par un vieux soldat du Premier Empire* (Marseille, 1861); its author, Jean-Baptiste Schweitzer, claimed that in 1852 he had sent the Minister of War a drawing of what would later become the Médaille de Sainte-Hélène.

30 L. Tripier, *Code des membres de la Légion d'Honneur* (Paris: Mayer-Odin, 1859), LII-LIII.

31 'Testament de Napoléon Ier', in Las Cases, *Mémorial de Sainte-Hélène* (op. cit.).

32 Louis-Henri Fleurence, 'Les survivants des campagnes de la République et de l'Empire et l'attribution de la médaille de Sainte-Hélène dans le département des Vosges en 1857', *Revue de l'Institut Napoléon*, No. 151 (Vol. II, 1988), 62; this figure comes from the Hôtel des Monnaies et Médailles in Paris, which was responsible for striking the commemorative medals.

33 'The Army of 1813 was in its immense majority an army of "minors"', Lucas-Dubreton, *Le culte de Napoléon* (op. cit.), 25.

34 François-Frédéric Lemetheyer, *La Médaille de Sainte-Hélène* (Pont Audemer, 1857), 5.

35 See Hazareesingh and Wright, 'Le Second Empire', in Louis Fougère,

Jean-Pierre Machelon and François Monnier (eds.), *Les communes et le pouvoir en France* (op. cit.).

36 See Françoise Job, 'Les anciens militaires de la République et de l'Empire dans le département de la Meurthe en 1857', *Annales Historiques de la Révolution Française* No. 245, Juillet–Septembre 1981, 419–436; Louis-Henri Fleurence, (op.cit.) and Petiteau, 'Les vétérans du Premier Empire', (op. cit.).

37 For further discussion of these aspects, see Sudhir Hazareesingh, 'La légende napoléonienne sous le Second Empire: les Médaillés de Sainte-Hélène et la fête du 15 août', *Revue Historique* CCCV, Vol. 3 (2003).

38 Françoise Job, 'Les anciens militaires' (op. cit.), 427.

39 Certificate issued by municipality of Saudrupt, 17 April 1856, in AD Marne, 16 M 1 (Médaille de Sainte-Hélène).

40 AD Marne, 16 M 1 (Médaille de Sainte-Hélène).

41 More cases are cited in Petiteau, *Lendemains d'Empire* (op. cit.), 340–343.

42 For example, the prefect of Corsica wrote to the Minister of the Interior on 22 March 1827 about ninety-six retired officers who were all 'without resources and in the greatest need' and urged Paris to intervene. The reply was scribbled on the letter: 'Nothing to do' (*rien à faire*). AN F7 6702 (Militaires).

43 His letter to the Emperor made its way to Lyons, where the Prefect assigned him a medal. AD Rhône, 1 M 263 (Médaille de Sainte-Hélène).

44 A copy of his letter to the Prefect of the Rhône, dated 19 August 1858, is in AD Rhône, 1 M 263 (Médaille de Sainte-Hélène).

45 Ibid., letter dated 30 March 1858.

46 Mayor of St Lager, letter dated 10 April 1858, in AD Rhône, 1 M 263 (Médaille de Sainte-Hélène).

47 For more on the civic and political dimensions of this festivity, see Hazareesingh, *The Saint Napoleon* (op. cit.).

48 Philippe Busoni, 'Courrier de Paris', *L'Illustration*, 21 August 1852.

49 Report of *Procureur-Général*, Besançon, 14 September 1852. AN BB30-373.

50 Report of Prefect, 20 August 1853. AN F1C^{III}/Indre (6).

51 Report of Prefect of Aude, 20 August 1854. AN F1C^{I} 110.

52 See, for example, the report of Mayor of Mormoiron, 17 August 1861. AD Vaucluse, 1 M 880.

53 For more on the ideological diversity of the veterans, and their shifting attitudes over time, see Petiteau, *Lendemains d'Empire* (op. cit.), 267–297.

54 This case is cited in Michel Pigenet, *Les ouvriers du Cher (fin XVIIIe siècle-1914). Travail, espace, et conscience sociale* (Paris: Institut CGT d'Histoire Sociale, 1990), 176.

55 *Lettre d'un vieux grognard de l'Ancienne Garde Impériale au citoyen Louis-Napoléon Bonaparte* (signed A. B. L) (Paris, 1848), 3.

56 Report of sub-prefect of Apt, 20 August 1858. AD Vaucluse 1 M 880.

57 Jean Lucas-Dubreton, *Soldats de Napoléon* (Paris: Tallandier, 1977 ed.), 437.

58 *Corporation des Membres Décorés de la Médaille de Sainte-Hélène en résidence à la Chapelle Saint-Denis. Règlement* (Paris, 1858). Bib. Nat. LL24-11.

59 Ibid., 7.

60 Ibid., 1.

61 Ibid., 8.

62 Ibid., 2–3.

63 Ibid., 4.

64 Ibid., 5–6.

65 Ibid., 7.

66 *Préambule et Statuts des Membres Décorés de la Médaille de Sainte-Hélène*, Maine et Loire (1859). Bib. Nat. LL24-10.

67 Report of mayor of Tours, 15 August 1859. AD Indre-et-Loire 1 M 255.

68 Report of sub-prefect, 16 August 1859. AD Bouches-du-Rhône 1 M 642.

69 AN F^{IC} IV 8 Ministère de l'Intérieur, *élections aux conseils généraux* (1852).

70 Letter dated 27 August 1859. AD Loire Atlantique, 1 M 675.

71 'Vieilles peaux'; quoted in Pierre Pierrard, *Histoire des curés de campagne* (Paris: Bartillat, 1990), 206.

72 Report of Mayor of Sacy, 23 August 1859. AD Marne 32 M 10.

73 Report of 16 August 1858. AD Meuse, 73 M 6.

74 Report of Police Commissioner, Avignon, 16 August 1861. AD Vaucluse 1 M 880.

75 Report of *Procureur-Général*, Colmar, 4 October 1858. AN BB30-376.

76 Report to the Prefect, Béziers, 17 August 1858. AD Hérault, 1 M 505.

77 Report of *Procureur-Général*, Toulouse, 16 August 1858. AN BB30-421.

78 Draft report of Prefect to Minister of Interior, 1859. AD Seine-Maritime, 1 M 351.

79 Report of Police Commissioner, 16 August 1858. AD Hérault, 1 M 505.

80 'Tell us about him, grandmother, grandmother, tell us about him.'

81 Report of Mayor of Chateaudouble, 18 August 1861. AD Var, 6 M 18 (5).

82 See, for example, the report of the Mayor of Villeneuve-les-Béziers on the celebration of 15 August 1857; the official procession contained 'one former soldier of the Empire.' AD Hérault, 1 M 505.

83 Louis-Henri Fleurance, 'Les survivants des campagnes', (op. cit.) 64.

84 For example, see *Almanach Historique, Anecdotique, et Populaire de l'Empire Français pour 1867* (Paris, 1866), 127.

85 See *Discours prononcé par M. Pellecat sur la tombe de M. Jacques-Louis Philippe, Médaillé de Sainte-Hélène* (Rouen, 1874). Bib. Nat. LN27-27729.

86 *Le Petit Caporal*, 17–18 August 1887, cited in Jean El Gammal, *Politique et poids du passé dans la France 'fin de siècle'* (Limoges: Presses Universitaires de Limoges, 1999), 142.

87 Cited in Gustave Schlumberger, *Derniers soldats de Napoléon* (Paris, 1905), 32.

88 Letter of Bureau of Association des Médaillés de Sainte-Hélène (Gironde) to prefect, Bordeaux, 8 August 1859. AD Gironde 1 M 707.

89 *Aux décorés de la Médaille de Sainte-Hélène. A propos de l'inauguration de la statue de*

Napoléon Ier à Rouen, le 15 août 1865. Bib. Nat. YE-37738. 'Despite so much suffering/Despite so many setbacks/Laurels of our France/You remain for ever green!'

90 *La Médaille de Sainte-Hélène. Couplets chantés á la réunion des Médaillés de Mulhouse, le 15 août 1858* (Mulhouse, 1858).

91 An example: the report of the Mayor of Béhonne (Meuse), 17 August 1858. AD Meuse 73 M 6.

92 There is a modest collection of this genre in the Bibliothèque Nationale. See, for example, Henry Courant, *Sur la Médaille de Sainte-Hélène* (Paris, 1858). LL24-2.

93 Report of the sub-prefect of Vitry-le-François, 18 August 1869. AD Marne 30 M 31 (reports to the prefect 1869–70).

94 See, for example, the report of the sub-prefect of Villefranche, 27 February 1857; and prefect letter to the Minister of the Interior, 17 August 1858. AD Aveyron 1 M (Fêtes du Second Empire) (unclassified).

95 Frédéric Chalaron, 'Le Bonapartisme dans la vie politique du Puy-de-Dôme (1848–79), *Revue d'Auvergne* 94-3 (1980), 329.

96 These qualities are all stressed by the Mayor of Maillys (Côte d'Or), in his report of 16 August 1859. AD Côte d'Or 1 M 467.

97 '[the medal] appeals to the rich man, as to the proletarian'; Justin Cabassol, *La Médaille de Sainte-Hélène* (Paris, 1858).

98 See, for example, 'Quelques mots adressés aux médaillés de Sainte-Hélène par leur Président, le 15 Août 1861.' AD Gironde 1 M 707.

99 Ménager also highlights the importance of the Médaillés as functional intermediaries; see *Les Napoléon du peuple* (op. cit.), 155.

100 'Ils grognaient mais le suivaient toujours'.

101 Napoleonic officer Philippe Benoît, quoted in Alain Pigeard, *L'Armée de Napoléon. Organisation et vie quotidienne* (Paris: Tallandier, 2000), 320–321.

102 For a study of the resonance of this theme in French nineteenth-century writings, see Gérard de Puymège, *Chauvin, le soldat-laboureur: contribution à l'étude des nationalismes* (Paris: Gallimard, 1993).

103 For a sample of this genre, see *Napoléon ou la gloire française* (n.d.) Bib. Nat. Ye 28422; and *La Médaille de Sainte-Hélène. Chant triomphal* (1857) Bib. Nat. Ye 55471.

104 Jean Claude Vittoz, *Le grand homme ou la légende napoléonienne* (Paris, 1866).

105 'And you, who in our bitter wars/never betrayed us/Italians and Poles/Rejoice with us too, my brothers !'. G. A. Montmain, *La Médaille de Sainte-Hélène. Couplets* (Paris, 1857).

106 Report of Mayor of Tourtour, 18 August 1859. AD Var 6 M 18 (5).

107 A. B. L. Adam, *La Médaille Ste. Hélène et les 4 rubans rouges. Anecdote militaire* (Paris, 1857), 11; the author served in the Grande Armée between 1809 and 1815, and became a primary schoolteacher in 1833.

108 Hilaire Le Gai, *Almanach des souvenirs de l'Empire. Bonapartiana* (Paris: Passard, 1853), 5.

109 *Discours prononcé à la distribution de la Médaille de Sainte-Hélène aux anciens soldats de la République et de l'Empire de la commune d'Albi, le 24 janvier 1858, par M. le Général Baron Gorsse* (Albi, 1858), 4; emphasis added. Bib. Nat. LL24-4.

110 *Chanson Napoléonienne par Girod-Genet, Hussard de l'Armée de la Loire* (Paris, n.d.) [1866]. Bib. Nat. Ye 55471.

111 *Chanson à double circonstance, improvisée dans une réunion d'amis sur les évènements du 2, 3, et 4 décembre 1851* (Oise, n.d.). Bib. Nat. Ye 55471 (351 bis).

112 'L'Echo Français', poem submitted to the prefect of Gironde by the Association of Médaillés de Sainte-Hélène (Gironde), 13 August 1859. AD Gironde 1 M 707.

113 Quoted in prefect of Isère report, Grenoble, 19 August 1868. AD Isère 54 M 15.

114 Ernest Lavisse, *Souvenirs* (Paris: Calmann-Lévy, 1988), 281.

Conclusion: The Legend Lives On

1 The last Médaillé de Sainte-Hélène known to the French authorities died in 1898.

2 M. de Lys, 'Le dernier soldat de Napoléon', *Le Journal*, 3 August 1901, cited in Schlumberger, *Derniers soldats* (op. cit.), 57–59.

3 See Elzbieta Stoinska, *La légende napoléonienne dans la poésie française et polonaise au XIXe siècle 1798-1871* (Lille, ANRT, 1986).

4 Edmond Rostand, *L'Aiglon* (Paris: Gallimard, 1986).

5 Maurice Barrès, *Le roman de l'énergie nationale. Les Déracinés* (Paris: Fasquelle, 1897), 232.

6 On the fate of Bonapartism under the Third Republic, see Ménager, *Les Napoléon du peuple* (op. cit.); and John Rothney, *Bonapartism after Sedan* (Ithaca: Cornell University Press, 1969).

7 See Jean El Gammal, *Politique et poids du passé dans la France 'fin de siècle'* (Limoges: Presses Universitaires de Limoges, 1999), 141–149.

8 Furet, *La Révolution* (op. cit.), II, 225.

9 Cited in Dansette, 'Légende et transfiguration' (op. cit.), 312.

10 Police report, Lyons, 12 August 1815. AD Rhône 4 M 237.

11 Stendhal, *Le Rouge et le Noir* (op. cit.), 205.

12 See the table in Christian Amalvi, 'L'exemple des grands hommes de l'histoire de France', *Romantisme* 100 (1998), 101. The 'runner-up' was Joan of Arc.

13 Petiteau, *Napoléon de la mythologie à l'histoire* (op. cit.), 179.

14 Max Gallo, *Napoléon* (Paris: Robert Laffont, 1997), 4 vols.

15 For examples of this genre, see the book by the journalist Jean-Paul Kauffmann, *La chambre noire de Longwood. Le voyage à Sainte-Hélène* (Paris: La Table Ronde, 1997) ; and the work by France's former Foreign Minister, Dominique de Villepin, *Les Cent-Jours ou l'esprit de sacrifice* (Paris: Perrin, 2001).

16 Its website is www.napoleon.org
17 Patrick Rambaud, *La Bataille* (Paris: Grasset, 1997). This was the first of a trilogy; it was followed by *Il neigeait* (2000) and *L'Absent* (2003), which ends with Napoleon's return to France in March 1815.
18 Letter to Eugène Noël, 19 July 1850; in Jules Michelet, *Correspondance générale* (Paris: Champion, 1996, ed. Louis Le Guillou), 473–474.
19 Antoine Chollier, *La vraie route Napoléon* (Paris : Editions Alpina, 1946), 25.
20 Besnard, *Le napoléonisme* (Paris, 1876), 3–4.
21 Amalvi, 'L'exemple des grands hommes de l'histoire de France' (op. cit.), 92.
22 Jean-François Chanet, *Les grands hommes du Panthéon* (Paris: Editions du Patrimoine, 1996), 13.
23 Mona Ozouf, 'Le Panthéon. L'Ecole Normale des Morts', in Pierre Nora (ed.), *Les lieux de mémoire* (Paris: Gallimard, 1984), Vol.I, 139–166.
24 For further discussion of the contrasting conception of the 'great man' in nineteenth-century French political culture, see Avner Ben-Amos, *Funerals, politics, and memory in modern France* (Oxford: Oxford University Press, 2000), 143–148.
25 Petiteau, *Napoléon de la mythologie à l'histoire* (op. cit.), 140–142.
26 *Bonaparte* (Paris: Lafitte, 1913).
27 According to CSA polls, cited in Jean-Noël Jeanneney and Philippe Joutard (eds.), *Du bon usage des grands hommes en Europe* (Paris: Perrin, 2003), 66.
28 Maurice Agulhon, *De Gaulle: histoire, symbole, mythe* (Paris: Hachette, 2000), 53.
29 See notably his *A demain de Gaulle* (Paris: Gallimard, 1996).
30 Alain Duhamel, *La politique imaginaire* (Paris: Gallimard, 1995), 247.
31 Denis Tillinac, 'Le gaullisme: un état d'esprit', *Le Figaro-Magazine*, 15 November 2003.
32 See Michel Winock, 'Jeanne d'Arc', in Pierre Nora, *Les lieux de mémoire* (Paris: Gallimard, 1992), Vol. III-3, 675–733.
33 See Hazareesingh, *Intellectual Founders of the Republic* (op. cit.), 294–297.
34 Yves Mény, 'The Republic and its territory: the persistence and adaptation of founding myths', in S. Hazareesingh (ed.), *The Jacobin legacy in modern France* (Oxford: Oxford University Press, 2002), 183–195.
35 On this theme see Pierre Rosanvallon, *Le peuple introuvable* (Paris: Gallimard, 1998); and *Le modèle politique français* (Paris: Seuil, 2004).

Napoleonic sources, sites, and further reading

Much of the source material I used to write this book came from French public archives. The Archives de la Préfecture de Police in Paris have some very interesting holdings on the pre-1870 period – mostly fragments, but very useful when set alongside material found elsewhere. The bulk of my research was drawn from the Archives Nationales (CARAN), also in Paris, where I explored the rich collections in the BB (justice) and F7 (police) series relating to the 1815–48 period, as well as the reports on the celebrations of national festivities under the Second Empire. I also looked through the Napoleon archives (400 AP), where among other things I found many of Louis Napoleon's letters.

This work was supplemented by research in departmental archives. I went to three 'Napoleonic' localities (Isère, Rhône, and Yonne), where the M series yielded much fascinating material on the 1815–48 period; the research for Chapter 9 also took me to ten other departments, where I looked at holdings on imperial veterans and the celebrations of national festivities from 1815 to 1870. These trips, which were very enjoyable, took me to the *chef-lieux* of the Aveyron, Gironde, Hérault, Indre-et-Loire, Loire-Atlantique, Marne, Meuse, Seine-Maritime, Var, and Vaucluse. These local archives were extremely welcoming and user-friendly; they also contain much material on the history of nineteenth-century Bonapartism which remains unexplored.

I also used some excellent libraries in Paris: the Bibliothèque Nationale in Tolbiac, of course, but also the Bibliothèque Napoléon, which is part of the Fondation Napoléon on Boulevard Haussmann; this is a particularly good place to read journals, which are directly accessible. Also remarkable for its Napoleonic collections (of books, objects, and images) is the Fondation Thiers. I found some equally captivating material at the Bibliothèque Paul Marmottan in Boulogne, which holds one of the largest collections of Napoleonic images in France.

France is full of monuments and museums commemorating the Emperor. There is a beautifully illustrated evocation of Napoleon's Paris by Diana Reid Haig, *Walks through Napoleon and Josephine's Paris* (London, 2004). Relics of imperial and Napoleonic France can be found in Paris, of course, starting with the Invalides, where the Emperor is buried, and the museums of the Louvre, Versailles, and Carnavalet; there are also superb collections at the Chateau de la Malmaison and at Fontainebleau. The passionate seeker of imperial remains can also visit the Père Lachaise cemetery in Paris, where Marshals Davout, Masséna, Ney, and Murat are buried; the truly adventurous can also travel along the Route Nationale 85, inaugurated in 1932, and known as the Route Napoléon. It connects Golfe-Juan to Grenoble, and many of the spots which the Emperor passed during his 'flight of the eagle' are marked and commemorated. At Laffrey, there is a magnificent statue of Napoleon on horseback at a place called La Prairie de la Rencontre.

Further afield, there are also very good Napoleonic museums in Corsica (Ajaccio), Boulogne-sur-mer (Pas-de-Calais) and Compiègne (Oise). There is an excellent world guide to the geographical 'sites of memory' dedicated to Napoleon, *Répertoire mondial des souvenirs napoléoniens* (Paris, 1993) edited by Alain Chappet, Martin Roger, and Alain Pigeard. It includes the present-day locations of famous battle sites, and the addresses of some superb Napoleonic museums outside France – notably in Italy (Rome); Switzerland (Arenenberg, where Louis Napoleon spent much of his youth); the USA (New Orleans); and Cuba (Havana).

Now for some suggestions for those interested in wider reading about Napoleon, the legend, and nineteenth-century politics more generally. There are plenty of biographies of Napoleon to choose from, but my favourites are Georges Lefebvre, *Napoléon* (Paris, 1941); Vincent Cronin, *Napoleon Bonaparte* (London, 1974); Jean Tulard,

Napoléon ou le mythe du sauveur (Paris, 1977); Robert Alexander, *Napoleon* (London, 2001), and Steven Englund, *Napoleon, a political life* (New York, 2004). Napoleon is still a subject of controversy and passion; for a contemporary example of the 'black legend', see Paul Johnson, *Napoleon* (London, 2002); conversely, for a wildly enthusiastic advocacy, see Max Gallo's four-volume *Napoléon* (Paris, 1997).

On the history of the Consulate and the First Empire, excellent works include Martin Lyons, *Napoleon Bonaparte and the legacy of the French Revolution* (London, 1974); Jacques-Olivier Boudon, *Le Consulat et l'Empire* (Paris, 1988); Annie Jourdan, *Napoléon: héros, imperator, mécène* (Paris, 1998), without of course forgetting older classics such as Adolphe Thiers's monumental work, *Histoire du Consulat et de l'Empire* (Paris, 1845–1860) and Henry Houssaye's *1815* (Paris, 1905). Jean Tulard's *Dictionnaire Napoléon* (Paris, new ed. 1999) is also a very good source, with concise entries on the principal events and personalities of the Napoleonic era (as well as the major battles).

On the wider history of Bonapartism in the nineteenth century, see Frédéric Bluche, *Le Bonapartisme* (Paris, 1980); Bernard Ménager, *Les Napoléon du peuple* (Paris, 1988); François Furet, *La Révolution* (Paris, 1988, 2 vols.); this work was translated as *Revolutionary France 1770-1880* (London, 1995); Natalie Petiteau, *Lendemains d'Empire. Les soldats de Napoléon dans la France du XIXe siècle* (Paris, 2003); and Sudhir Hazareesingh, *The Saint-Napoleon: celebrations of sovereignty in 19th Century France* (Cambridge, Massachusetts, 2004). Napoleon III has been the subject of some good political biographies, notably Adrien Dansette's *Louis Napoléon à la conquête du pouvoir* (Paris, 1961) and *Du 2 Décembre au 4 Septembre* (Paris, 1972). William H. C. Smith's *Napoleon III* (London, 1982) and Louis Girard's *Napoléon III* (Paris, 1986) are also authoritative. I refer those interested in the wider history of Bonapartism under the Second Empire to the bibliography of my other work, *From subject to citizen: the Second Empire and the emergence of modern French democracy* (Princeton, NJ, 1998).

Lastly, some recommendations on the legend and its modern manifestations. There are some excellent works on the treatment of Napoleon in French literature. See Maurice Descotes, *La légende de Napoléon et les écrivains français au XIXe siècle* (Paris, 1967) ; and Saint-Paulien, *Napoléon, Balzac et l'Empire de la Comédie Humaine* (Paris, 1979). Despite its contestable conclusions, there is much to be taken from

Philippe Gonnard's classic work, *Les origines de la légende napoléonienne. L'œuvre historique de Napoléon à Sainte-Hélène* (Paris, 1906; reprinted in 1979). My favourite work on the legend is Jean Lucas-Dubreton, *Le culte de Napoléon (1815–1848)* (Paris, 1960), which is superbly written and draws widely from memoir literature; more recent studies include Jean Tulard, *Le mythe de Napoléon* (Paris, 1971); Natalie Petiteau, *Napoléon de la mythologie à l'histoire* (Paris, 1999); Maurice Agulhon, *De Gaulle: histoire, symbole, mythe* (Paris, 2000); and Gérard Gengembre, *Napoléon: la vie, la légende* (Paris, 2001). For an excellent study of the impact of Napoleon in Britain, see Stuart Semmel, *Napoleon in the British Imagination* (New Haven, 2004).

Picture credits

Cover images: *Les Huit Epoques de Napoléon*. Painting by Charles Auguste Guillaume Steuben. *Son Ombre Les Epouvante*. Anonymous drawing. Reprinted with kind permission of Réunion des Musées Nationaux, Paris.

The following photographs are reproduced with kind permission:

The landing of Napoleon. Imprimerie Pellerin, Epinal. Bibliothèque Marmottan, Paris.

The evening of 20 March 1815: the return of Napoleon to the Tuileries. Drawing by Charles Motte. Musée Carnavalet, Paris.

Return from Elba, 7 March 1815. From a painting by Charles August Guillaume Steuben. Bibliothèque Marmottan, Paris.

Each to his profession. Print by François Georgin, Imprimerie Pellerin, Epinal. Bibliothèque Marmottan, Paris.

Allegorical representation of the return of the ultras. Anonymous drawing, 1816. Musée Carnavalet, Paris.

Death of Napoleon, 5 May 1821. Drawing used to illustrate Marchand's account of the Emperor's death (first published in 1836). Musée Carnavalet, Paris.

The tomb of Napoleon at Saint-Helena. Anonymous drawing, Chateaux de Malmaison et Bois-Préau. Réunion des Musées Nationaux, Paris.

The imperial leap. Anonymous drawing, 1815. Musée Carnavalet, Paris.

'I take my bonnet and leave you with your skullcap.' Anonymous drawing, 1815. Bibliothèque Marmottan, Paris.

Seditious Bonapartist placard. Archives Nationales, F7 6705, Paris.

Cover of tobacco box, representing General Cambronne at the Battle of Waterloo. Musée Carnavalet, Paris.

Glorious reign of 19 years. As he has governed for 15 years. Anonymous drawing, 1815. Musée Carnavalet, Paris.

'Is it true, as they say, that things are going so badly?' Drawing by Charlet (1824). Bibliothèque Marmottan, Paris.

Entry of Napoleon into Grenoble. Imprimerie Pellerin, Epinal. Bibliothèque Marmottan, Paris.

Entry of the procession bearing Napoleon's remains in Paris, under the Arc de Triomphe, 15 December 1840. Drawing by Victor Adam, 1840.

Napoleon and Benjamin Constant in the gardens of the Elysée Palace in June 1815. Drawing by Félix-Henri-Emmanuel Philippoteaux. Chateaux de Malmaison et Bois-Préau. Réunion des Musées Nationaux, Paris.

The man of the people. Drawing by Raffet (1836). Bibliothèque Marmottan, Paris.

Faithful as a Pole. Drawing by Raffet (1833). Bibliothèque Marmottan, Paris.

Reflection. Drawing by Raffet (1834). Bibliothèque Marmottan, Paris.

Prince Louis Napoleon Bonaparte. Drawing by T. H. Ryall. Bibliothèque Nationale, Paris.

Manifesto of Louis-Napoleon Bonaparte to the electors. Poster, November 1848. Musée Carnavalet, Paris.

Louis Napoleon receiving deputies from the provinces. Drawing by Philippoteaux. Private collection.

'Sire you can rely on us as much as on the Old Guard.' Drawing by Raffet (1831). Bibliothèque Marmottan, Paris.

The veterans of the First Empire gathered before the Vendôme Column, on the occasion of the anniversary of the death of Napoleon. Drawing by Godefroy-Durand, in *L'Univers Illustré.* Musée Carnavalet, Paris.

Blind survivor of the Grande Armée 1858 and *Last survivors of the Grande Armée 1861.* Anonymous drawings, Chateaux de Malmaison et Bois-Préau. Reunion des Musées Nationaux, Paris.

Index

Note: Napoleon I Bonaparte is referred to as N in sub-entries